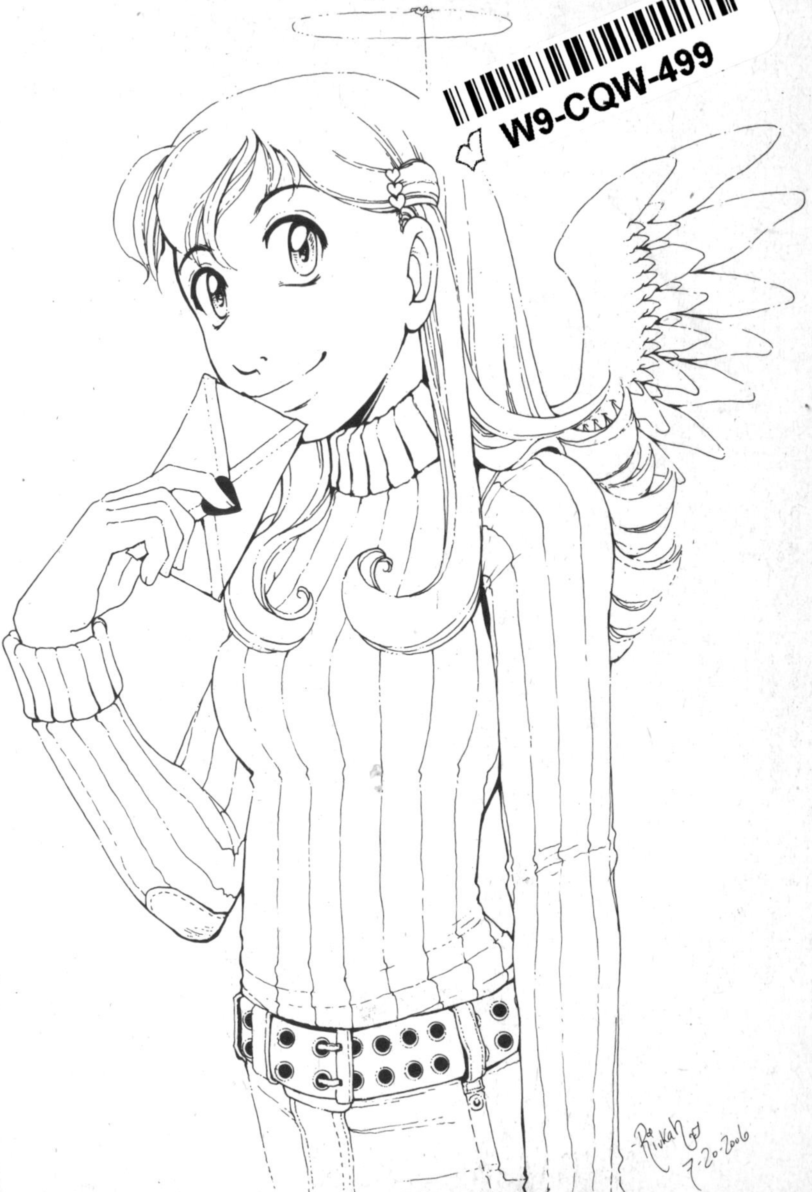
Rivkah
7-20-2006

## *Steady Beat Vol. 2*
## Created by Rivkah

---

Toning - Rivkah, Nathaniel Merriam &
Hon Lam Chow
Production Artist & Lettering - Bowen Park
Cover Design - Jose Macasocol, Jr.

Editor - Rob Valois
Digital Imaging Manager - Chris Buford
Managing Editor - Elisabeth Brizzi
Production Manager - Vy Nguyen
VP of Production - Ron Klamert
Editor in Chief - Rob Tokar
Publisher - Mike Kiley
President and C.O.O. - John Parker
C.E.O. and Chief Creative Officer - Stuart Levy

A  Manga

TOKYOPOP Inc.
5900 Wilshire Blvd. Suite 2000
Los Angeles, CA 90036

E-mail: info@TOKYOPOP.com
Come visit us online at www.TOKYOPOP.com

ISBN: 1-59816-136-9

First TOKYOPOP printing: October 2006
10  9  8  7  6  5  4  3  2  1
Printed in the USA

# STEADY BEAT™

## Volume 2

### by
### Rivkah

TOKYOPOP®

HAMBURG // LONDON // LOS ANGELES // TOKYO

# contents

"LOVE, JESSICA"

THAT'S WHAT LEAH WINTERS FOUND ON THE BACK OF A LOVE LETTER TO HER SISTER. BUT WHO IS JESSICA? LEAH IS ON THE HUNT WITH HER BEST FRIEND, JUNE, TO DISCOVER THIS PARAMOUR'S SECRET IDENTITY. HOWEVER, THINGS GET A LITTLE DISTRACTING WHEN SHE RUNS INTO ELIJAH PETERSON, A WEALTHY YOUNG MAN FROM A NEIGHBORING PRIVATE SCHOOL. BUT THERE'S MORE TO ELIJAH THAN MEETS THE EYE, AND THE CLOSER LEAH GETS TO HIM, THE MORE SHE LEARNS NOT TO JUDGE SIMPLY BY FIRST IMPRESSIONS.

BEAT 6

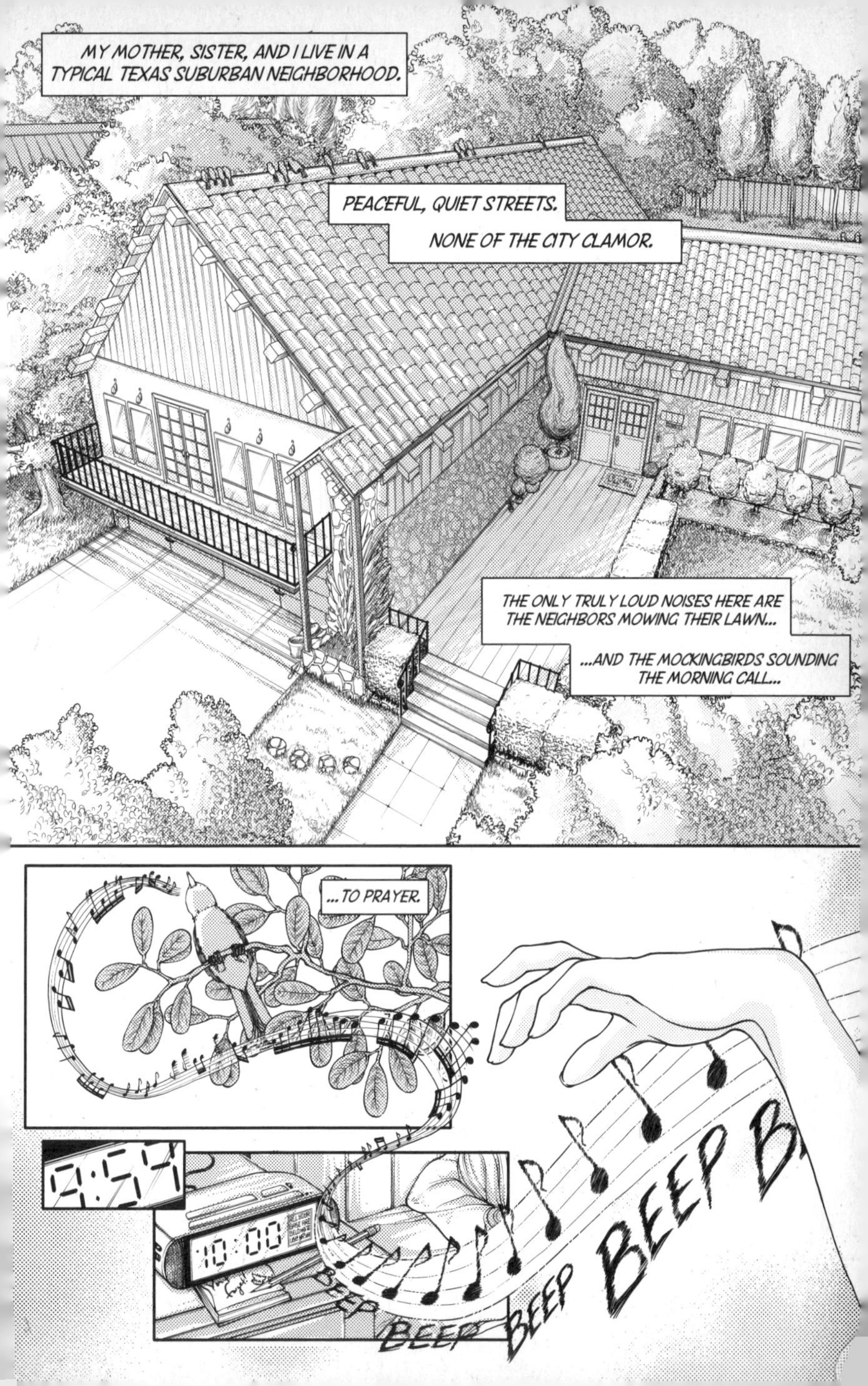
MY MOTHER, SISTER, AND I LIVE IN A TYPICAL TEXAS SUBURBAN NEIGHBORHOOD.
PEACEFUL, QUIET STREETS.
NONE OF THE CITY CLAMOR.
THE ONLY TRULY LOUD NOISES HERE ARE THE NEIGHBORS MOWING THEIR LAWN...
...AND THE MOCKINGBIRDS SOUNDING THE MORNING CALL...
...TO PRAYER.
9:59
10:00
BEEP
BEEP
BEEP
B

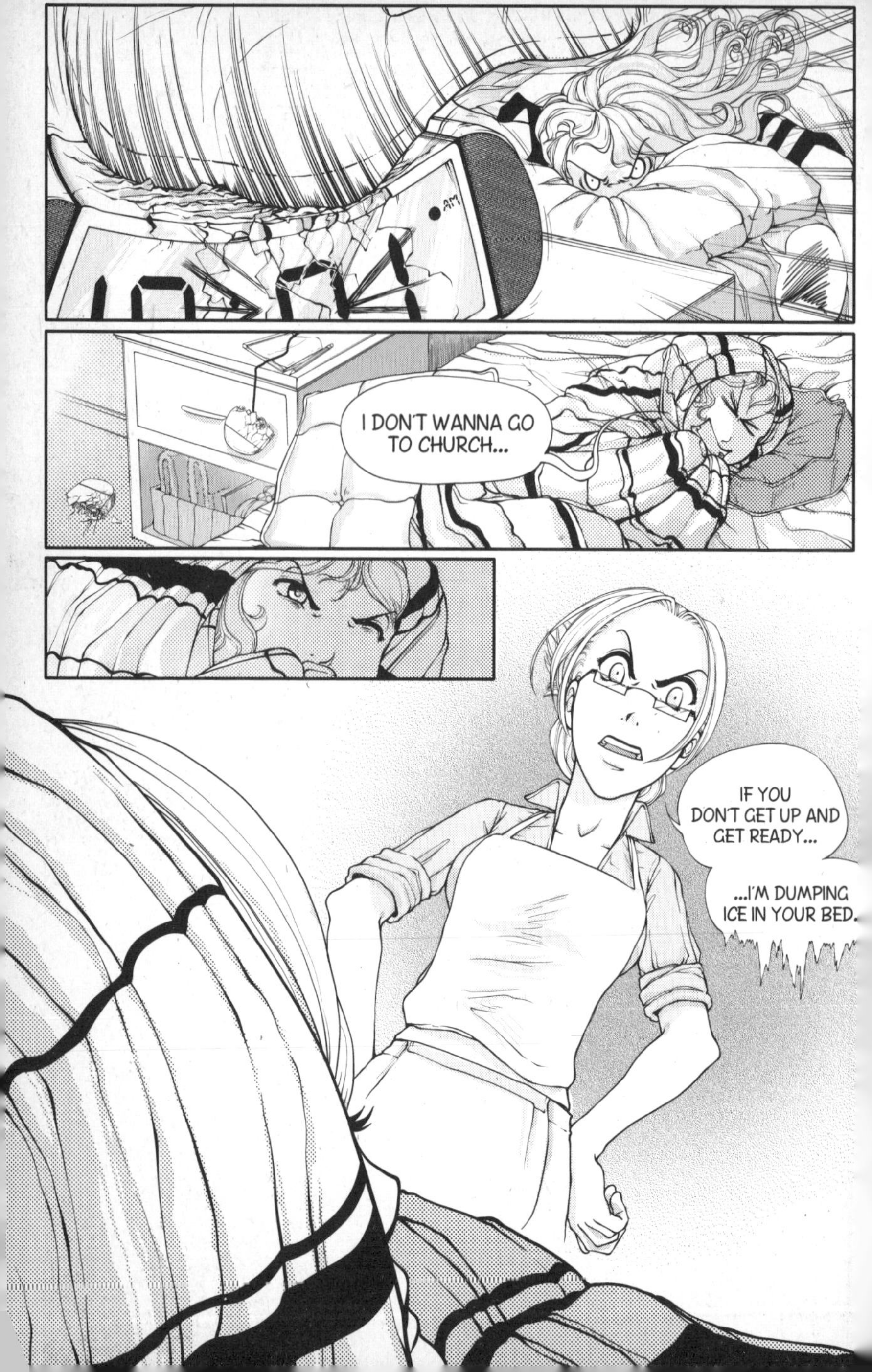
AM
I DON'T WANNA GO TO CHURCH...
IF YOU DON'T GET UP AND GET READY...
...I'M DUMPING ICE IN YOUR BED.

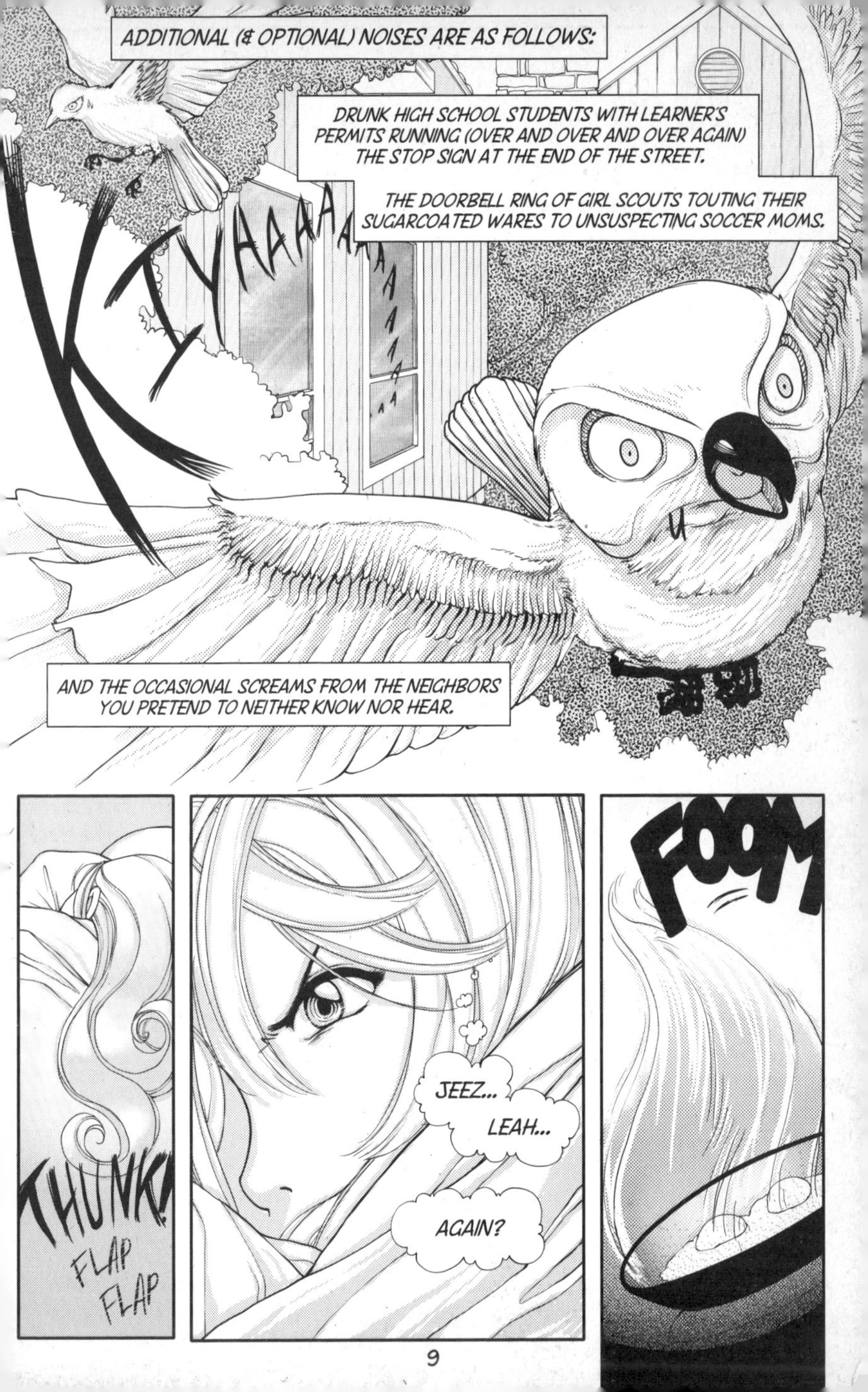
ADDITIONAL (& OPTIONAL) NOISES ARE AS FOLLOWS:
DRUNK HIGH SCHOOL STUDENTS WITH LEARNER'S PERMITS RUNNING (OVER AND OVER AND OVER AGAIN) THE STOP SIGN AT THE END OF THE STREET.
THE DOORBELL RING OF GIRL SCOUTS TOUTING THEIR SUGARCOATED WARES TO UNSUSPECTING SOCCER MOMS.
KIYAAAAAAAAAAAAA
AND THE OCCASIONAL SCREAMS FROM THE NEIGHBORS YOU PRETEND TO NEITHER KNOW NOR HEAR.
THUNK!
FLAP
FLAP
JEEZ...
LEAH...
AGAIN?
FOOM

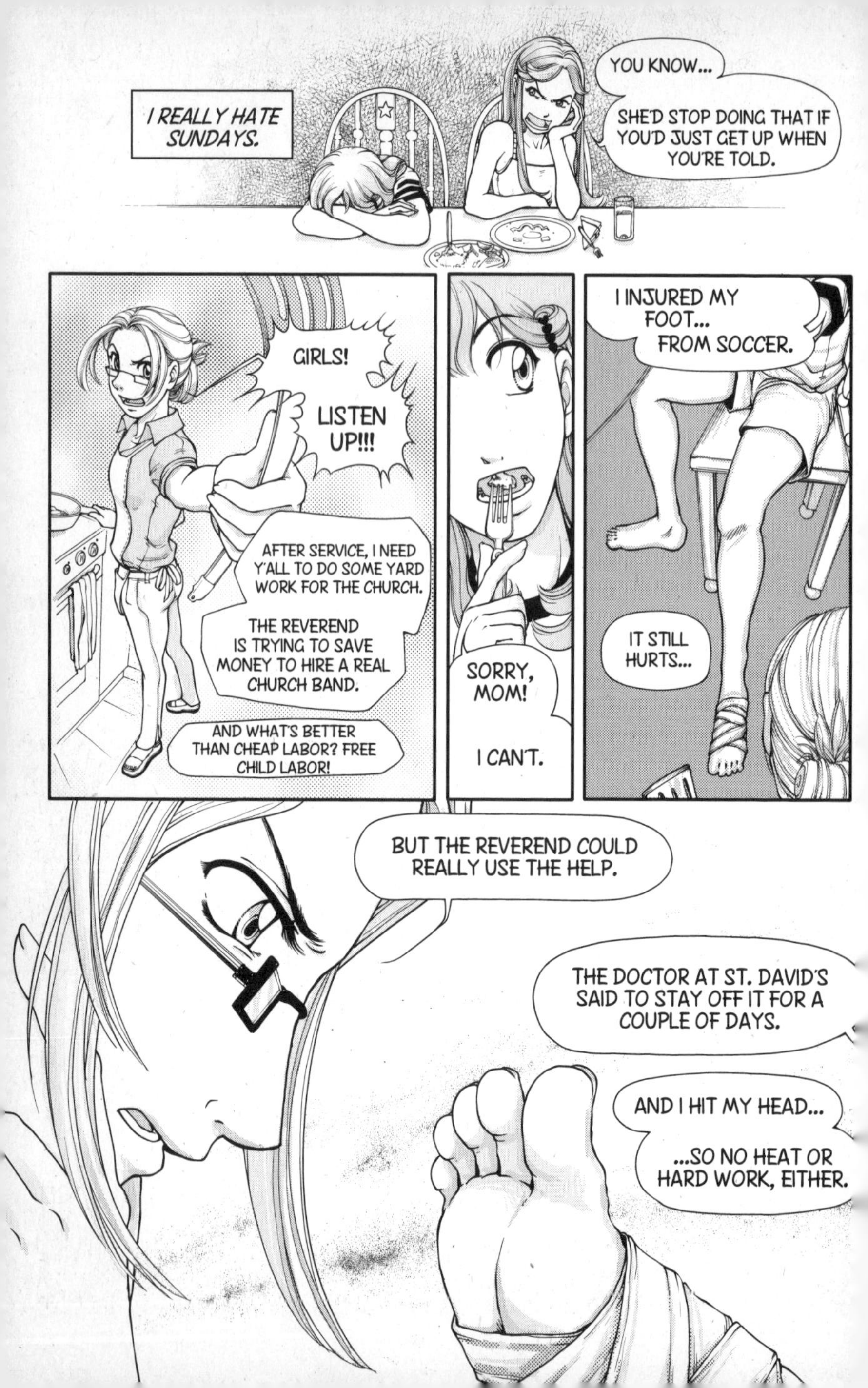
I REALLY HATE SUNDAYS.
YOU KNOW...
SHE'D STOP DOING THAT IF YOU'D JUST GET UP WHEN YOU'RE TOLD.
GIRLS!
LISTEN UP!!!
AFTER SERVICE, I NEED Y'ALL TO DO SOME YARD WORK FOR THE CHURCH.
THE REVEREND IS TRYING TO SAVE MONEY TO HIRE A REAL CHURCH BAND.
AND WHAT'S BETTER THAN CHEAP LABOR? FREE CHILD LABOR!
SORRY, MOM!
I CAN'T.
I INJURED MY FOOT... FROM SOCCER.
IT STILL HURTS...
BUT THE REVEREND COULD REALLY USE THE HELP.
THE DOCTOR AT ST. DAVID'S SAID TO STAY OFF IT FOR A COUPLE OF DAYS.
AND I HIT MY HEAD...
...SO NO HEAT OR HARD WORK, EITHER.

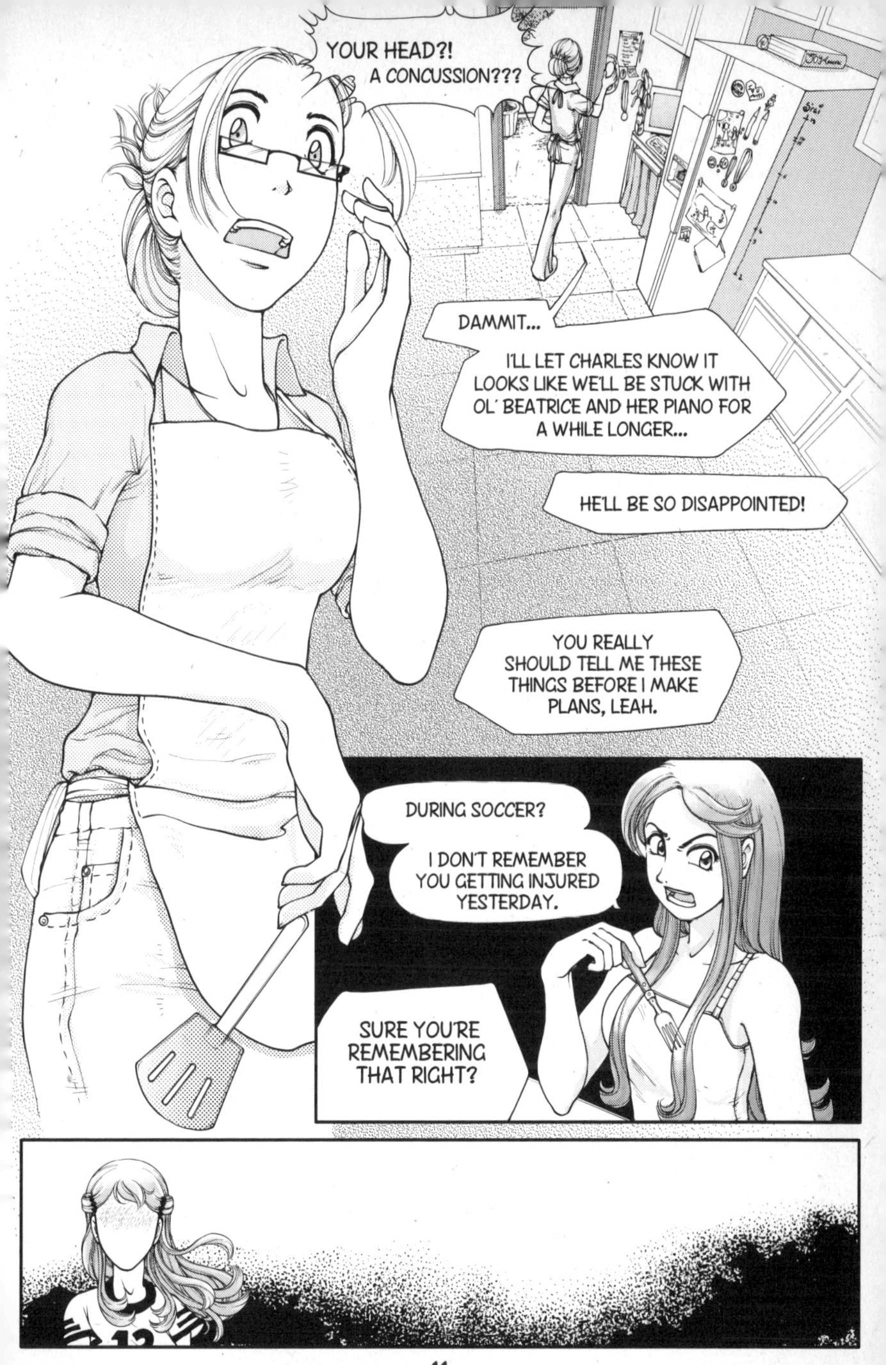
YOUR HEAD?! A CONCUSSION???
DAMMIT...
I'LL LET CHARLES KNOW IT LOOKS LIKE WE'LL BE STUCK WITH OL' BEATRICE AND HER PIANO FOR A WHILE LONGER...
HE'LL BE SO DISAPPOINTED!
YOU REALLY SHOULD TELL ME THESE THINGS BEFORE I MAKE PLANS, LEAH.
DURING SOCCER?
I DON'T REMEMBER YOU GETTING INJURED YESTERDAY.
SURE YOU'RE REMEMBERING THAT RIGHT?

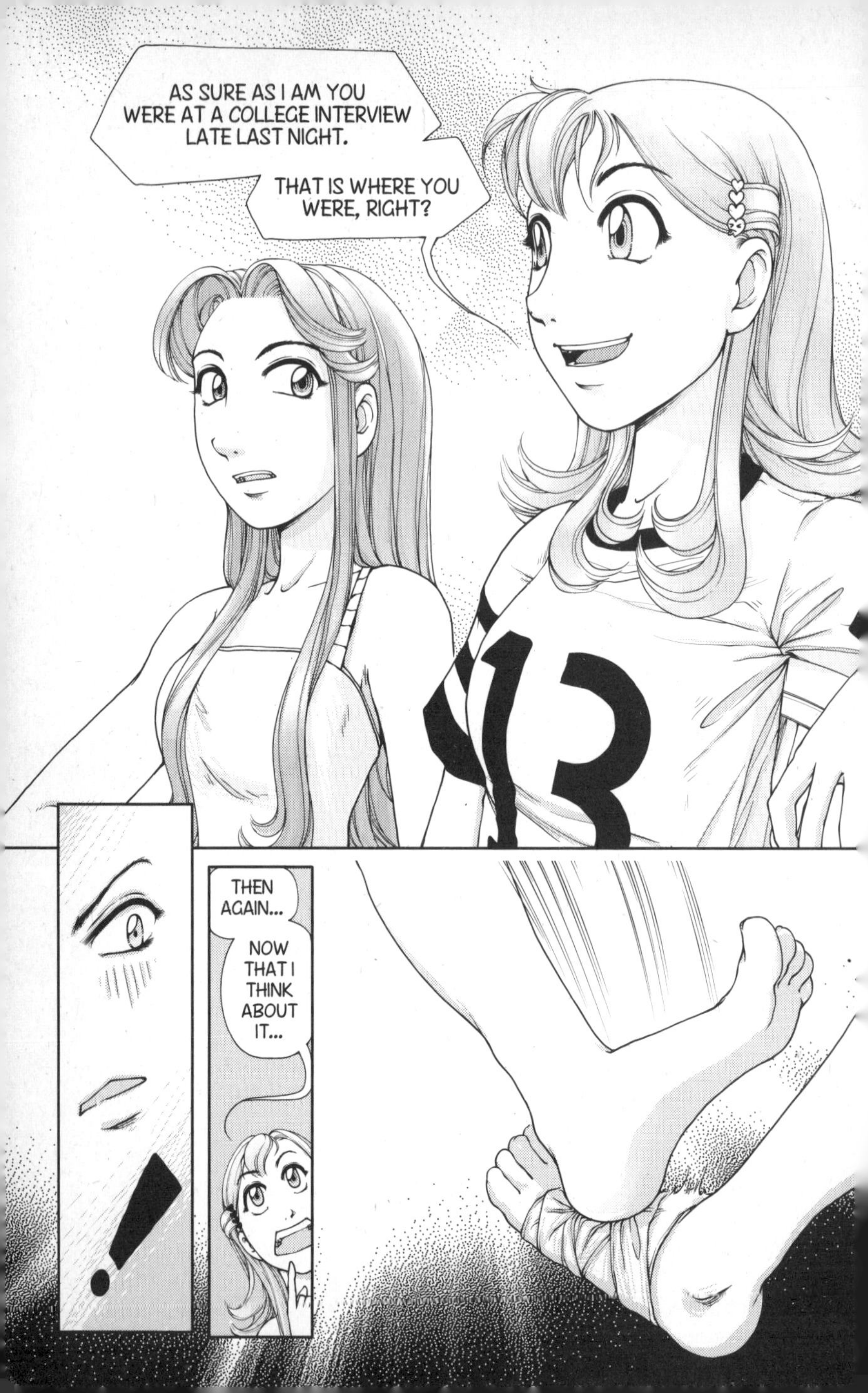
AS SURE AS I AM YOU WERE AT A COLLEGE INTERVIEW LATE LAST NIGHT.
THAT IS WHERE YOU WERE, RIGHT?
THEN AGAIN...
NOW THAT I THINK ABOUT IT...

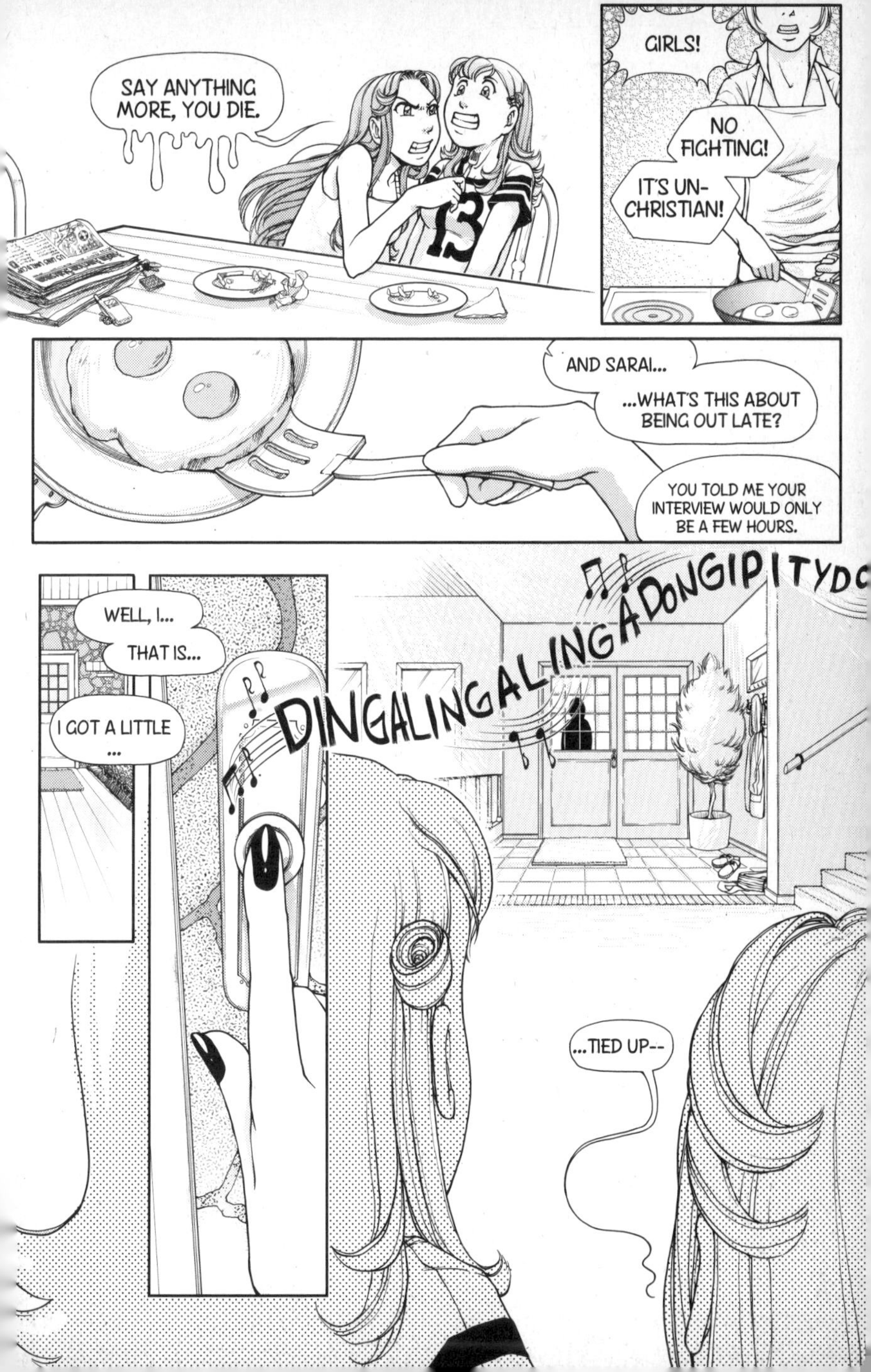
SAY ANYTHING MORE, YOU DIE.
GIRLS!
NO FIGHTING!
IT'S UN-CHRISTIAN!
AND SARAI...
...WHAT'S THIS ABOUT BEING OUT LATE?
YOU TOLD ME YOUR INTERVIEW WOULD ONLY BE A FEW HOURS.
WELL, I...
THAT IS...
I GOT A LITTLE ...
DINGALINGALINGADONGIPITYDO
...TIED UP--

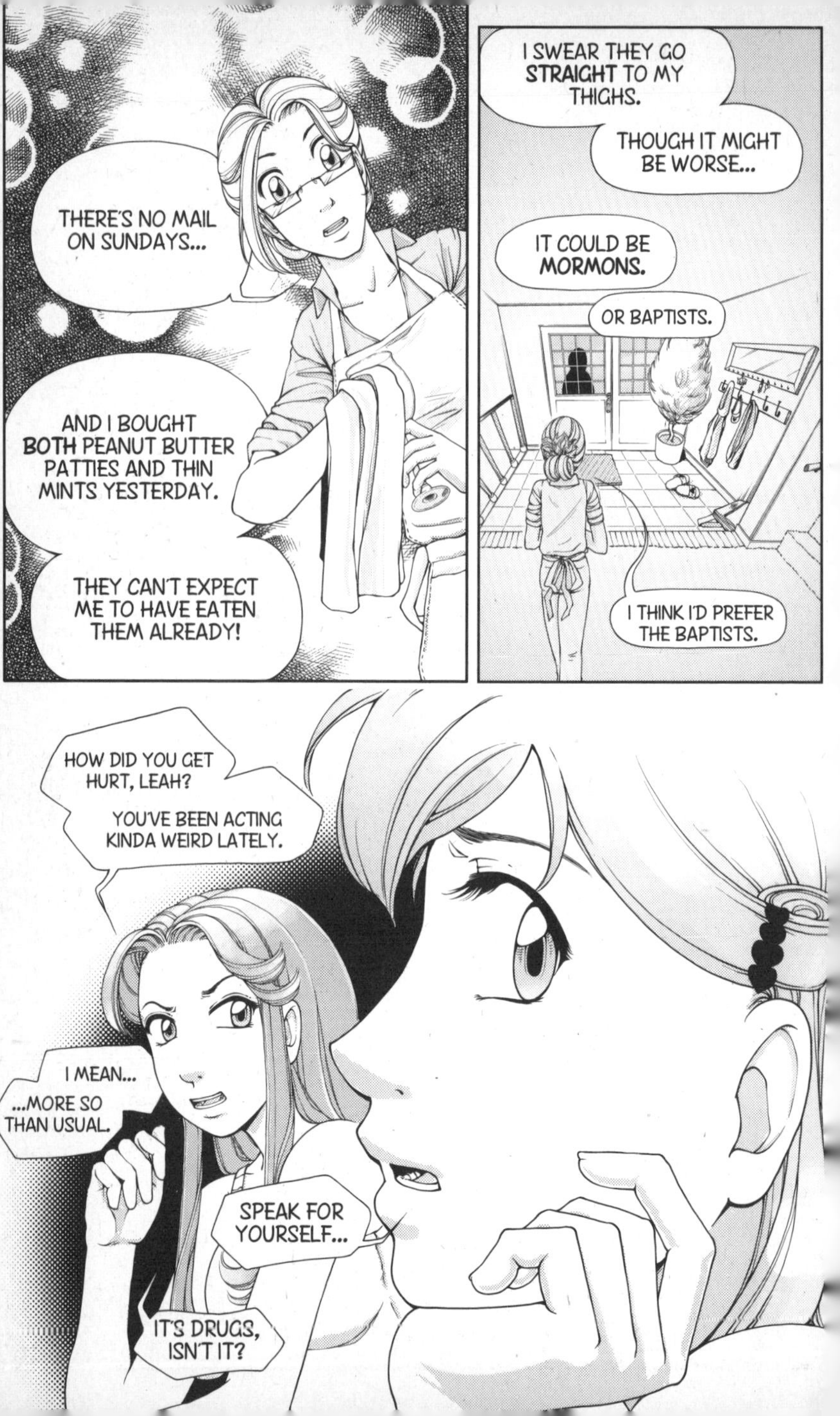
THERE'S NO MAIL ON SUNDAYS...
AND I BOUGHT **BOTH** PEANUT BUTTER PATTIES AND THIN MINTS YESTERDAY.
THEY CAN'T EXPECT ME TO HAVE EATEN THEM ALREADY!
I SWEAR THEY GO **STRAIGHT** TO MY THIGHS.
THOUGH IT MIGHT BE WORSE...
IT COULD BE **MORMONS.**
OR BAPTISTS.
I THINK I'D PREFER THE BAPTISTS.
HOW DID YOU GET HURT, LEAH?
YOU'VE BEEN ACTING KINDA WEIRD LATELY.
I MEAN...
...MORE SO THAN USUAL.
SPEAK FOR YOURSELF...
IT'S DRUGS, ISN'T IT?

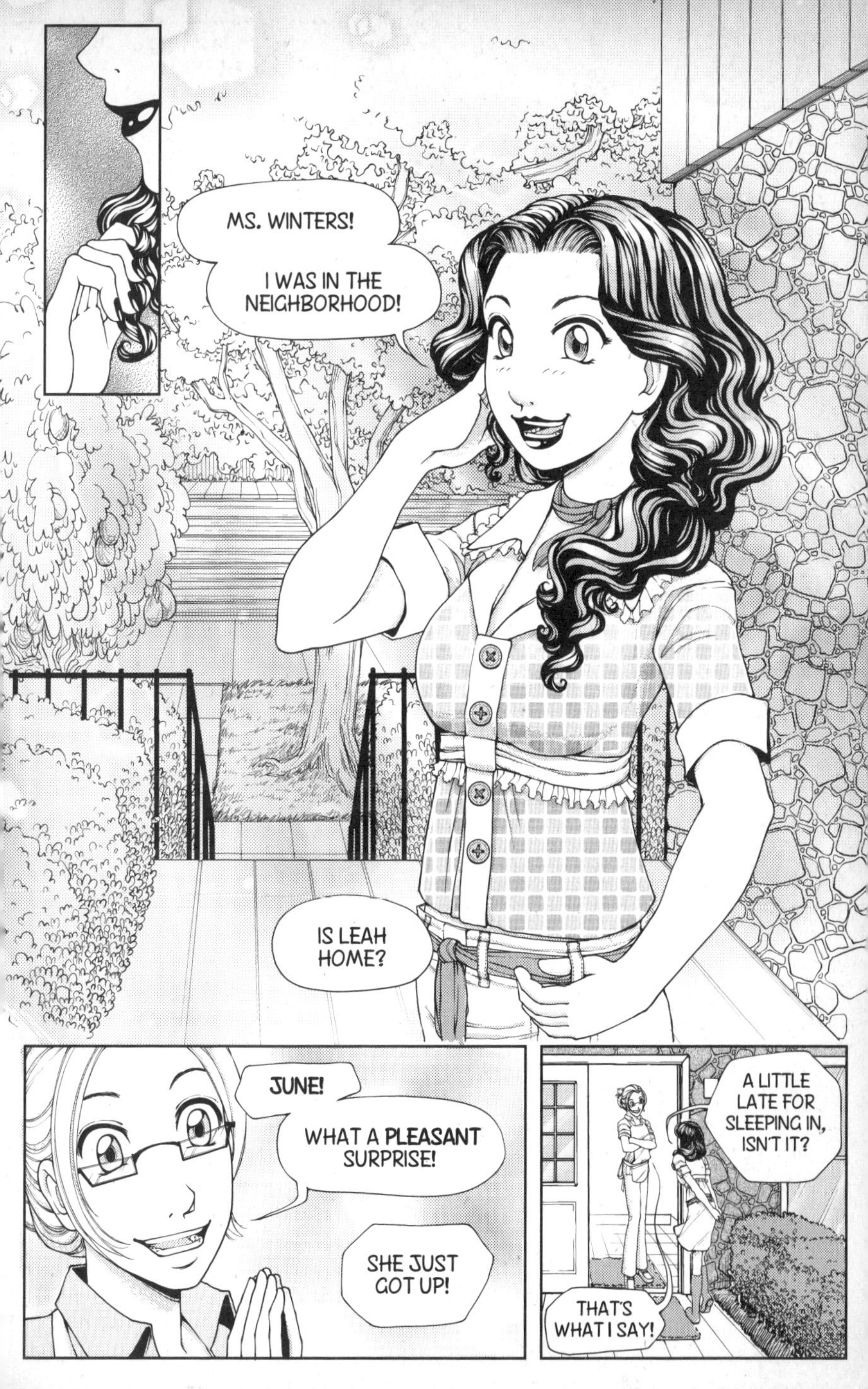
MS. WINTERS!
I WAS IN THE NEIGHBORHOOD!
IS LEAH HOME?
JUNE!
WHAT A PLEASANT SURPRISE!
SHE JUST GOT UP!
A LITTLE LATE FOR SLEEPING IN, ISN'T IT?
THAT'S WHAT I SAY!

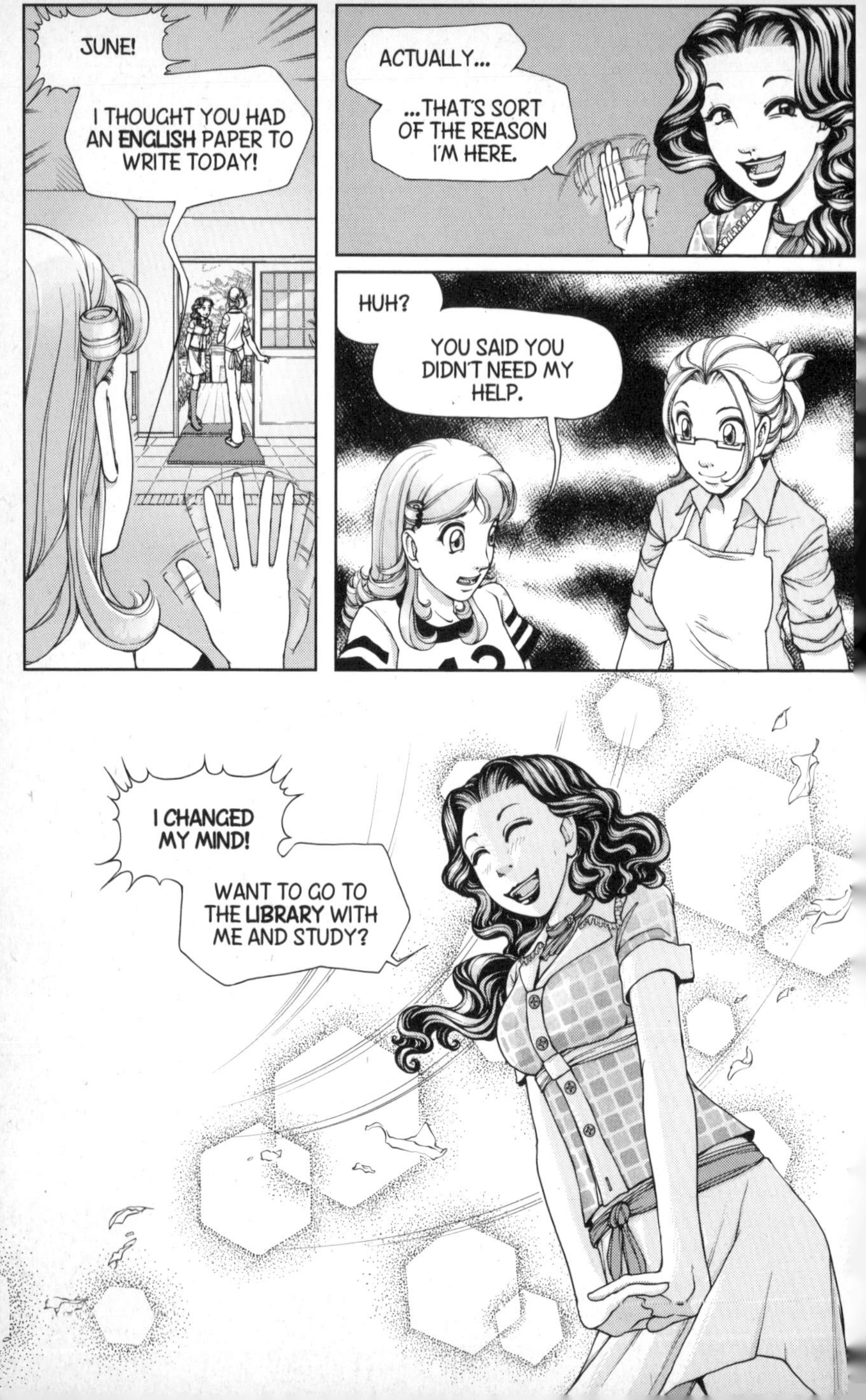
JUNE!
I THOUGHT YOU HAD AN **ENGLISH** PAPER TO WRITE TODAY!
ACTUALLY...
...THAT'S SORT OF THE REASON I'M HERE.
HUH?
YOU SAID YOU DIDN'T NEED MY HELP.
I CHANGED MY MIND!
WANT TO GO TO THE **LIBRARY** WITH ME AND STUDY?

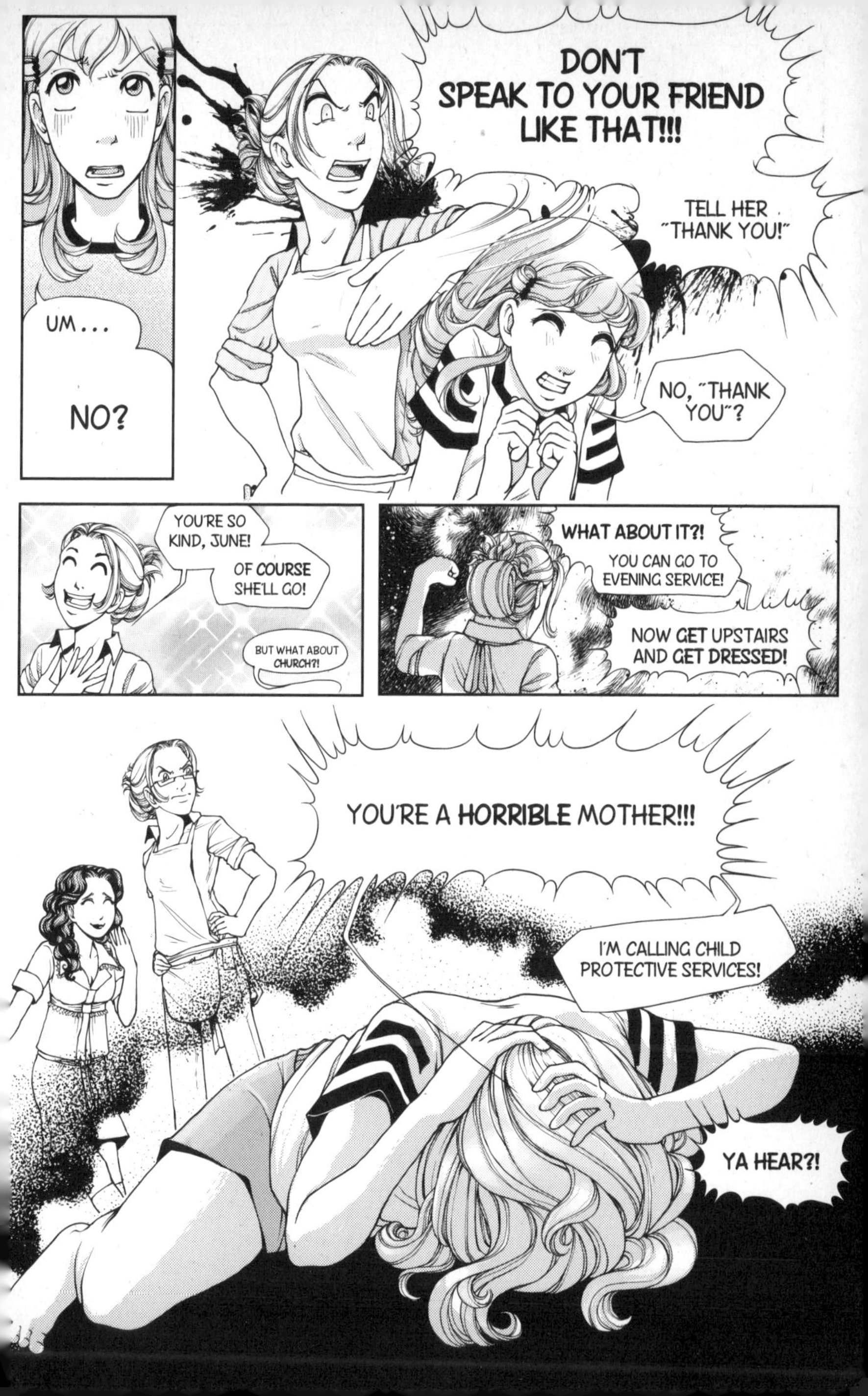
DON'T SPEAK TO YOUR FRIEND LIKE THAT!!!
TELL HER "THANK YOU!"
UM . . .
NO?
NO, "THANK YOU"?
YOU'RE SO KIND, JUNE!
OF COURSE SHE'LL GO!
BUT WHAT ABOUT CHURCH?!
WHAT ABOUT IT?!
YOU CAN GO TO EVENING SERVICE!
NOW GET UPSTAIRS AND GET DRESSED!
YOU'RE A HORRIBLE MOTHER!!!
I'M CALLING CHILD PROTECTIVE SERVICES!
YA HEAR?!

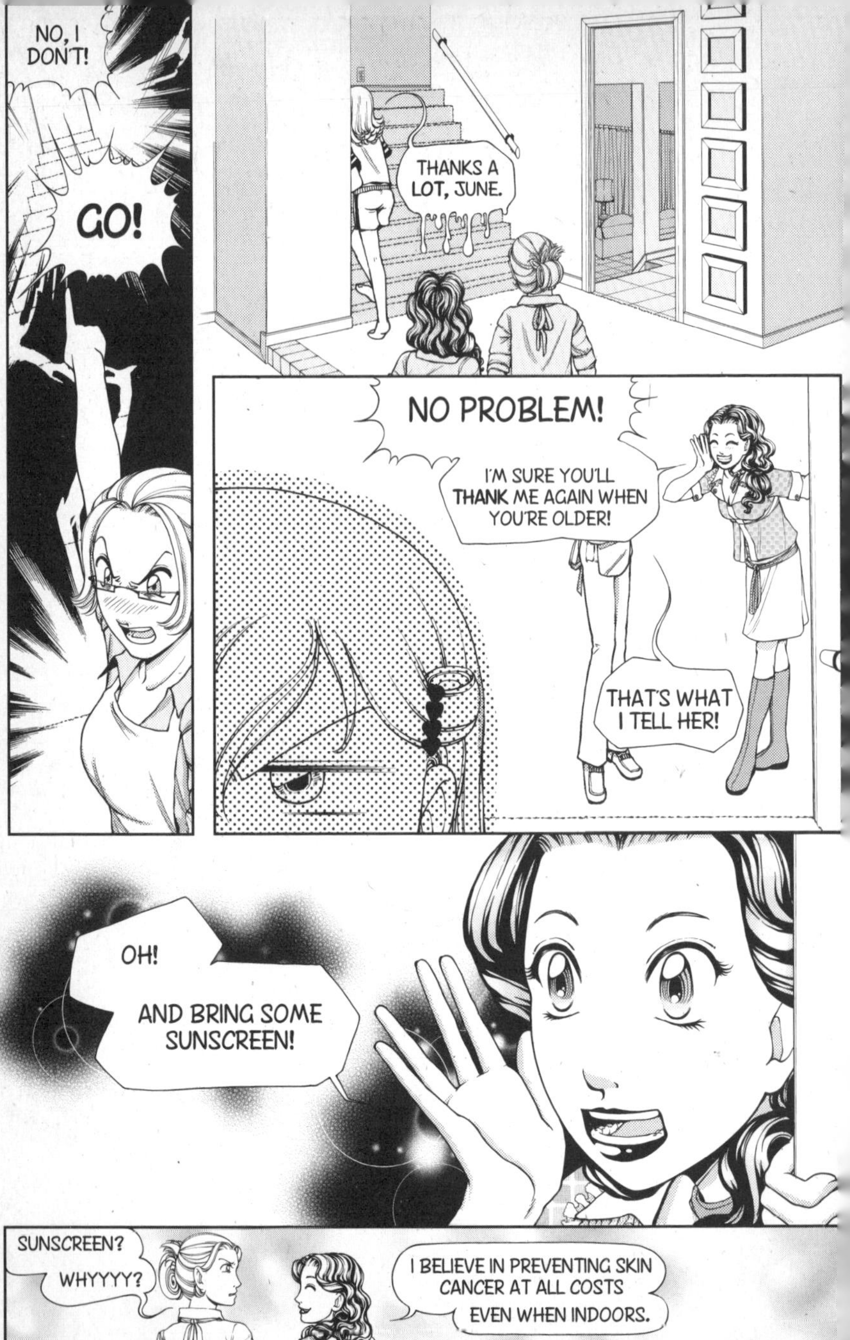
NO, I DON'T!
GO!
THANKS A LOT, JUNE.
NO PROBLEM!
I'M SURE YOU'LL **THANK** ME AGAIN WHEN YOU'RE OLDER!
THAT'S WHAT I TELL HER!
OH!
AND BRING SOME SUNSCREEN!
SUNSCREEN?
WHYYYY?
I BELIEVE IN PREVENTING SKIN CANCER AT ALL COSTS
EVEN WHEN INDOORS.

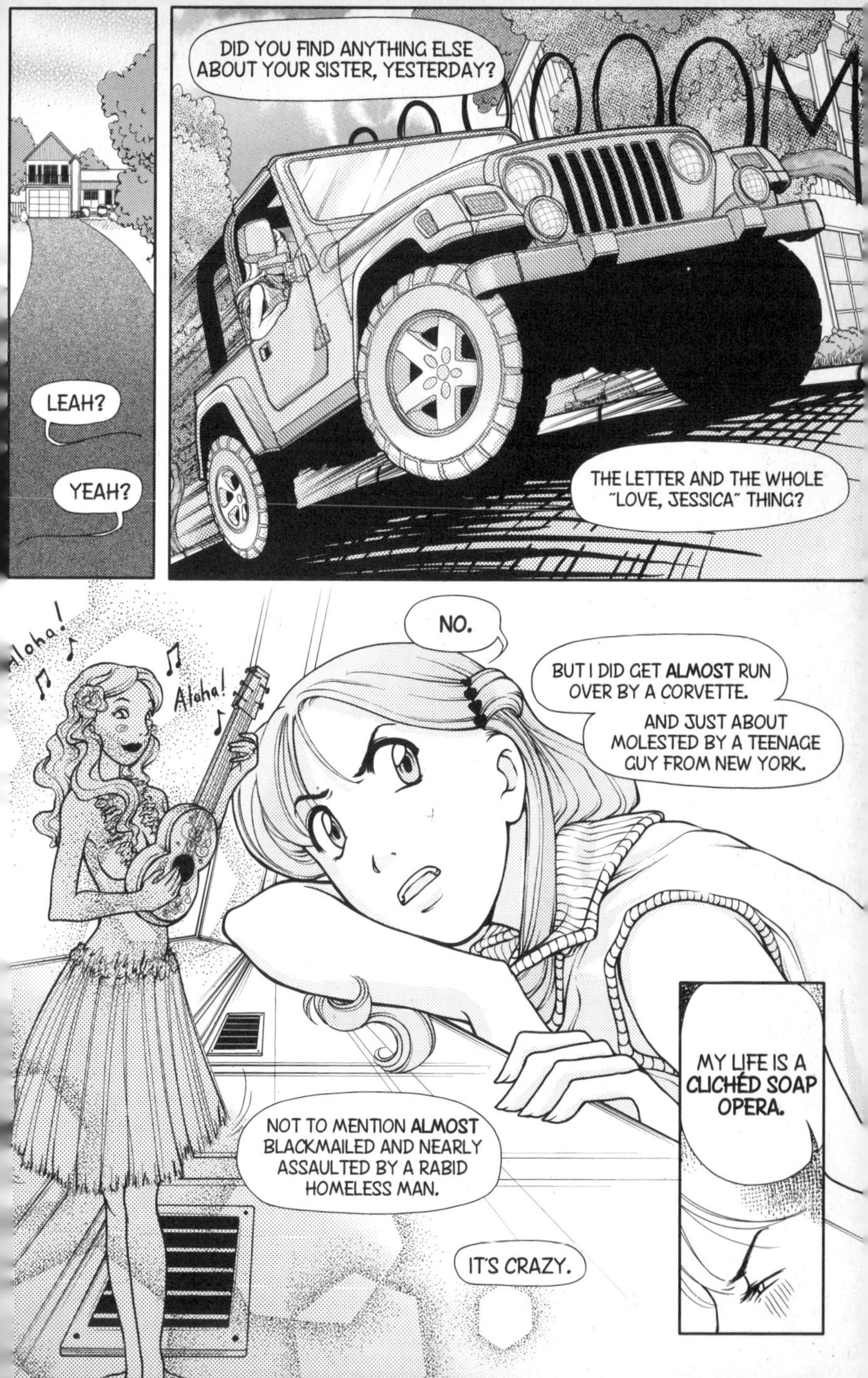
LEAH?
YEAH?
DID YOU FIND ANYTHING ELSE ABOUT YOUR SISTER, YESTERDAY?
VROOOOM
THE LETTER AND THE WHOLE "LOVE, JESSICA" THING?
Aloha!
Aloha!
NO.
BUT I DID GET ALMOST RUN OVER BY A CORVETTE.
AND JUST ABOUT MOLESTED BY A TEENAGE GUY FROM NEW YORK.
NOT TO MENTION ALMOST BLACKMAILED AND NEARLY ASSAULTED BY A RABID HOMELESS MAN.
IT'S CRAZY.
MY LIFE IS A CLICHÉD SOAP OPERA.

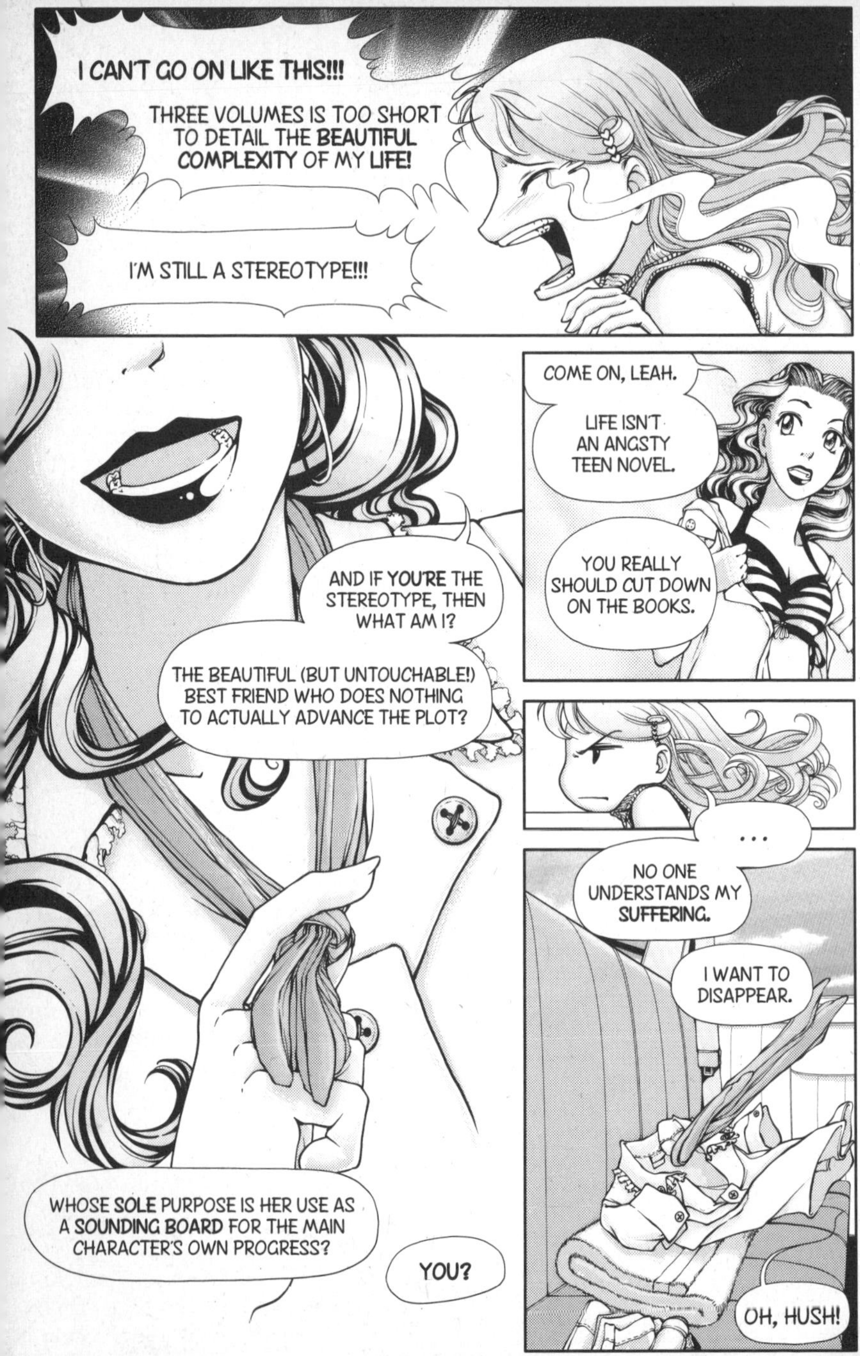
I CAN'T GO ON LIKE THIS!!!
THREE VOLUMES IS TOO SHORT TO DETAIL THE **BEAUTIFUL COMPLEXITY** OF MY **LIFE!**
I'M STILL A STEREOTYPE!!!
AND IF **YOU'RE** THE STEREOTYPE, THEN WHAT AM I?
THE BEAUTIFUL (BUT UNTOUCHABLE!) BEST FRIEND WHO DOES NOTHING TO ACTUALLY ADVANCE THE PLOT?
WHOSE **SOLE** PURPOSE IS HER USE AS A **SOUNDING BOARD** FOR THE MAIN CHARACTER'S OWN PROGRESS?
YOU?
COME ON, LEAH.
LIFE ISN'T AN ANGSTY TEEN NOVEL.
YOU REALLY SHOULD CUT DOWN ON THE BOOKS.
...
NO ONE UNDERSTANDS MY **SUFFERING.**
I WANT TO DISAPPEAR.
OH, HUSH!

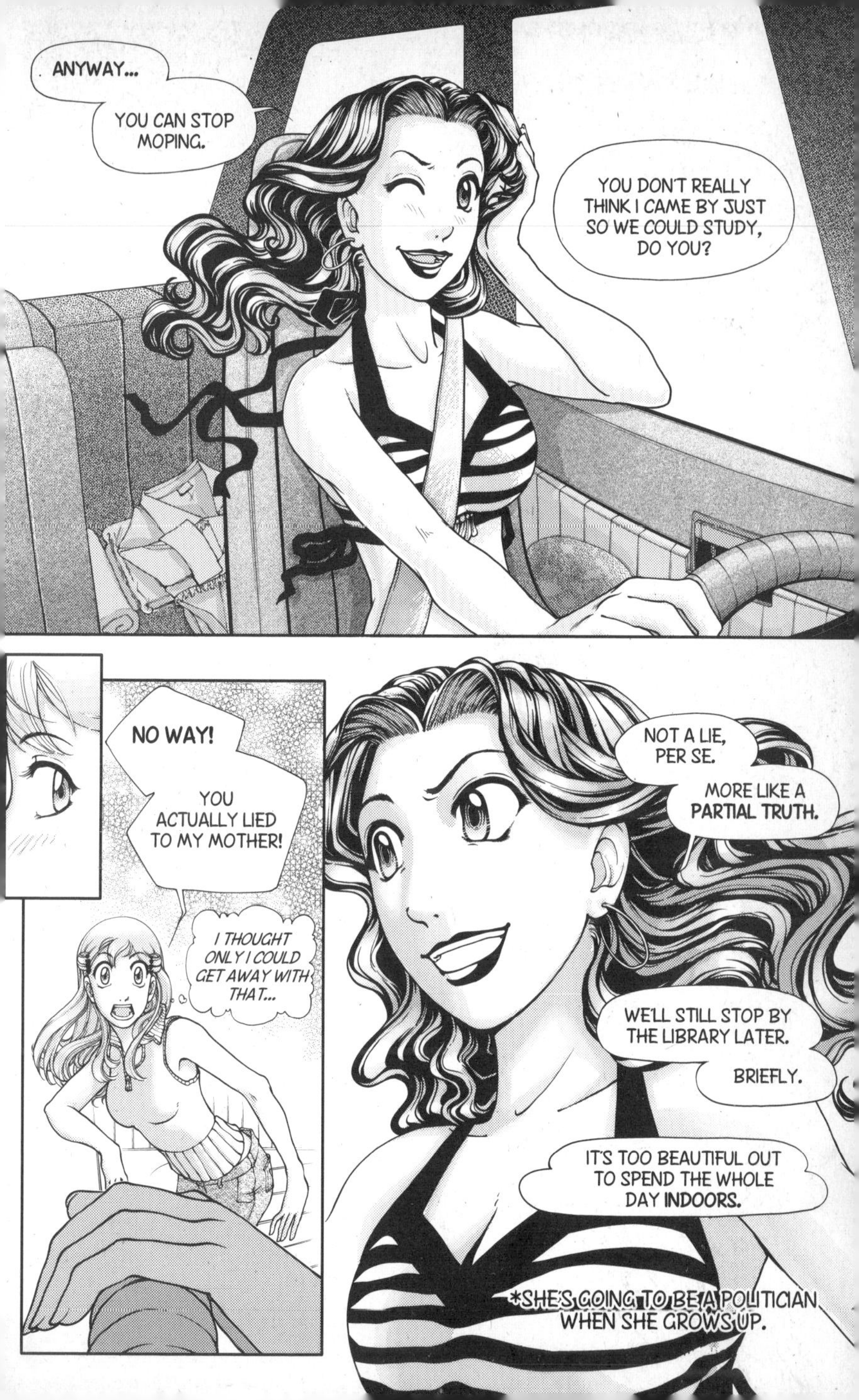
ANYWAY...
YOU CAN STOP MOPING.
YOU DON'T REALLY THINK I CAME BY JUST SO WE COULD STUDY, DO YOU?
NO WAY!
YOU ACTUALLY LIED TO MY MOTHER!
I THOUGHT ONLY I COULD GET AWAY WITH THAT...
NOT A LIE, PER SE.
MORE LIKE A PARTIAL TRUTH.
WE'LL STILL STOP BY THE LIBRARY LATER.
BRIEFLY.
IT'S TOO BEAUTIFUL OUT TO SPEND THE WHOLE DAY INDOORS.
*SHE'S GOING TO BE A POLITICIAN WHEN SHE GROWS UP.

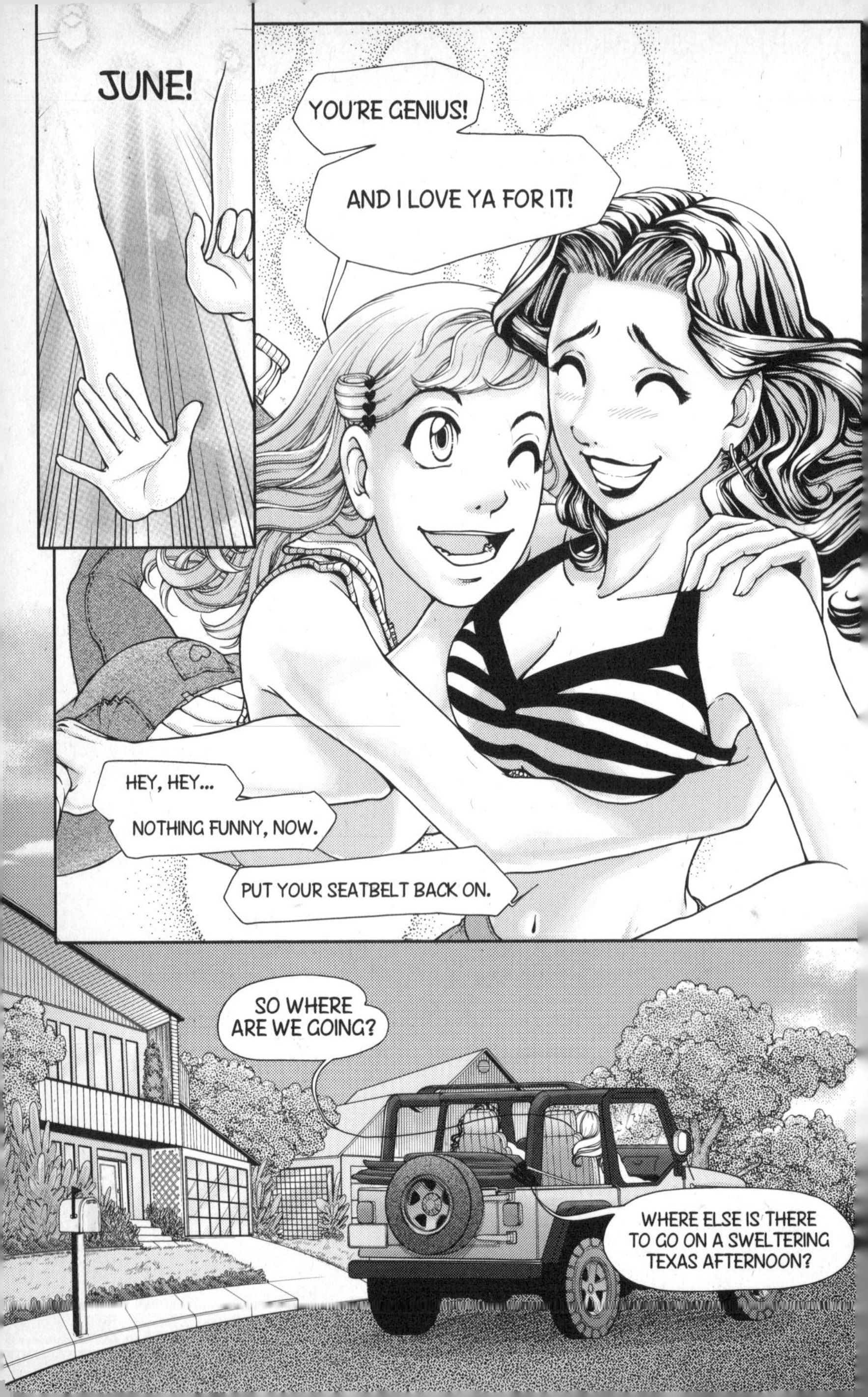
JUNE!
YOU'RE GENIUS!
AND I LOVE YA FOR IT!
HEY, HEY...
NOTHING FUNNY, NOW.
PUT YOUR SEATBELT BACK ON.
SO WHERE ARE WE GOING?
WHERE ELSE IS THERE TO GO ON A SWELTERING TEXAS AFTERNOON?

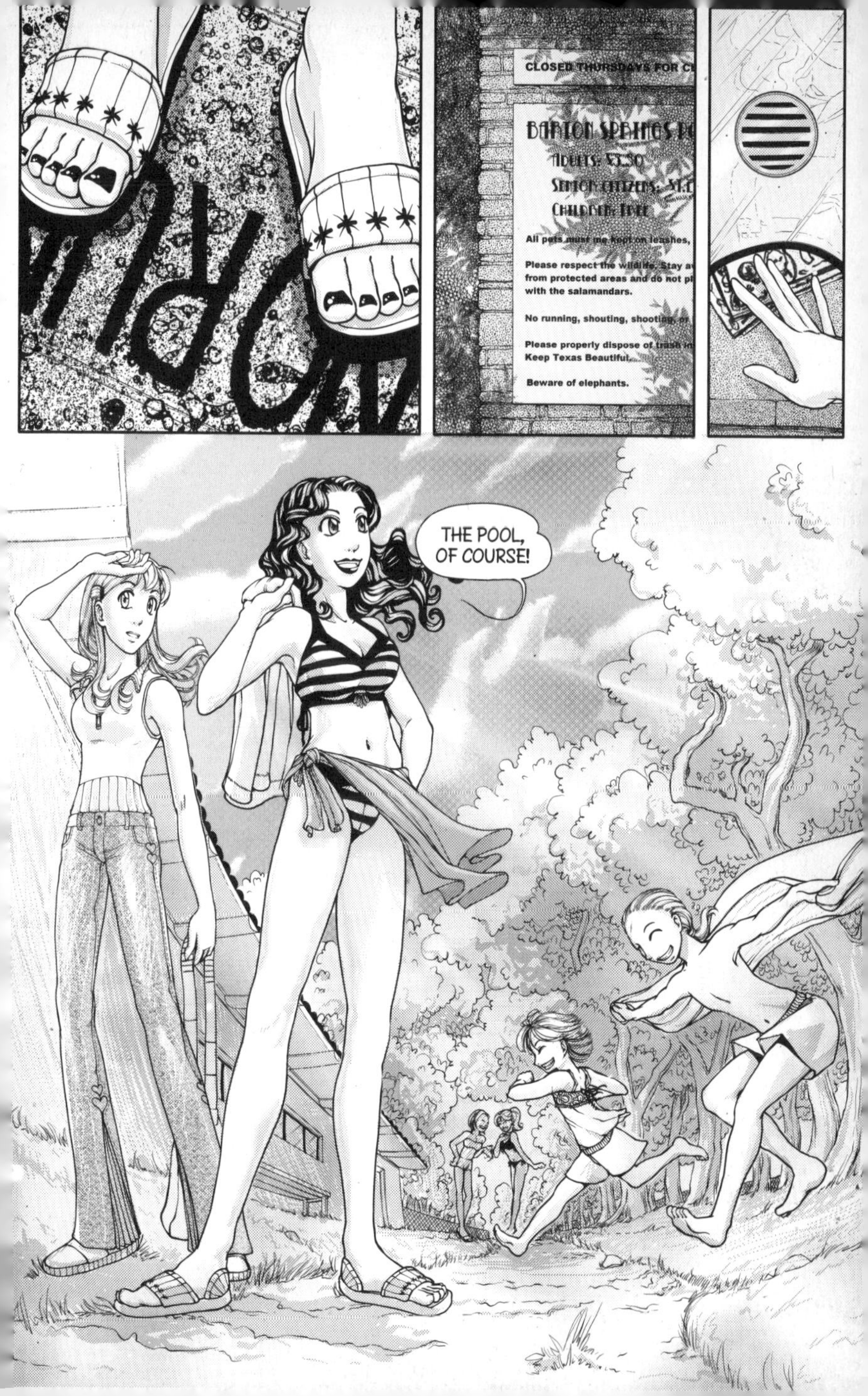
CLOSED THURSDAYS FOR
BARTON SPRINGS
ADULTS: $3.50
SENIOR CITIZENS:
CHILDREN: FREE
All pets must me kept on leashes,
Please respect the wildlife. Stay
from protected areas and do not
with the salamandars.
No running, shouting, shooting, or
Please properly dispose of trash
Keep Texas Beautiful.
Beware of elephants.
THE POOL, OF COURSE!

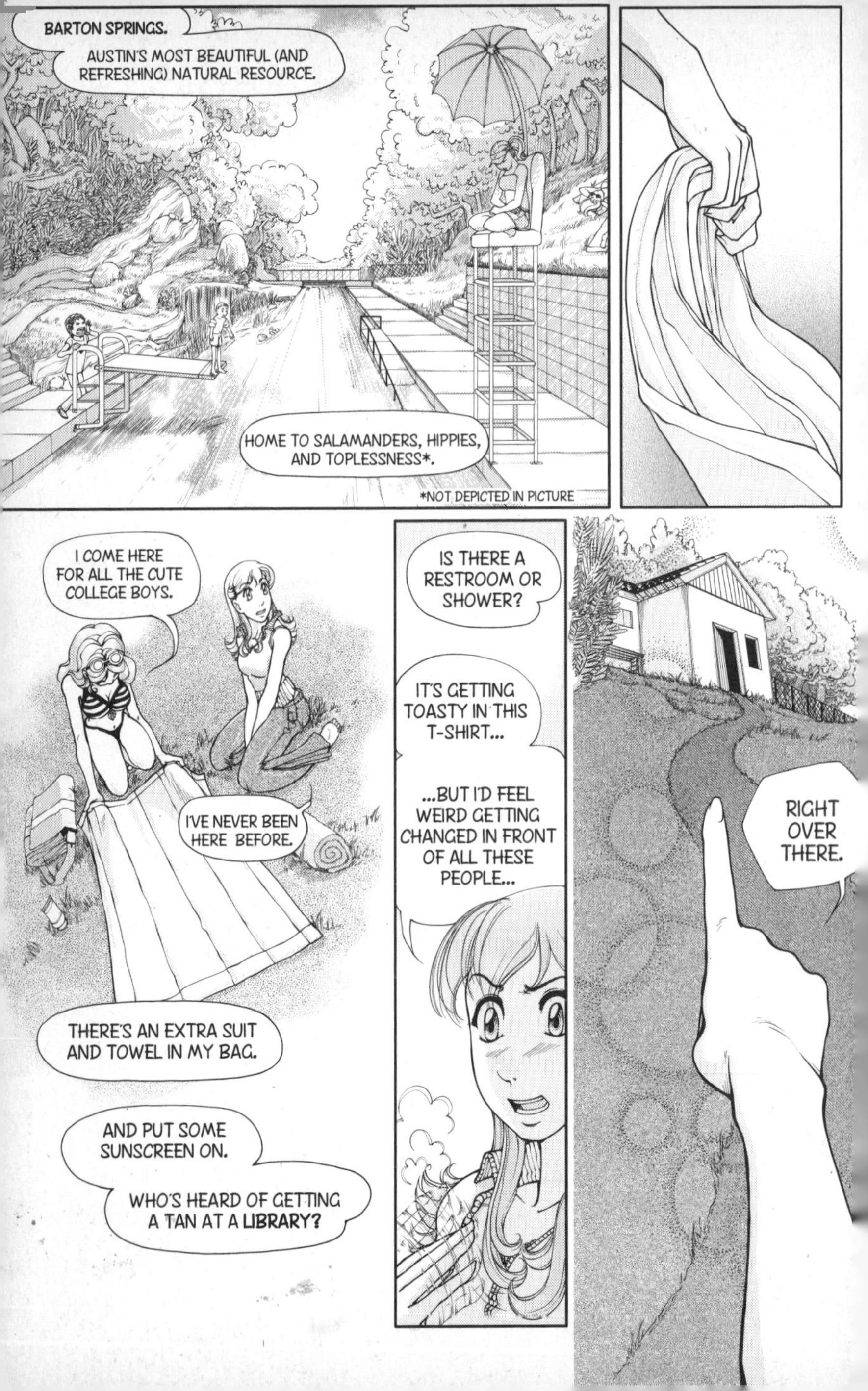
BARTON SPRINGS.
AUSTIN'S MOST BEAUTIFUL (AND REFRESHING) NATURAL RESOURCE.
HOME TO SALAMANDERS, HIPPIES, AND TOPLESSNESS*.
*NOT DEPICTED IN PICTURE
I COME HERE FOR ALL THE CUTE COLLEGE BOYS.
I'VE NEVER BEEN HERE BEFORE.
THERE'S AN EXTRA SUIT AND TOWEL IN MY BAG.
AND PUT SOME SUNSCREEN ON.
WHO'S HEARD OF GETTING A TAN AT A LIBRARY?
IS THERE A RESTROOM OR SHOWER?
IT'S GETTING TOASTY IN THIS T-SHIRT...
...BUT I'D FEEL WEIRD GETTING CHANGED IN FRONT OF ALL THESE PEOPLE...
RIGHT OVER THERE.

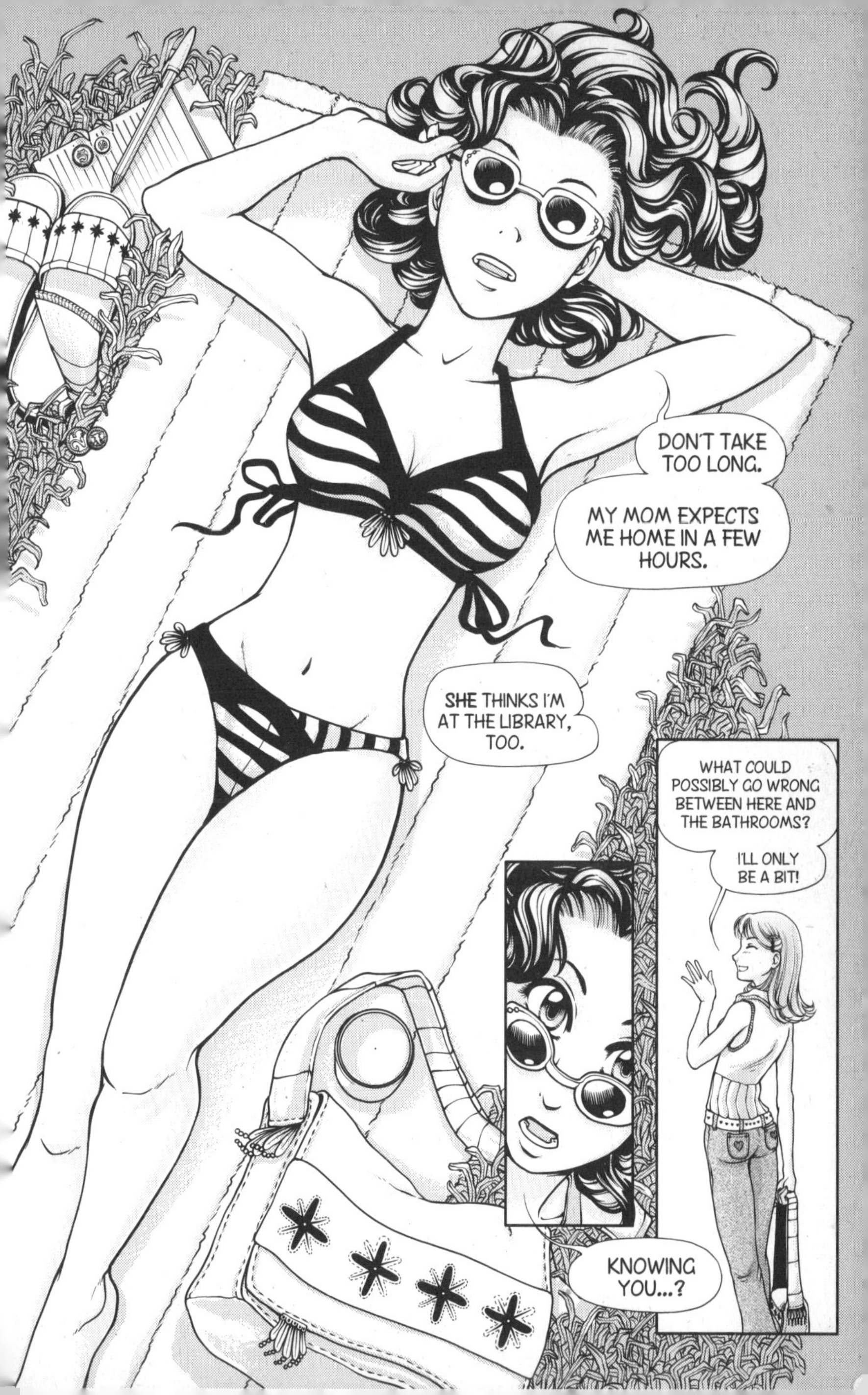
DON'T TAKE TOO LONG.
MY MOM EXPECTS ME HOME IN A FEW HOURS.
SHE THINKS I'M AT THE LIBRARY, TOO.
WHAT COULD POSSIBLY GO WRONG BETWEEN HERE AND THE BATHROOMS?
I'LL ONLY BE A BIT!
KNOWING YOU...?

Dear Diary,                                September 1st

     Why do people always write "dear diary"
I mean, it's dear diary. It isn't as
though a diary can actually think (or
read). I guess it's because we're
writing to ourselves, but then, shouldn't
it be "Dear Me"??? Or maybe "Dear
God"? Because God's gonna be reading it anyway, right?
     Right.

     ANYway... doodoodoo... hmm. Now I
don't know what to write. -- Weird
how you always know what you
want to write, but then when you
actually sit down, nothing actually
comes out. Or everything comes
out looking stupid.

     Anyway. Whatever.
I'm gonna get back
to bed. This diary's
boring.

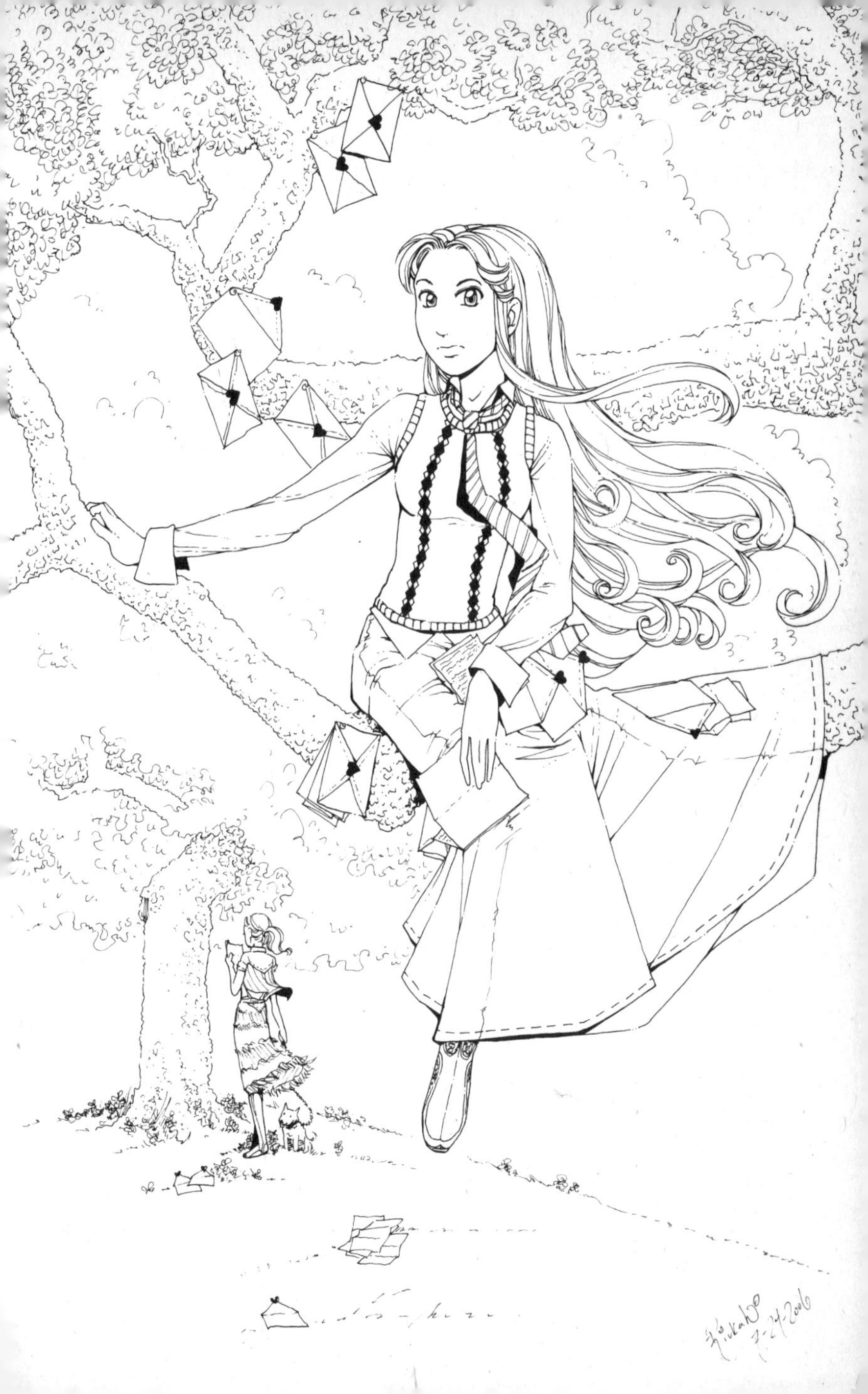

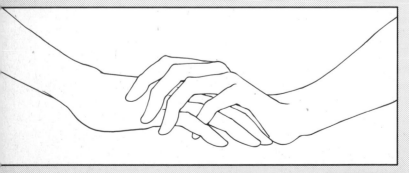

BEAT 7

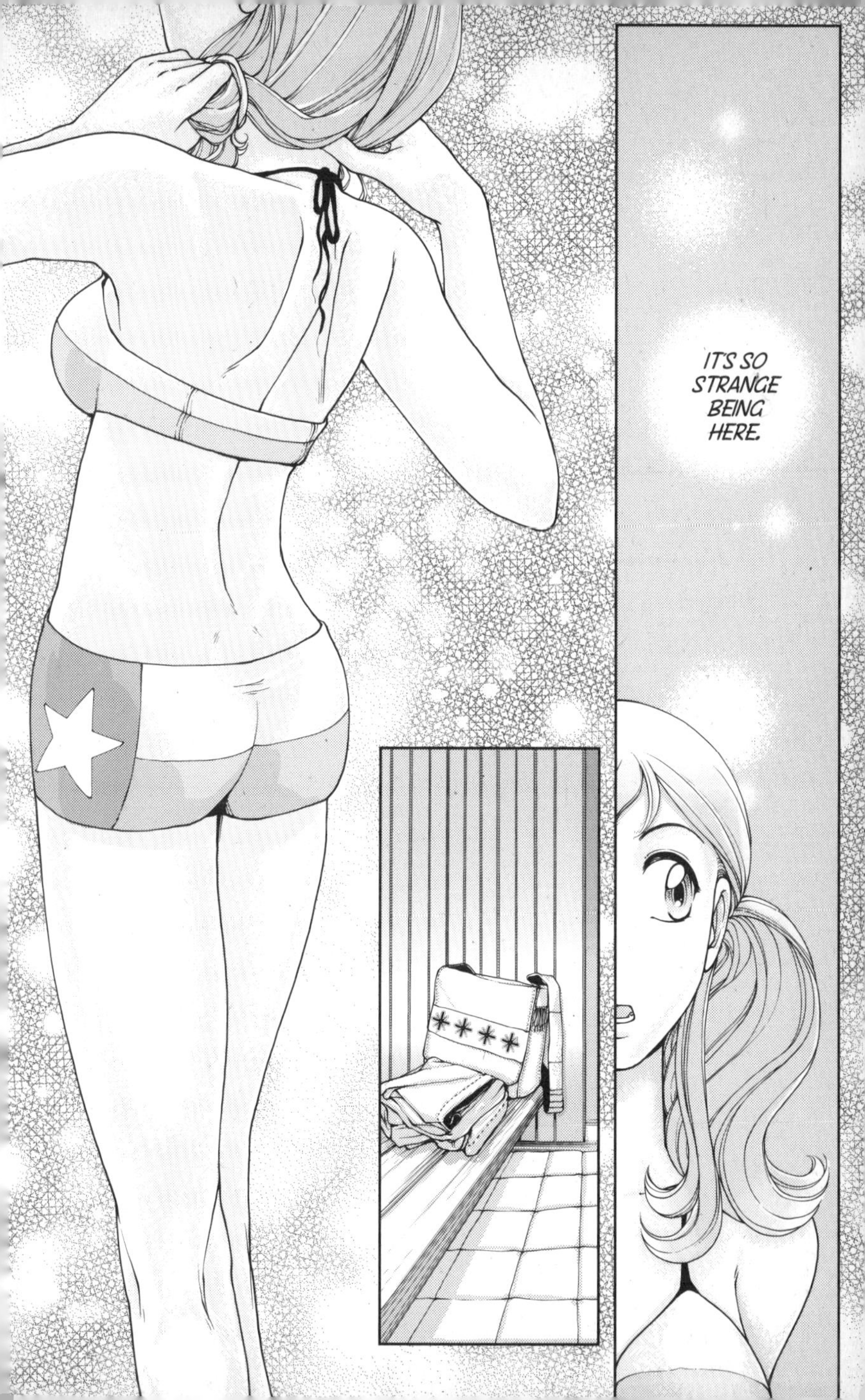
IT'S SO STRANGE BEING HERE.

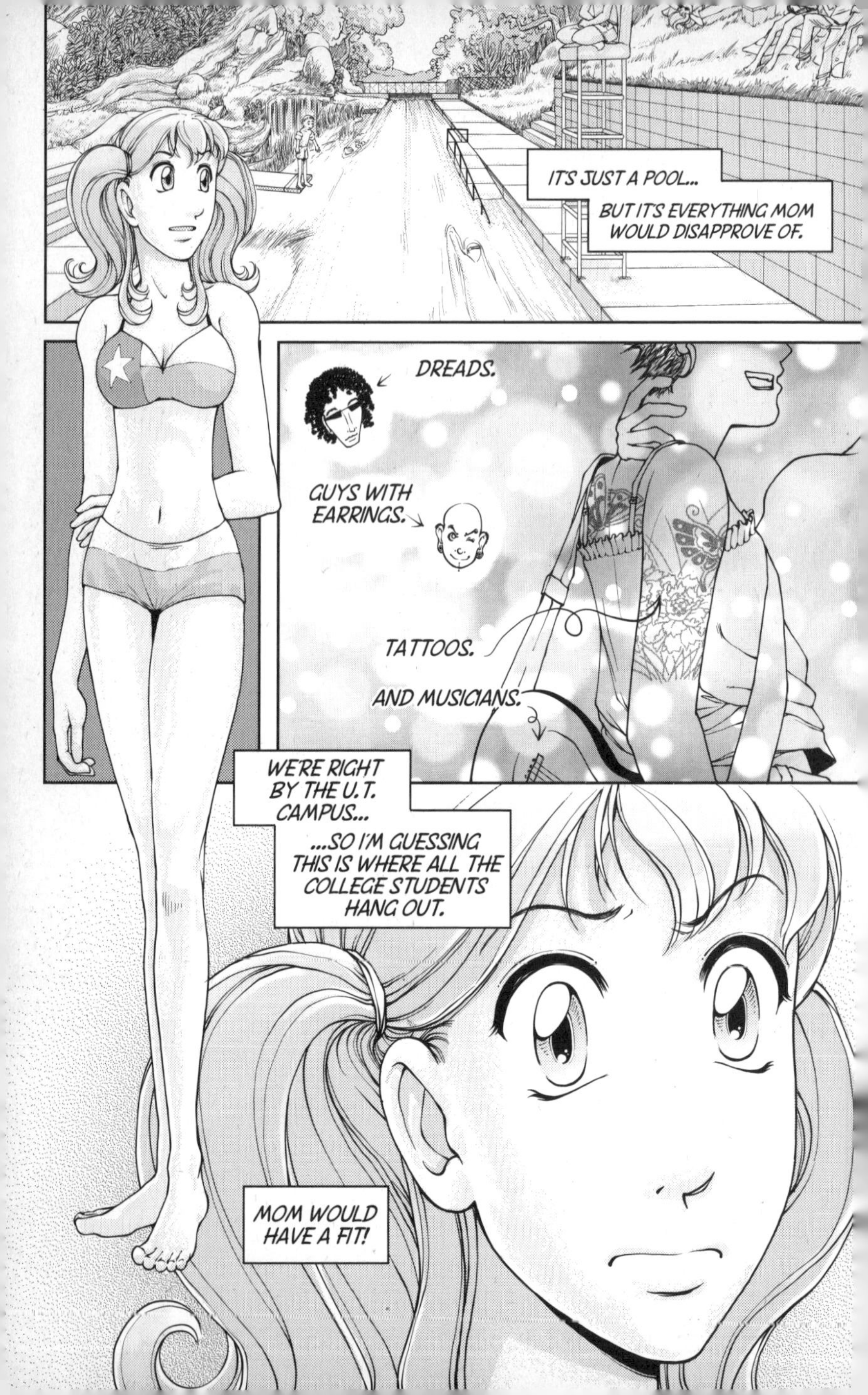
IT'S JUST A POOL...
BUT IT'S EVERYTHING MOM WOULD DISAPPROVE OF.
DREADS.
GUYS WITH EARRINGS.
TATTOOS.
AND MUSICIANS.
WE'RE RIGHT BY THE U.T. CAMPUS...
...SO I'M GUESSING THIS IS WHERE ALL THE COLLEGE STUDENTS HANG OUT.
MOM WOULD HAVE A FIT!

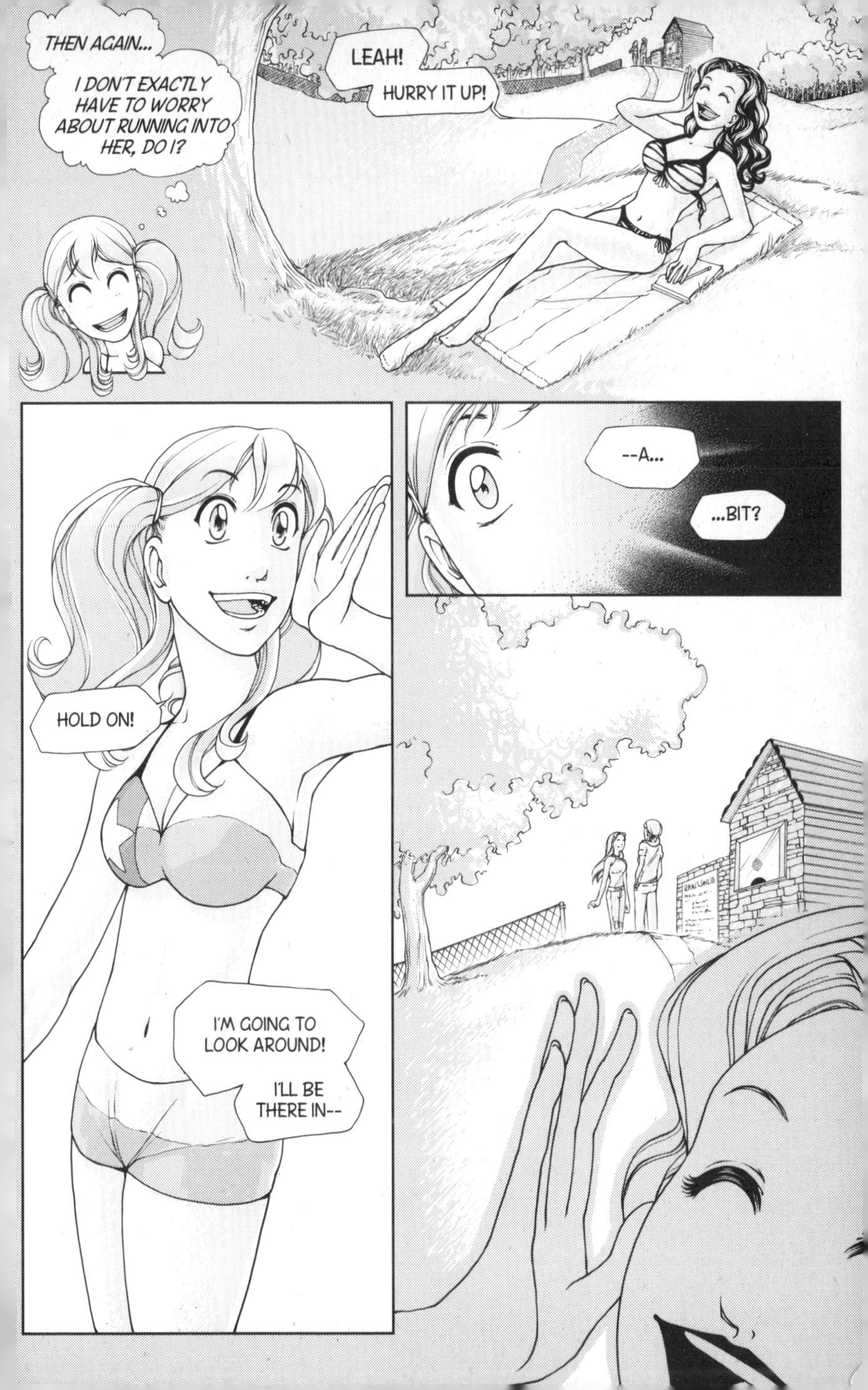
THEN AGAIN...
I DON'T EXACTLY HAVE TO WORRY ABOUT RUNNING INTO HER, DO I?
LEAH!
HURRY IT UP!
HOLD ON!
I'M GOING TO LOOK AROUND!
I'LL BE THERE IN--
--A...
...BIT?

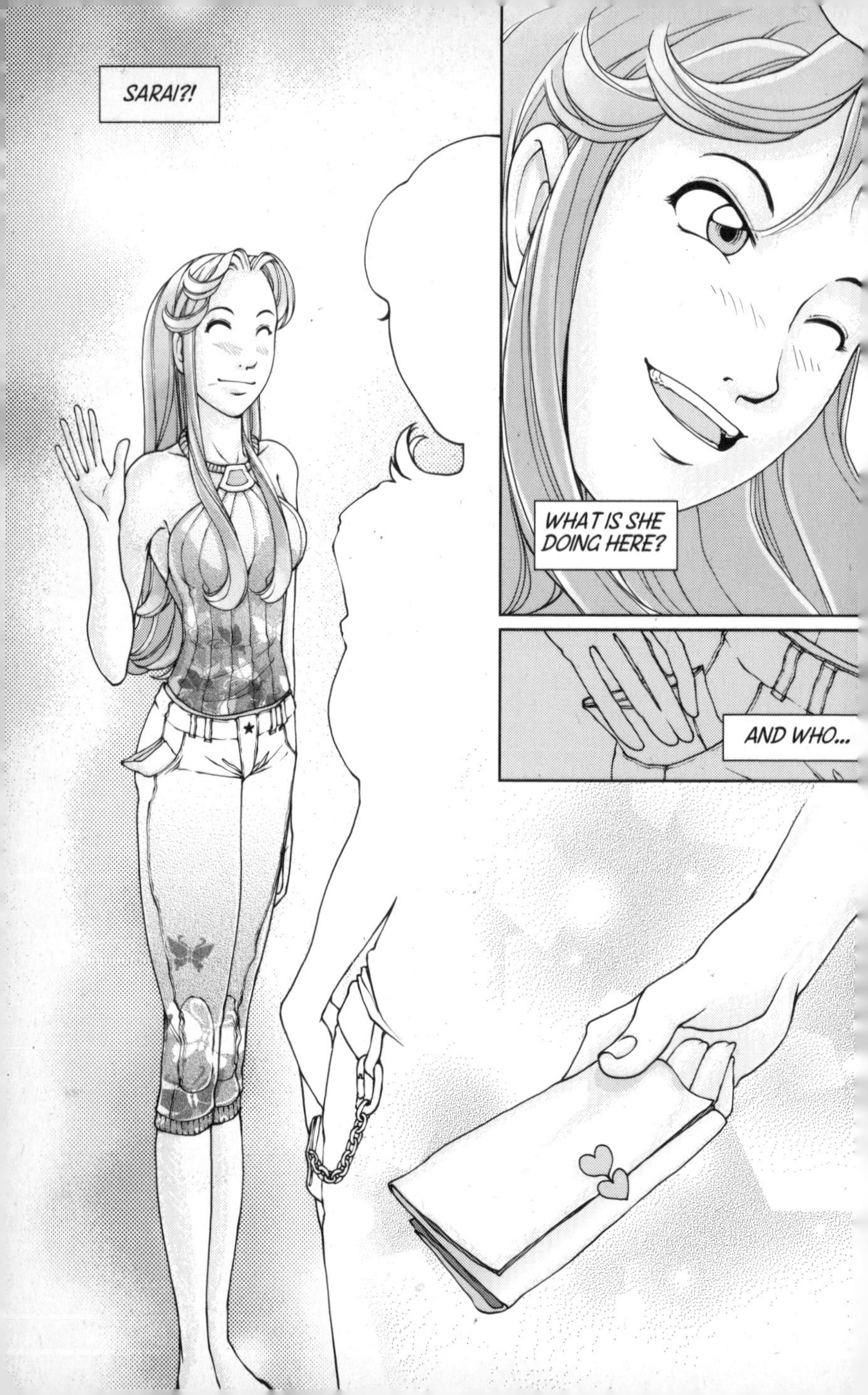
SARAI?!
WHAT IS SHE DOING HERE?
AND WHO...

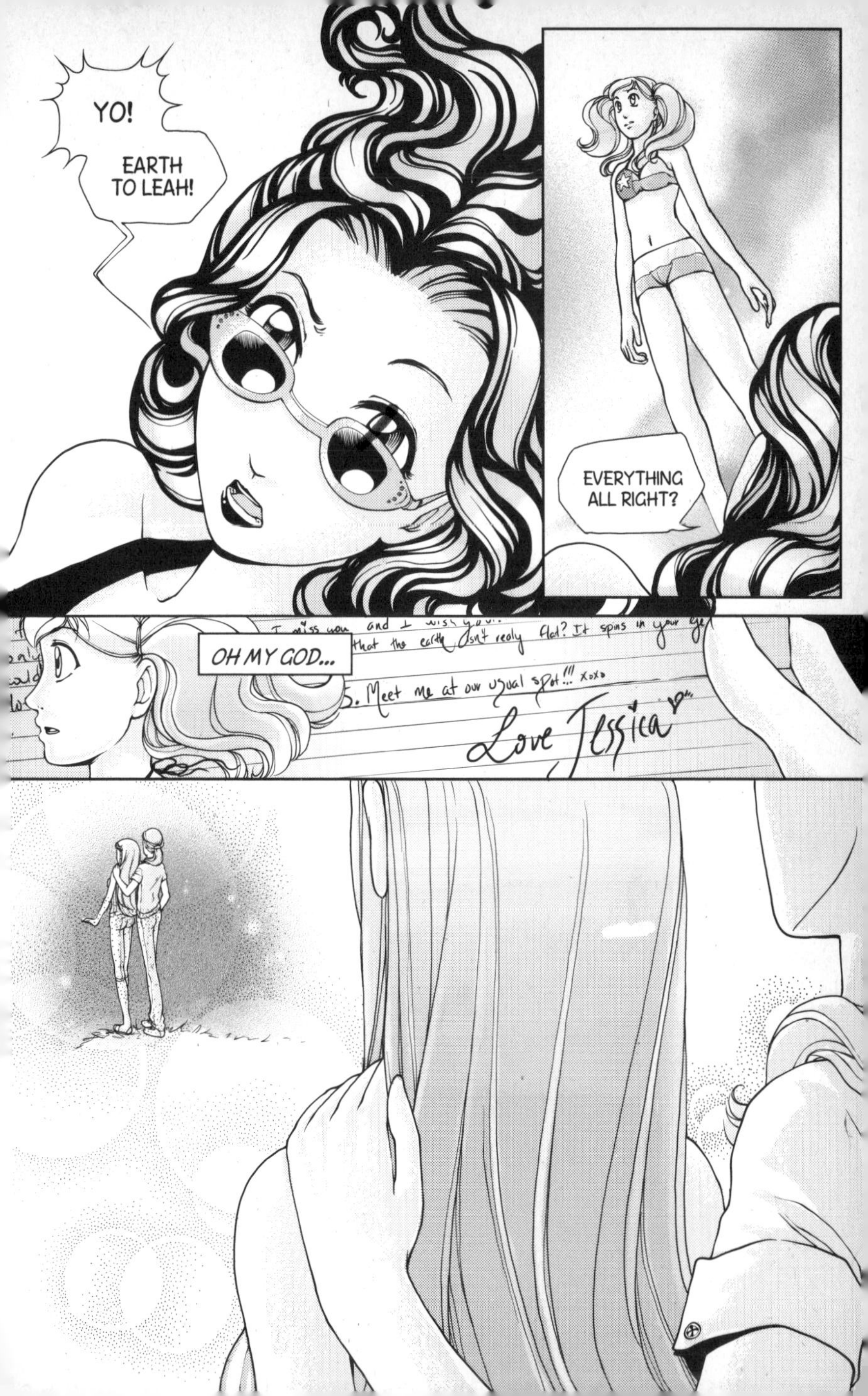
YO!
EARTH TO LEAH!
EVERYTHING ALL RIGHT?
OH MY GOD...
that the earth isn't really flat? It spins in your
5. Meet me at our usual spot!!! xoxo
Love Jessica

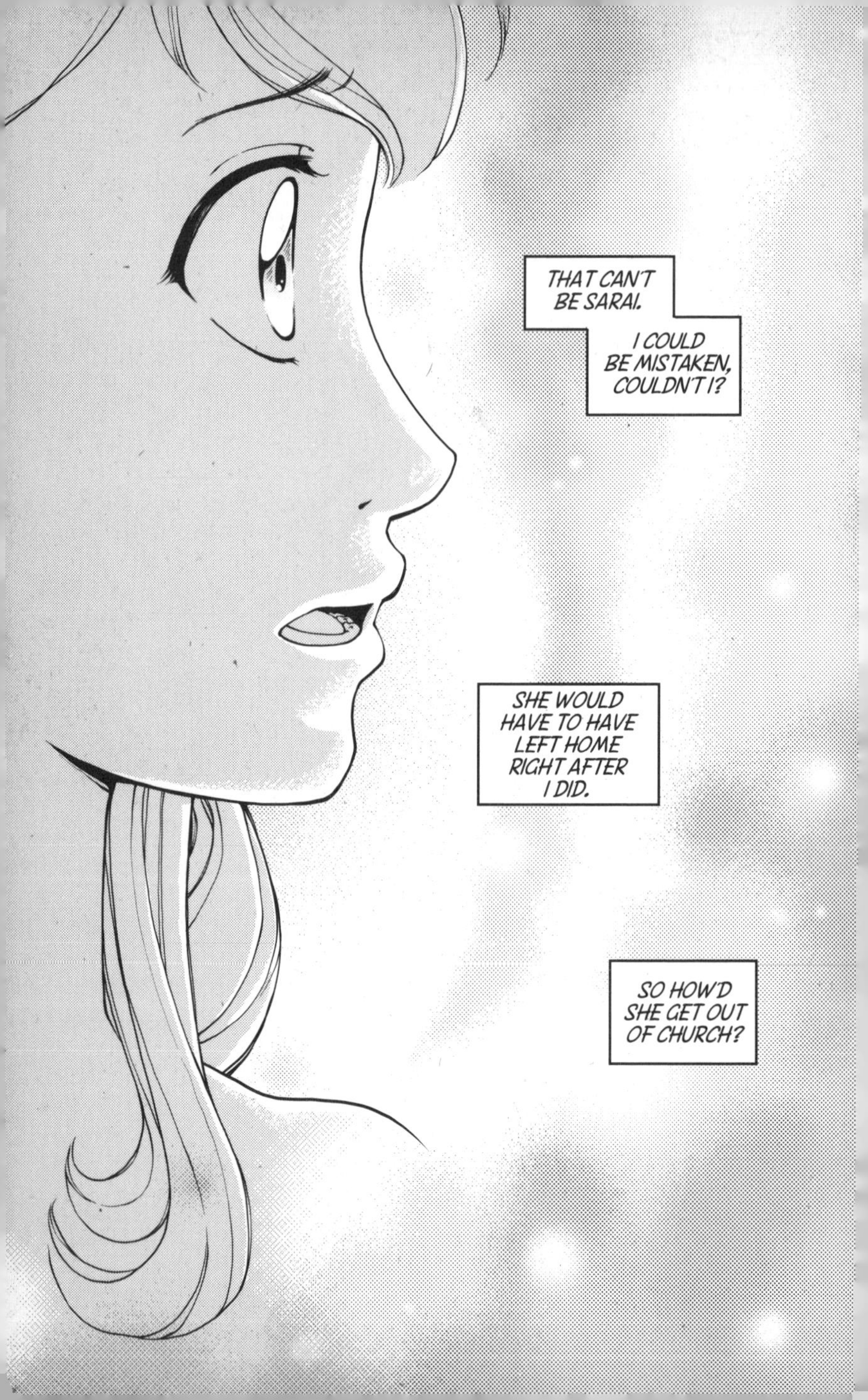
THAT CAN'T BE SARAI.
I COULD BE MISTAKEN, COULDN'T I?
SHE WOULD HAVE TO HAVE LEFT HOME RIGHT AFTER I DID.
SO HOW'D SHE GET OUT OF CHURCH?

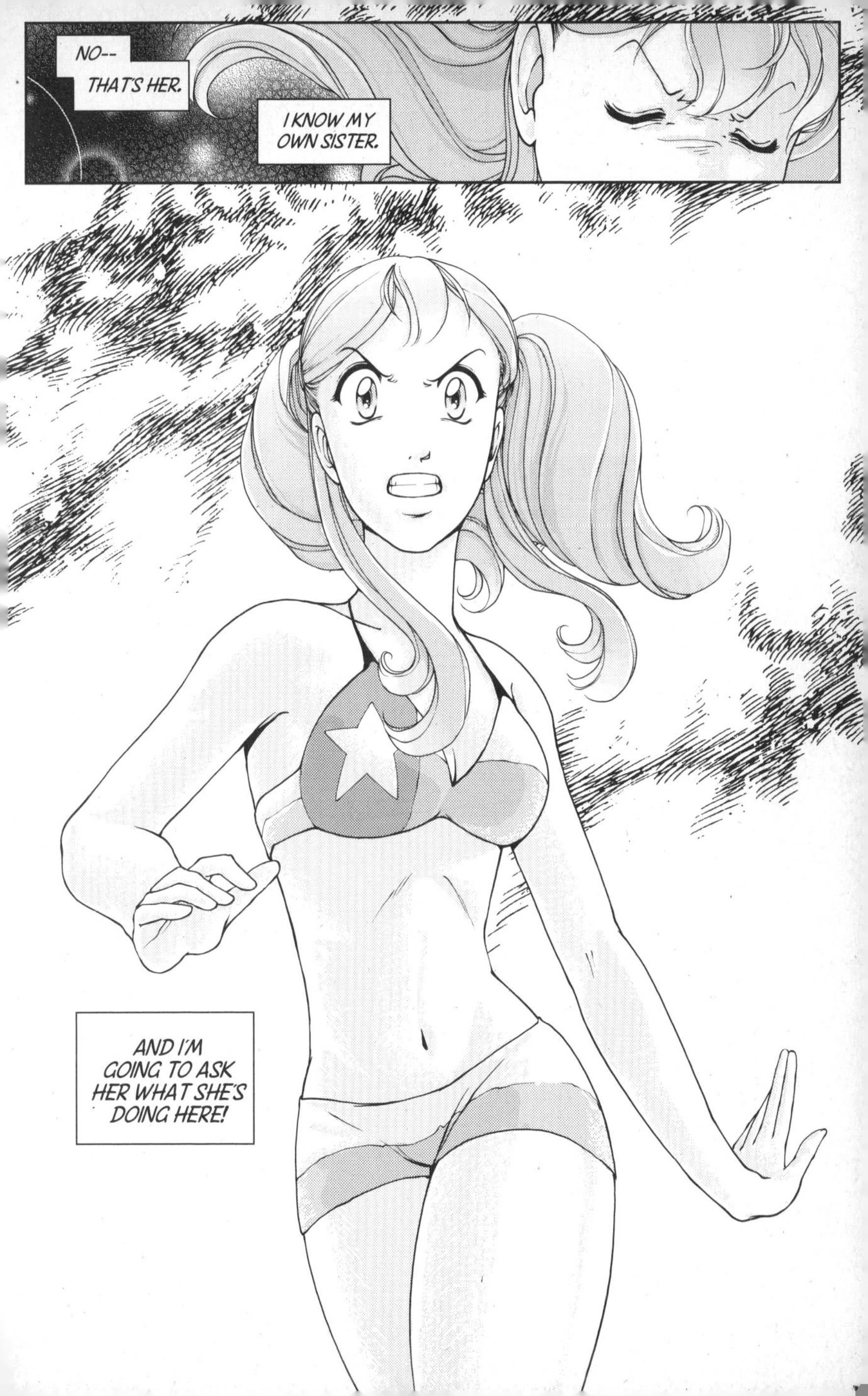
NO--
THAT'S HER.
I KNOW MY OWN SISTER.
AND I'M GOING TO ASK HER WHAT SHE'S DOING HERE!

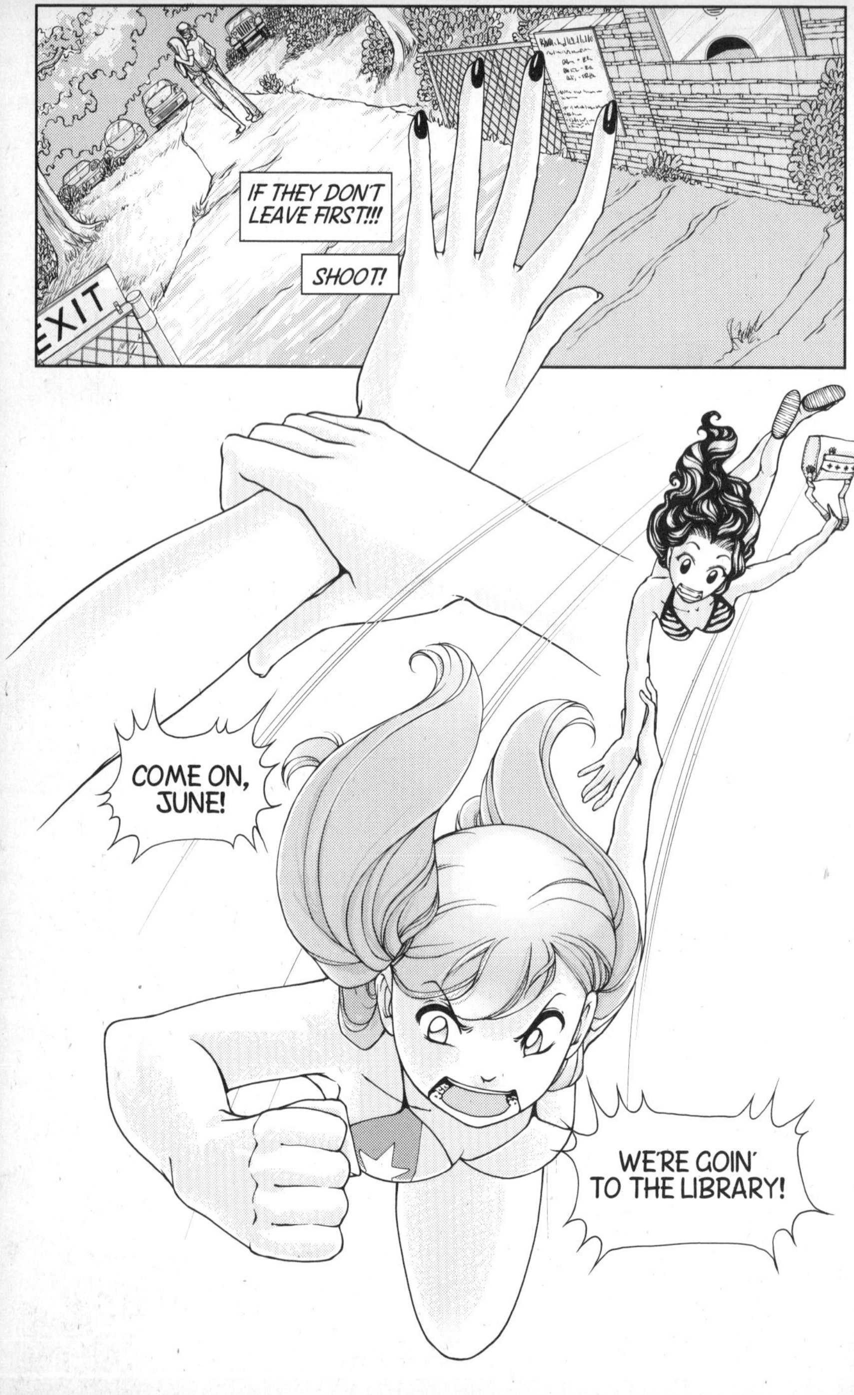
EXIT
IF THEY DON'T LEAVE FIRST!!!
SHOOT!
COME ON, JUNE!
WE'RE GOIN' TO THE LIBRARY!

Dear Reader,

Our heroine's in hot pursuit of the protagonist's sister and her ... friend?/ girlfriend?/ lover? (I guess we're about to find out), I wanted to take a moment to introduce the actual setting of "Steady Beat." This is my hometown – born and raised – Austin, Texas, good ol' U.S.A.!

And it's _the_ perfect setting for the theme of our book. Texas is conservative Christian by nature (like my parents), and yet Austin remains relatively liberal. A tiny blue dot awash in a sea of red (thanks to the gerrymandering politics of our politicians ...)

If you haven't noticed yet. I love politics, so you'll be seeing a lot of the capital dome (it's pretty hard to miss) and getting a lot of political references in the book. Texas is a wonderful state with wonderful people ... if a little misguided at times.

So while Leah and June run around downtown (in a car of course, our public transportation sucks), I hope that you enjoy the scenery of some of the things that make this city uniquelly _Austin._

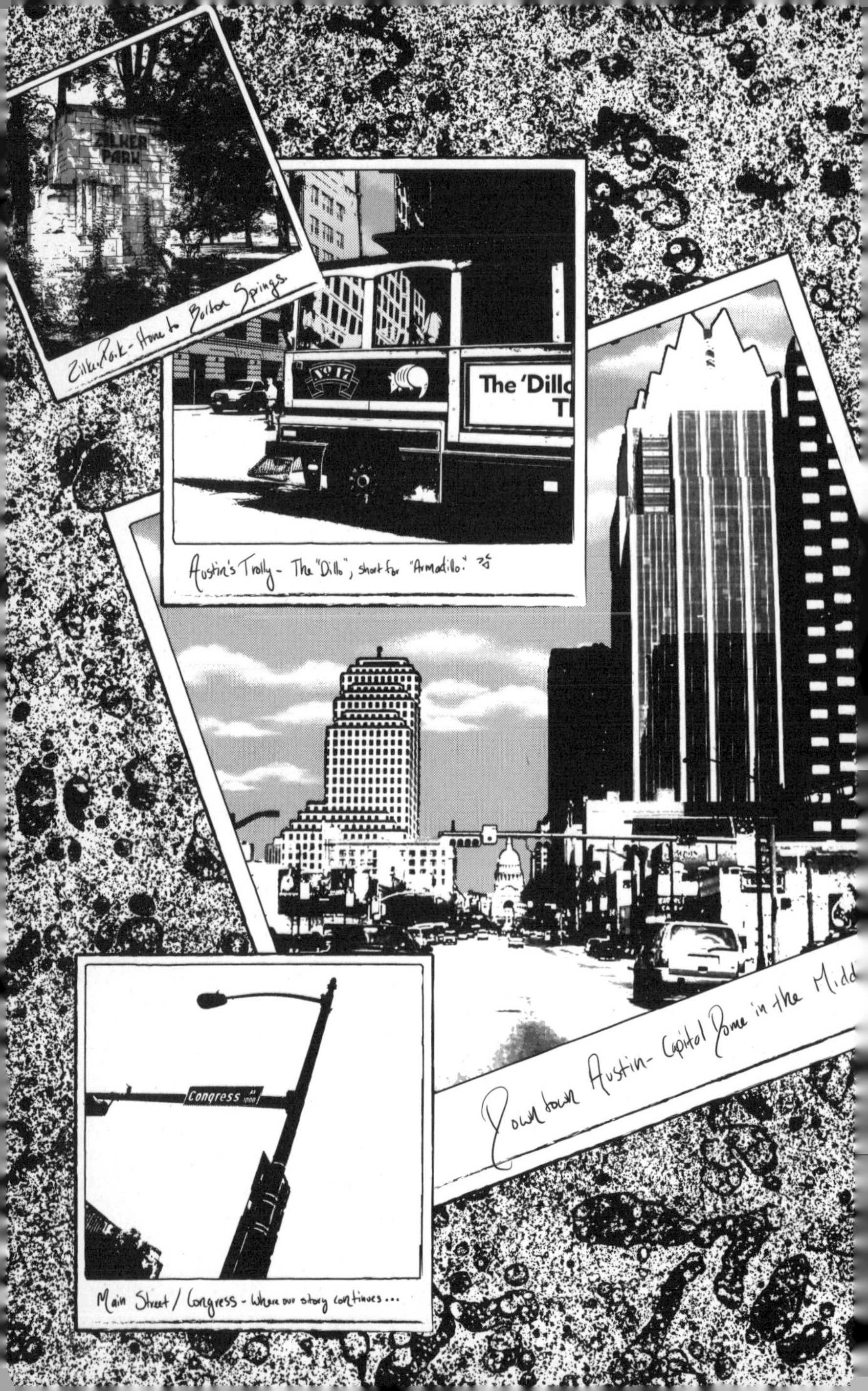
ZILKER PARK
Zilker Park - Home to Barton Springs.
1917
The 'Dillo
Austin's Trolly - The "Dillo", short for "Armadillo."
Downtown Austin - Capital Dome in the Midd
Congress
Main Street / Congress - Where our story continues...

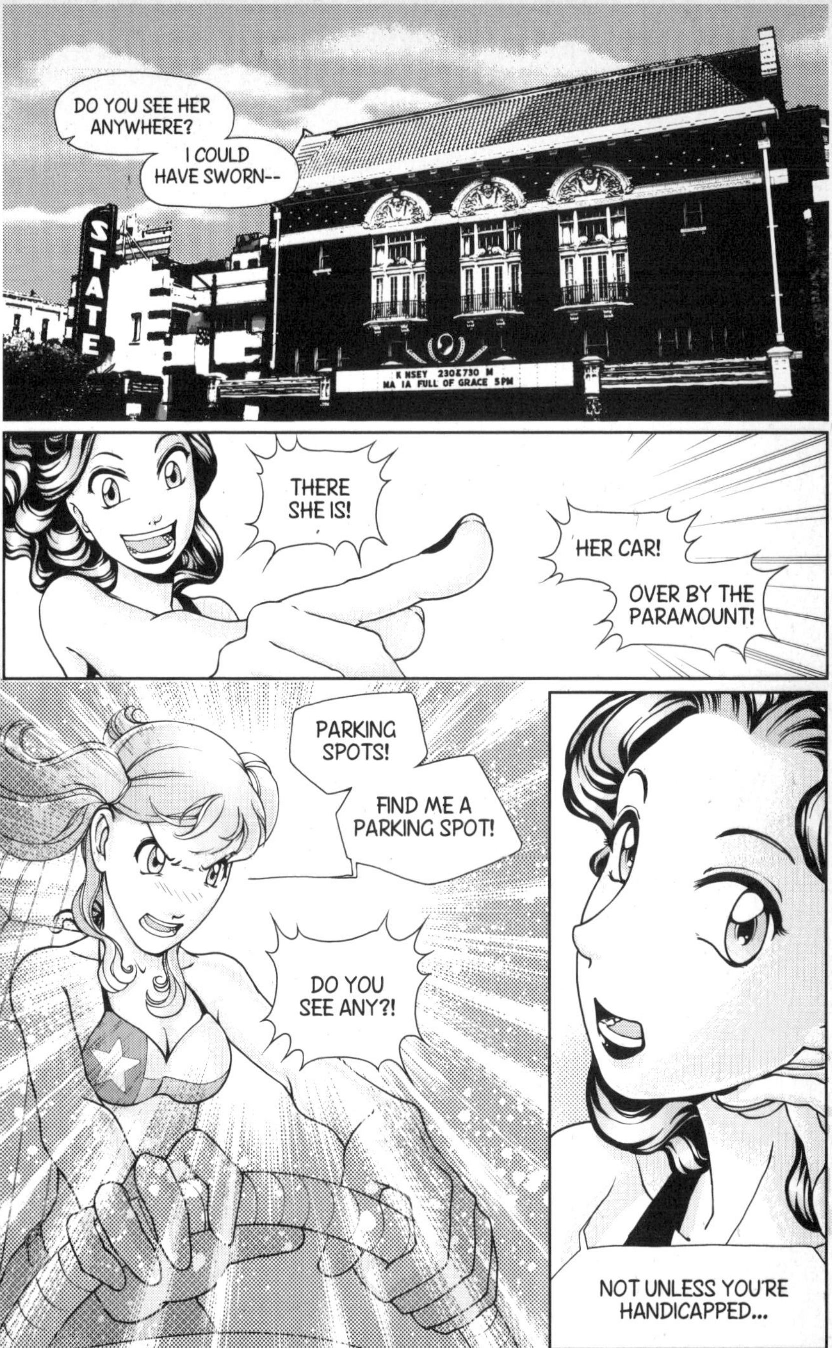
DO YOU SEE HER ANYWHERE?
I COULD HAVE SWORN--
STATE
K NSEY 230&730 M
MA IA FULL OF GRACE 5PM
THERE SHE IS!
HER CAR!
OVER BY THE PARAMOUNT!
PARKING SPOTS!
FIND ME A PARKING SPOT!
DO YOU SEE ANY?!
NOT UNLESS YOU'RE HANDICAPPED...

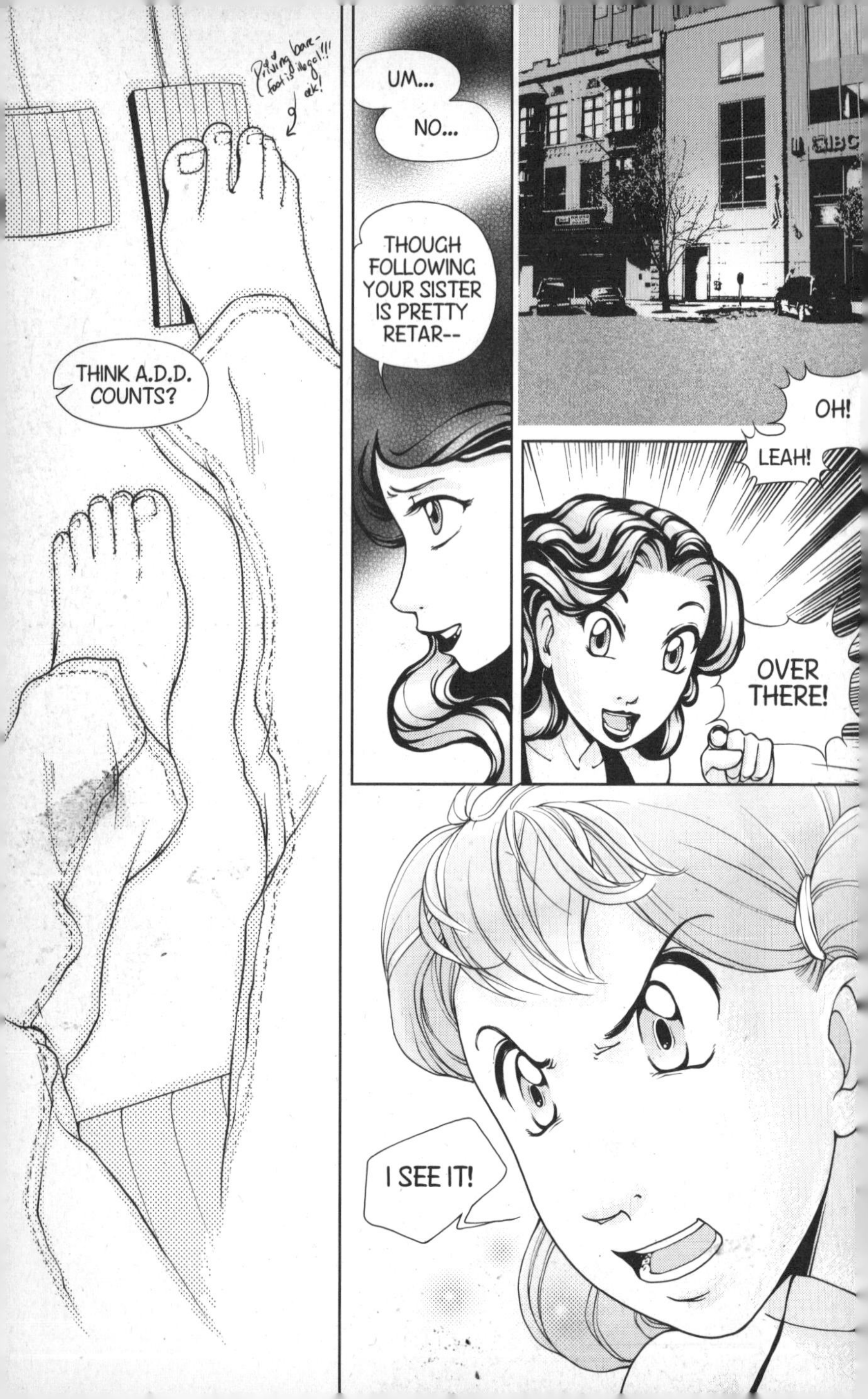
Driving bare-foot is illegal!!! eek!
THINK A.D.D. COUNTS?
UM... NO...
THOUGH FOLLOWING YOUR SISTER IS PRETTY RETAR--
OH!
LEAH!
OVER THERE!
I SEE IT!

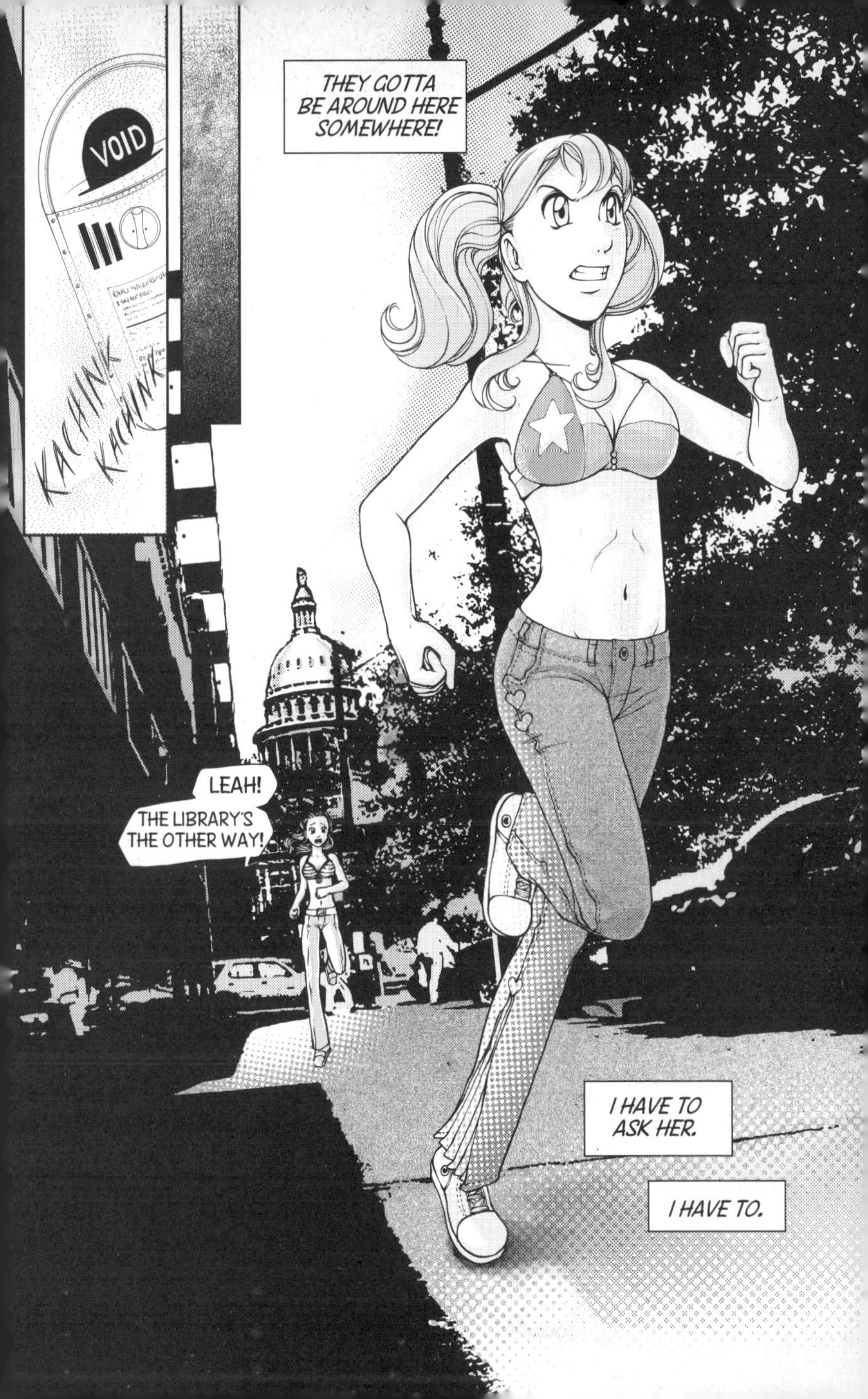
VOID
KACHINK KACHINK
THEY GOTTA BE AROUND HERE SOMEWHERE!
LEAH!
THE LIBRARY'S THE OTHER WAY!
I HAVE TO ASK HER.
I HAVE TO.

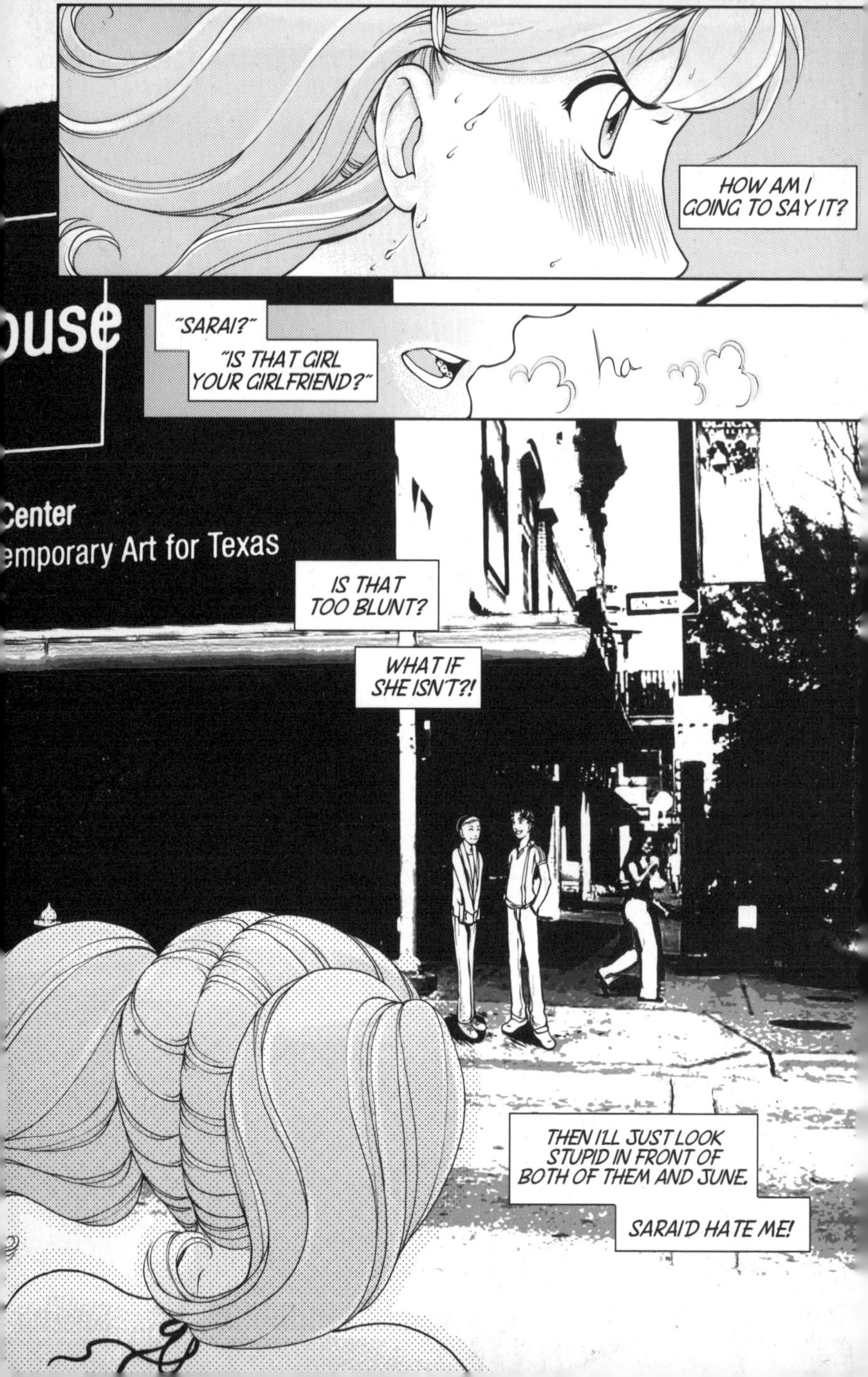
HOW AM I GOING TO SAY IT?
"SARAI?"
"IS THAT GIRL YOUR GIRLFRIEND?"
ha
ouse
Center
emporary Art for Texas
IS THAT TOO BLUNT?
WHAT IF SHE ISN'T?!
THEN I'LL JUST LOOK STUPID IN FRONT OF BOTH OF THEM AND JUNE.
SARAI'D HATE ME!

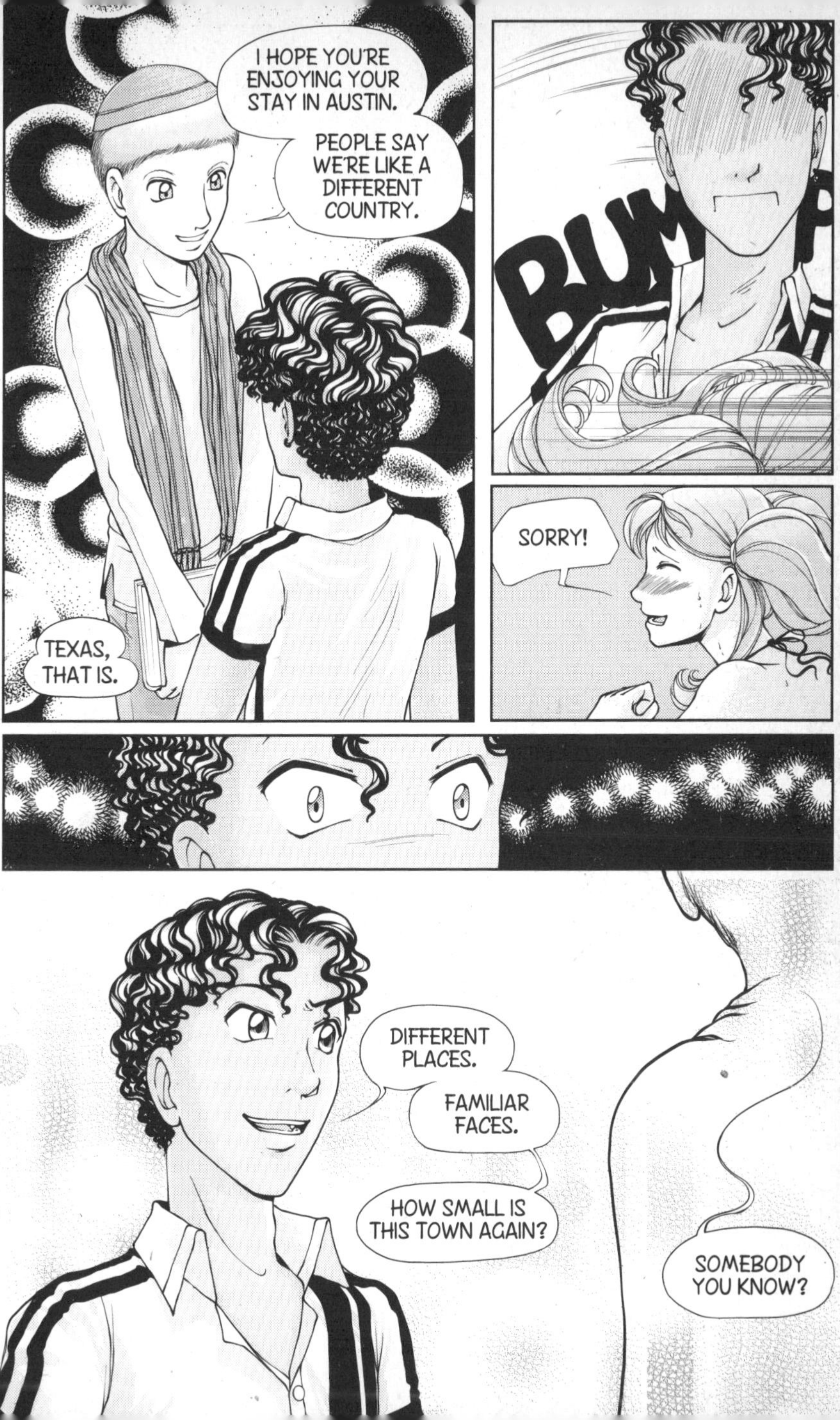
I HOPE YOU'RE ENJOYING YOUR STAY IN AUSTIN.
PEOPLE SAY WE'RE LIKE A DIFFERENT COUNTRY.
TEXAS, THAT IS.
BUMP
SORRY!
DIFFERENT PLACES.
FAMILIAR FACES.
HOW SMALL IS THIS TOWN AGAIN?
SOMEBODY YOU KNOW?

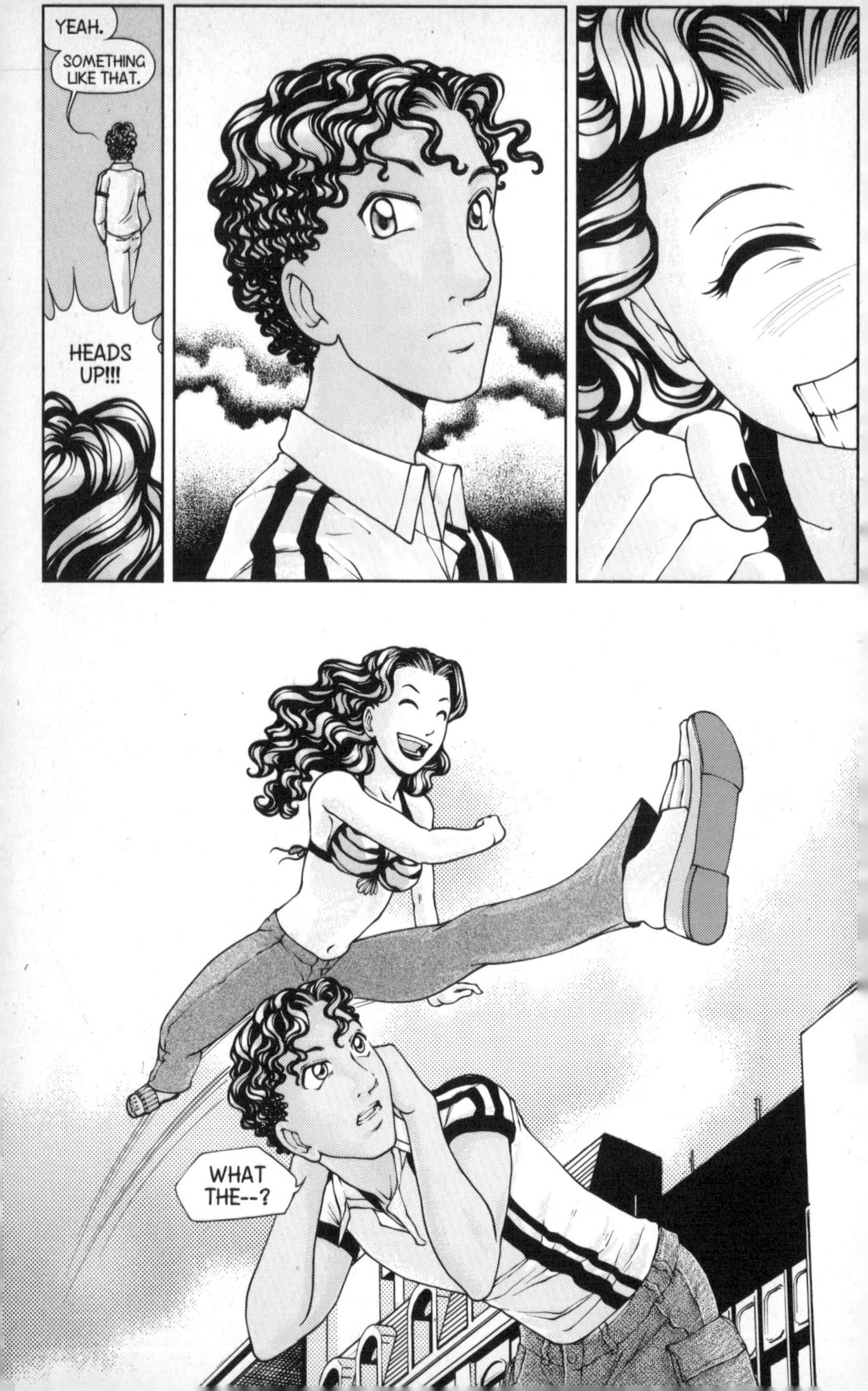
YEAH.
SOMETHING LIKE THAT.
HEADS UP!!!
WHAT THE--?

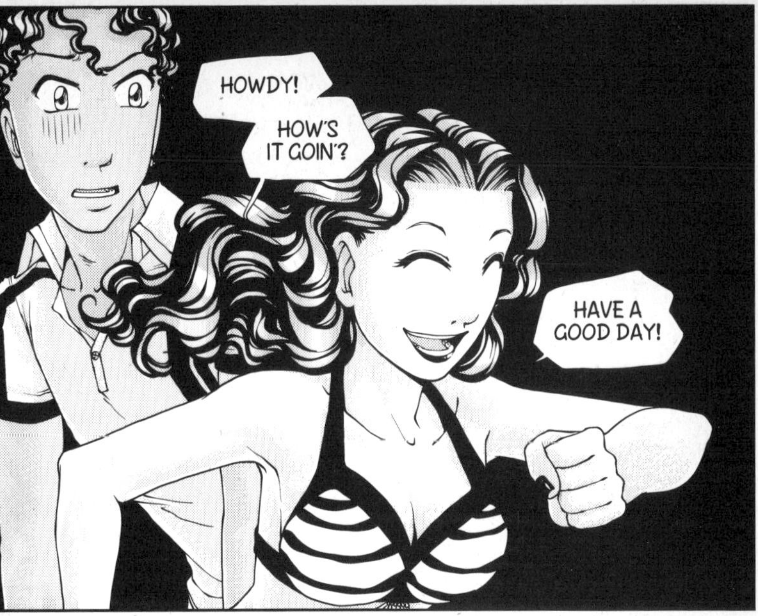
HOWDY!
HOW'S IT GOIN'?
HAVE A GOOD DAY!

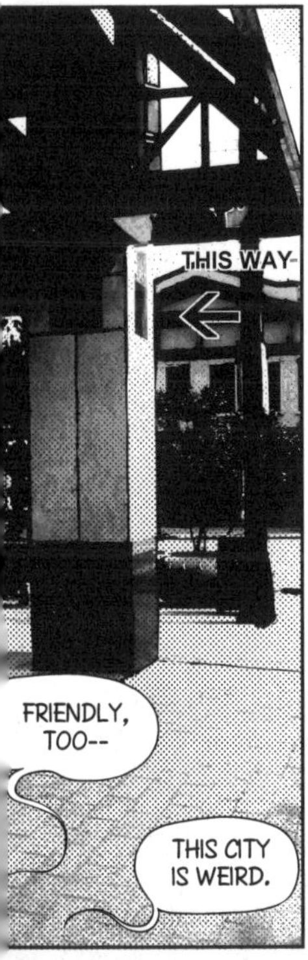
THIS WAY
FRIENDLY, TOO--
THIS CITY IS WEIRD.

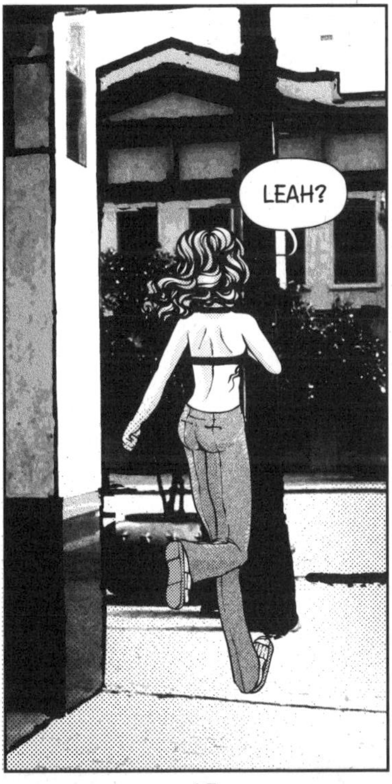
LEAH?

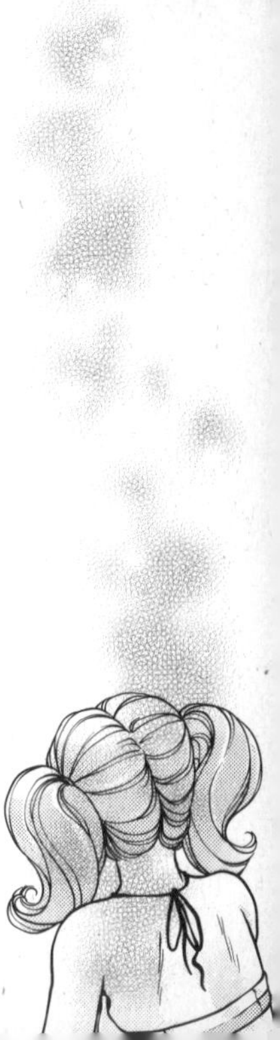

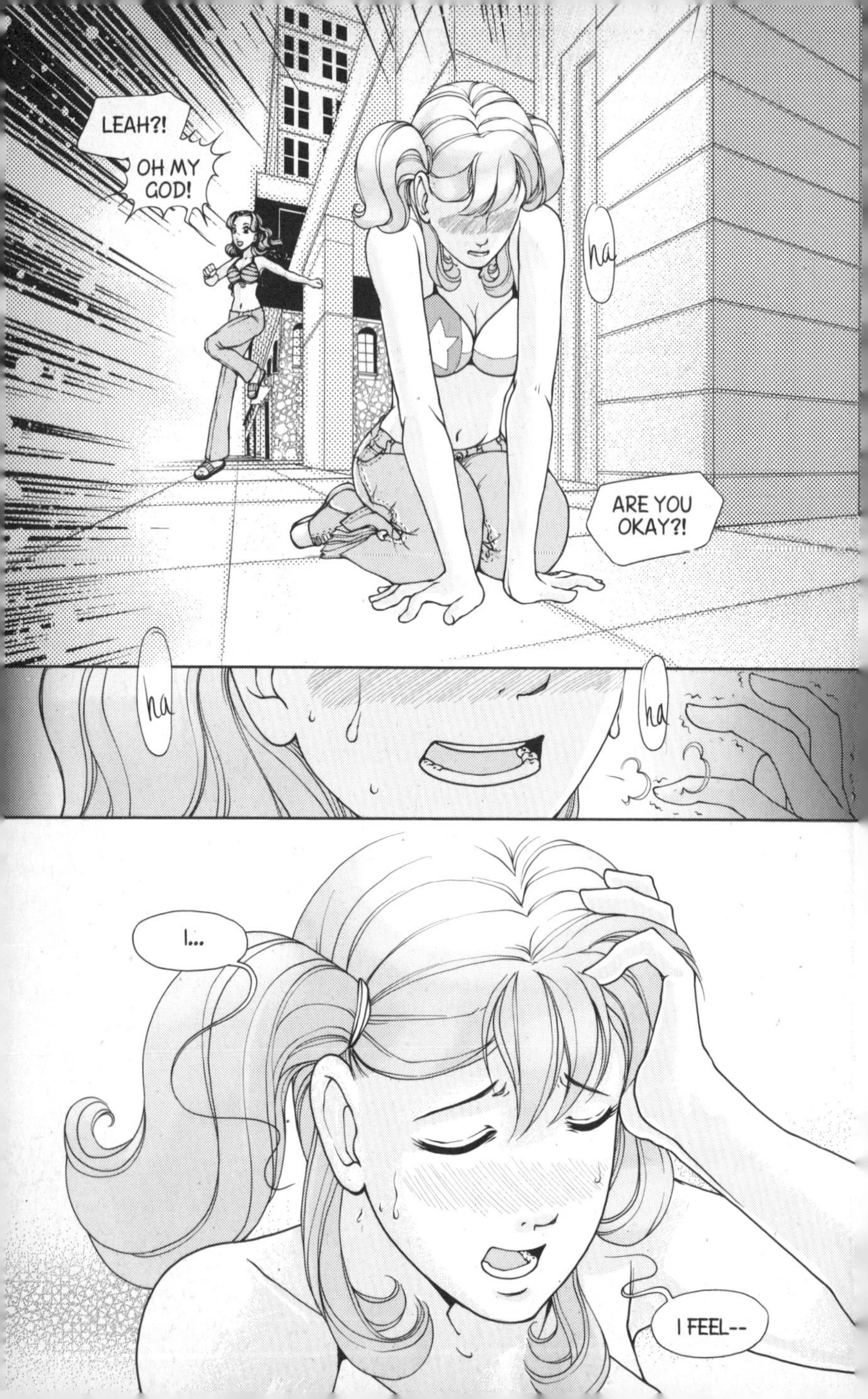
LEAH?!
OH MY GOD!
ha
ARE YOU OKAY?!
ha
ha
I...
I FEEL--

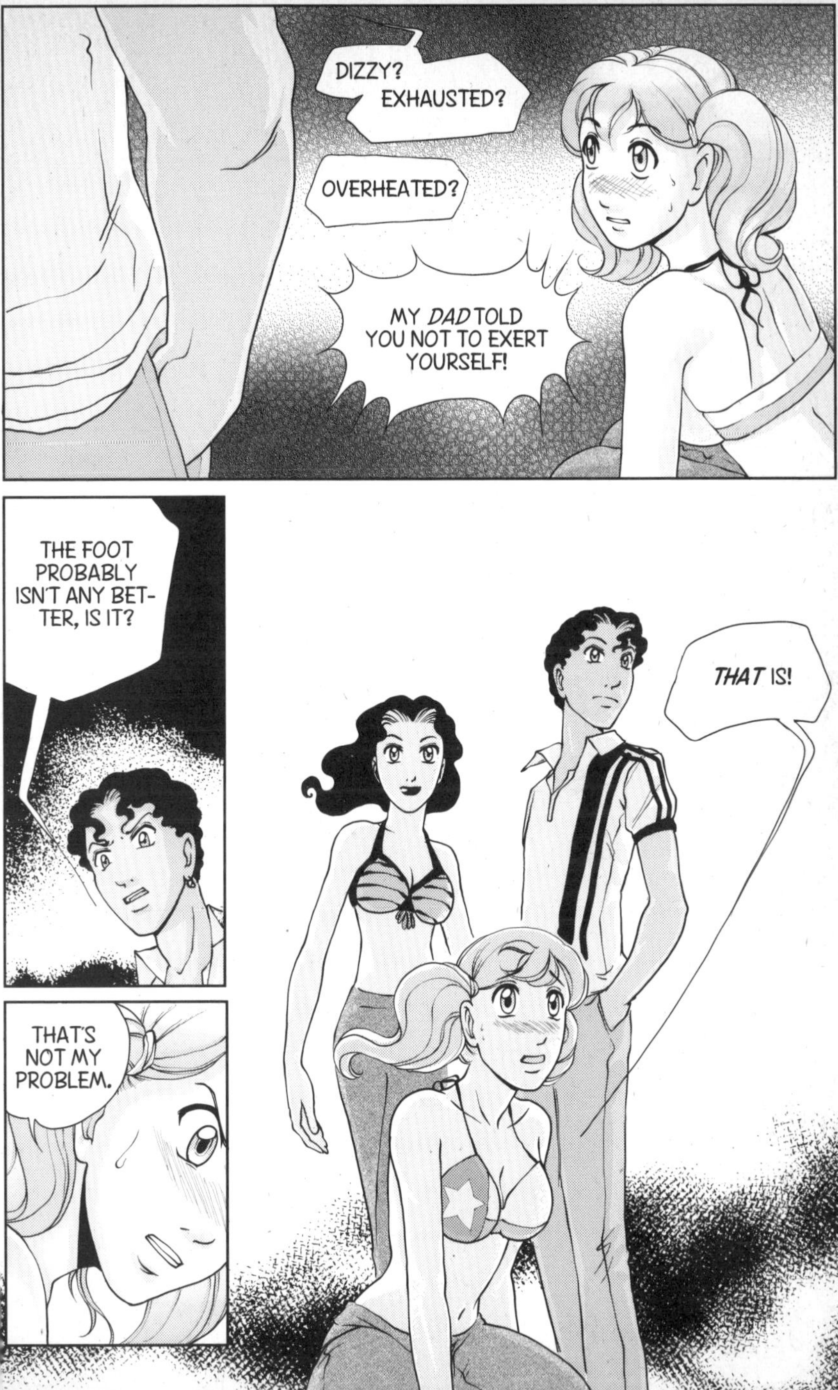
DIZZY?
EXHAUSTED?
OVERHEATED?
MY *DAD* TOLD YOU NOT TO EXERT YOURSELF!
THE FOOT PROBABLY ISN'T ANY BETTER, IS IT?
THAT'S NOT MY PROBLEM.
*THAT* IS!

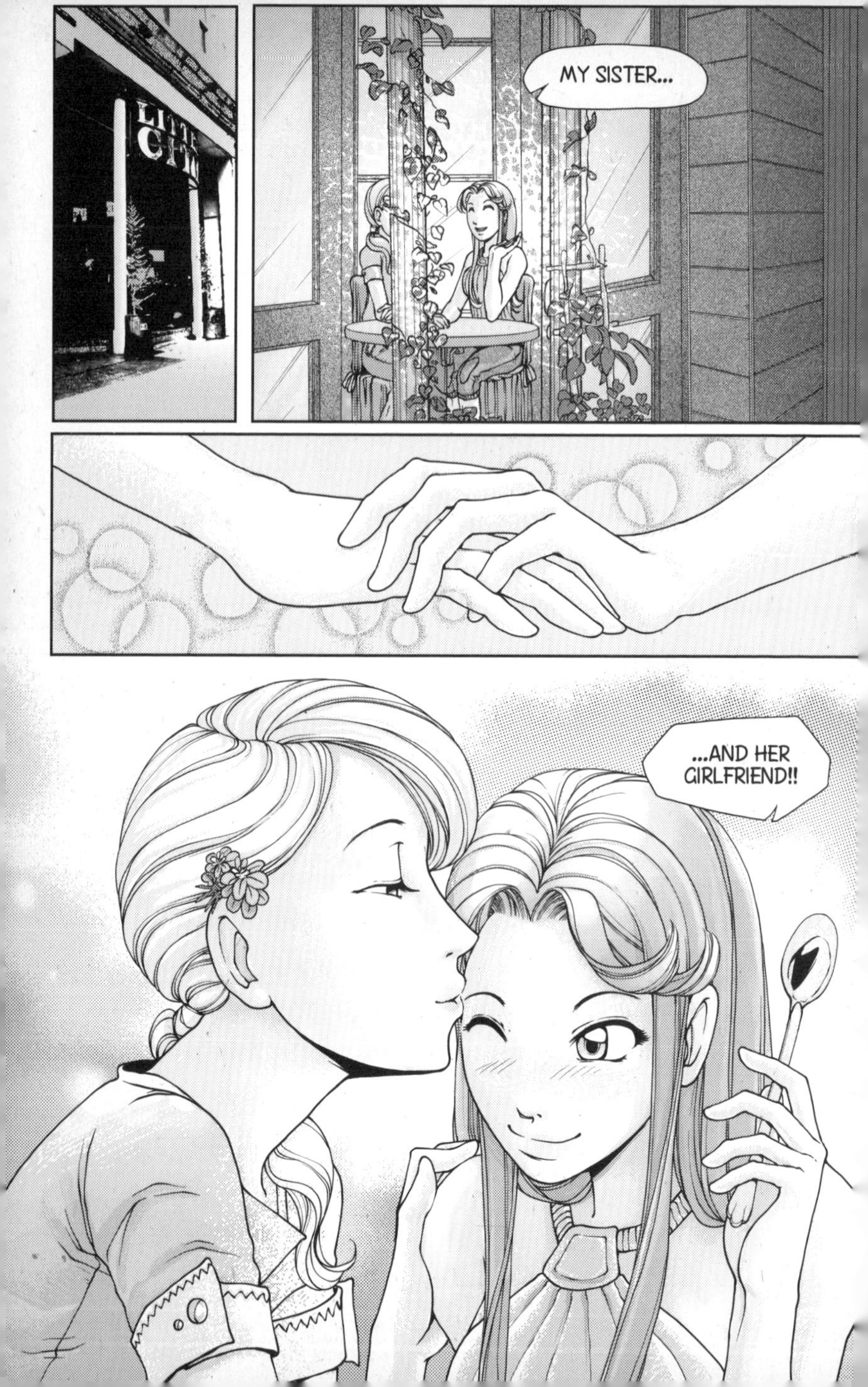
MY SISTER...
...AND HER GIRLFRIEND!!

Dear Me,
September 2nd

Hmm. What to write? I wonder how personal I should make this journal thingy ("diary's lame, but "journal" sounds kinda spiff) you always read these books and see these shows where the mother finds the daughter's diary and blows up (not literally) I really don't think my mom would go through my things. I guess I'm lucky? Who knows.

She really isn't very nosy. Even if we aren't allowed to watch certain shows or movies or listen to certain stations on the radio (etc), I just realized she never actually checks to see if we're obeying her. I wonder why that is? Even Sarai, she kinda ignores her as long as she's doing her homework or whatnot. Mom doesn't believe in grounding (and neither does dad), but then again, neither Sarai nor I have ever done anything wrong. Not really. We don't do drugs. We don't party. And we almost never stay out late. What would happen if we ever did actually do something, though? →

September 2nd

Would Mom even notice?

Anyway, whatever. Sometimes I wish Mom were a little more nosey. (maybe then I'd actually do homework), but then again, I kinda like her not paying attention. Because then at least I don't have to worry about her reading this journal, right?

Anyway, I'm going to bed.

Goodnight Me.

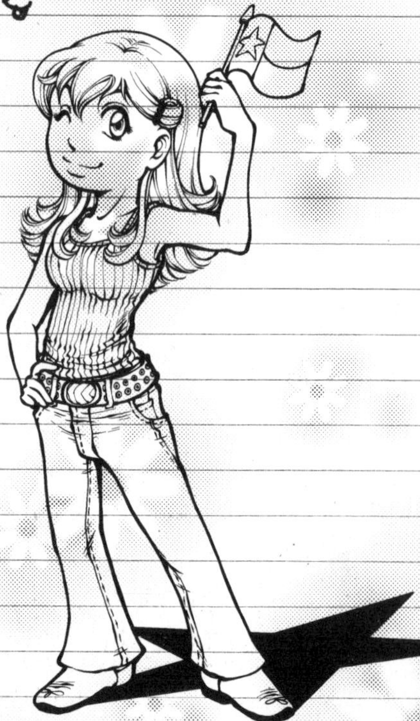

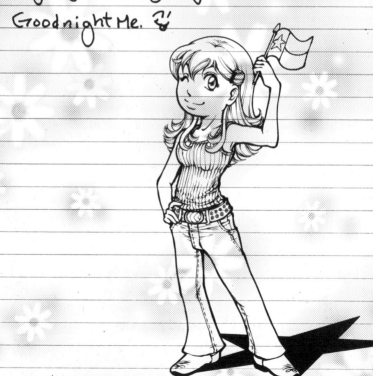

BEAT 8

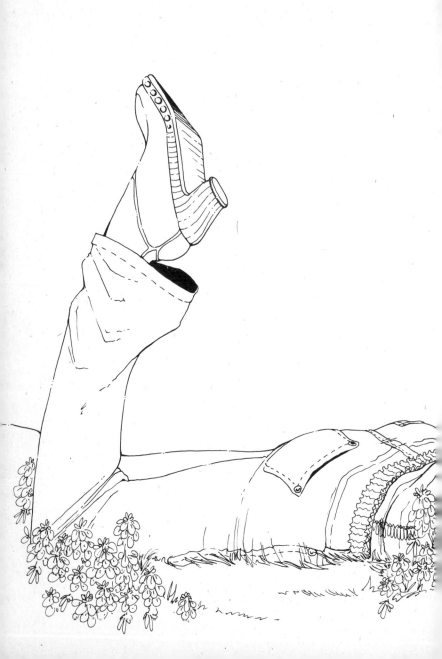

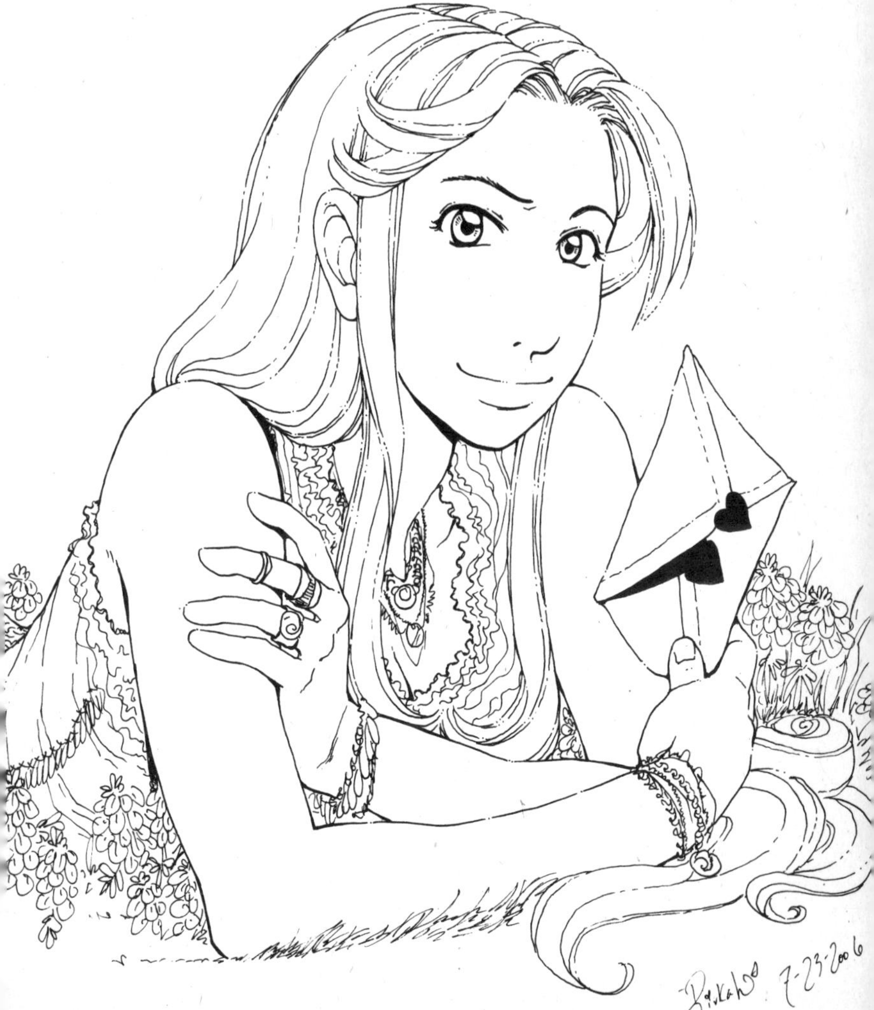
Rivkah 7-23-2006

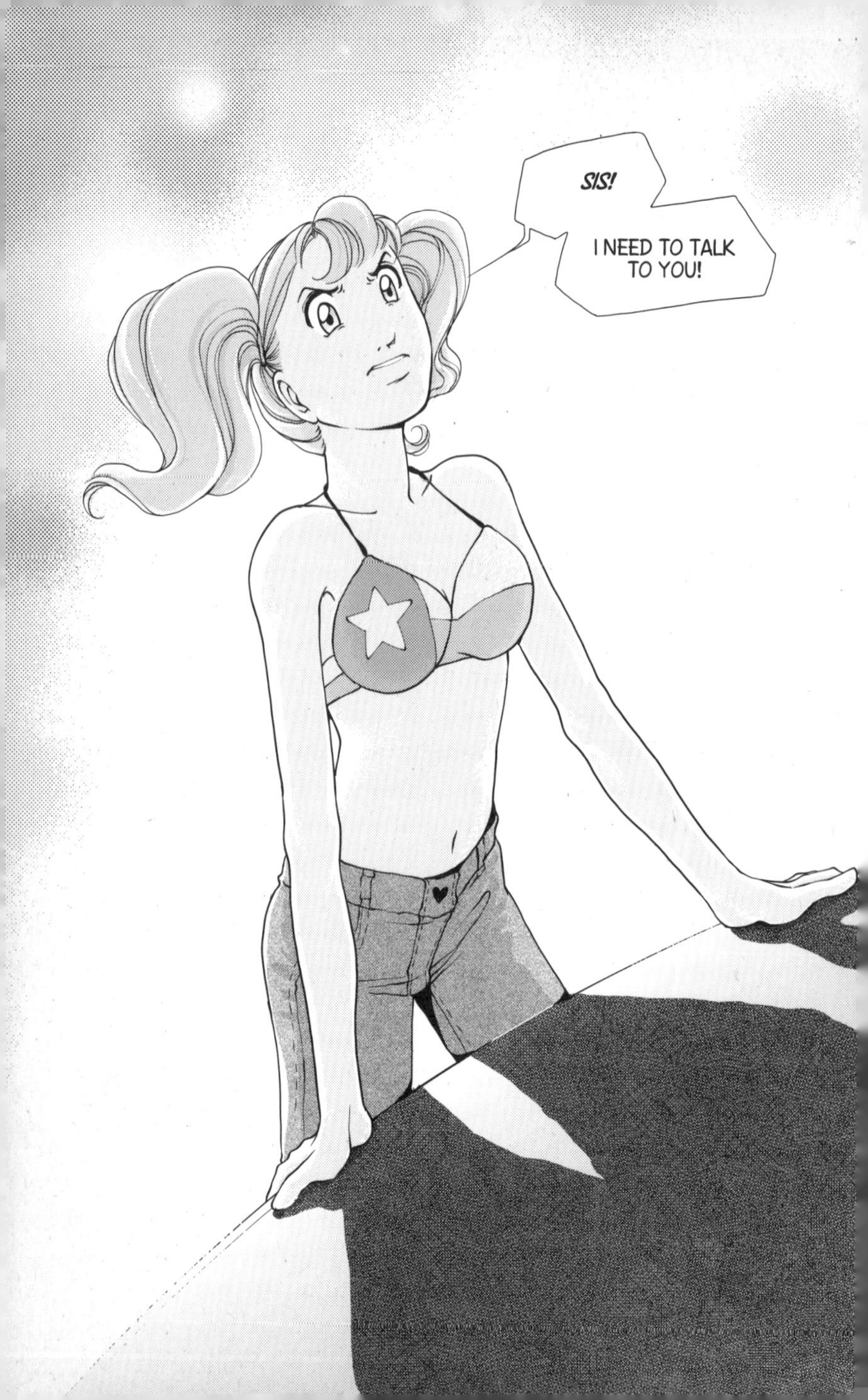
SIS!
I NEED TO TALK TO YOU!

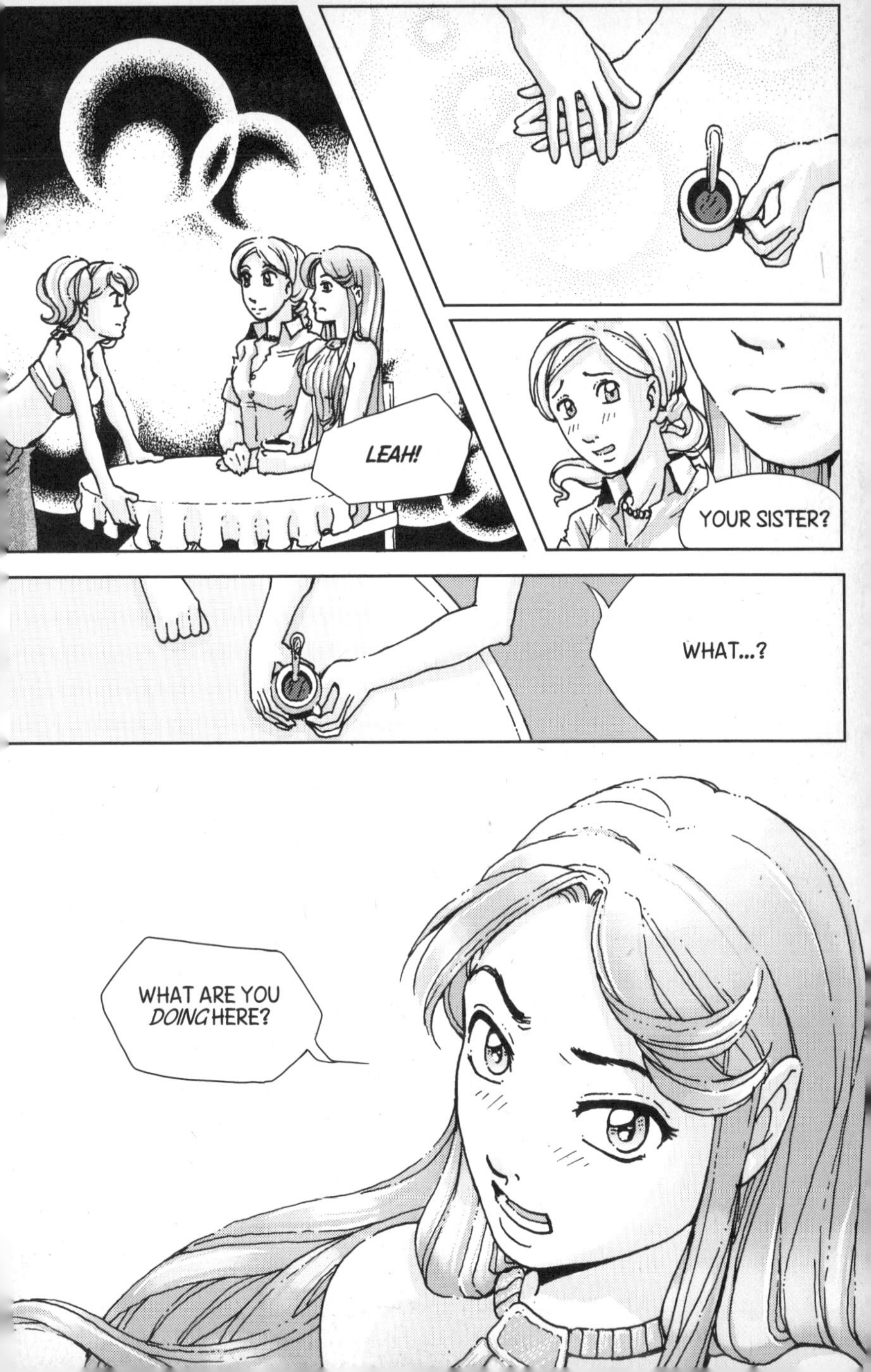
LEAH!
YOUR SISTER?
WHAT...?
WHAT ARE YOU *DOING* HERE?

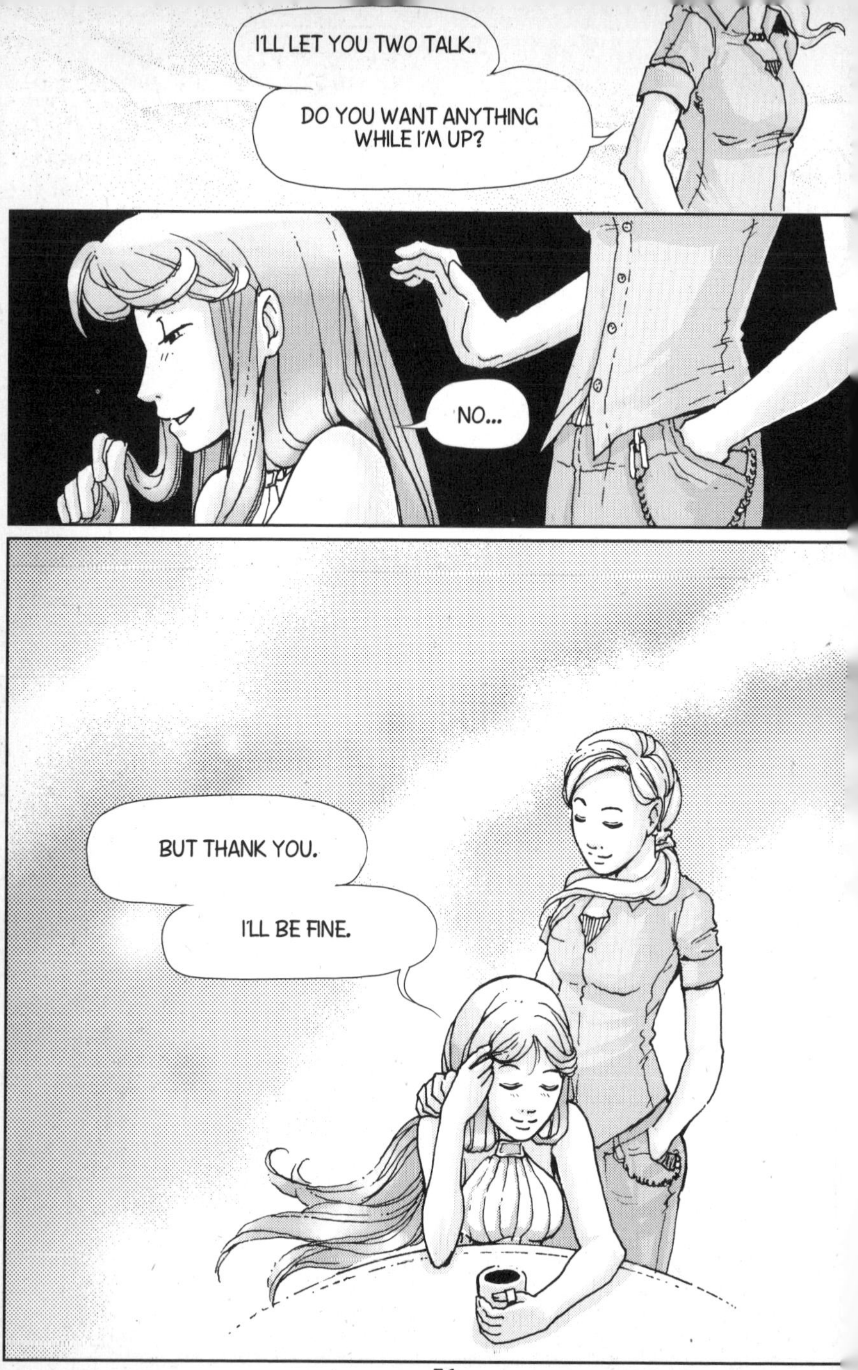

I'LL LET YOU TWO TALK.
DO YOU WANT ANYTHING WHILE I'M UP?
NO...
BUT THANK YOU.
I'LL BE FINE.

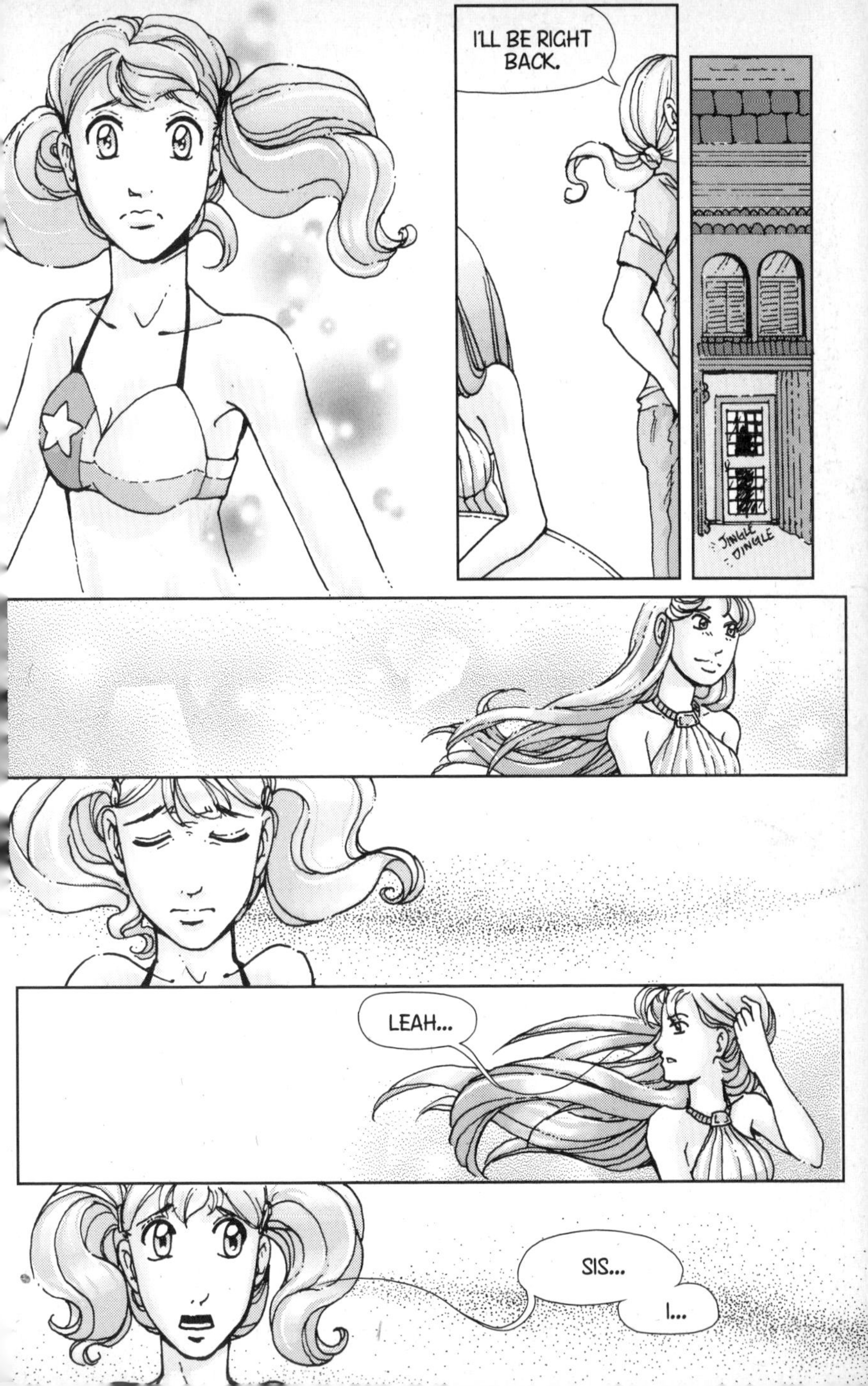
I'LL BE RIGHT BACK.
JINGLE JINGLE
LEAH...
SIS...
I...

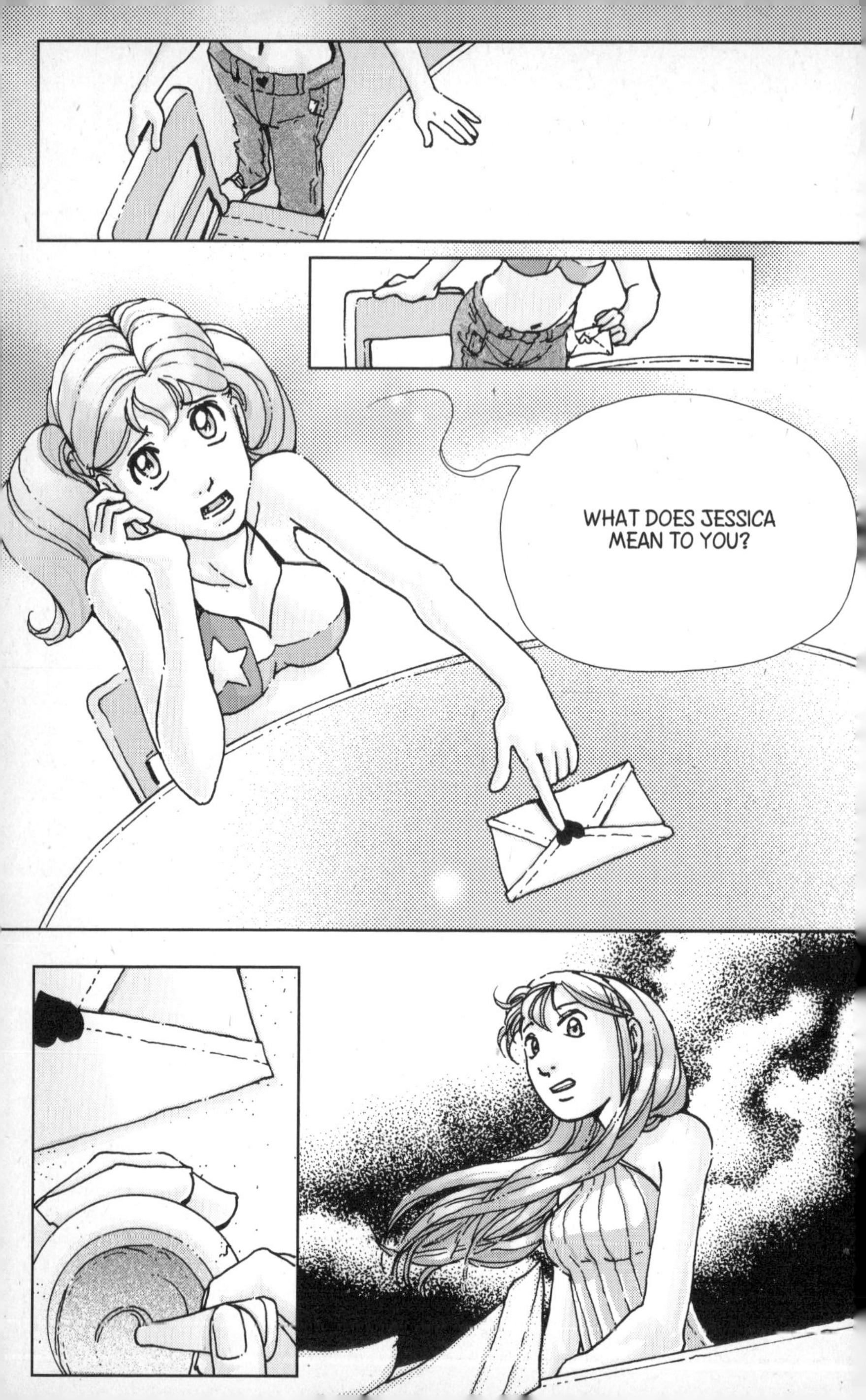
WHAT DOES JESSICA MEAN TO YOU?

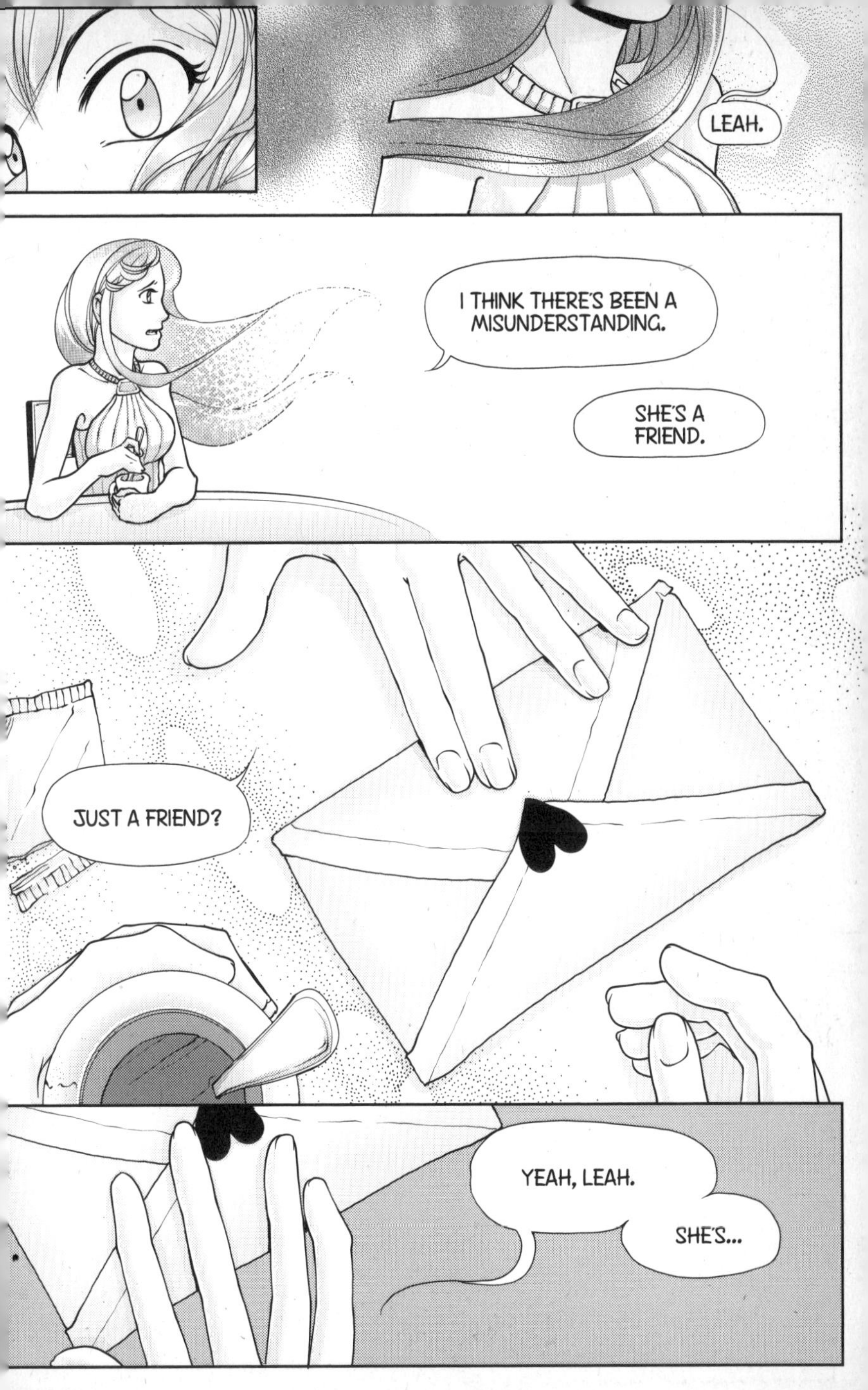
LEAH.
I THINK THERE'S BEEN A MISUNDERSTANDING.
SHE'S A FRIEND.
JUST A FRIEND?
YEAH, LEAH.
SHE'S...

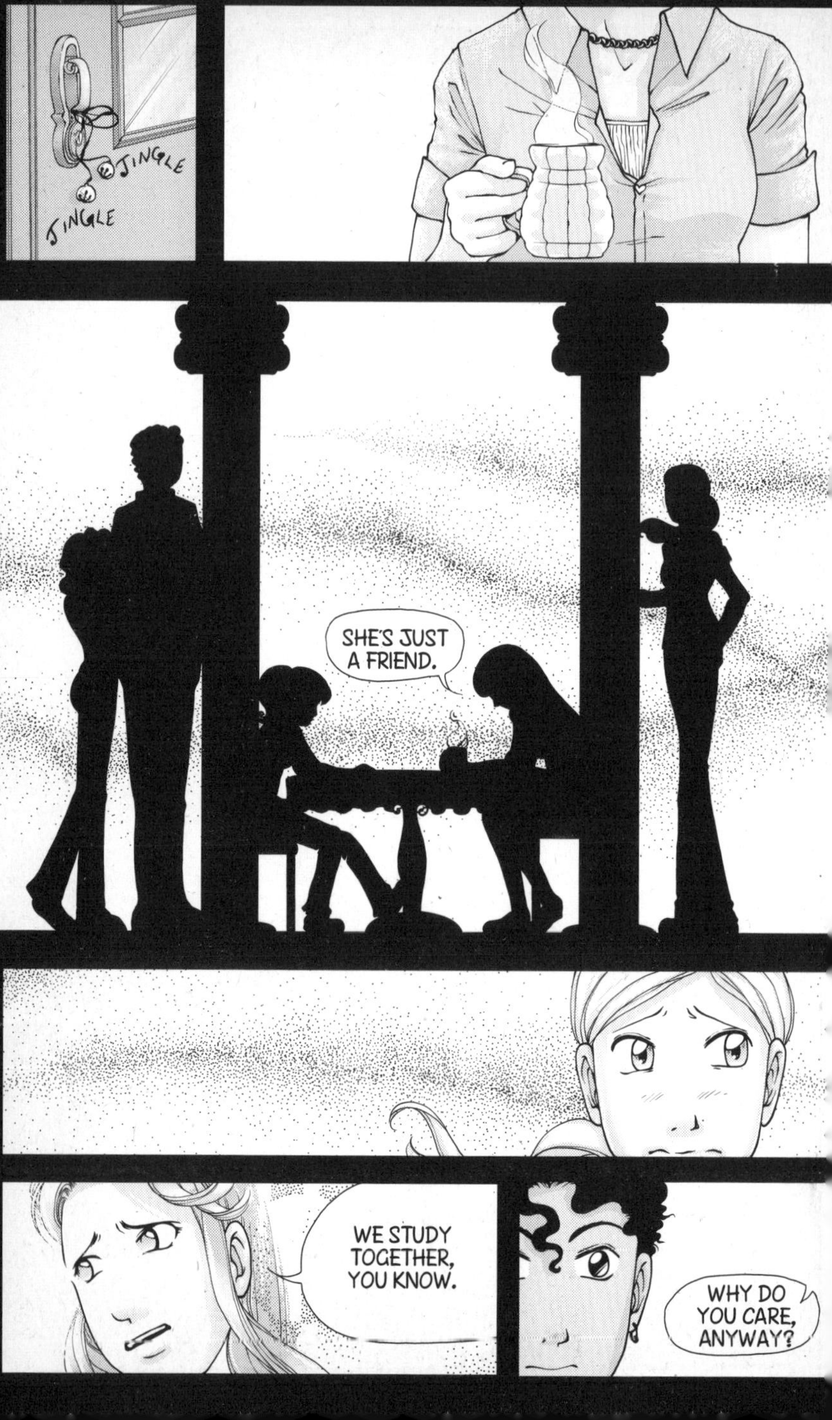
JINGLE
JINGLE
SHE'S JUST A FRIEND.
WE STUDY TOGETHER, YOU KNOW.
WHY DO YOU CARE, ANYWAY?

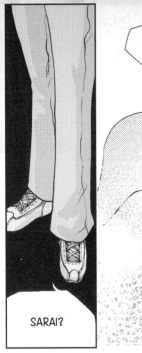

SARAI WINTERS?

SARAI?

ARE YOU TWO THE DAUGHTERS OF REPRESENTATIVE WINTERS?

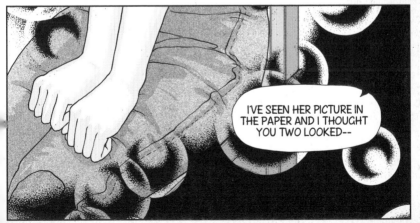

I'VE SEEN HER PICTURE IN THE PAPER AND I THOUGHT YOU TWO LOOKED--

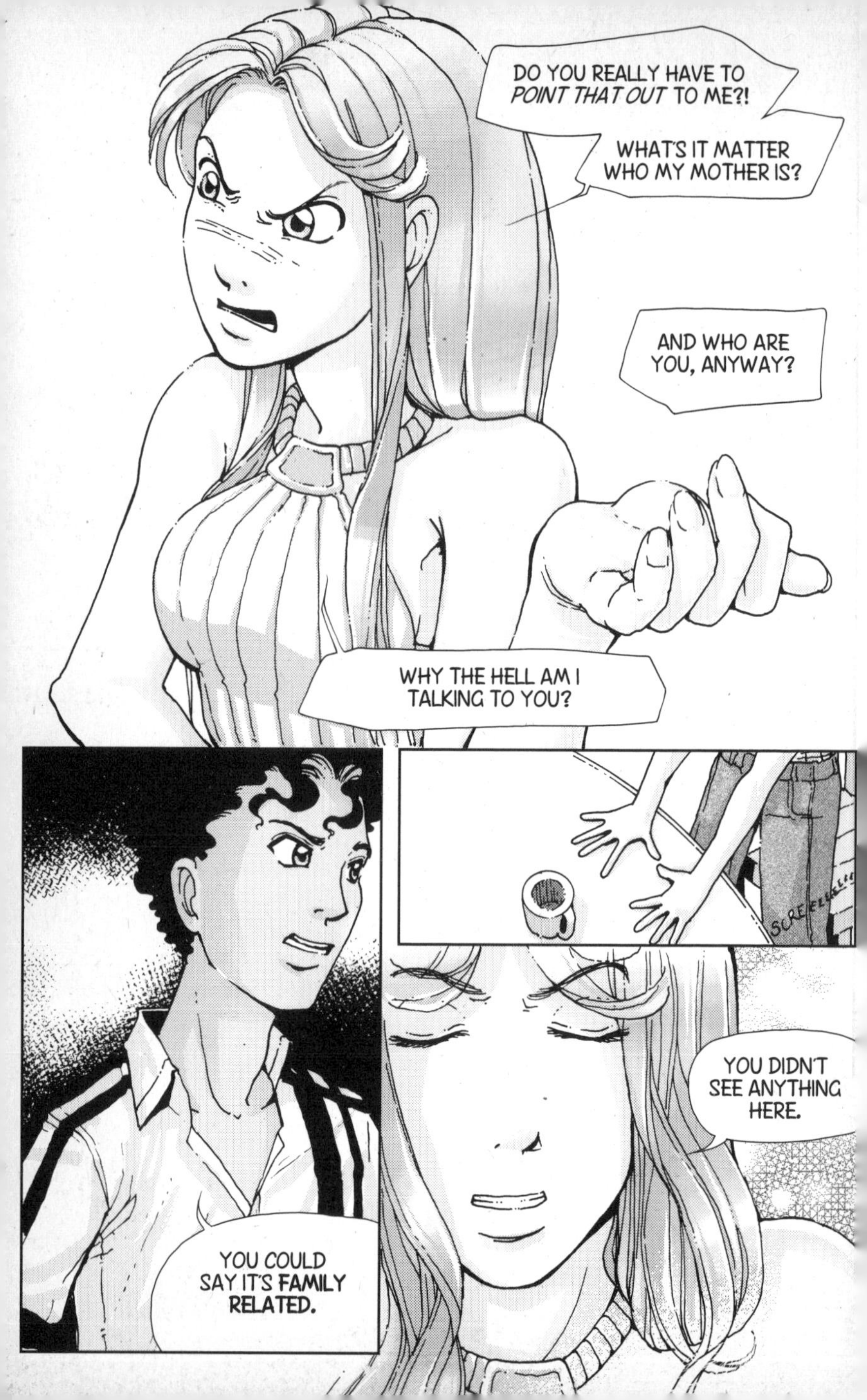
DO YOU REALLY HAVE TO *POINT THAT OUT* TO ME?!
WHAT'S IT MATTER WHO MY MOTHER IS?
AND WHO ARE YOU, ANYWAY?
WHY THE HELL AM I TALKING TO YOU?
YOU COULD SAY IT'S **FAMILY RELATED.**
SCREEEEEEEE
YOU DIDN'T SEE ANYTHING HERE.

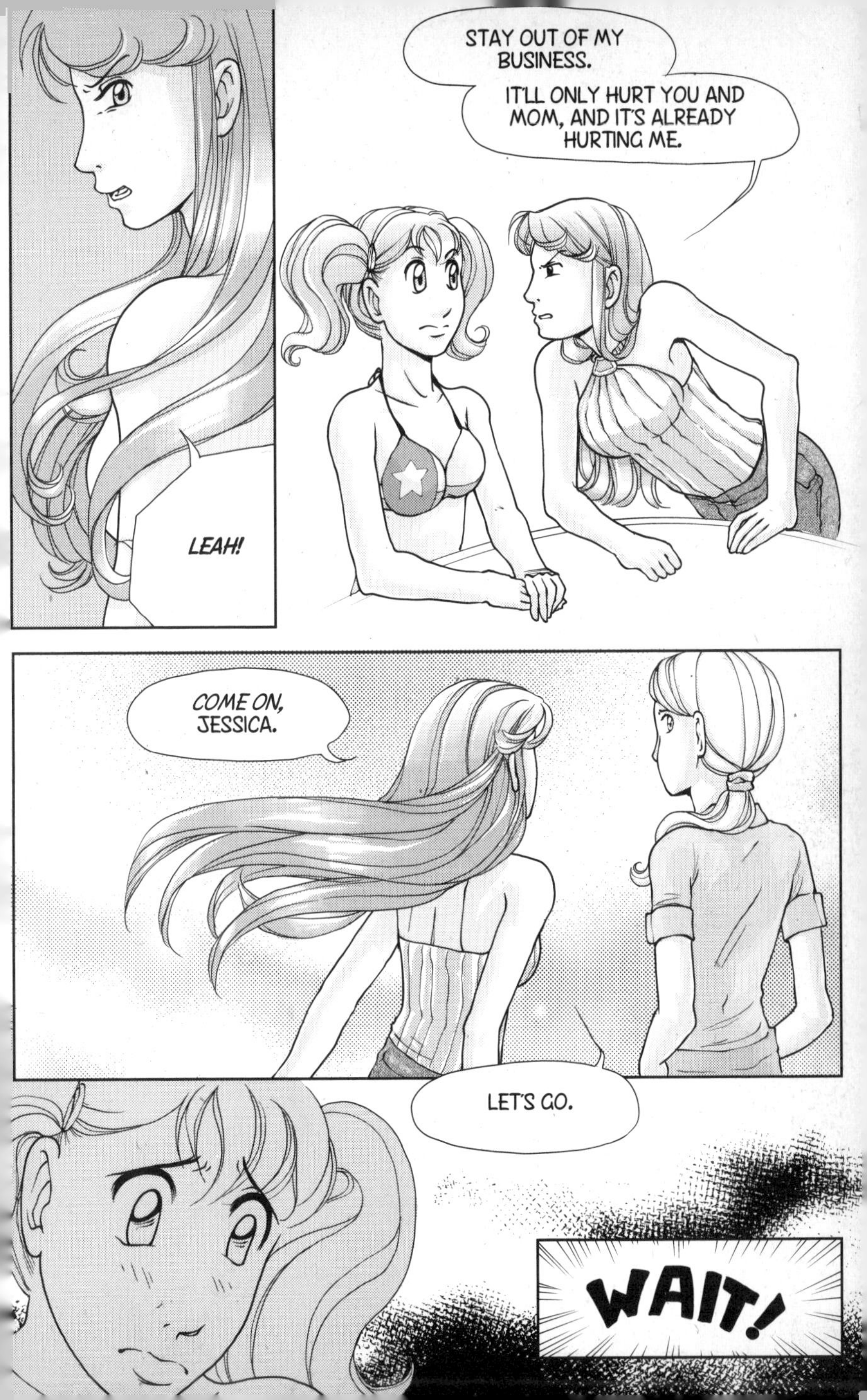
LEAH!
STAY OUT OF MY BUSINESS.
IT'LL ONLY HURT YOU AND MOM, AND IT'S ALREADY HURTING ME.
COME ON, JESSICA.
LET'S GO.
WAIT!

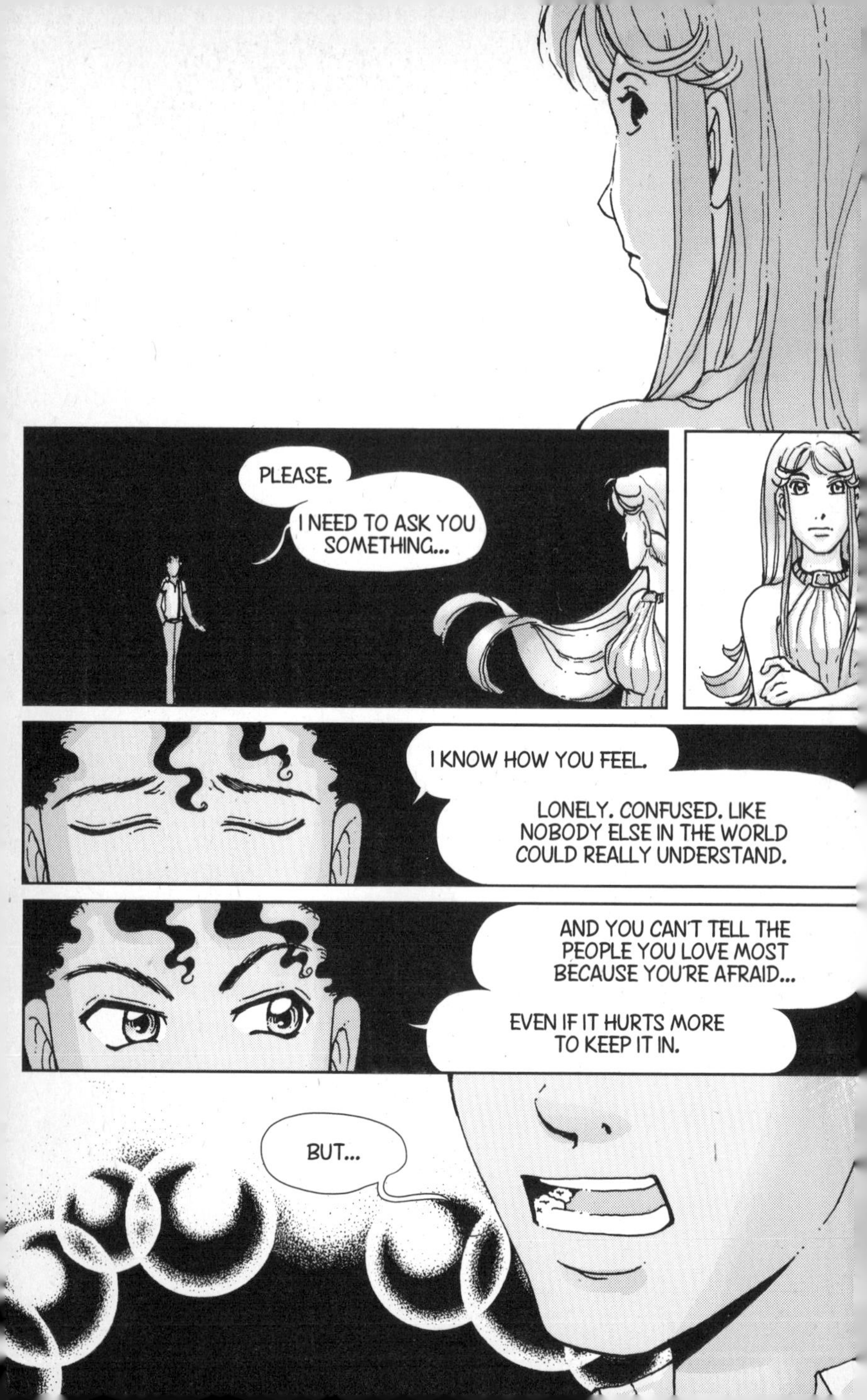
PLEASE.
I NEED TO ASK YOU SOMETHING...
I KNOW HOW YOU FEEL.
LONELY. CONFUSED. LIKE NOBODY ELSE IN THE WORLD COULD REALLY UNDERSTAND.
AND YOU CAN'T TELL THE PEOPLE YOU LOVE MOST BECAUSE YOU'RE AFRAID...
EVEN IF IT HURTS MORE TO KEEP IT IN.
BUT...

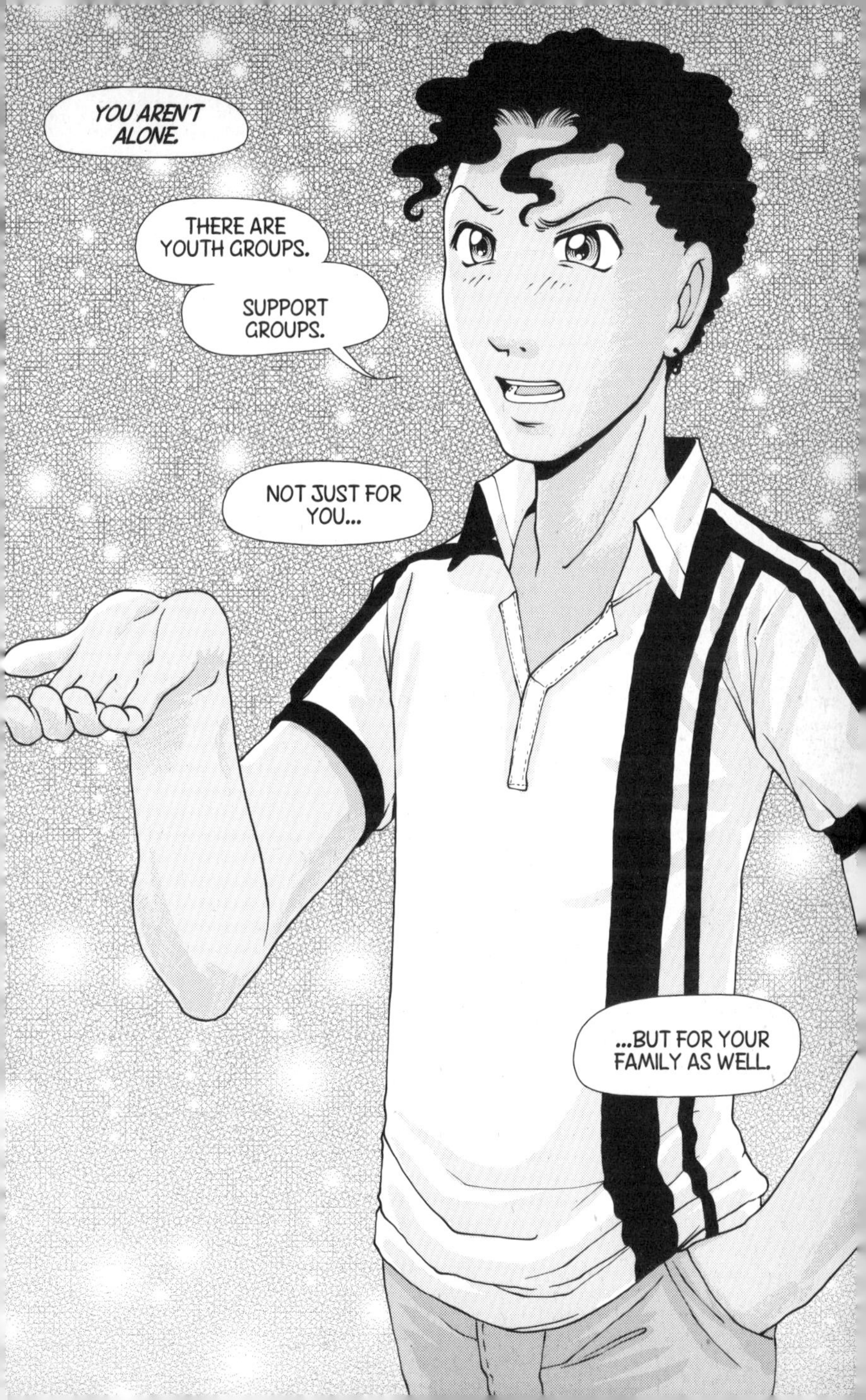
YOU AREN'T ALONE.
THERE ARE YOUTH GROUPS.
SUPPORT GROUPS.
NOT JUST FOR YOU...
...BUT FOR YOUR FAMILY AS WELL.

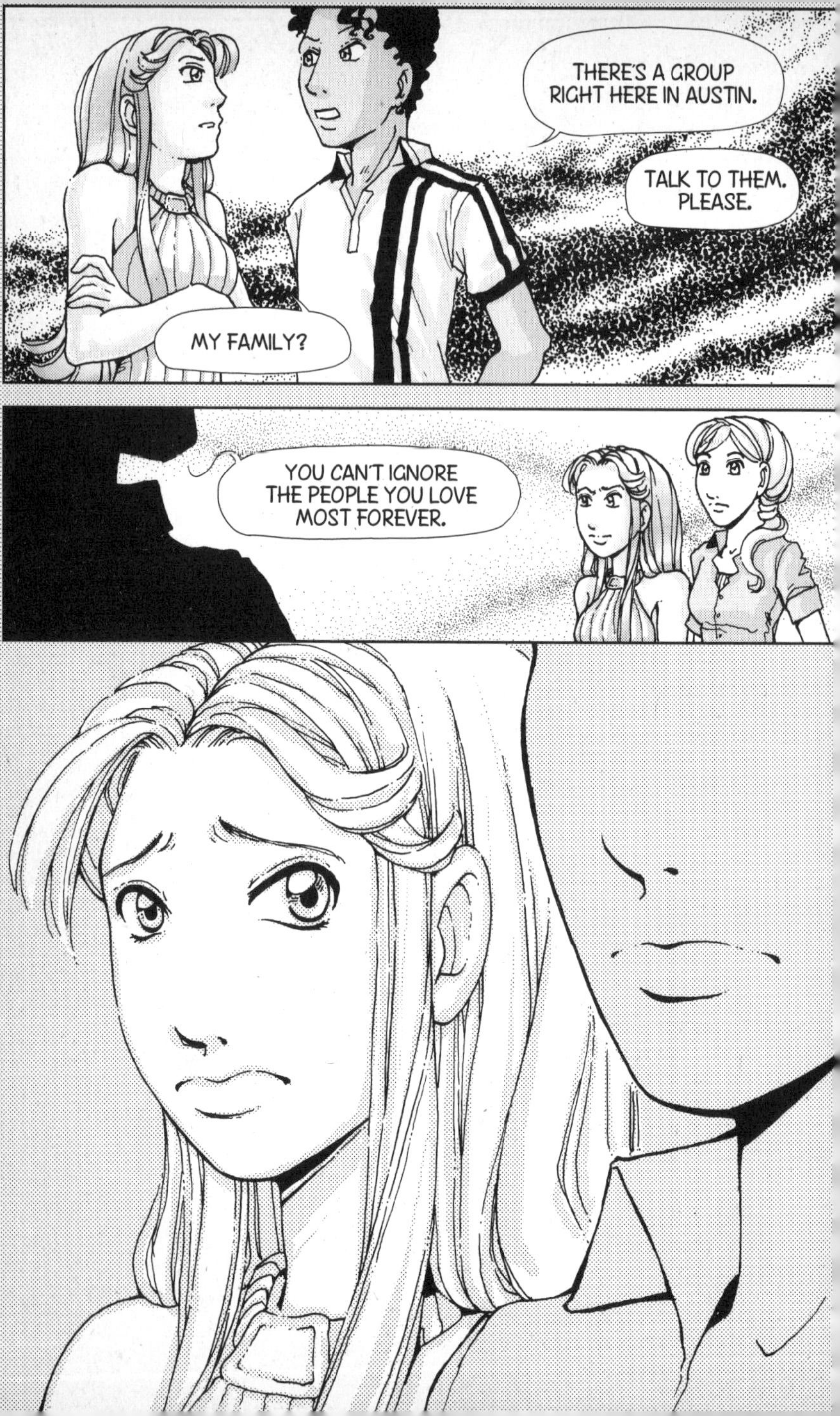
THERE'S A GROUP RIGHT HERE IN AUSTIN.
MY FAMILY?
TALK TO THEM. PLEASE.
YOU CAN'T IGNORE THE PEOPLE YOU LOVE MOST FOREVER.

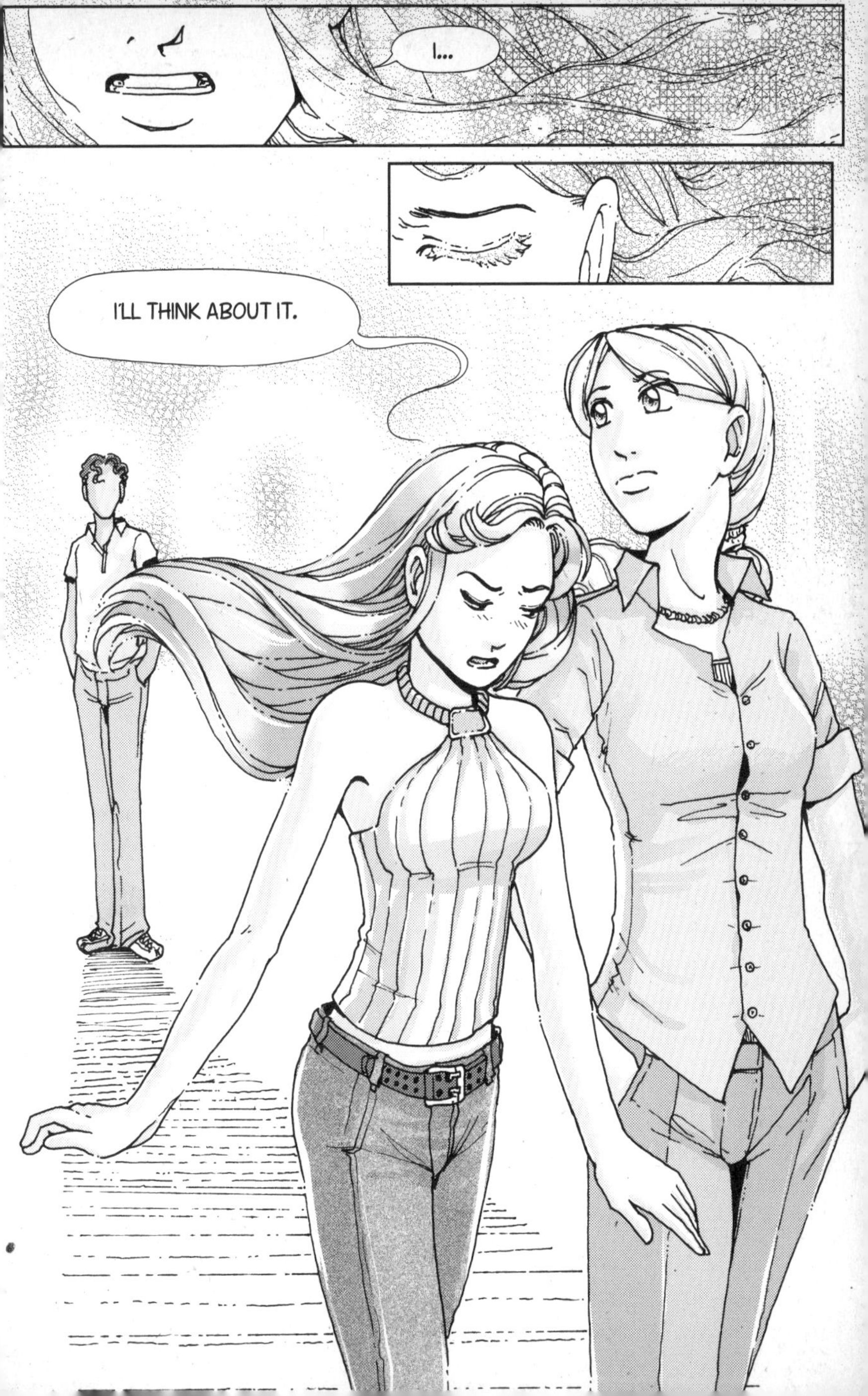
I...
I'LL THINK ABOUT IT.

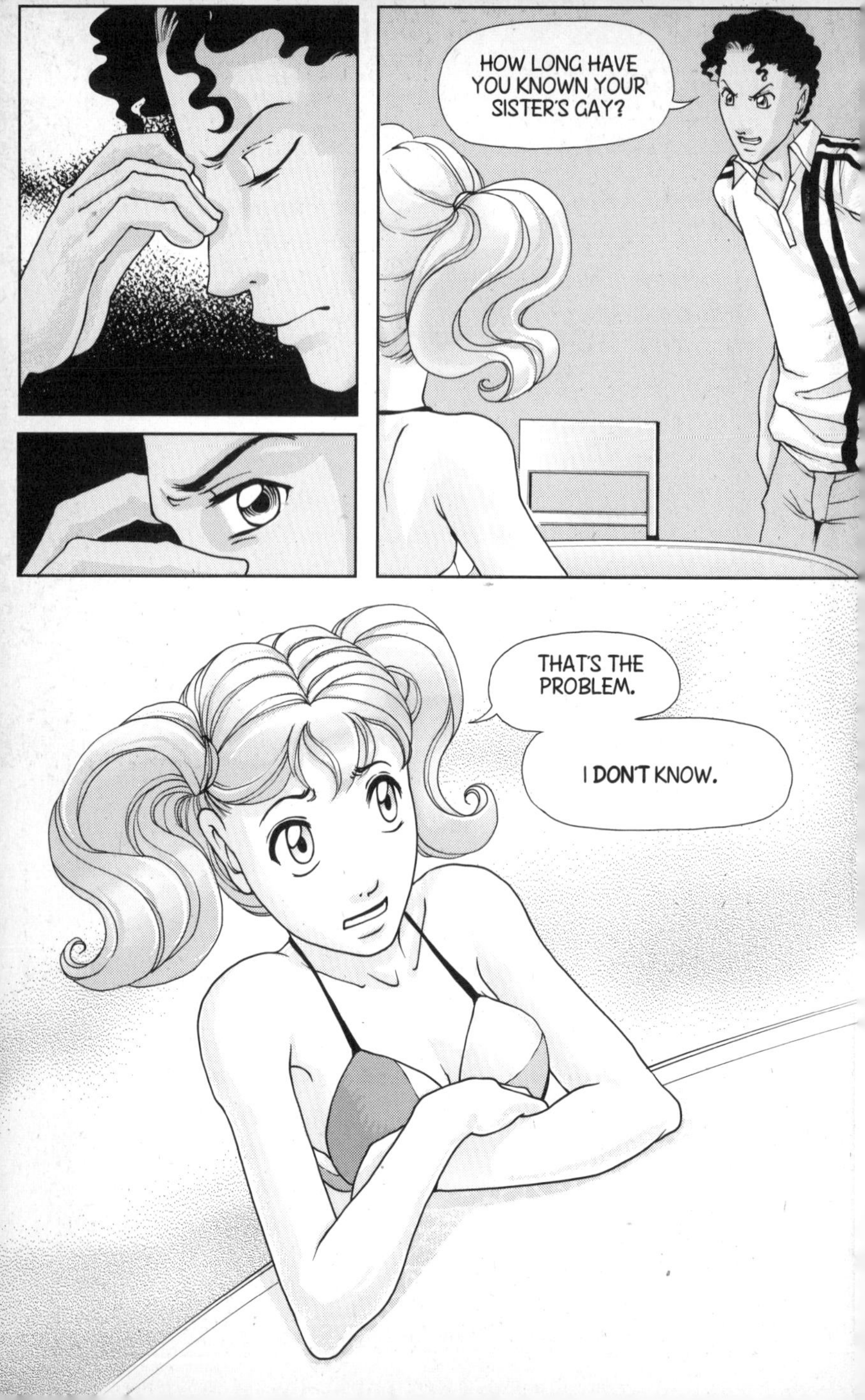
HOW LONG HAVE YOU KNOWN YOUR SISTER'S GAY?
THAT'S THE PROBLEM.
I DON'T KNOW.

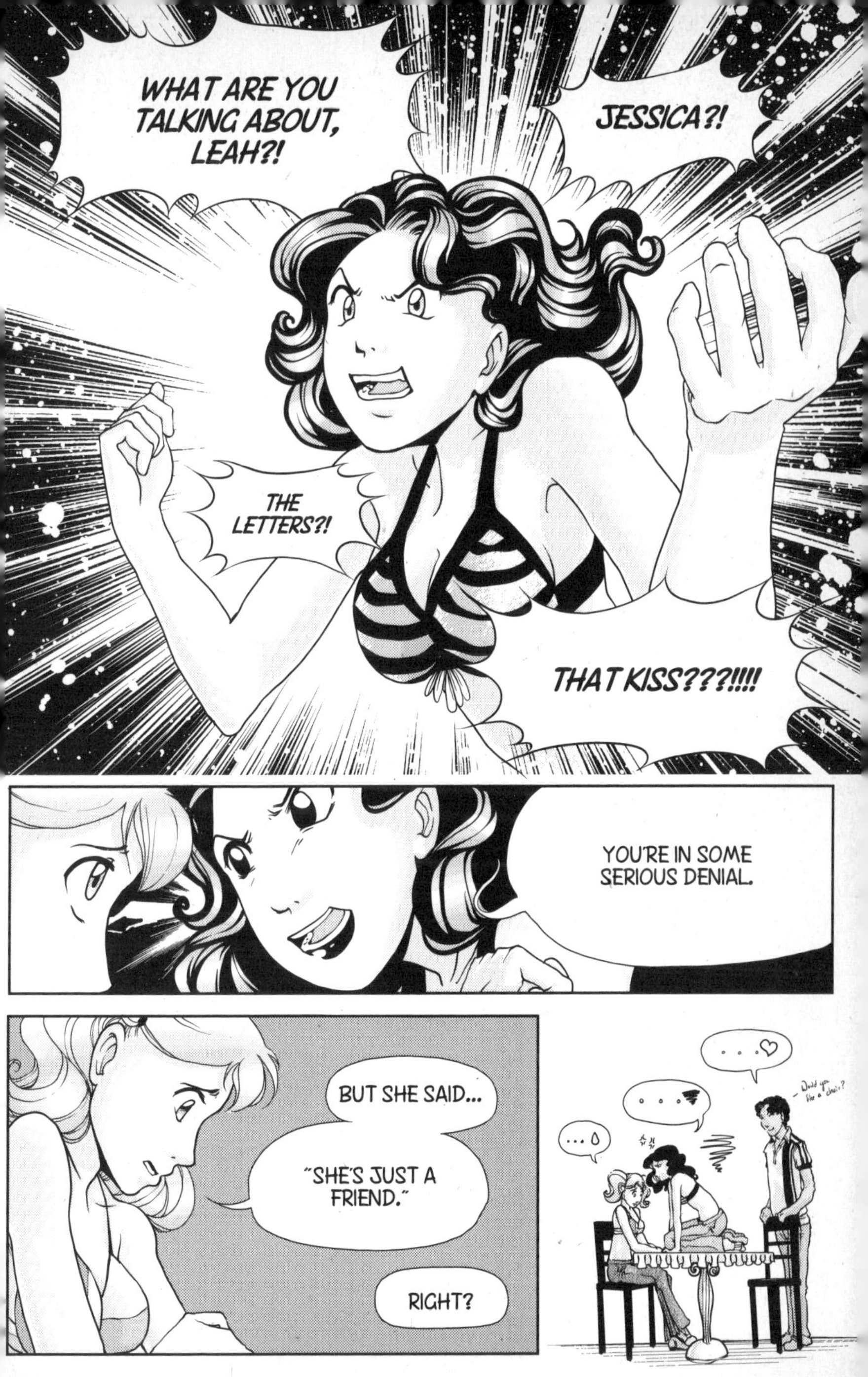
WHAT ARE YOU TALKING ABOUT, LEAH?!
JESSICA?!
THE LETTERS?!
THAT KISS???!!!!
YOU'RE IN SOME SERIOUS DENIAL.
BUT SHE SAID...
"SHE'S JUST A FRIEND."
RIGHT?
- Would you like a chair?

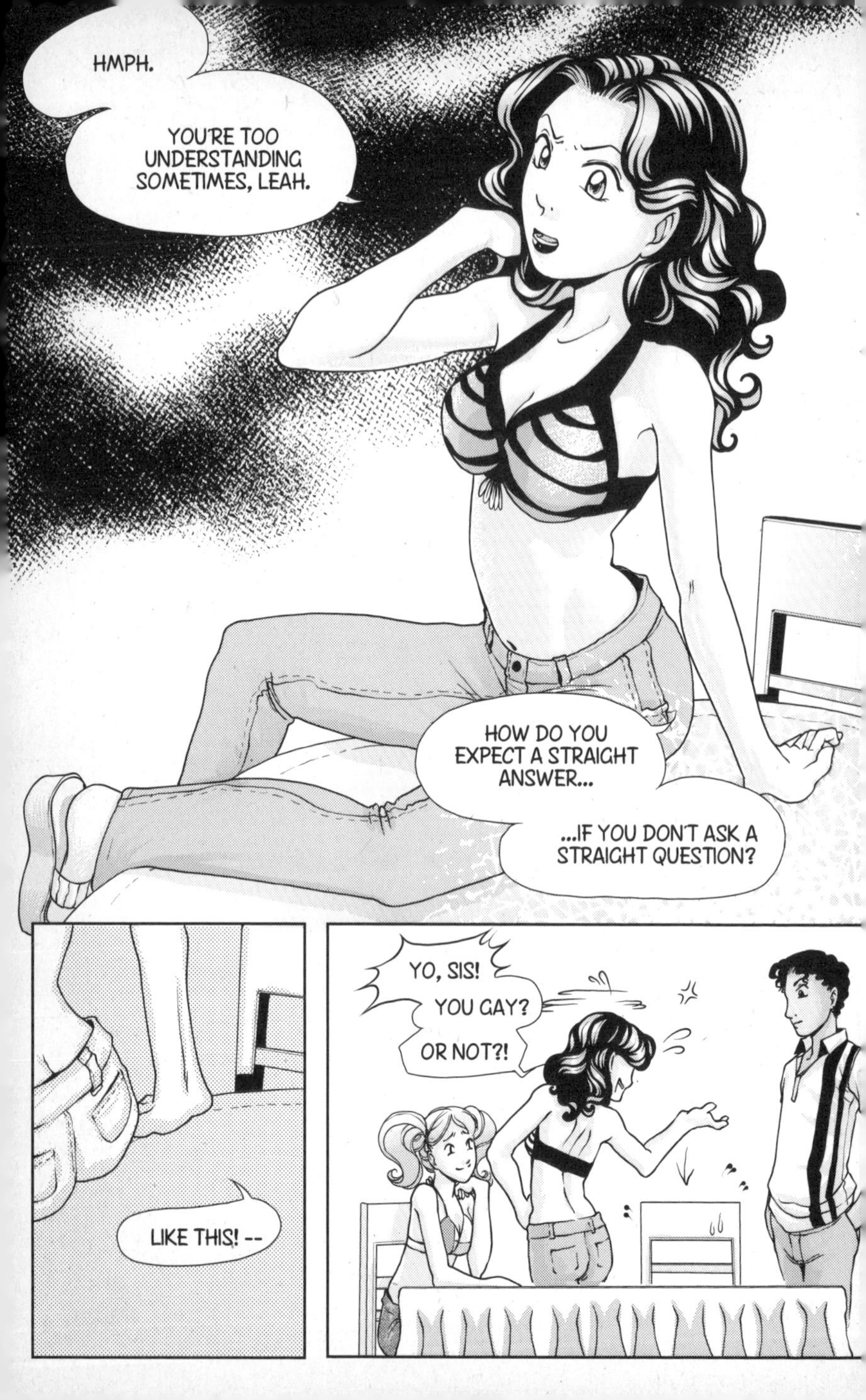
HMPH.
YOU'RE TOO UNDERSTANDING SOMETIMES, LEAH.
HOW DO YOU EXPECT A STRAIGHT ANSWER...
...IF YOU DON'T ASK A STRAIGHT QUESTION?
LIKE THIS! --
YO, SIS!
YOU GAY?
OR NOT?!

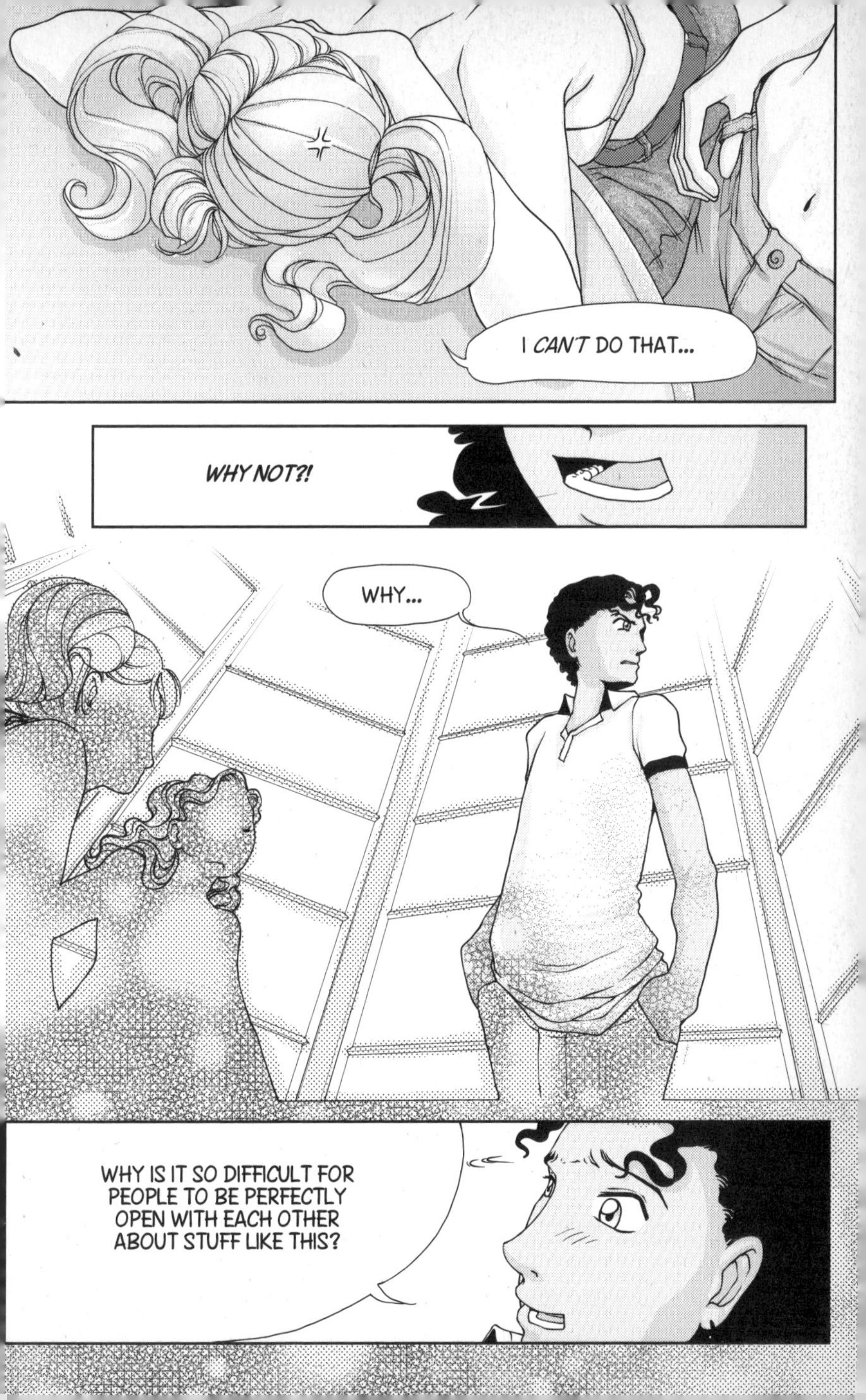
I *CAN'T* DO THAT...
*WHY NOT?!*
WHY...
WHY IS IT SO DIFFICULT FOR PEOPLE TO BE PERFECTLY OPEN WITH EACH OTHER ABOUT STUFF LIKE THIS?

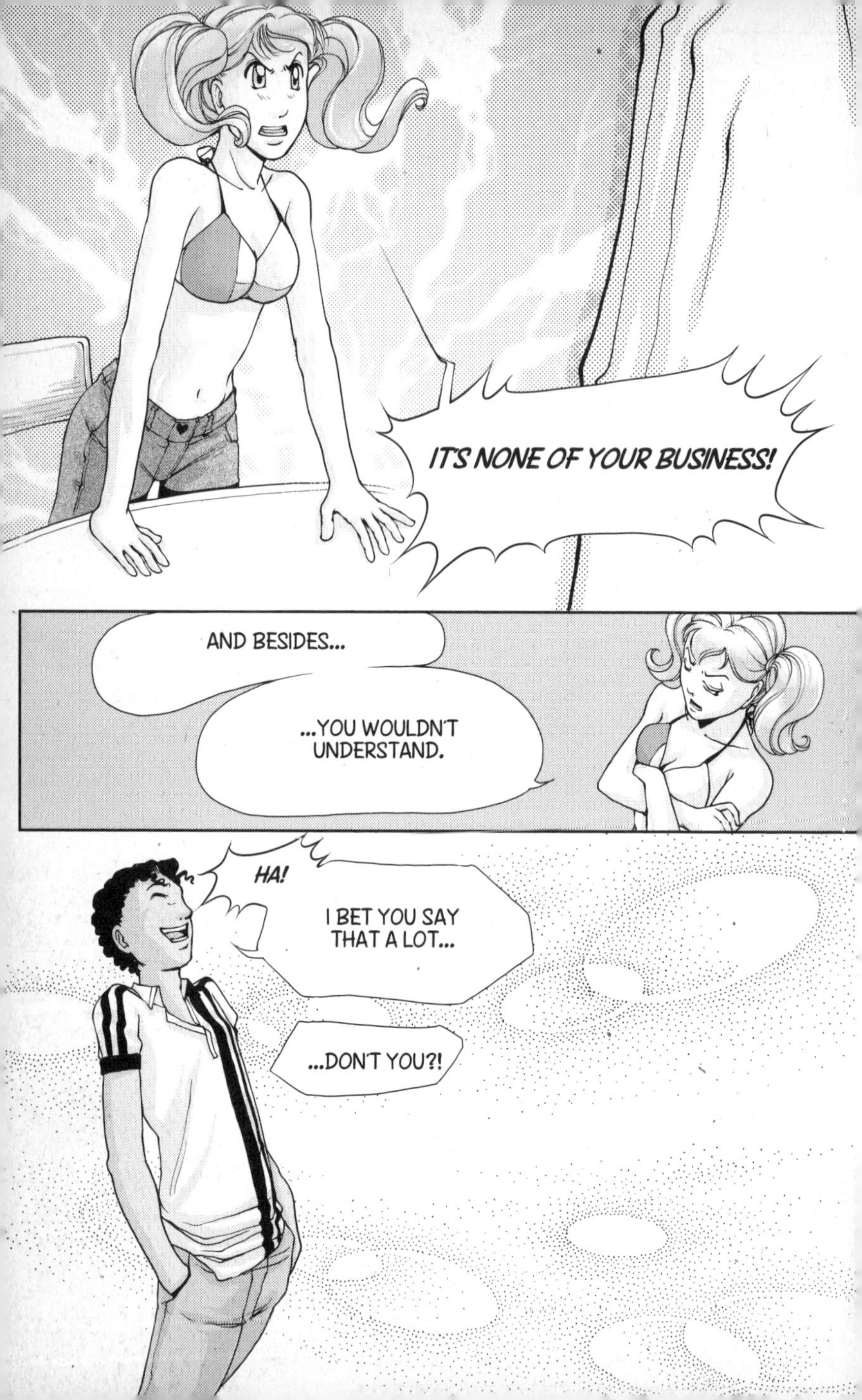
IT'S NONE OF YOUR BUSINESS!
AND BESIDES...
...YOU WOULDN'T UNDERSTAND.
HA!
I BET YOU SAY THAT A LOT...
...DON'T YOU?!

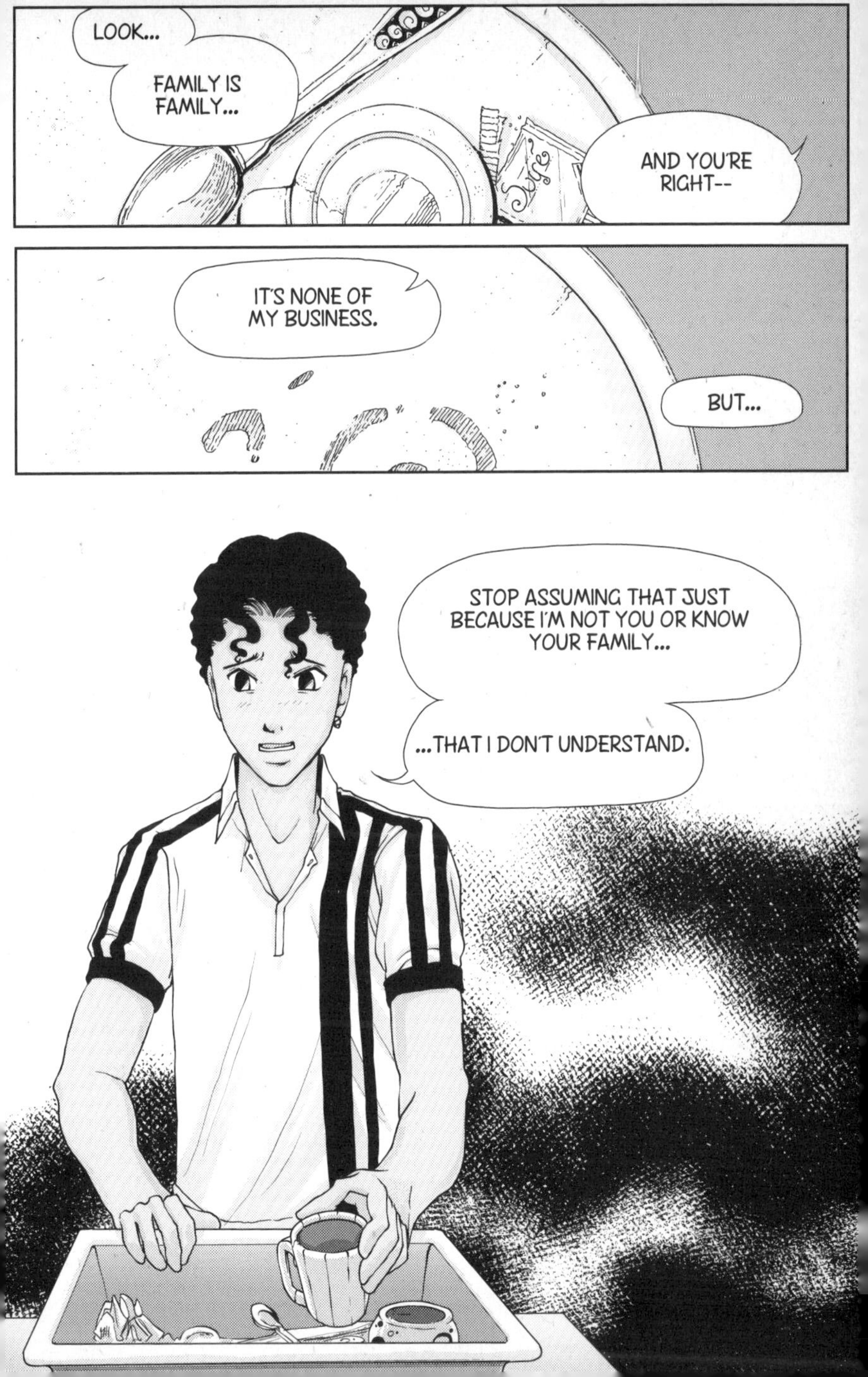
LOOK...
FAMILY IS FAMILY...
AND YOU'RE RIGHT--
IT'S NONE OF MY BUSINESS.
BUT...
STOP ASSUMING THAT JUST BECAUSE I'M NOT YOU OR KNOW YOUR FAMILY...
...THAT I DON'T UNDERSTAND.

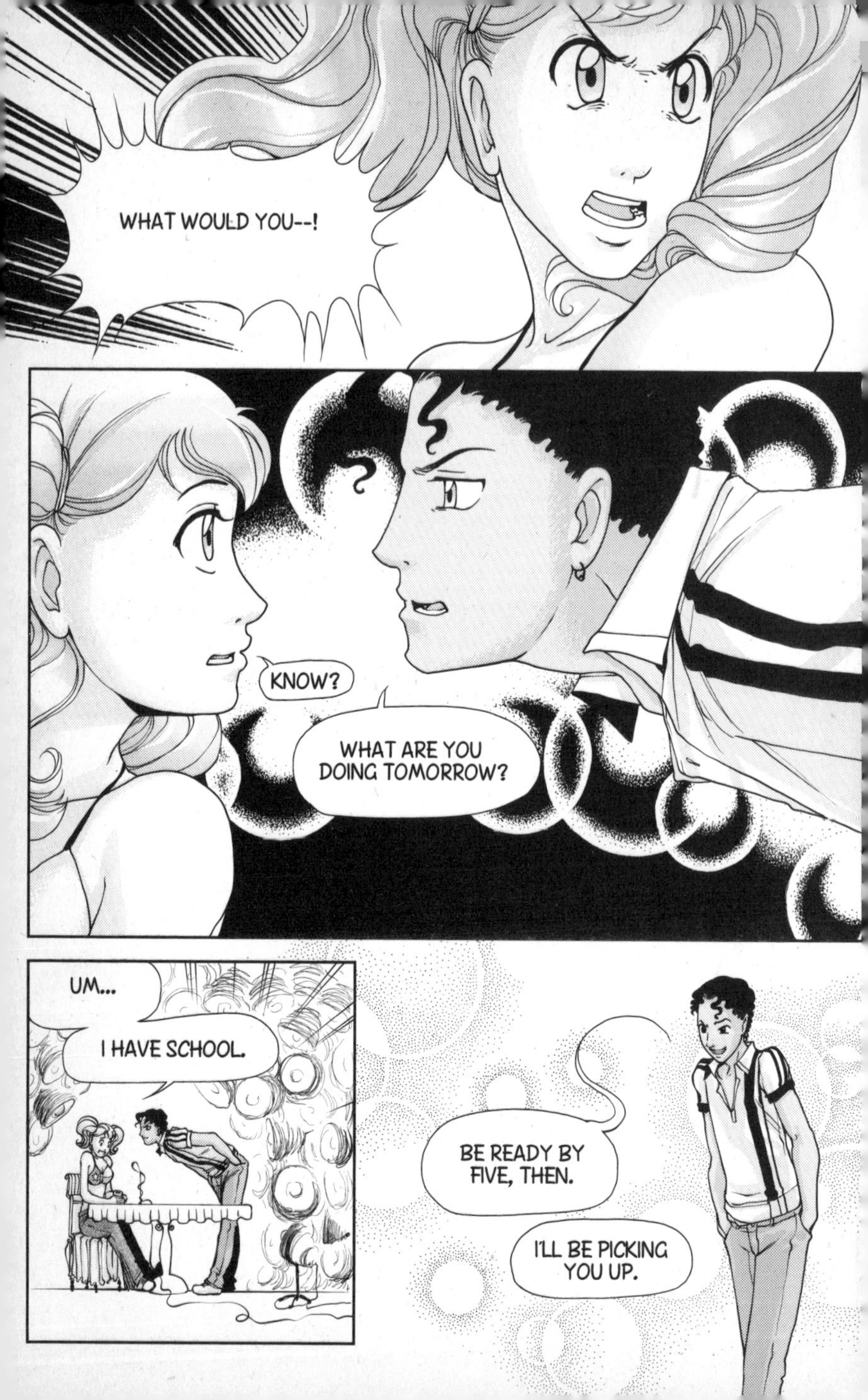
WHAT WOULD YOU--!
KNOW?
WHAT ARE YOU DOING TOMORROW?
UM...
I HAVE SCHOOL.
BE READY BY FIVE, THEN.
I'LL BE PICKING YOU UP.

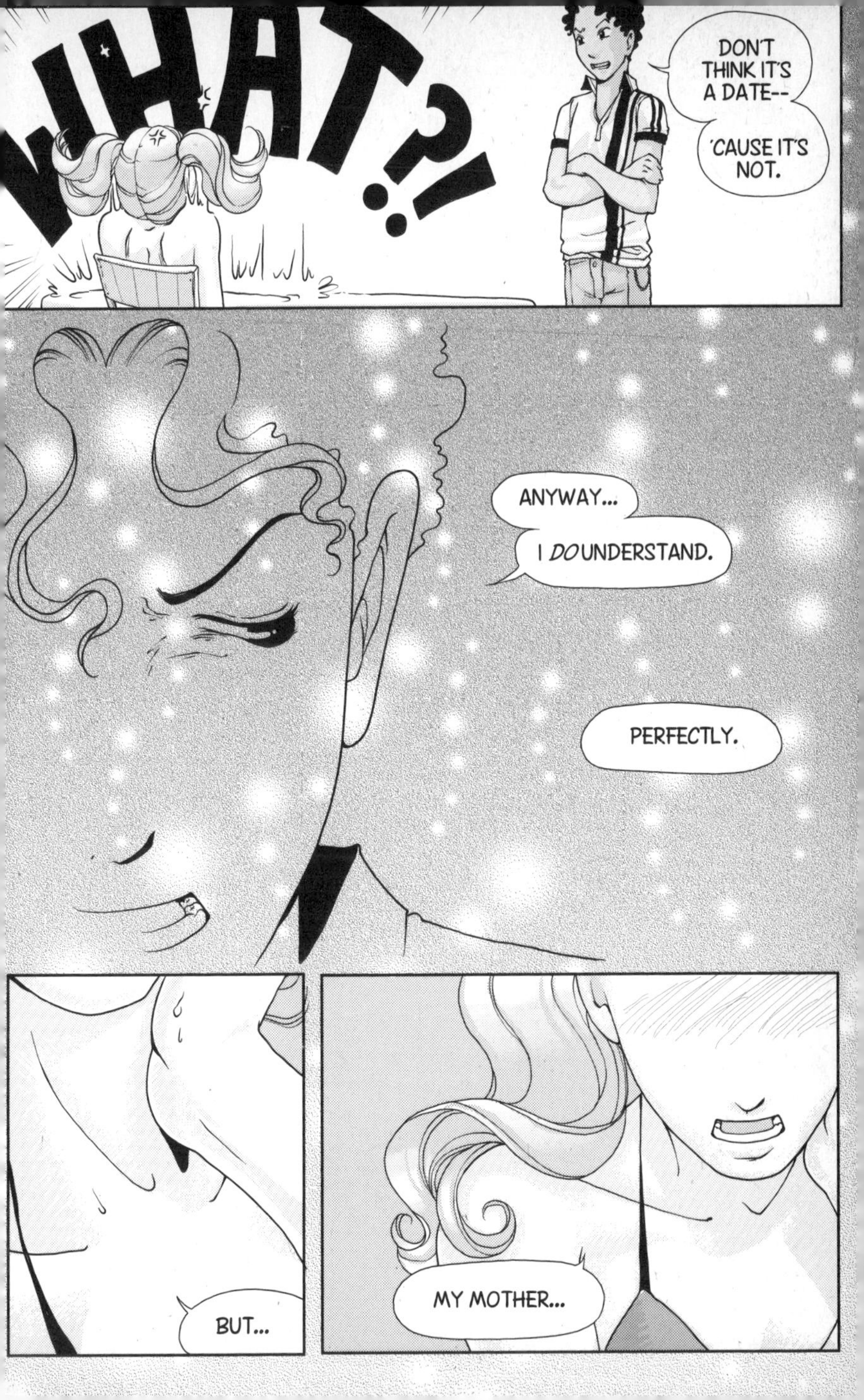
WHAT?!
DON'T THINK IT'S A DATE--
'CAUSE IT'S NOT.
ANYWAY...
I *DO* UNDERSTAND.
PERFECTLY.
BUT...
MY MOTHER...

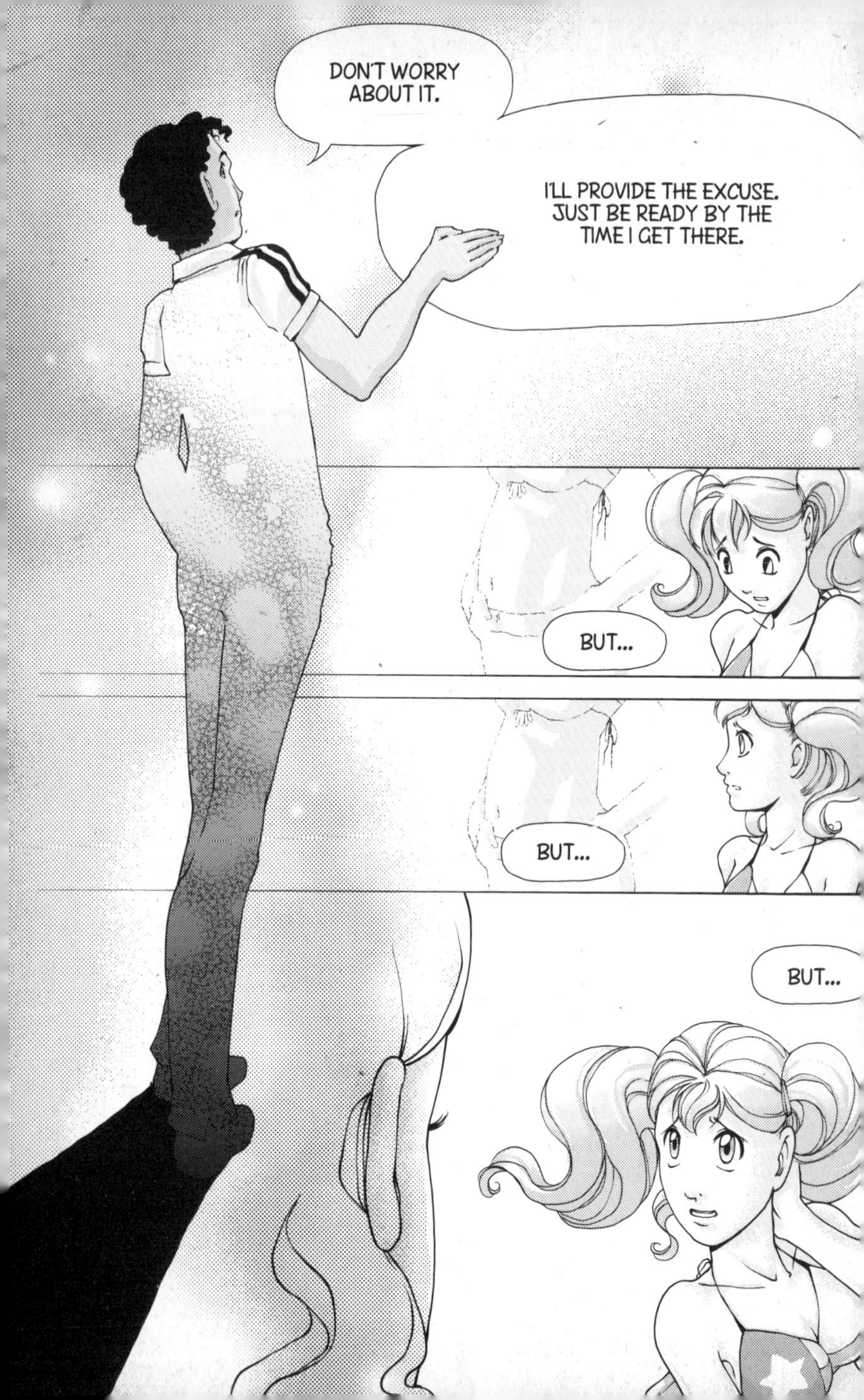
DON'T WORRY ABOUT IT.
I'LL PROVIDE THE EXCUSE. JUST BE READY BY THE TIME I GET THERE.
BUT...
BUT...
BUT...

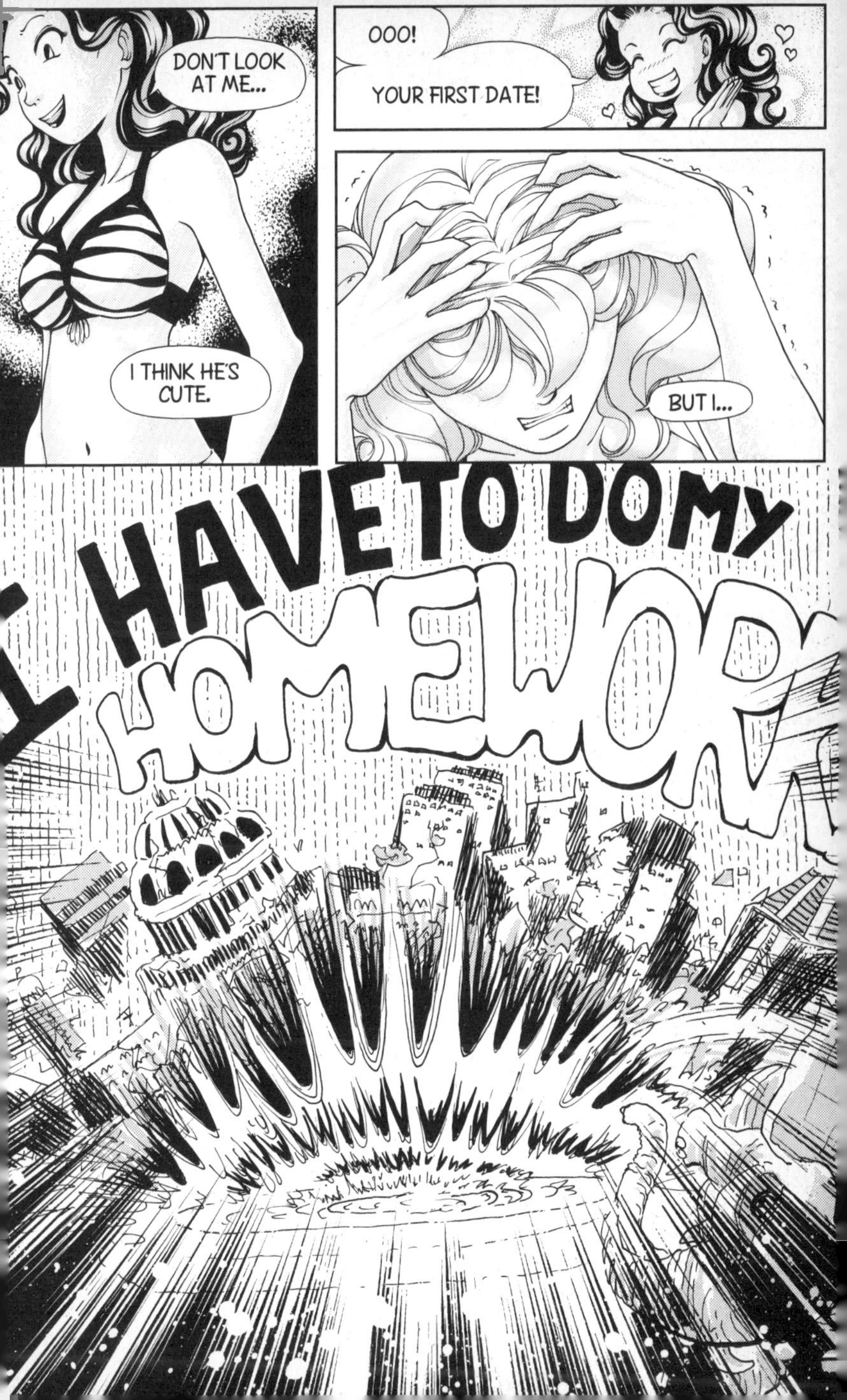
DON'T LOOK AT ME...
I THINK HE'S CUTE.
OOO!
YOUR FIRST DATE!
BUT I...
I HAVE TO DO MY
HOMEWOR

Dear Me,                                    September 4th

        Why can't they make school so
it's your choice of all tests or all
homework? I'd make A's if all we
had to do was take a few tests and
write a few essays (no deductions for
being late? Please?!) I just got back
my English paper, and it
    would have been a 104 (hurray
for bonus questions!), but instead
it was a 74 for being three days
late. --i Ugh.
        Oh well. Nothing I can do
about it. Story of my life.

        I hate busy work. Stupid
homework. *grumble*

**BEAT 9**

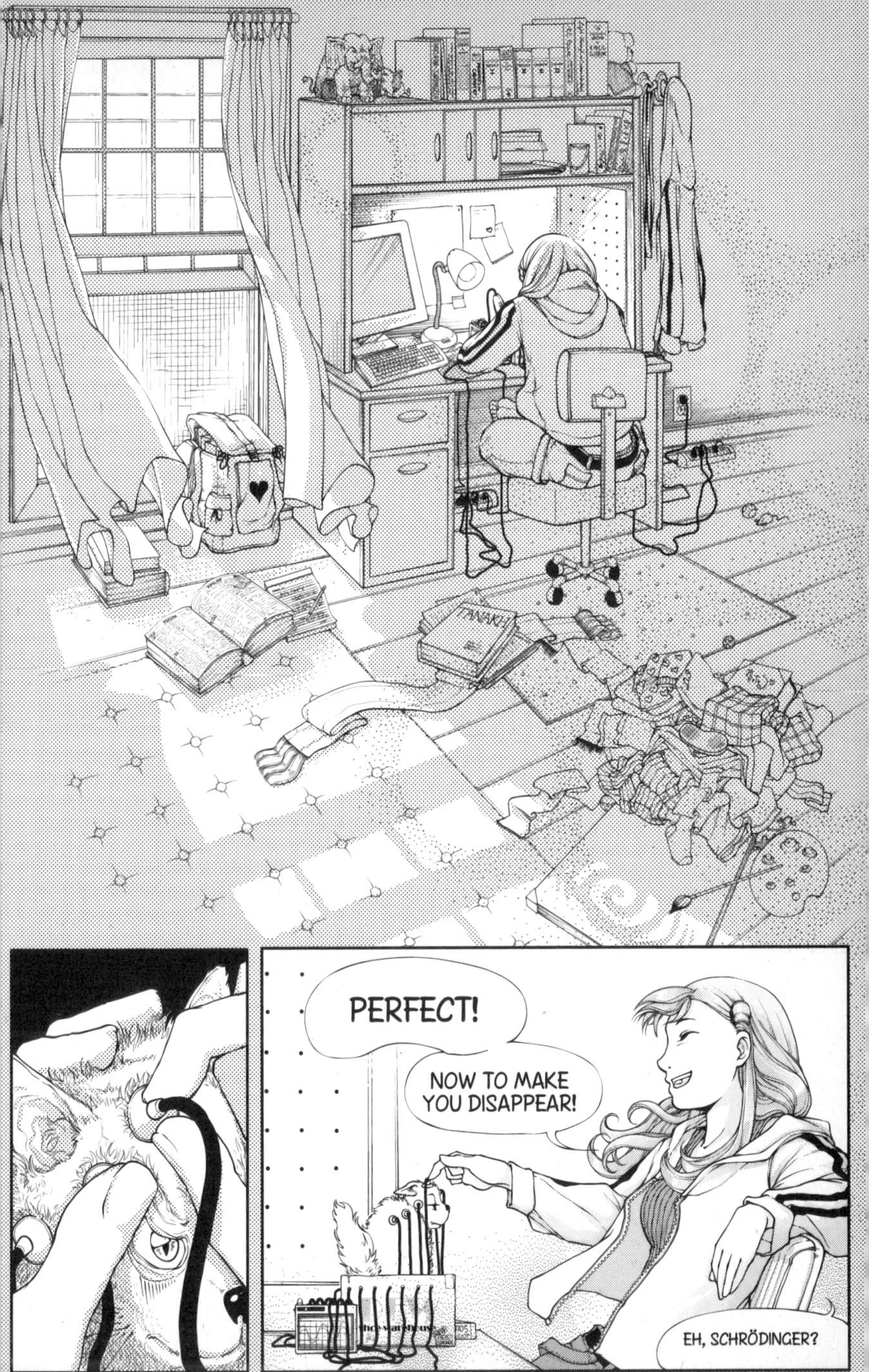
TANAKH
PERFECT!
NOW TO MAKE YOU DISAPPEAR!
EH, SCHRÖDINGER?

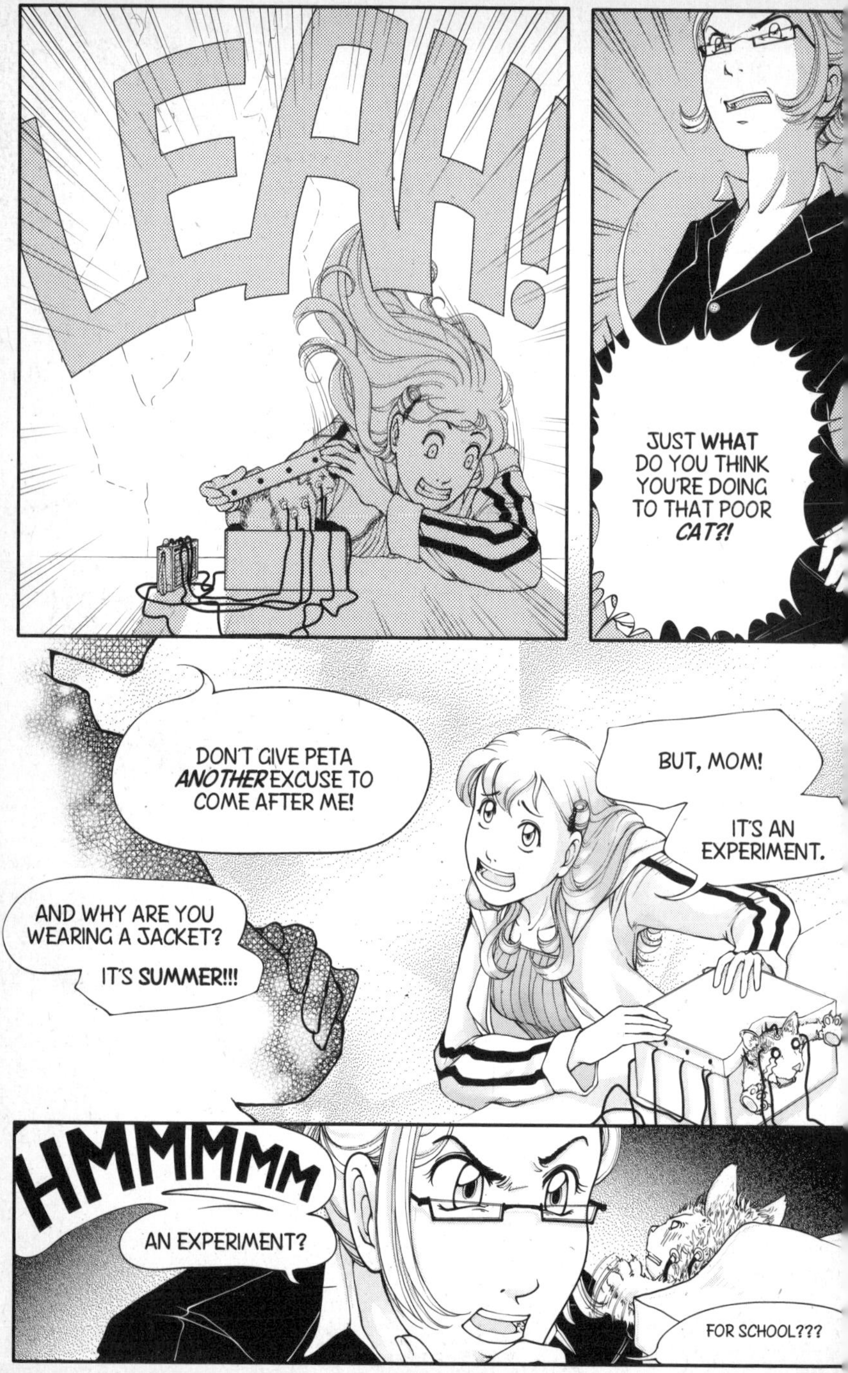
LEAH!!
JUST **WHAT** DO YOU THINK YOU'RE DOING TO THAT POOR ***CAT?!***
DON'T GIVE PETA ***ANOTHER*** EXCUSE TO COME AFTER ME!
AND WHY ARE YOU WEARING A JACKET?
IT'S **SUMMER!!!**
BUT, MOM!
IT'S AN EXPERIMENT.
HMMMMM
AN EXPERIMENT?
FOR SCHOOL???

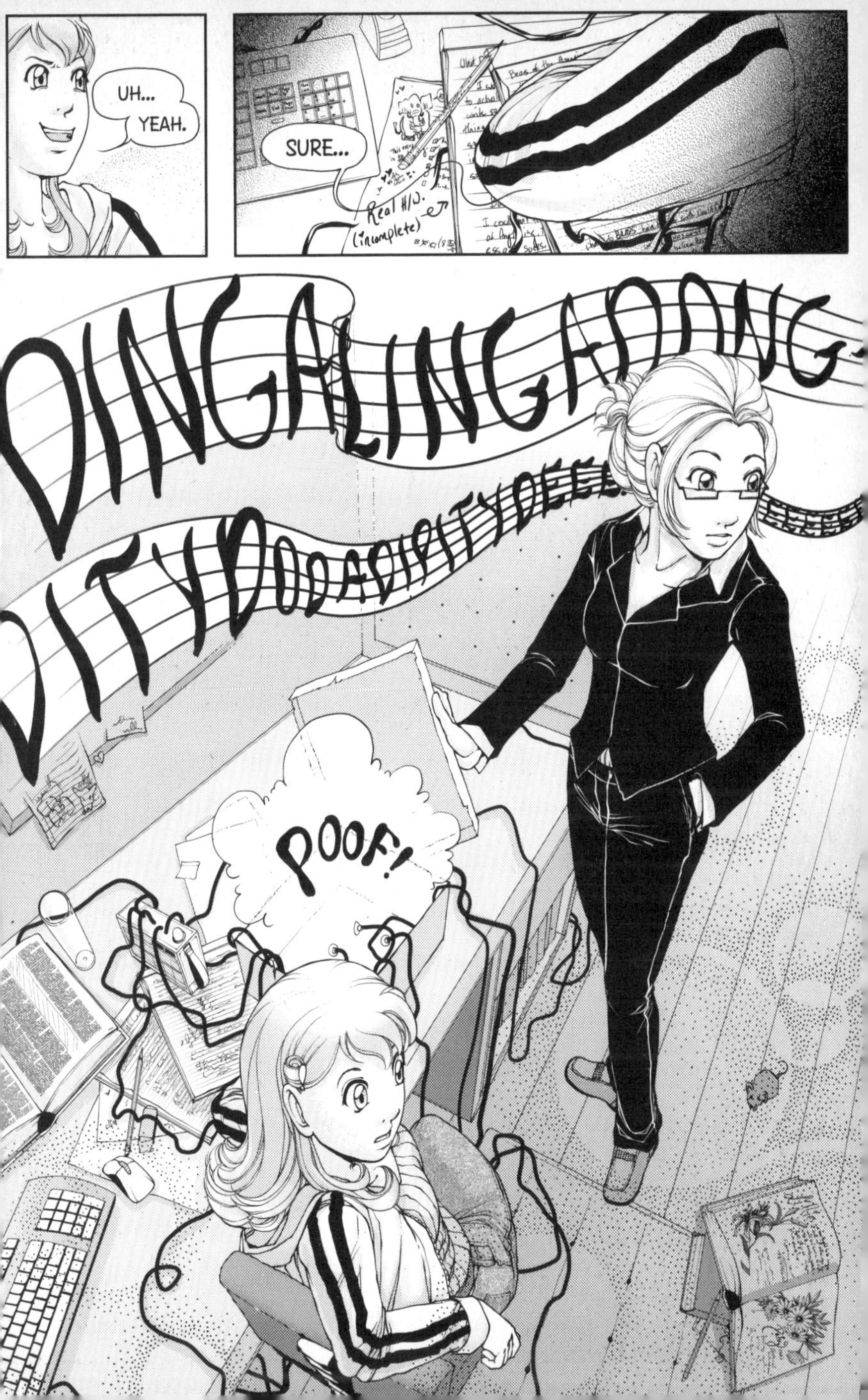
UH... YEAH.
SURE...
Real H/W. (incomplete)
DINGALINGADOONG-
DITYDOODADIPITYDEE
POOF!

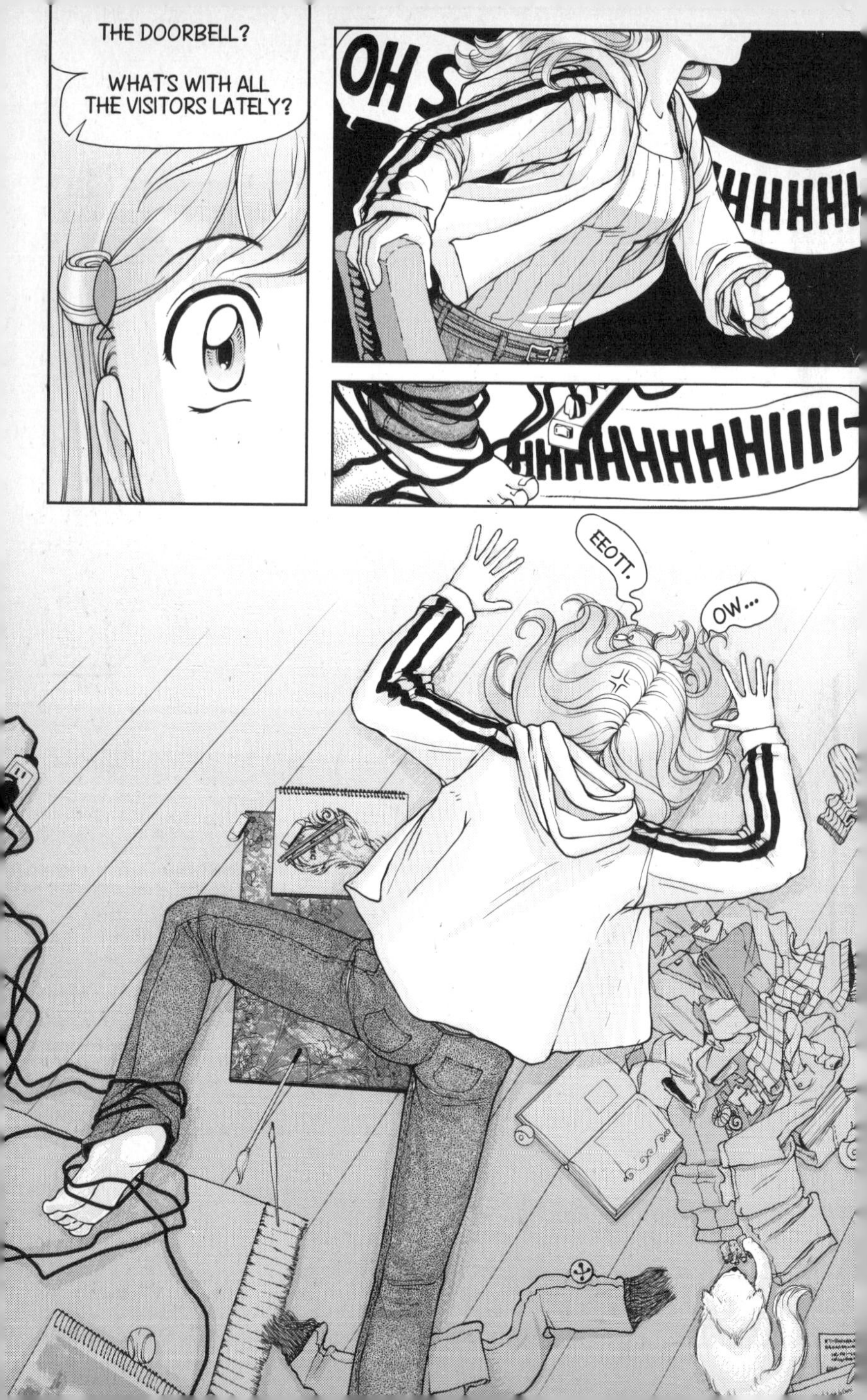
THE DOORBELL?
WHAT'S WITH ALL THE VISITORS LATELY?
OH S
HHHHH
HHHHHHHHHHIIII-
EEOTT.
OW...

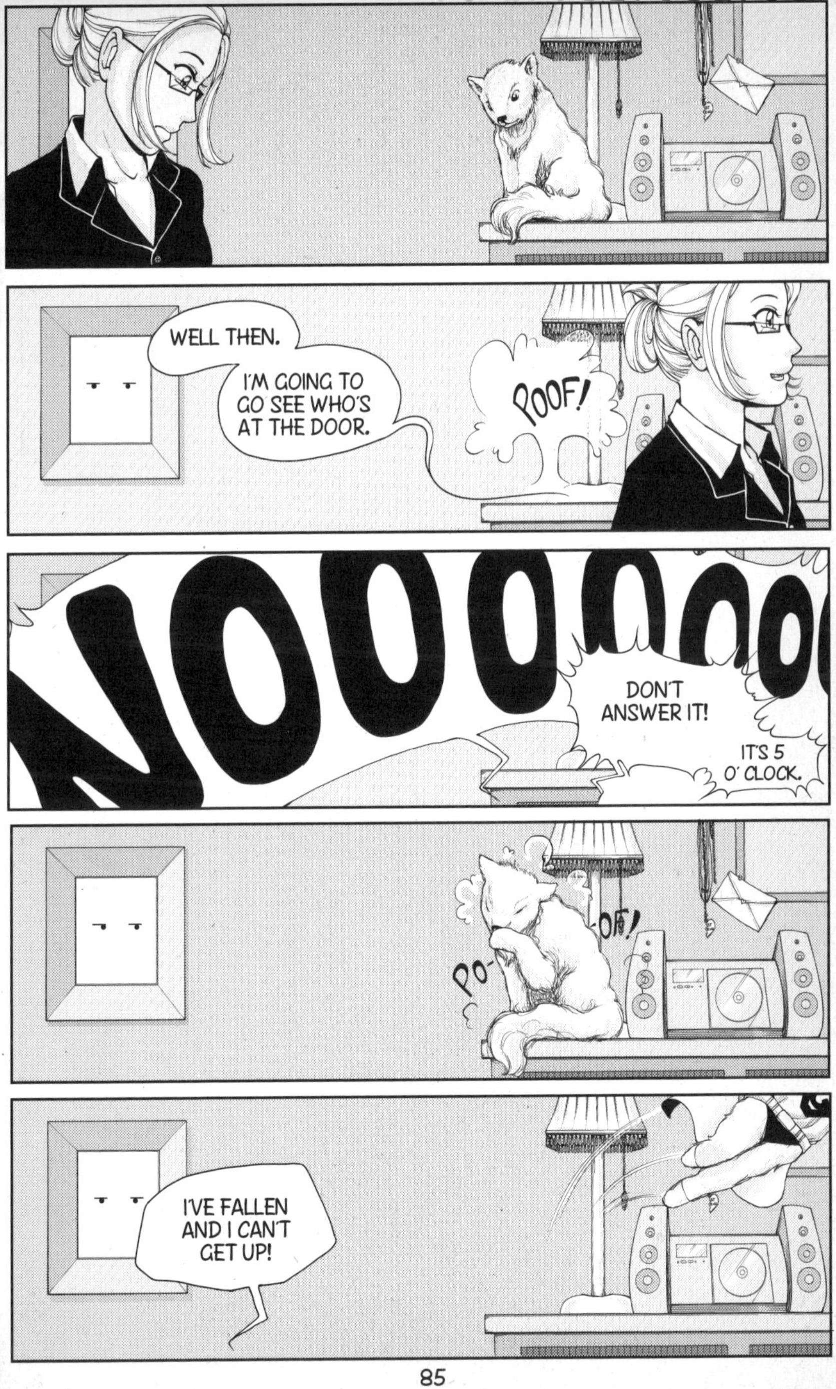
WELL THEN.
I'M GOING TO GO SEE WHO'S AT THE DOOR.
POOF!
NOOOOOOO
DON'T ANSWER IT!
IT'S 5 O' CLOCK.
PO-
-OF!
I'VE FALLEN AND I CAN'T GET UP!

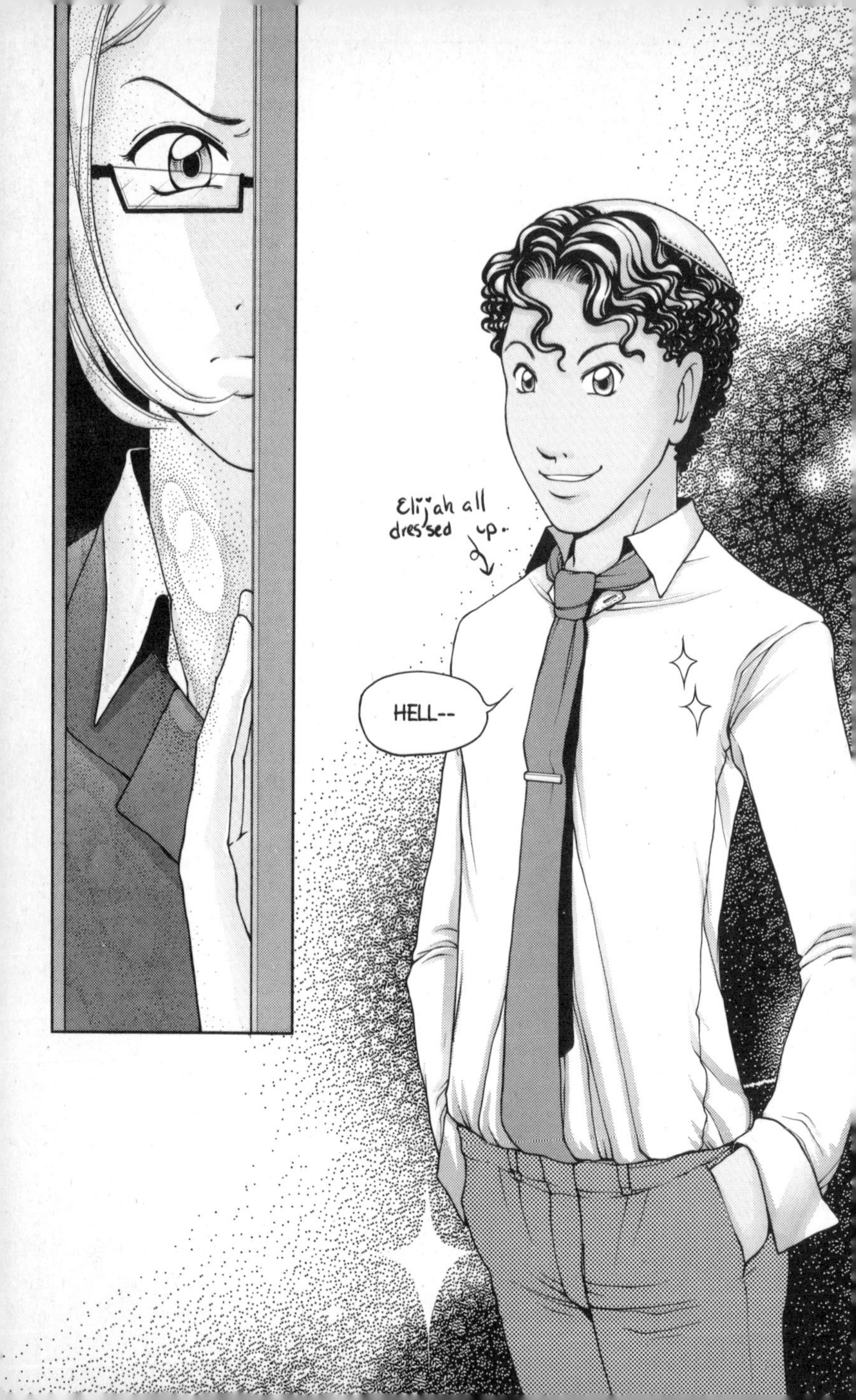
Elijah all dressed up..
HELL--

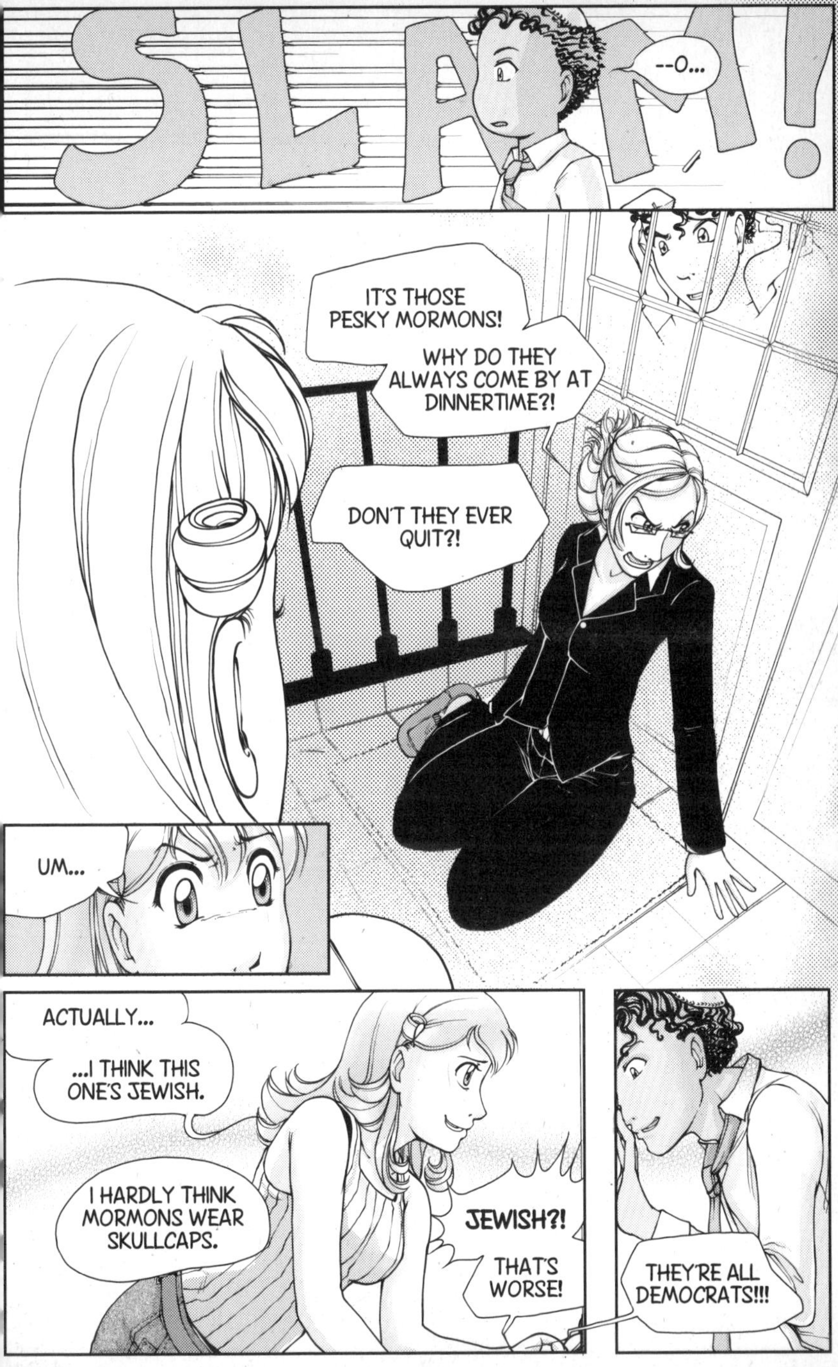
SLAM!
--O...
IT'S THOSE PESKY MORMONS!
WHY DO THEY ALWAYS COME BY AT DINNERTIME?!
DON'T THEY EVER QUIT?!
UM...
ACTUALLY...
...I THINK THIS ONE'S JEWISH.
I HARDLY THINK MORMONS WEAR SKULLCAPS.
JEWISH?!
THAT'S WORSE!
THEY'RE ALL DEMOCRATS!!!

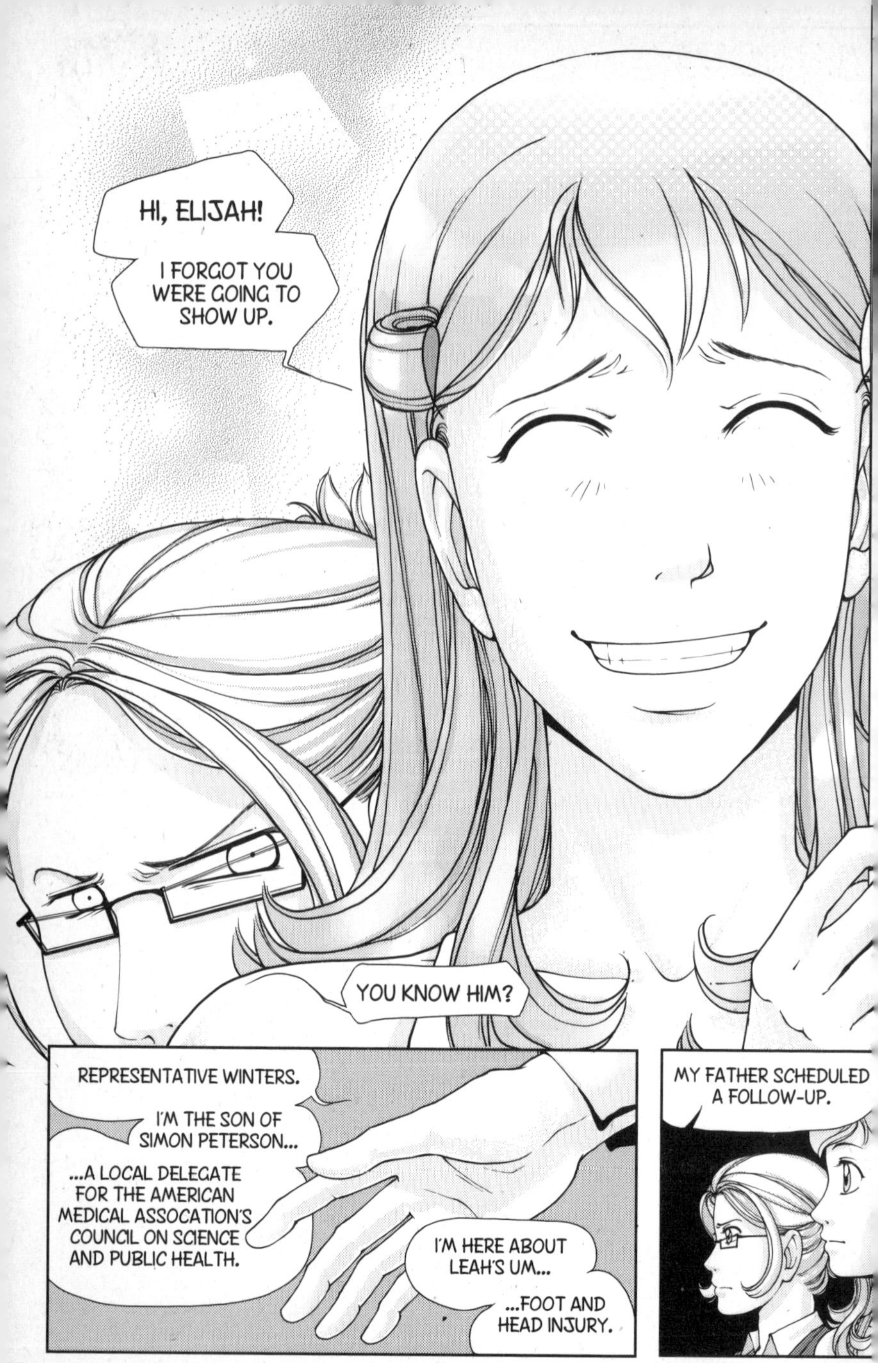
HI, ELIJAH!
I FORGOT YOU WERE GOING TO SHOW UP.
YOU KNOW HIM?
REPRESENTATIVE WINTERS.
I'M THE SON OF SIMON PETERSON...
...A LOCAL DELEGATE FOR THE AMERICAN MEDICAL ASSOCATION'S COUNCIL ON SCIENCE AND PUBLIC HEALTH.
I'M HERE ABOUT LEAH'S UM...
...FOOT AND HEAD INJURY.
MY FATHER SCHEDULED A FOLLOW-UP.

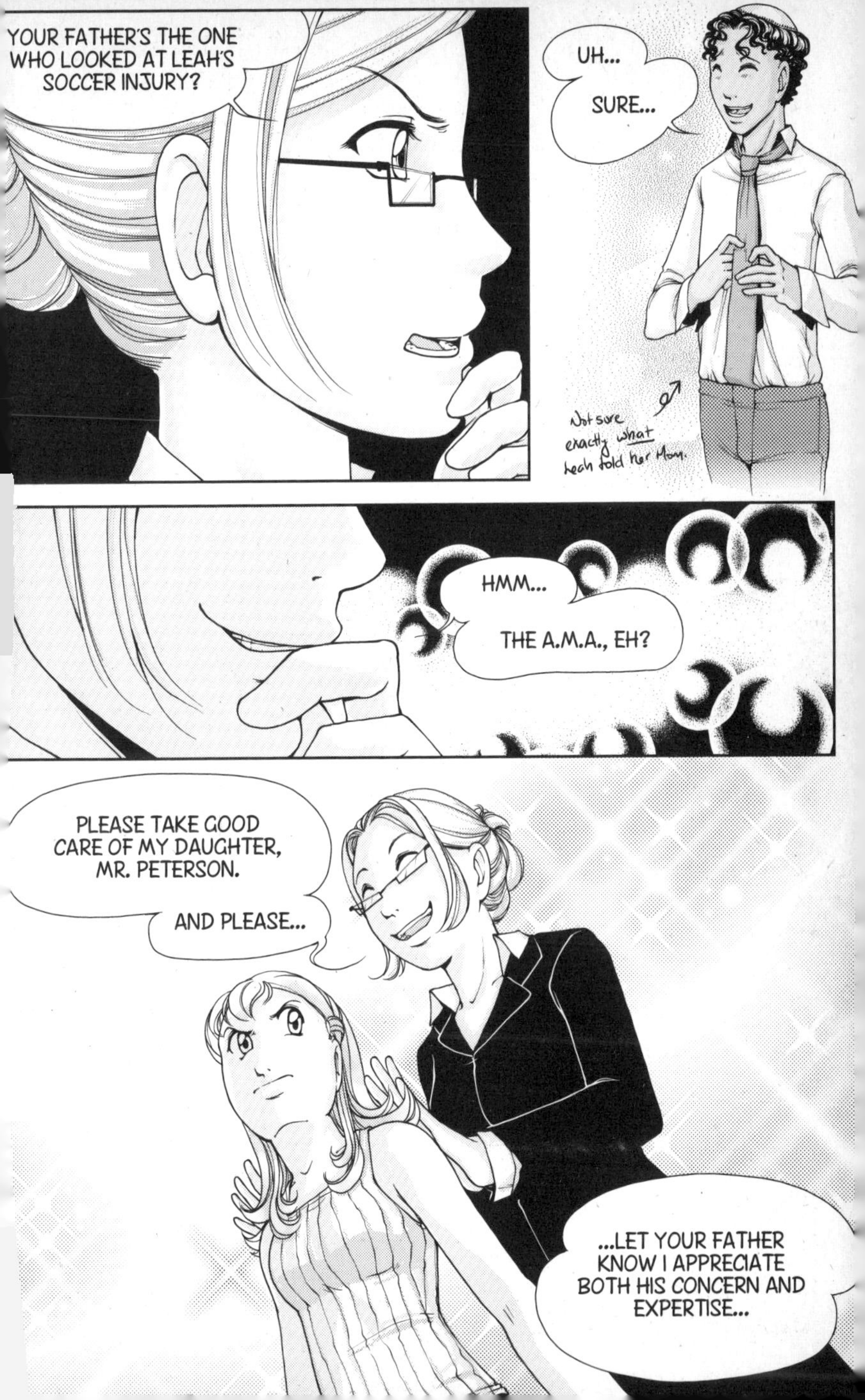
YOUR FATHER'S THE ONE WHO LOOKED AT LEAH'S SOCCER INJURY?
UH...
SURE...
Not sure exactly what Leah told her Mom.
HMM...
THE A.M.A., EH?
PLEASE TAKE GOOD CARE OF MY DAUGHTER, MR. PETERSON.
AND PLEASE...
...LET YOUR FATHER KNOW I APPRECIATE BOTH HIS CONCERN AND EXPERTISE...

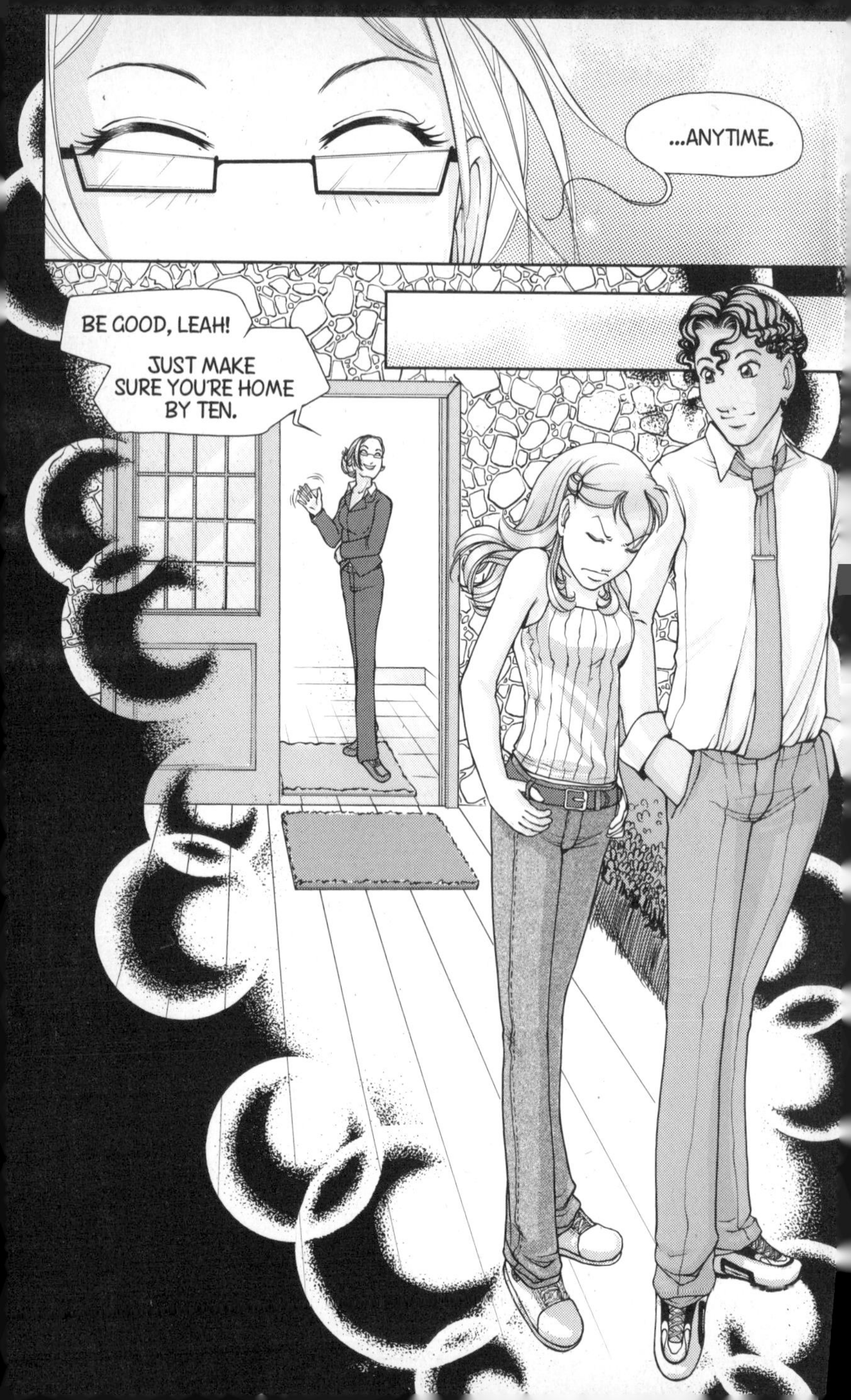
...ANYTIME.
BE GOOD, LEAH!
JUST MAKE SURE YOU'RE HOME BY TEN.

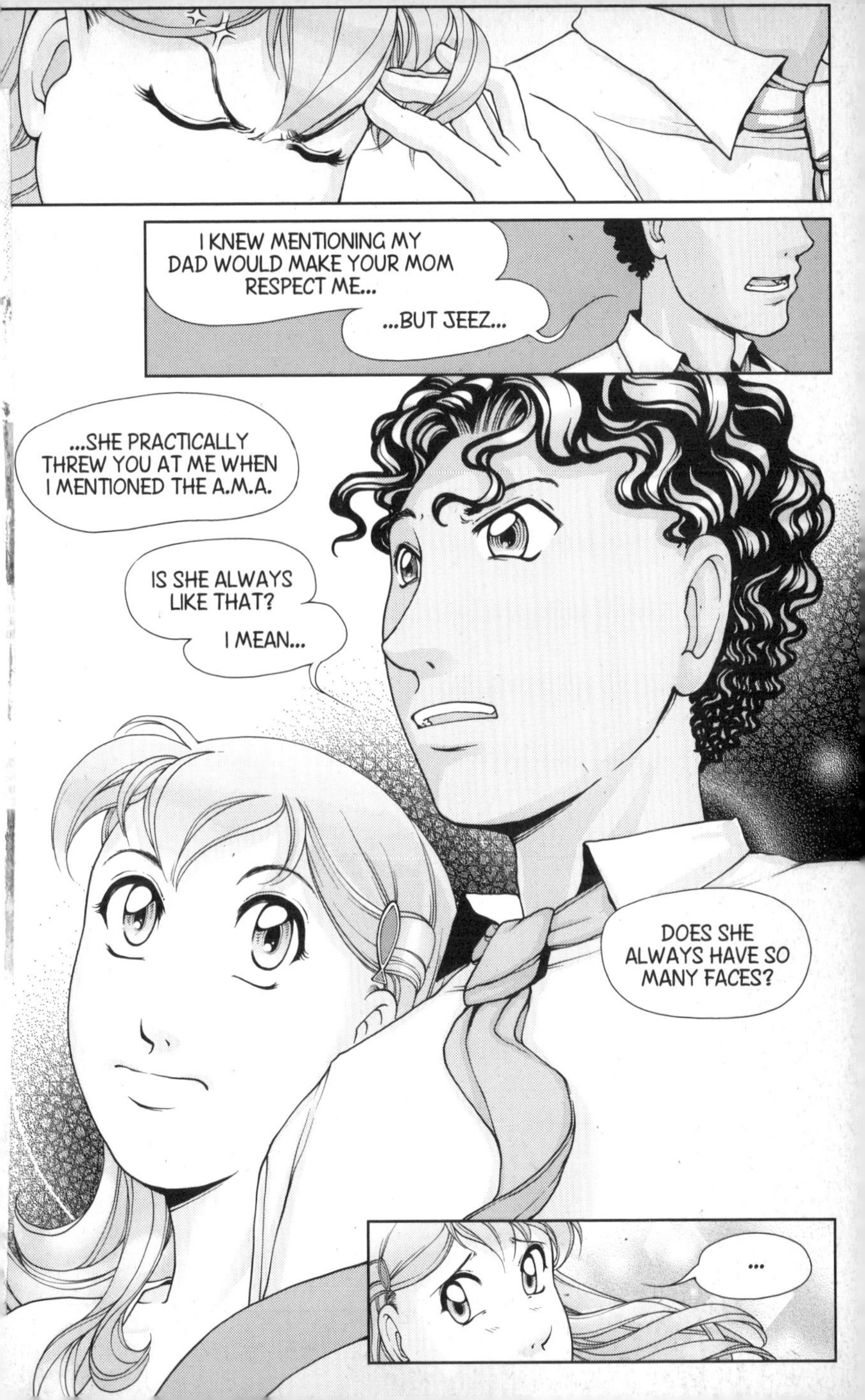

I KNEW MENTIONING MY DAD WOULD MAKE YOUR MOM RESPECT ME...
...BUT JEEZ...
...SHE PRACTICALLY THREW YOU AT ME WHEN I MENTIONED THE A.M.A.
IS SHE ALWAYS LIKE THAT?
I MEAN...
DOES SHE ALWAYS HAVE SO MANY FACES?
...

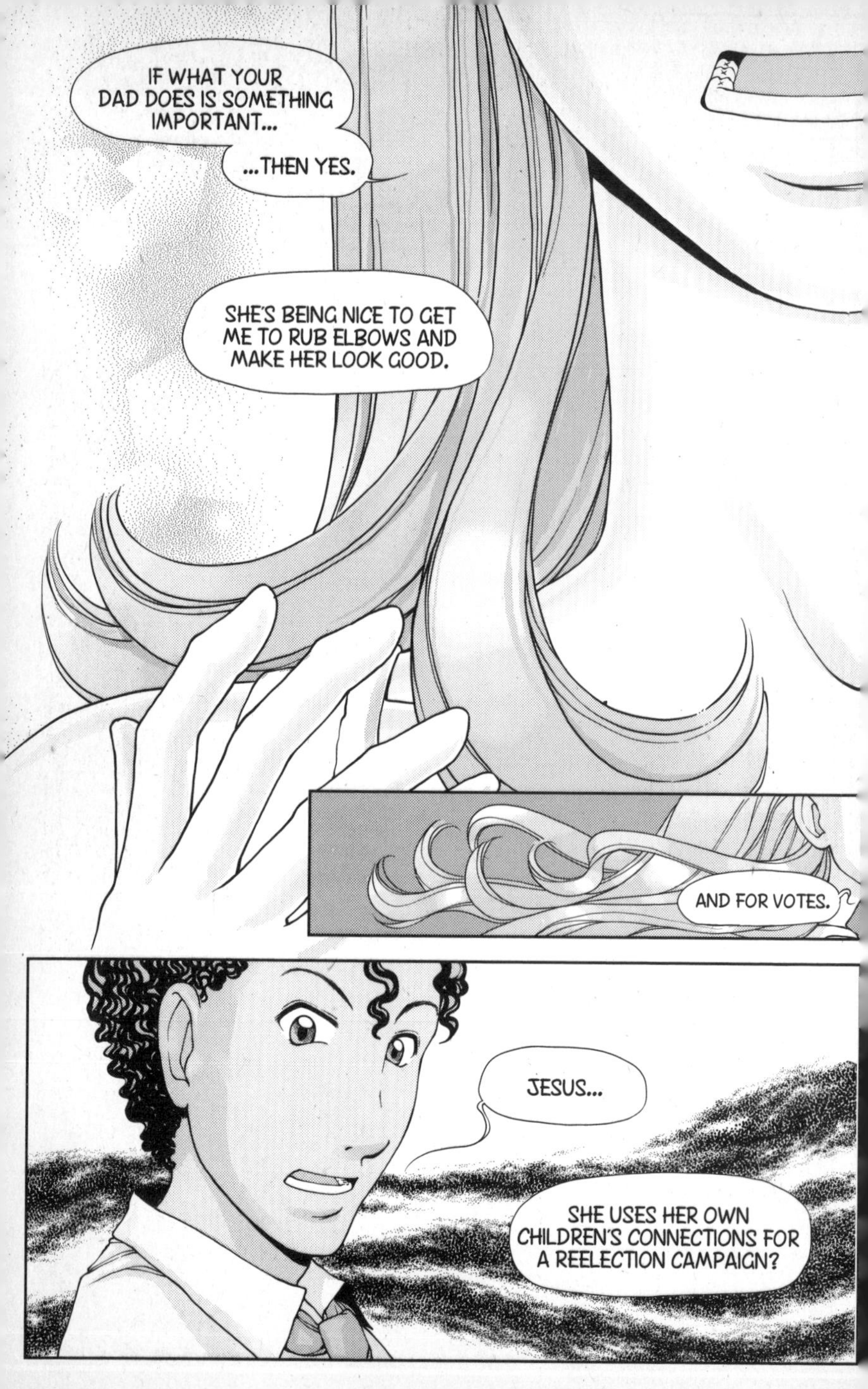
IF WHAT YOUR DAD DOES IS SOMETHING IMPORTANT...
...THEN YES.
SHE'S BEING NICE TO GET ME TO RUB ELBOWS AND MAKE HER LOOK GOOD.
AND FOR VOTES.
JESUS...
SHE USES HER OWN CHILDREN'S CONNECTIONS FOR A REELECTION CAMPAIGN?

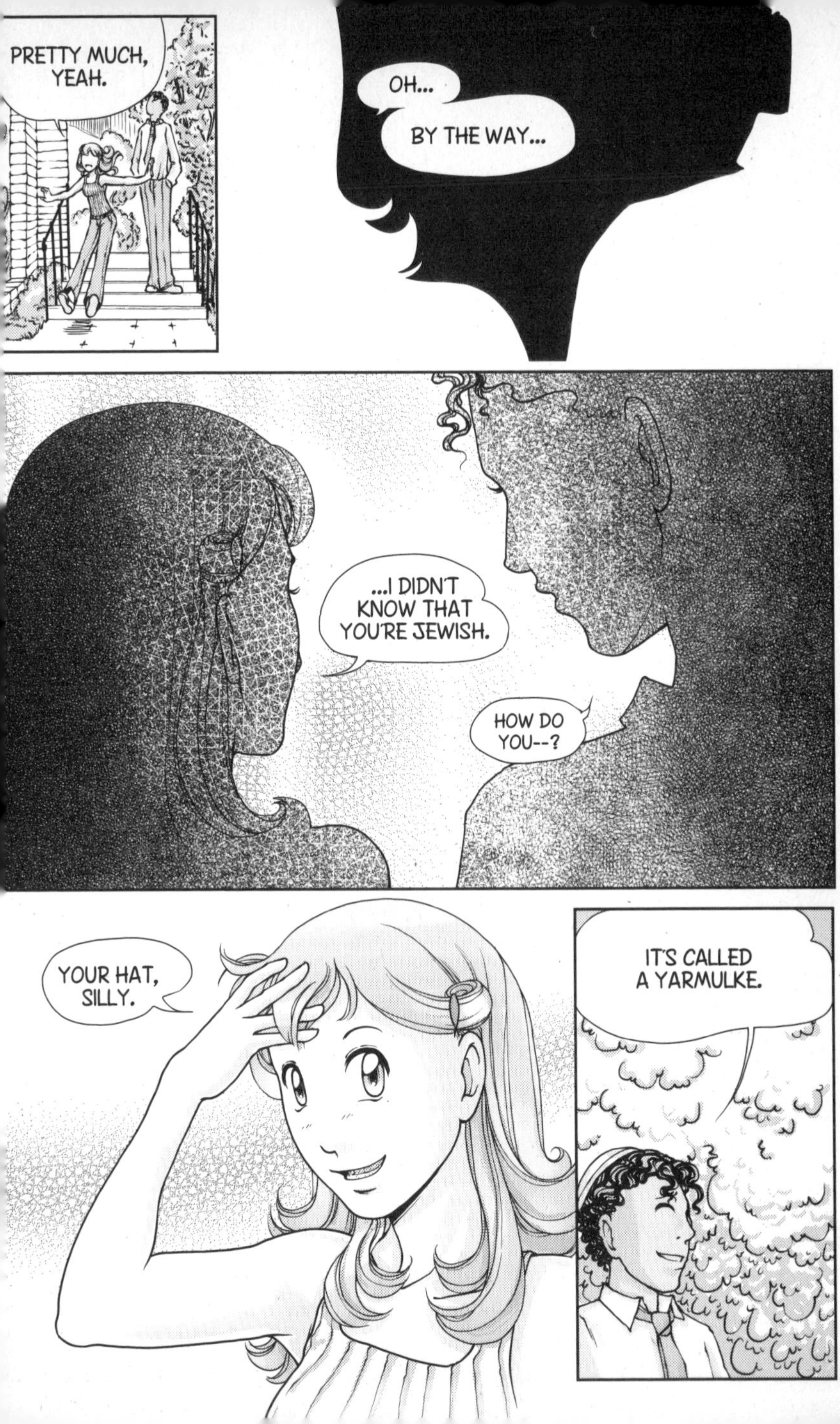
PRETTY MUCH, YEAH.
OH...
BY THE WAY...
...I DIDN'T KNOW THAT YOU'RE JEWISH.
HOW DO YOU--?
YOUR HAT, SILLY.
IT'S CALLED A YARMULKE.

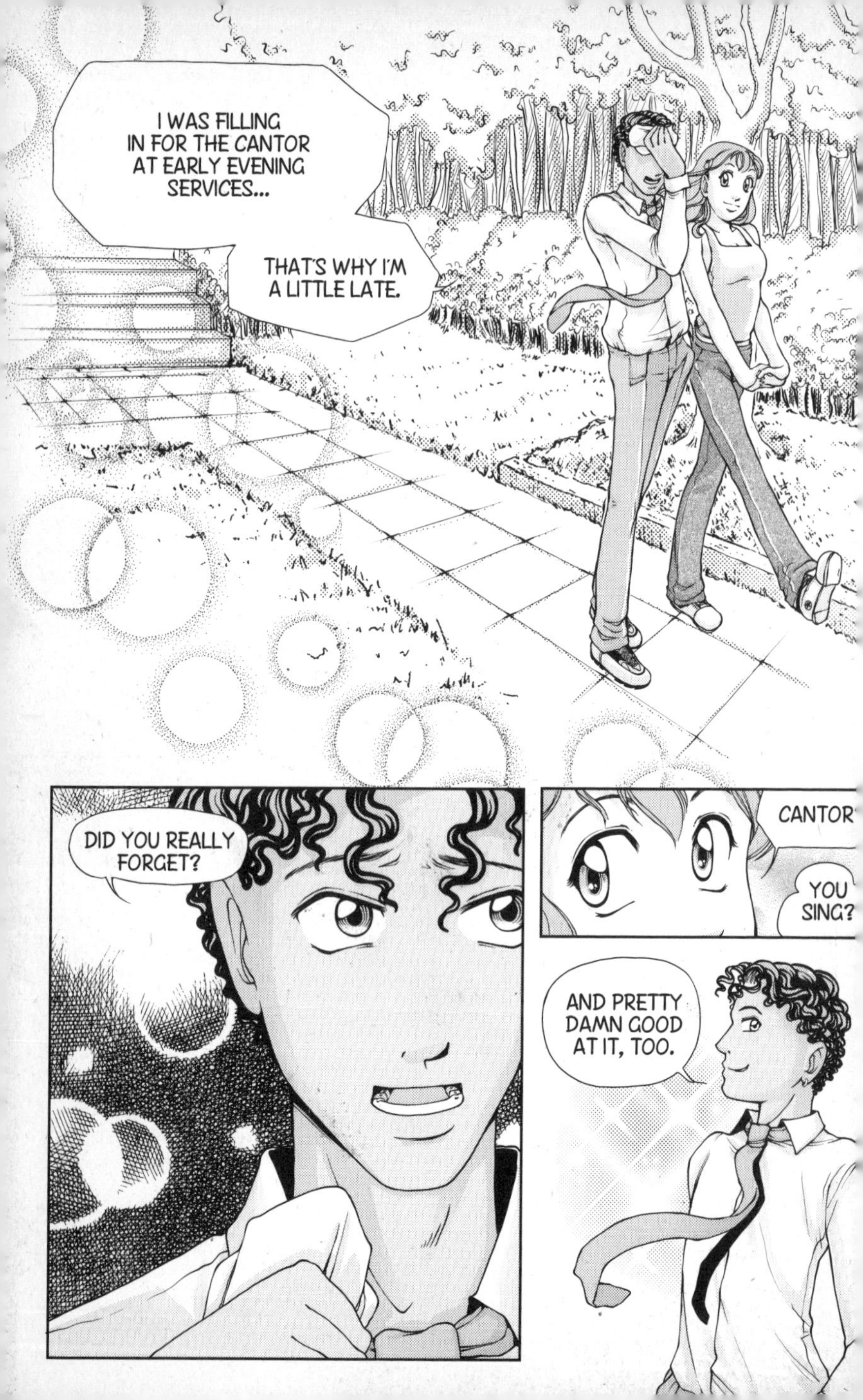
I WAS FILLING IN FOR THE CANTOR AT EARLY EVENING SERVICES...
THAT'S WHY I'M A LITTLE LATE.
DID YOU REALLY FORGET?
CANTOR
YOU SING?
AND PRETTY DAMN GOOD AT IT, TOO.

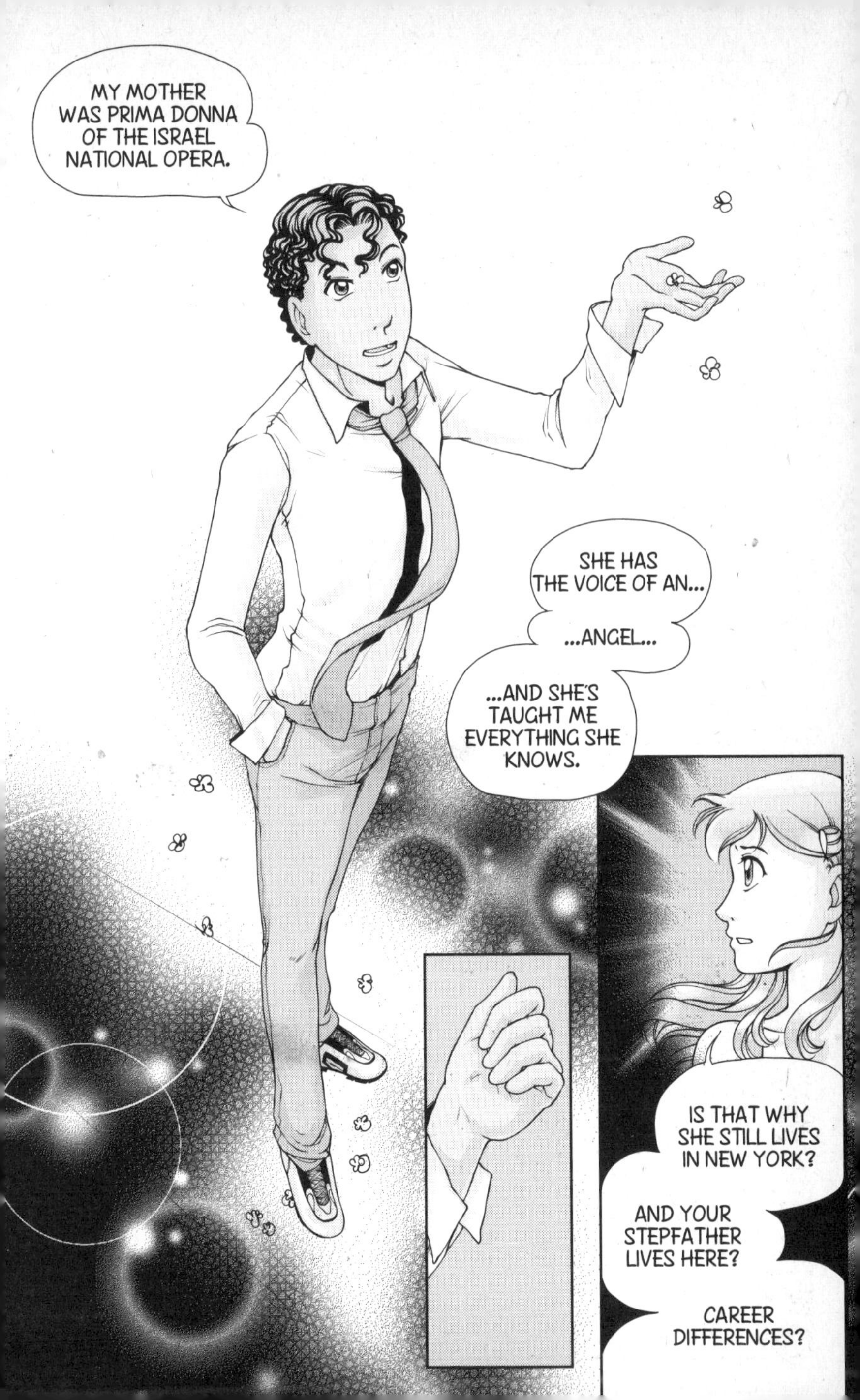
MY MOTHER WAS PRIMA DONNA OF THE ISRAEL NATIONAL OPERA.
SHE HAS THE VOICE OF AN...
...ANGEL...
...AND SHE'S TAUGHT ME EVERYTHING SHE KNOWS.
IS THAT WHY SHE STILL LIVES IN NEW YORK?
AND YOUR STEPFATHER LIVES HERE?
CAREER DIFFERENCES?

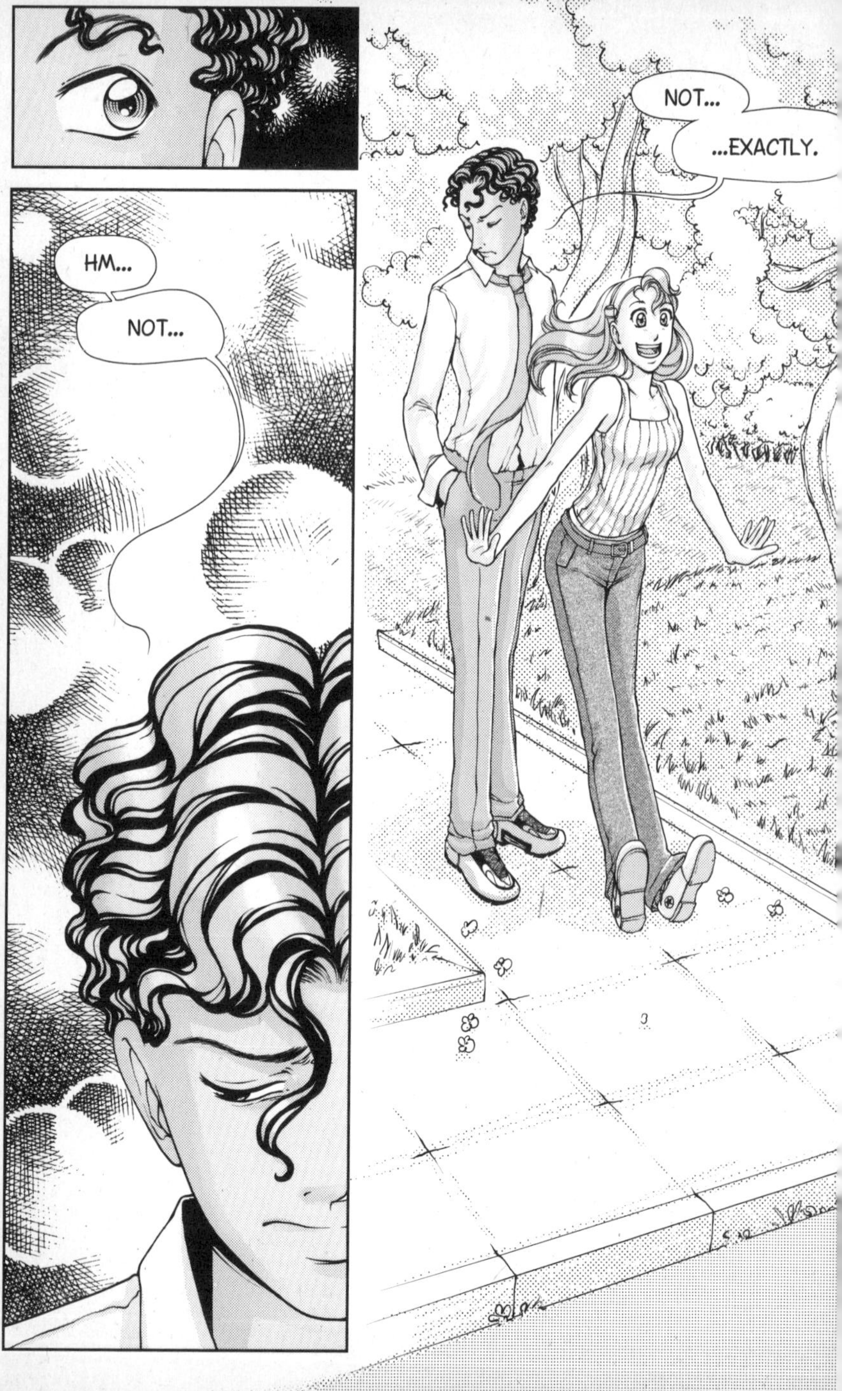
HM...
NOT...
NOT...
...EXACTLY.

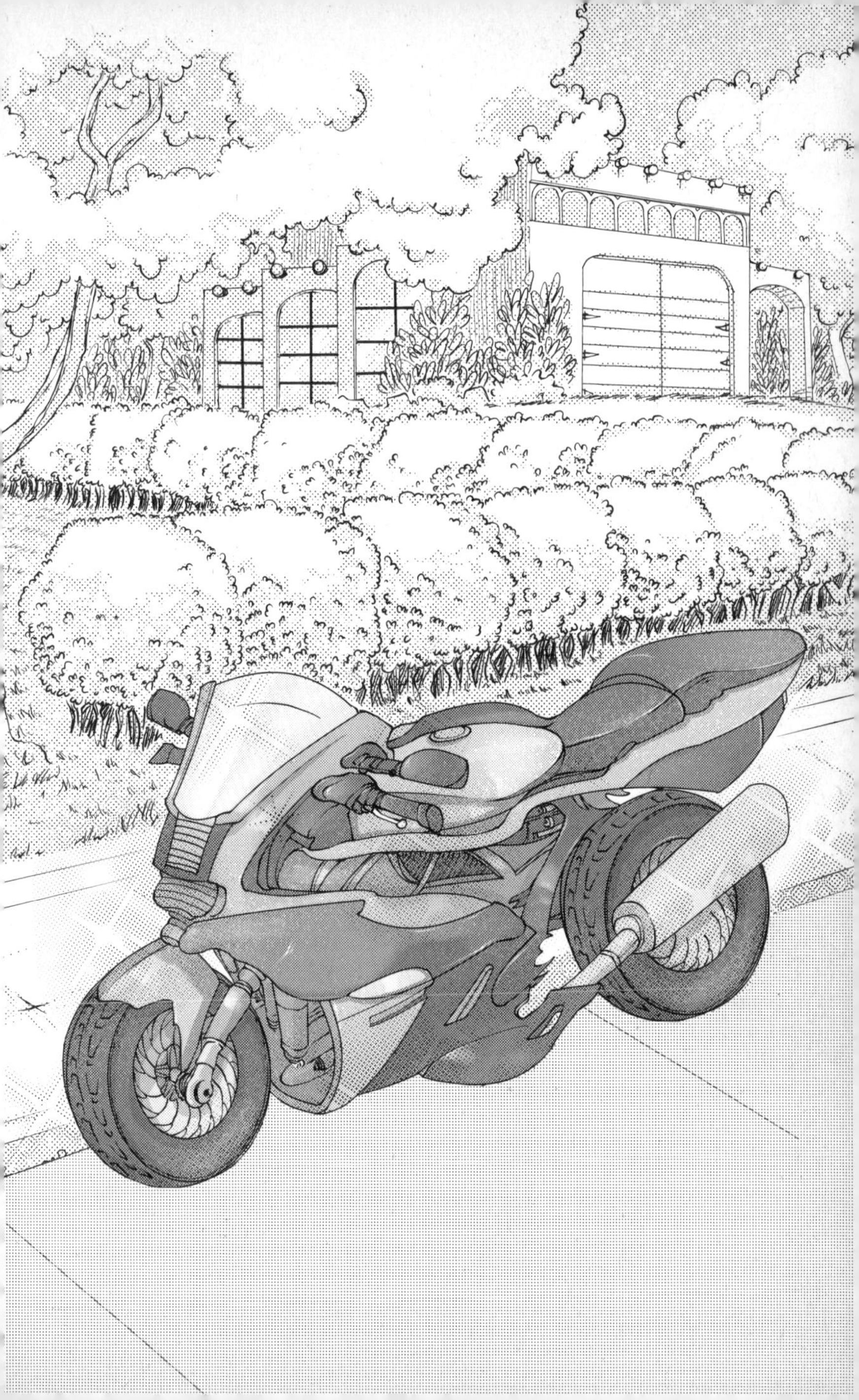

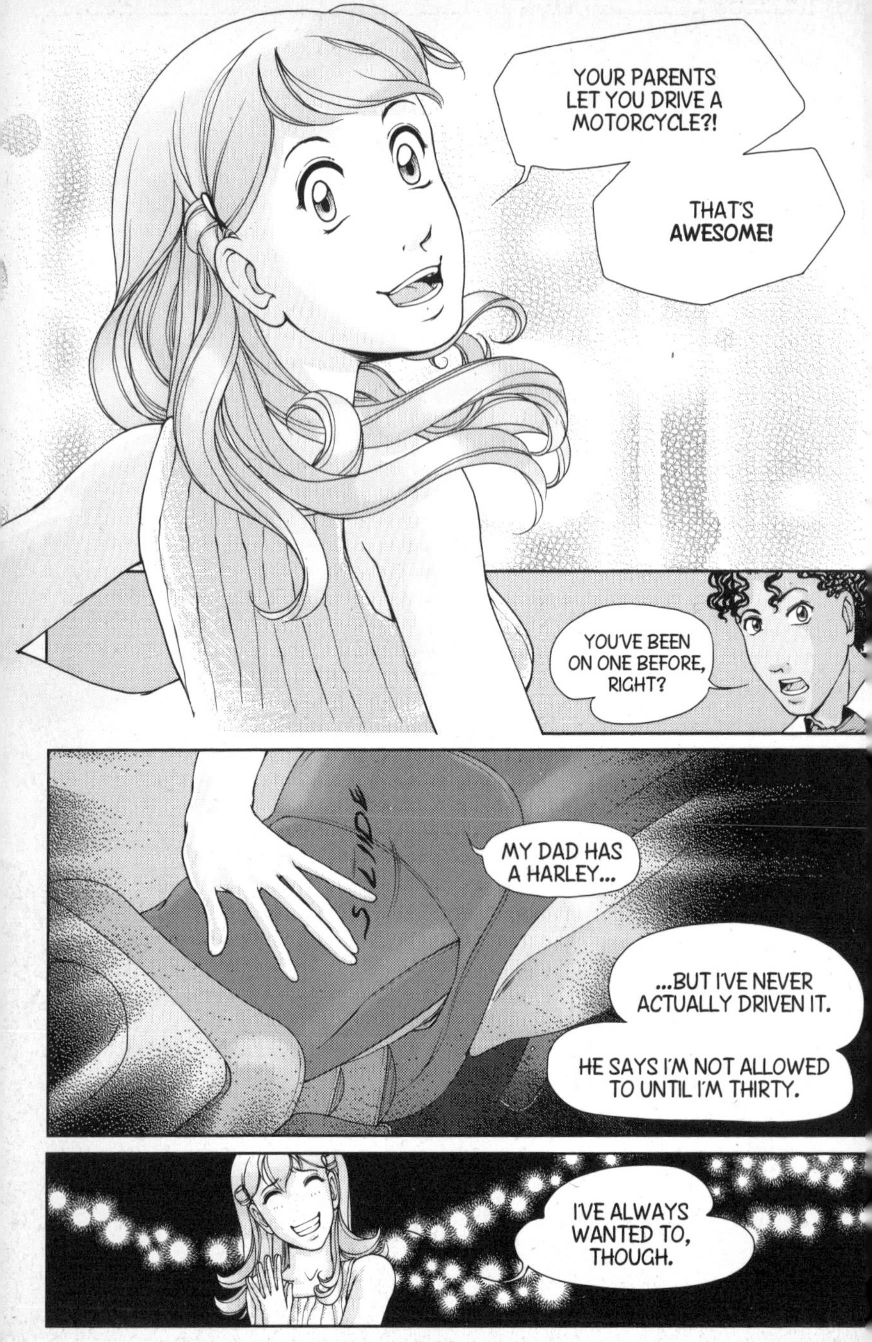
YOUR PARENTS LET YOU DRIVE A MOTORCYCLE?!
THAT'S **AWESOME!**
YOU'VE BEEN ON ONE BEFORE, RIGHT?
SLIDE
MY DAD HAS A HARLEY...
...BUT I'VE NEVER ACTUALLY DRIVEN IT.
HE SAYS I'M NOT ALLOWED TO UNTIL I'M THIRTY.
I'VE ALWAYS WANTED TO, THOUGH.

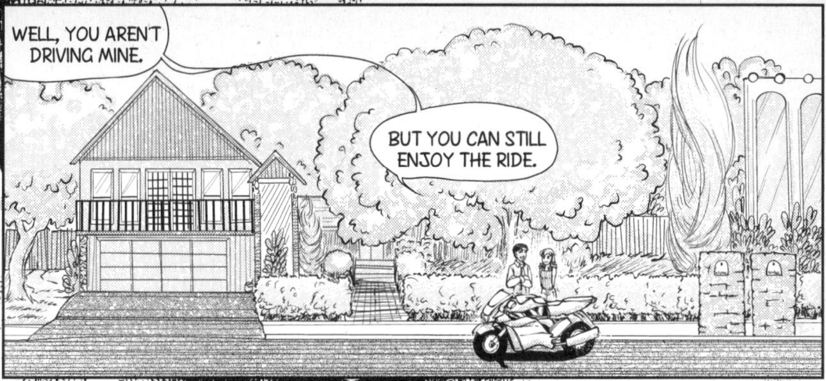
WELL, YOU AREN'T DRIVING MINE.
BUT YOU CAN STILL ENJOY THE RIDE.
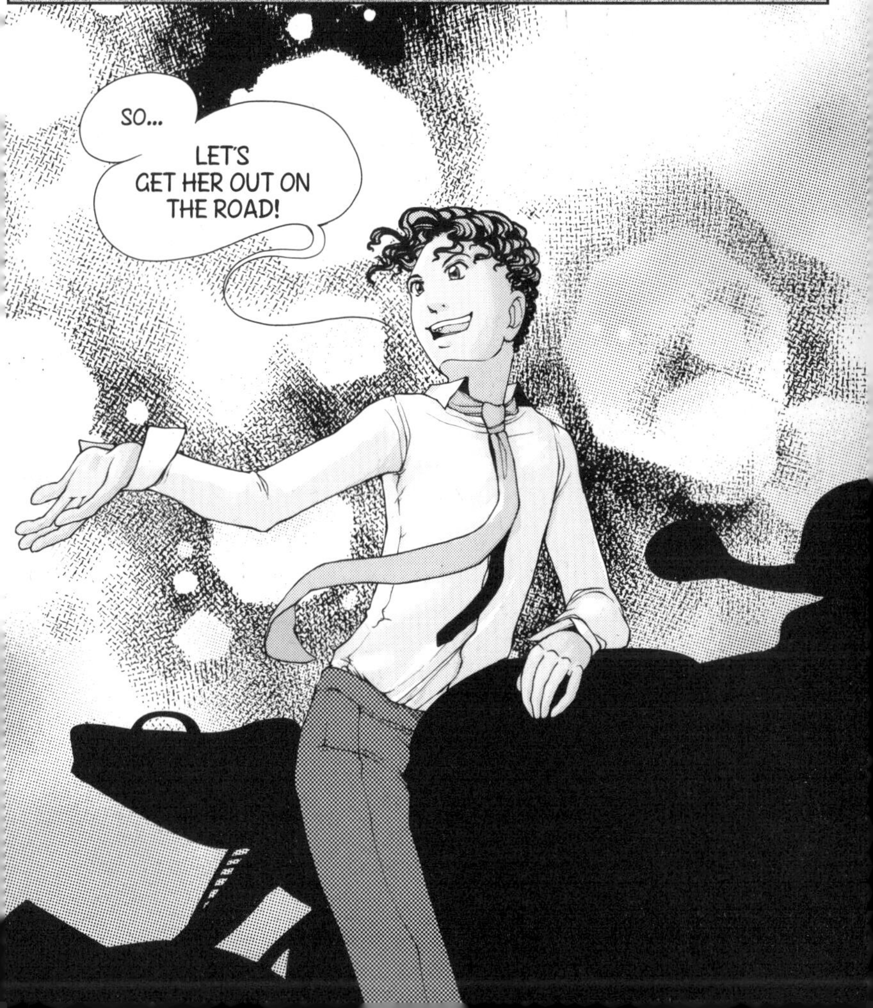
SO...
LET'S GET HER OUT ON THE ROAD!

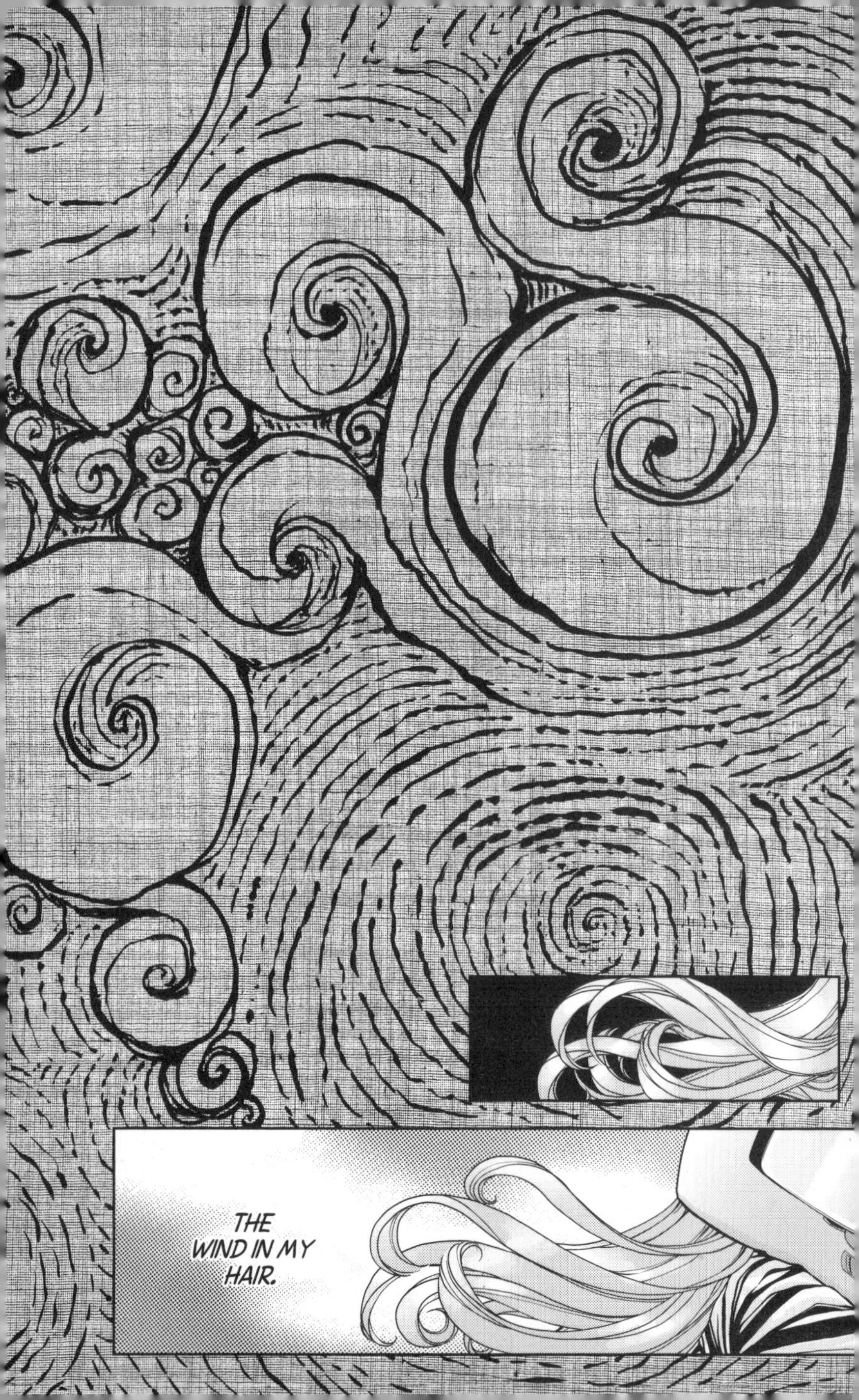
THE WIND IN MY HAIR.

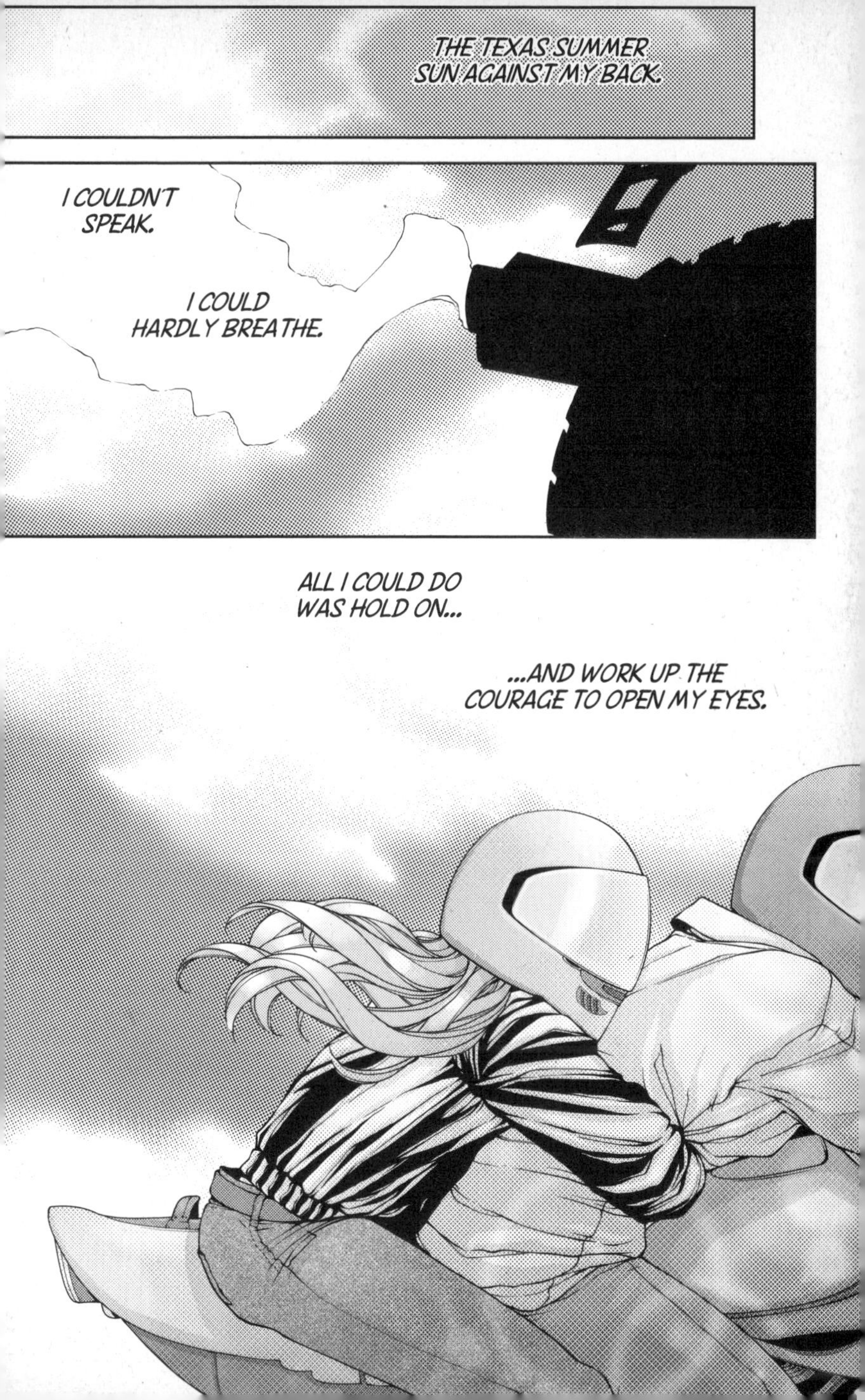
THE TEXAS SUMMER SUN AGAINST MY BACK.
I COULDN'T SPEAK.
I COULD HARDLY BREATHE.
ALL I COULD DO WAS HOLD ON...
...AND WORK UP THE COURAGE TO OPEN MY EYES.

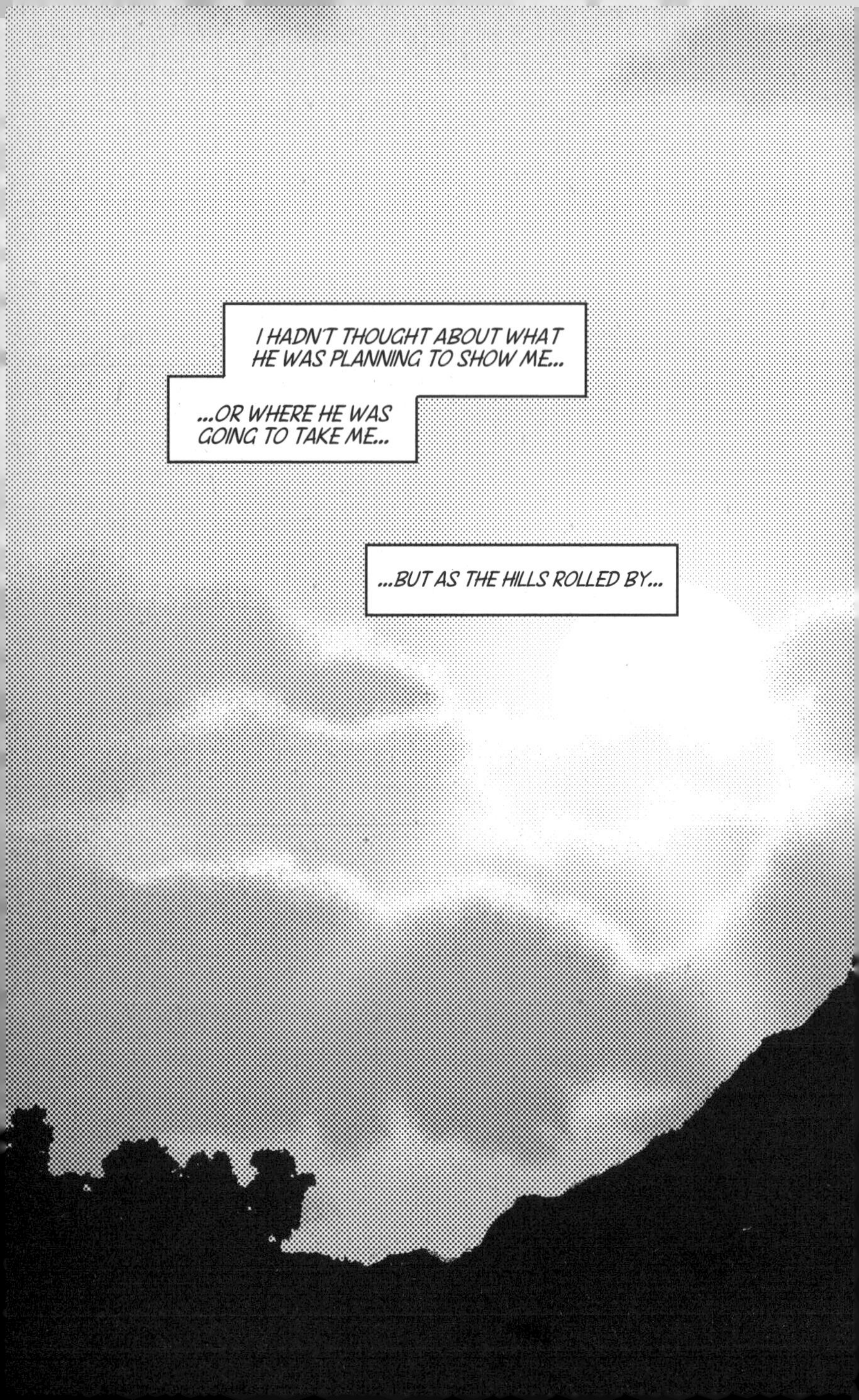
I HADN'T THOUGHT ABOUT WHAT HE WAS PLANNING TO SHOW ME...
...OR WHERE HE WAS GOING TO TAKE ME...
...BUT AS THE HILLS ROLLED BY...

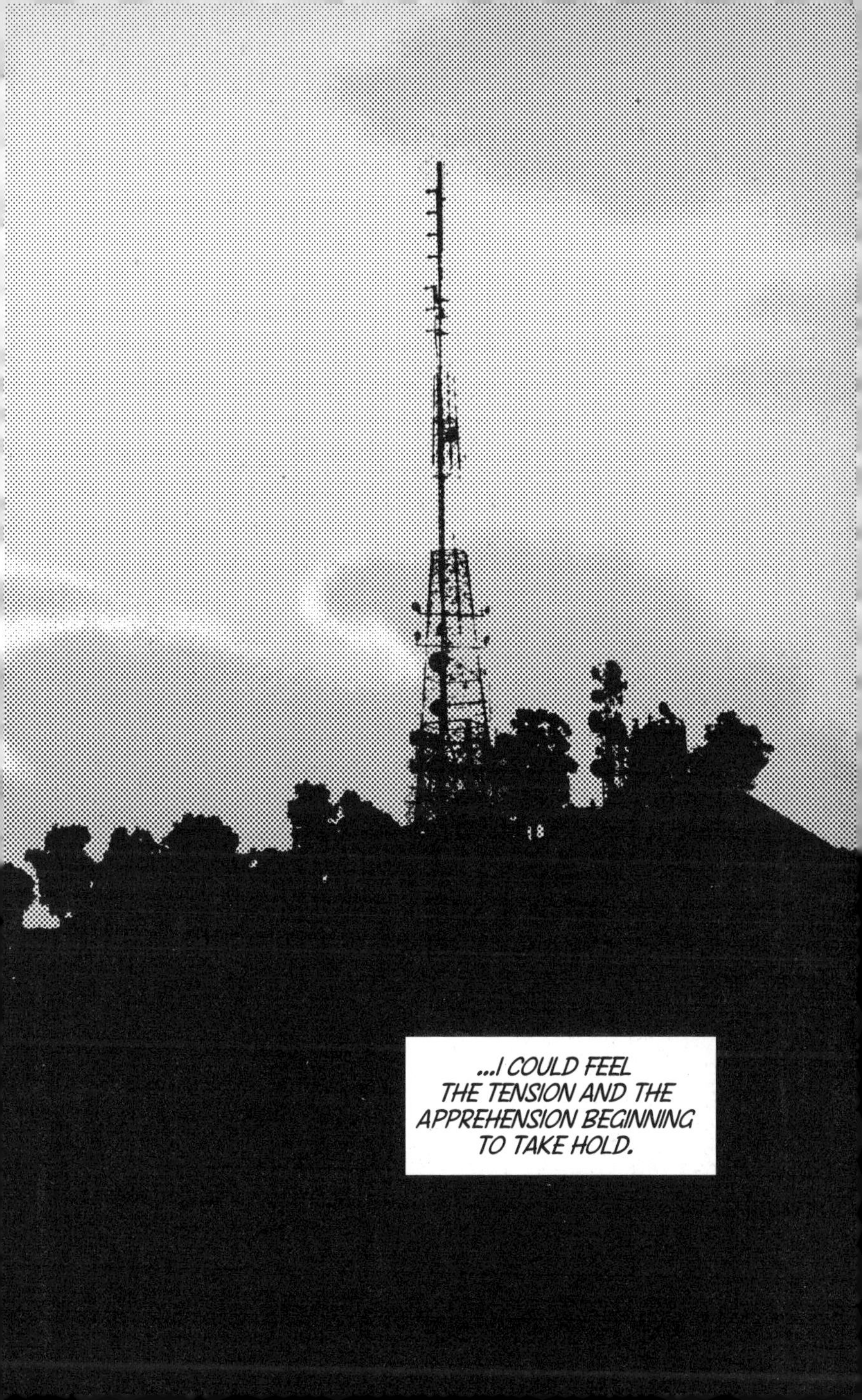
...I COULD FEEL THE TENSION AND THE APPREHENSION BEGINNING TO TAKE HOLD.

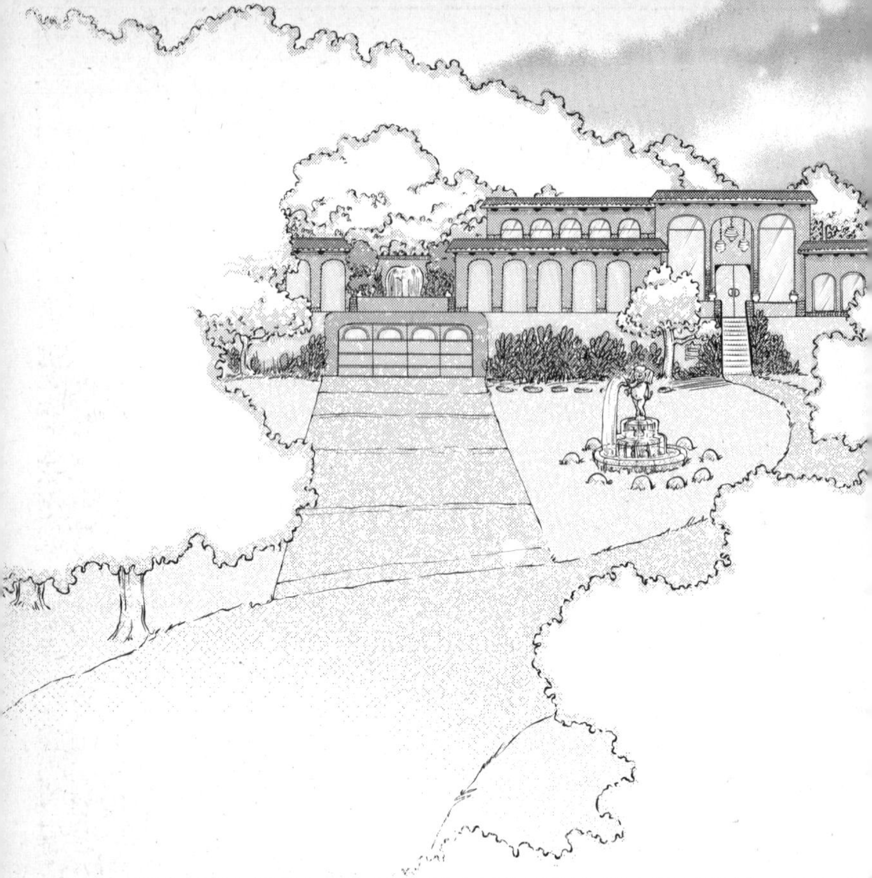
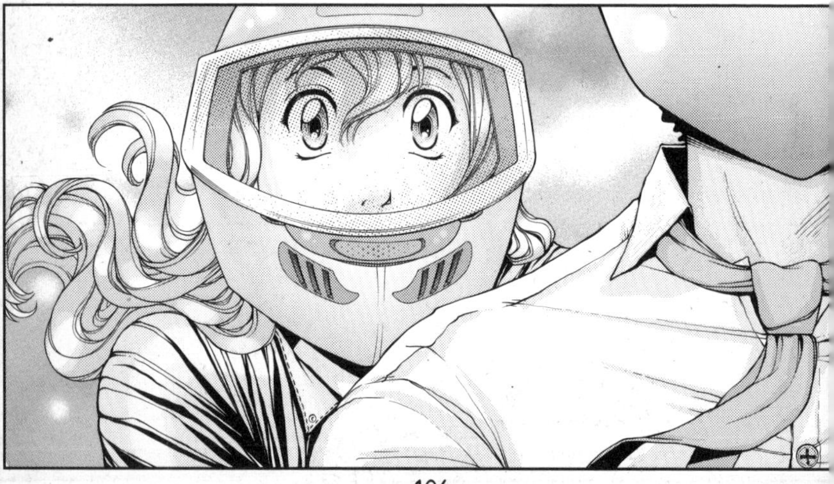

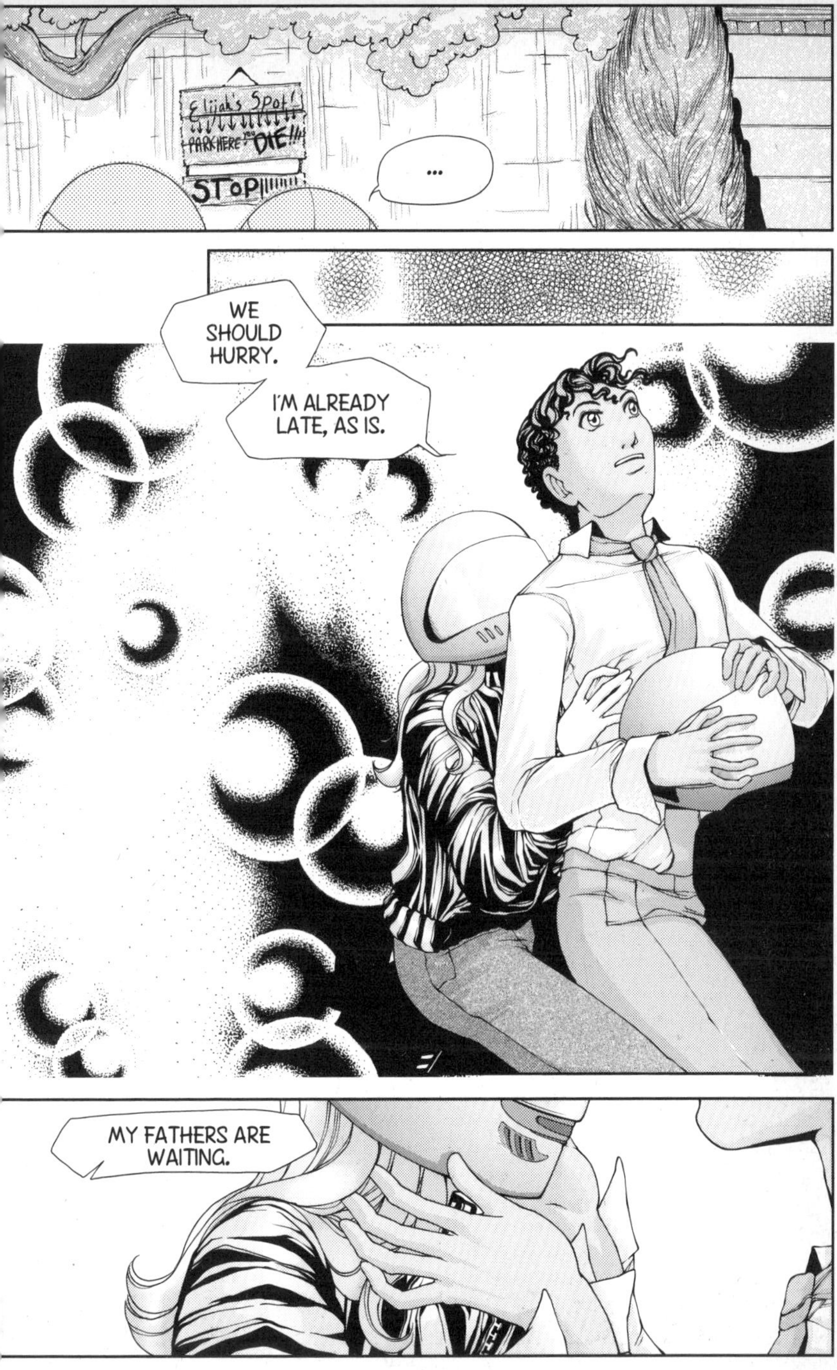
Elijah's Spot!
PARK HERE YOU DIE!!!
STOP!
...
WE SHOULD HURRY.
I'M ALREADY LATE, AS IS.
MY FATHERS ARE WAITING.

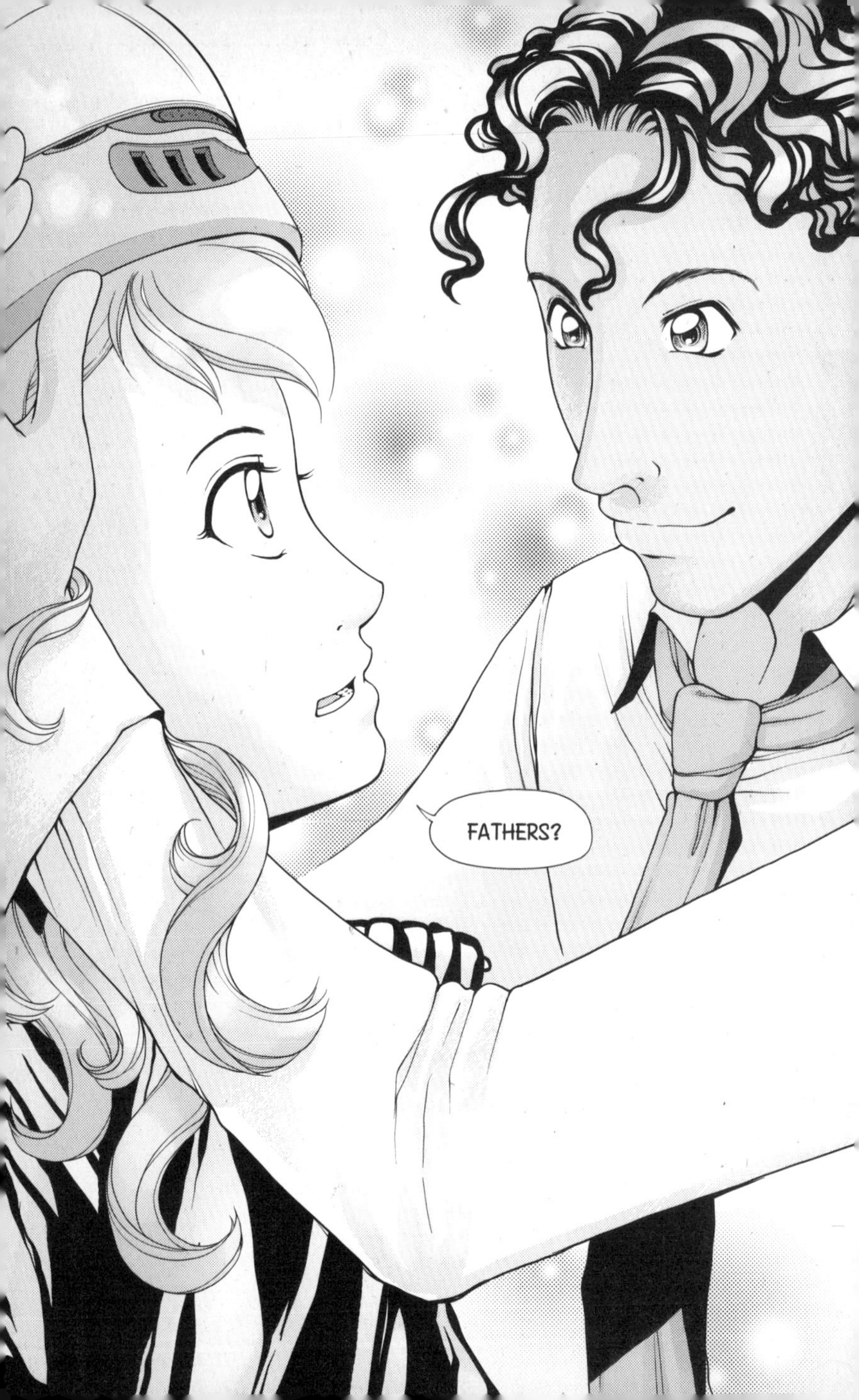
FATHERS?

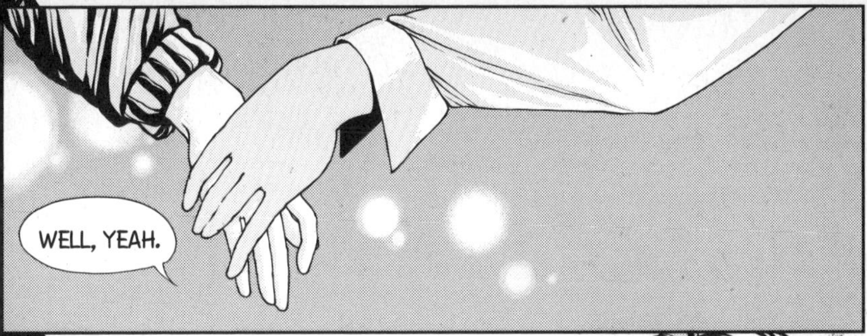
WELL, YEAH.

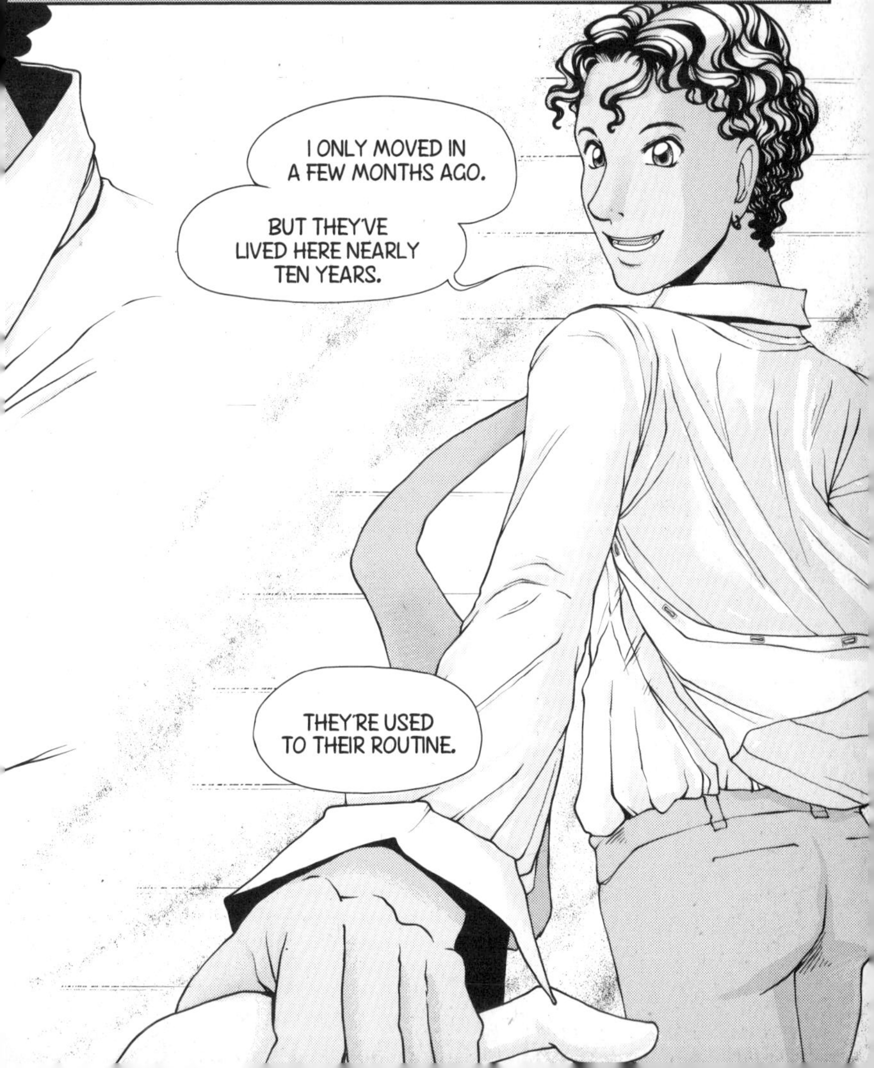
I ONLY MOVED IN A FEW MONTHS AGO.
BUT THEY'VE LIVED HERE NEARLY TEN YEARS.
THEY'RE USED TO THEIR ROUTINE.

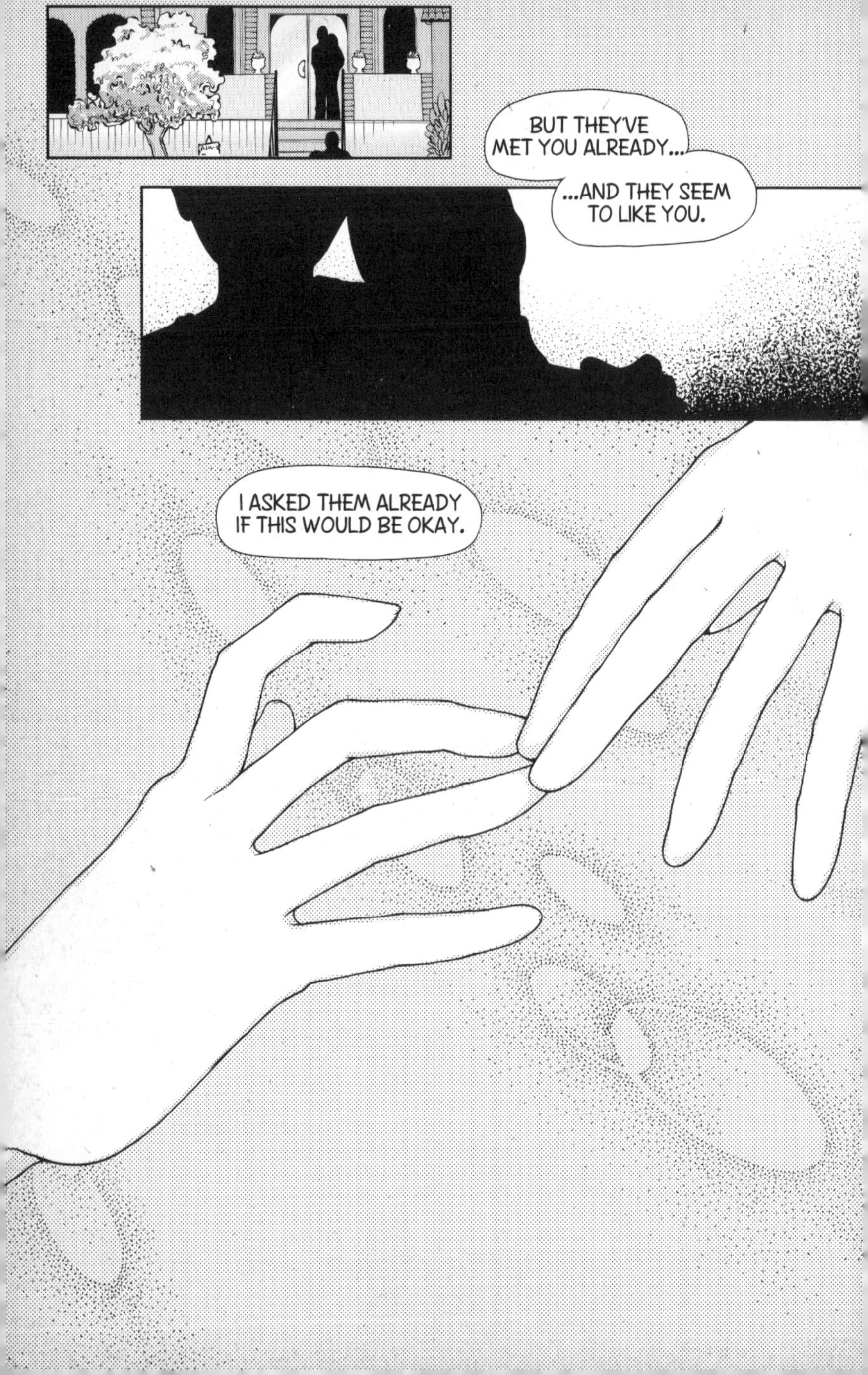
BUT THEY'VE MET YOU ALREADY...
...AND THEY SEEM TO LIKE YOU.
I ASKED THEM ALREADY IF THIS WOULD BE OKAY.

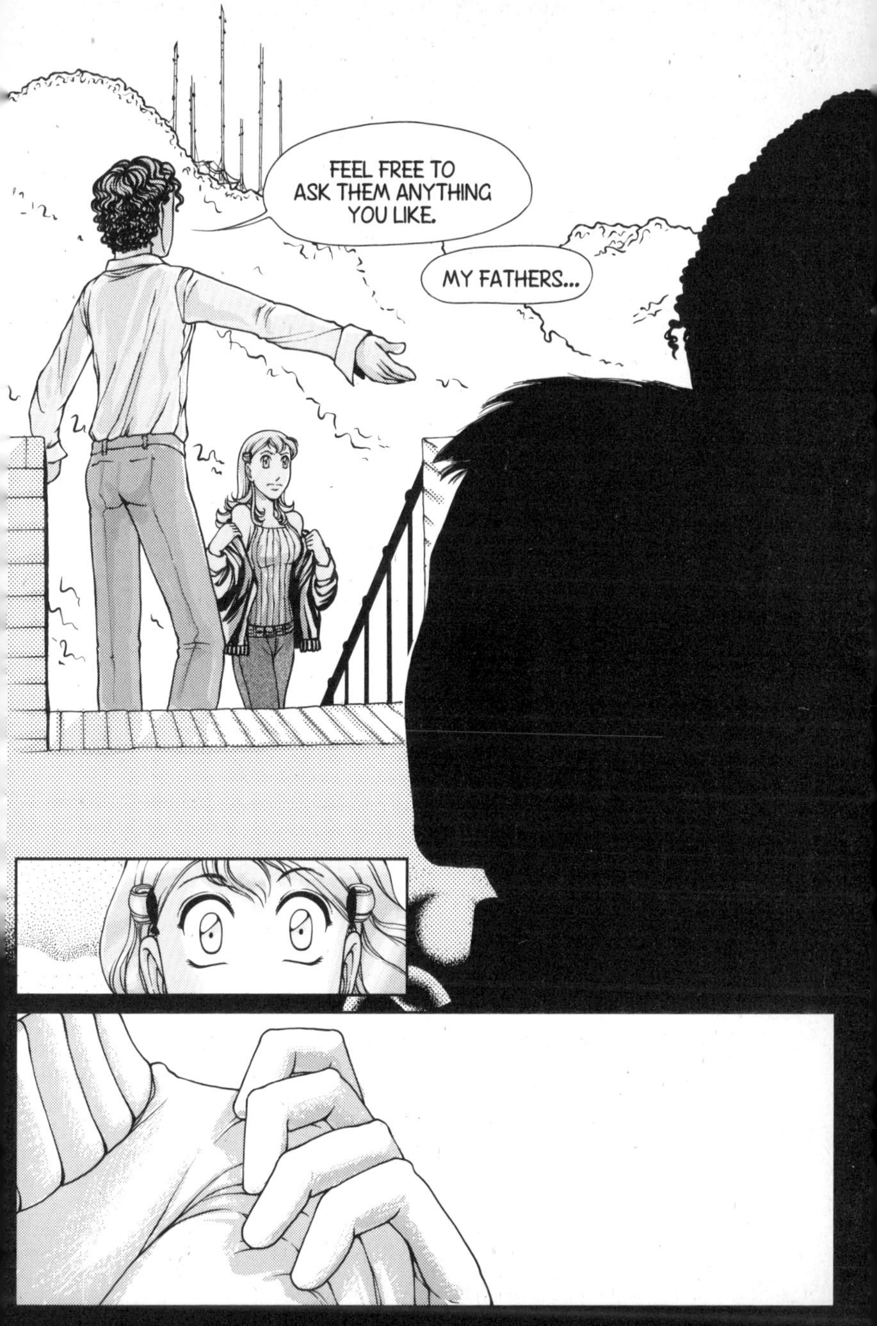
FEEL FREE TO ASK THEM ANYTHING YOU LIKE.
MY FATHERS...

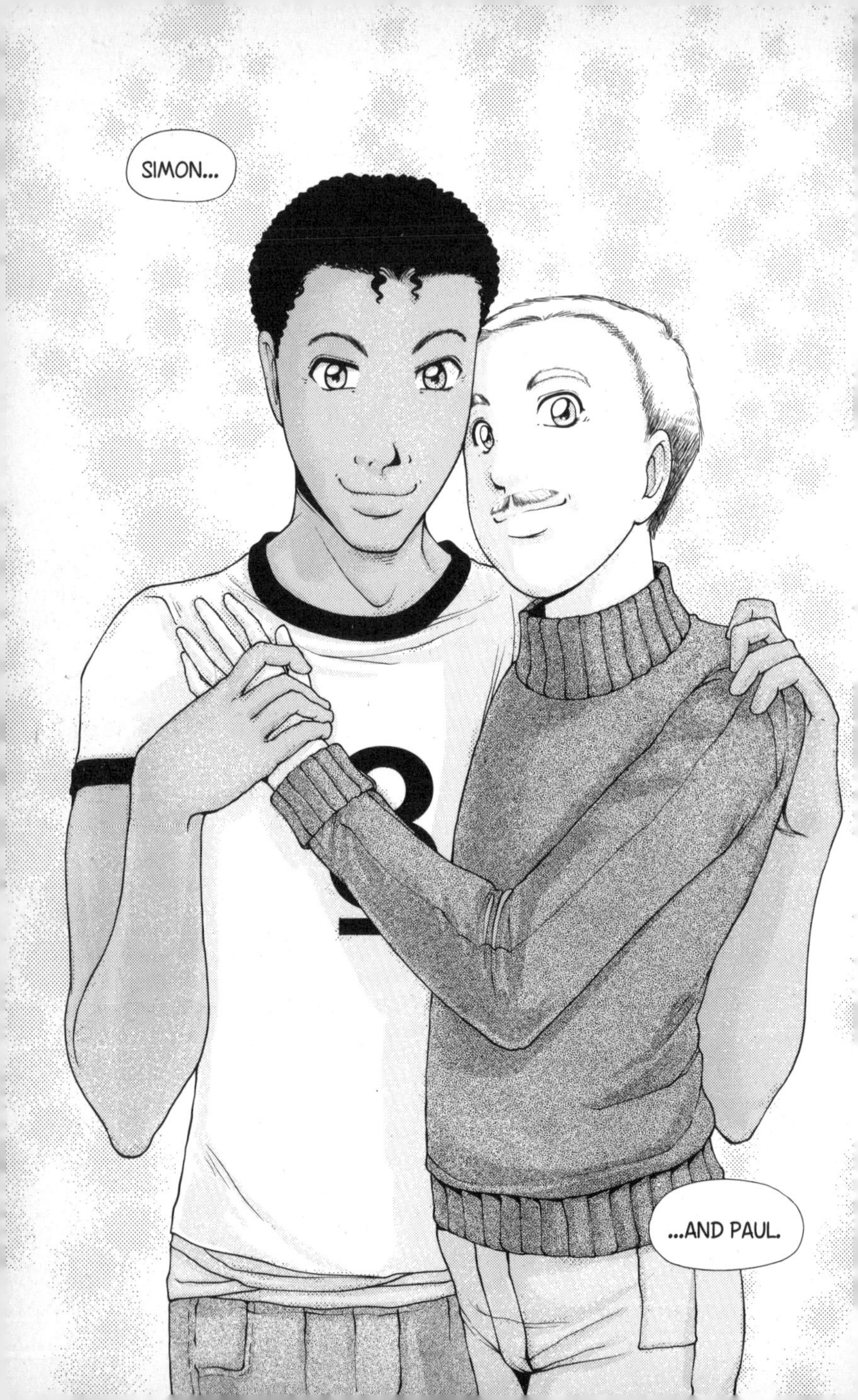
SIMON...
...AND PAUL.

Dear Me,                              September 5th

    I'm sitting in the Kitchen now, and I should be doing homework, but instead I'm doing this. Writing. Writing about.... nothing. It's gorgeous outside. So beautiful. Even if it _is_ 104 degrees (really. that's what the thermometer says). I like the heat, though.
—

    Okay, I'm outside now. Mmm. yummy. I love how sitting in the sun makes you want to just close your eyes and drift.

    So I'm thinking of writing a book. I have so many ideas... I even wrote a couple pages of one story... but I'm a little stuck because I know where I want to go, but I don't know how to get there.

    Oh! And I'm reading a _really good_ book right now. _Joan of Arc_ by Mark Twain. I didn't like the Tom Sawyer books we read in school, but his other stuff is really quite excellent. I just finished "A Connecticut Yankee in King Arthur's Court," but I really ⇒

think that his "Joan of Arc" (it's Jeanne d'Arc, ~~people~~!!!) is going to turn out to be a favorite. Mark Twain apparently spent nearly ~~fourteen~~ years doing research for the book and dear God... it's so beautiful. I checked out a couple other books on her, and she really was a fascinating person.

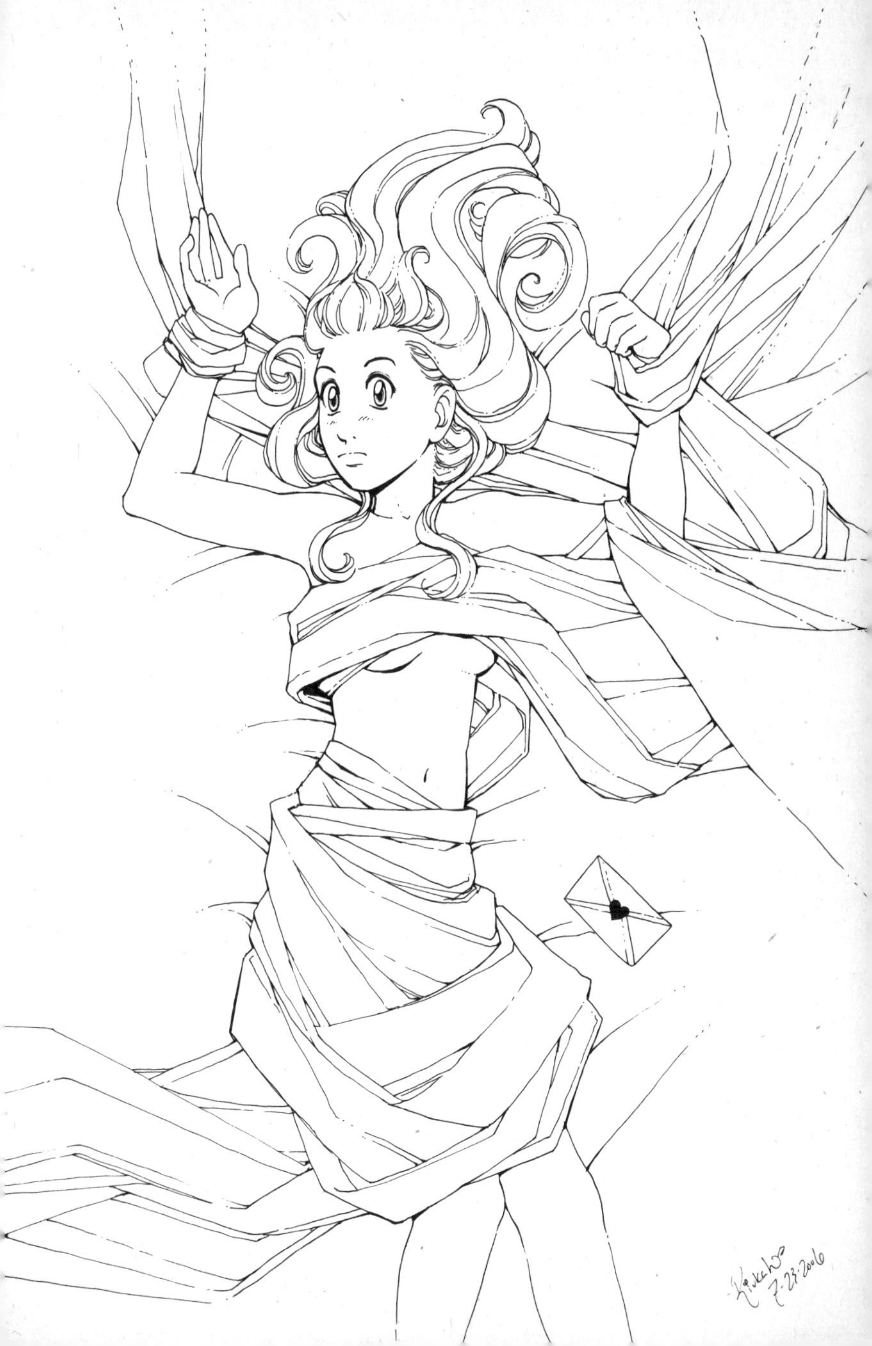
7-23-2006

BEAT 10

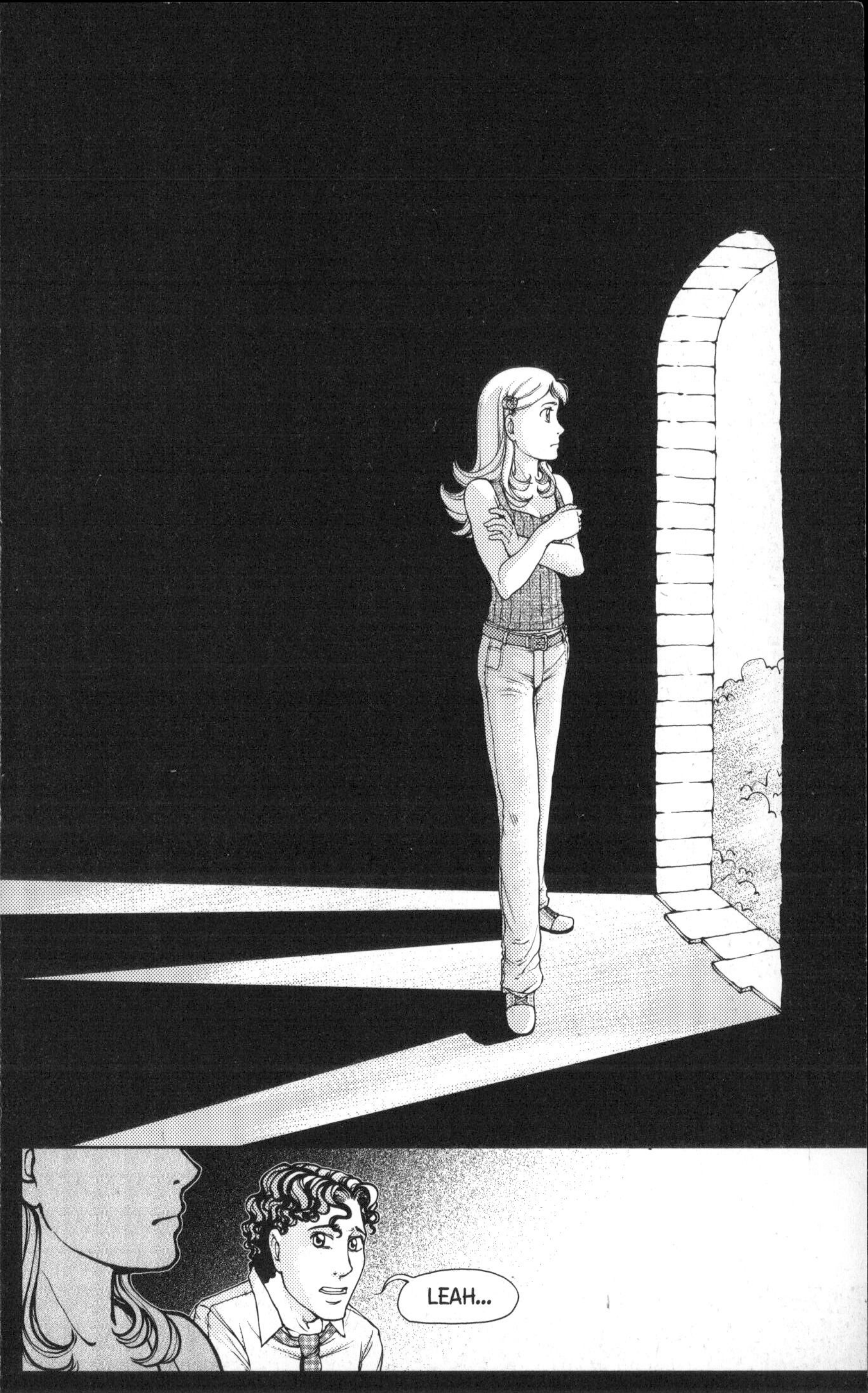
LEAH...

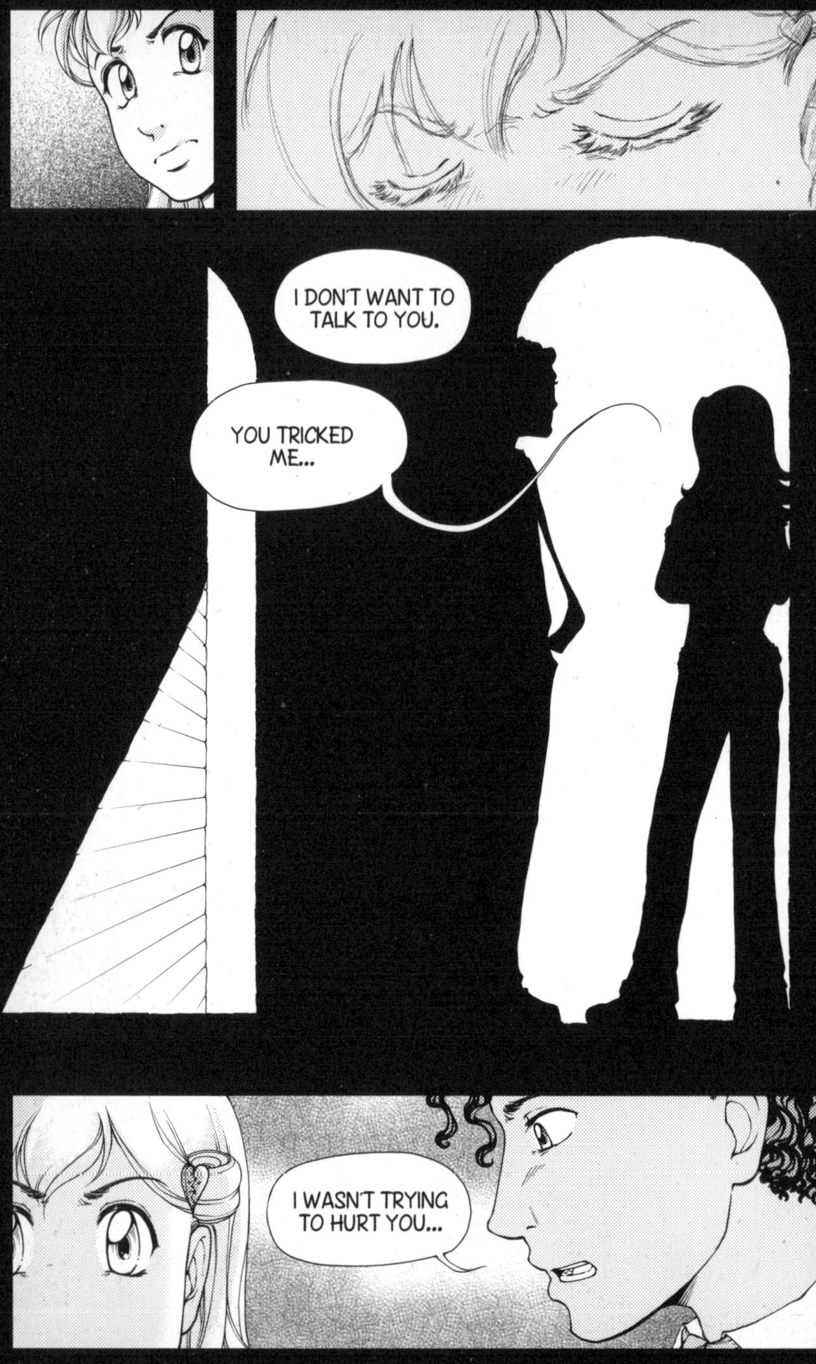
I DON'T WANT TO TALK TO YOU.
YOU TRICKED ME...
I WASN'T TRYING TO HURT YOU...

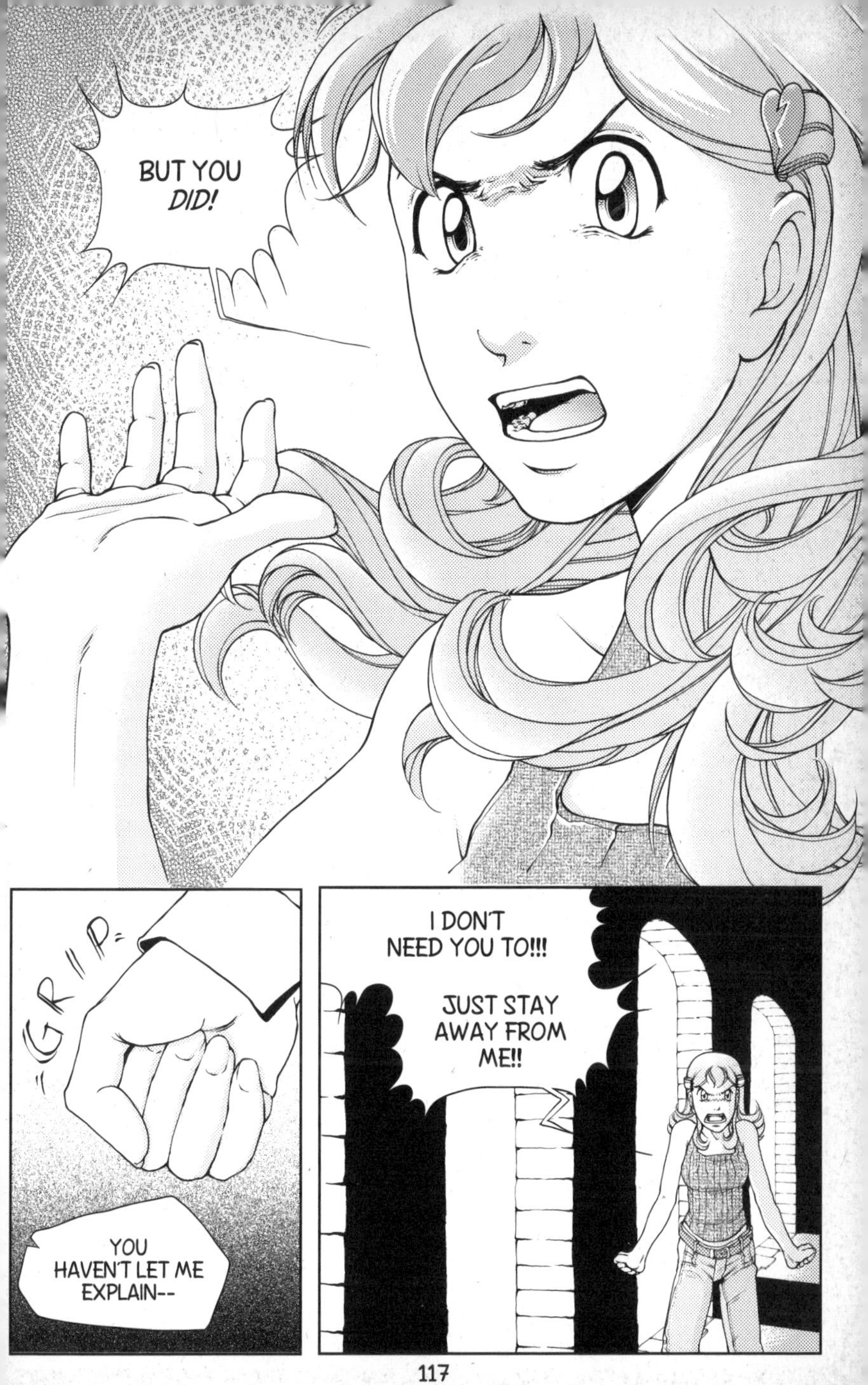
BUT YOU *DID!*
GRIP
YOU HAVEN'T LET ME EXPLAIN--
I DON'T NEED YOU TO!!!
JUST STAY AWAY FROM ME!!

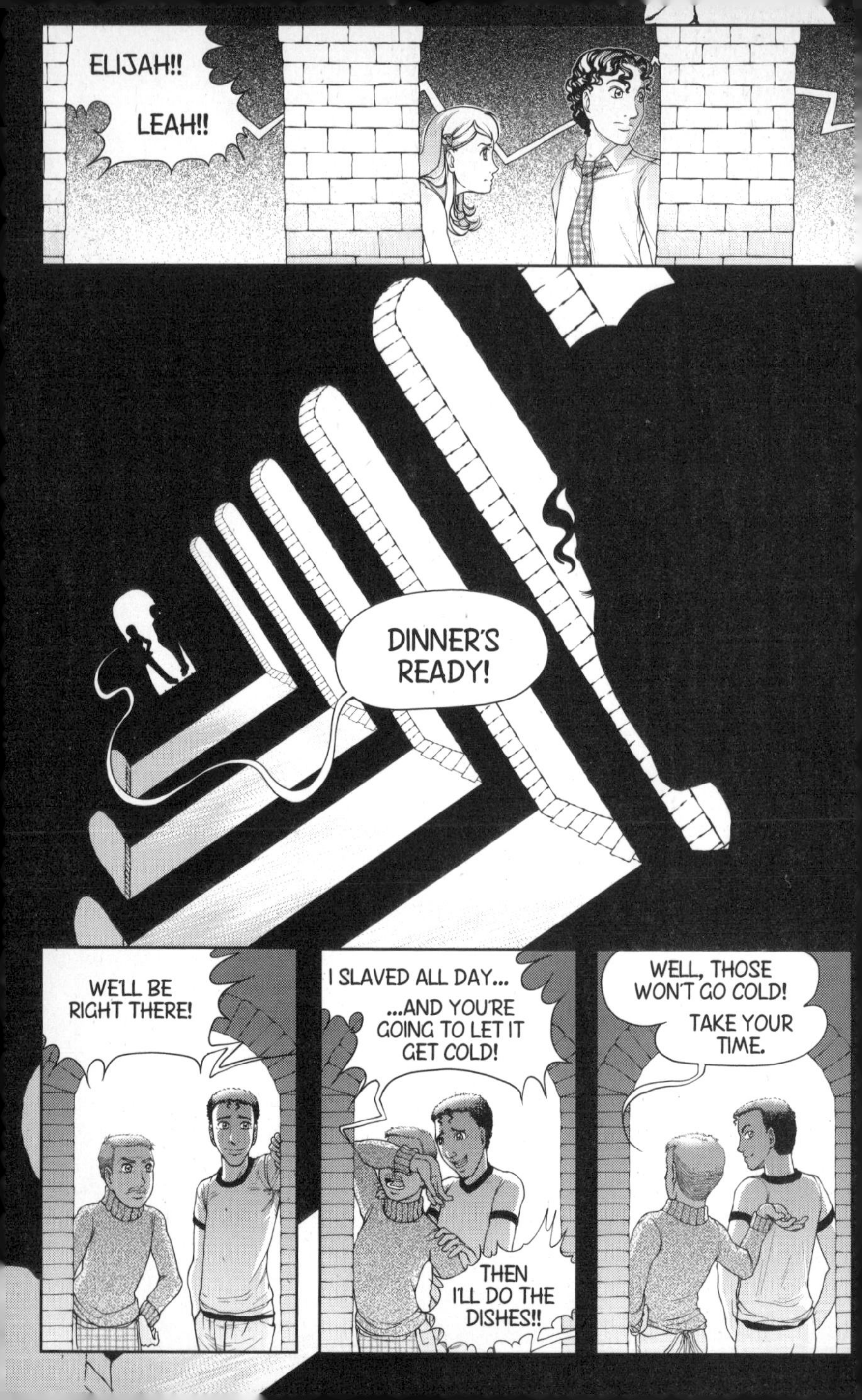
ELIJAH!!
LEAH!!
DINNER'S READY!
WE'LL BE RIGHT THERE!
I SLAVED ALL DAY...
...AND YOU'RE GOING TO LET IT GET COLD!
THEN I'LL DO THE DISHES!!
WELL, THOSE WON'T GO COLD!
TAKE YOUR TIME.

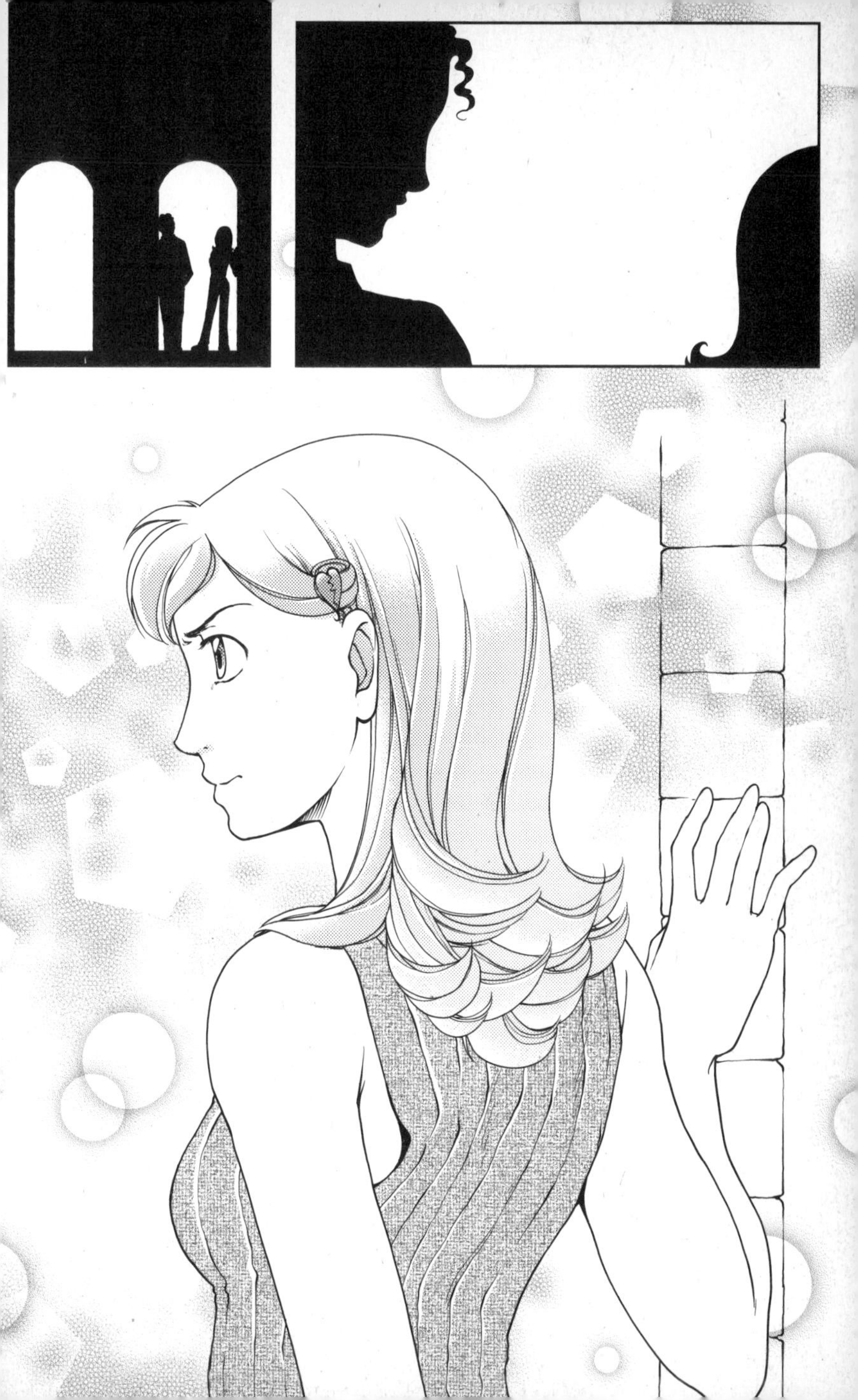

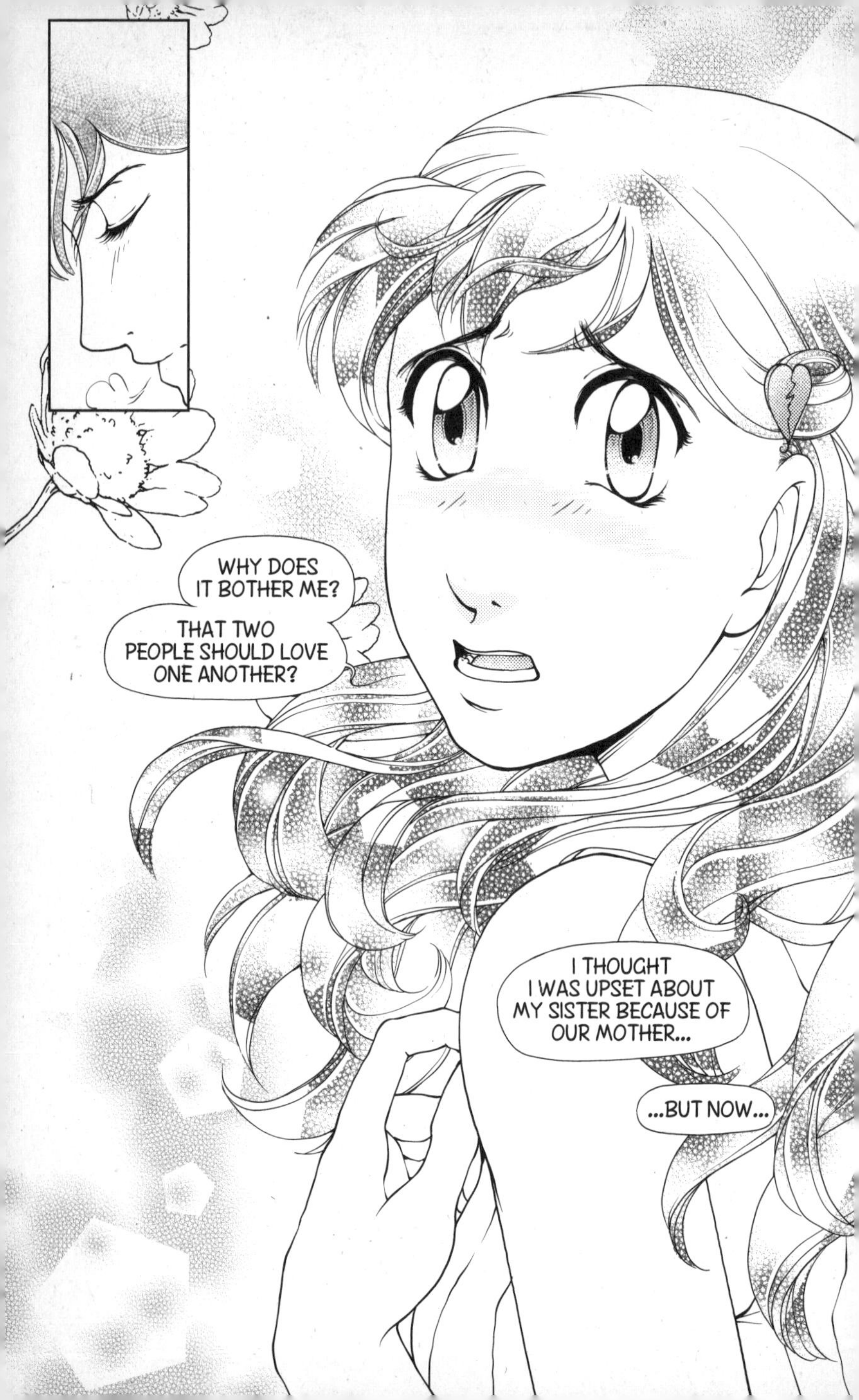
WHY DOES IT BOTHER ME?
THAT TWO PEOPLE SHOULD LOVE ONE ANOTHER?
I THOUGHT I WAS UPSET ABOUT MY SISTER BECAUSE OF OUR MOTHER...
...BUT NOW...

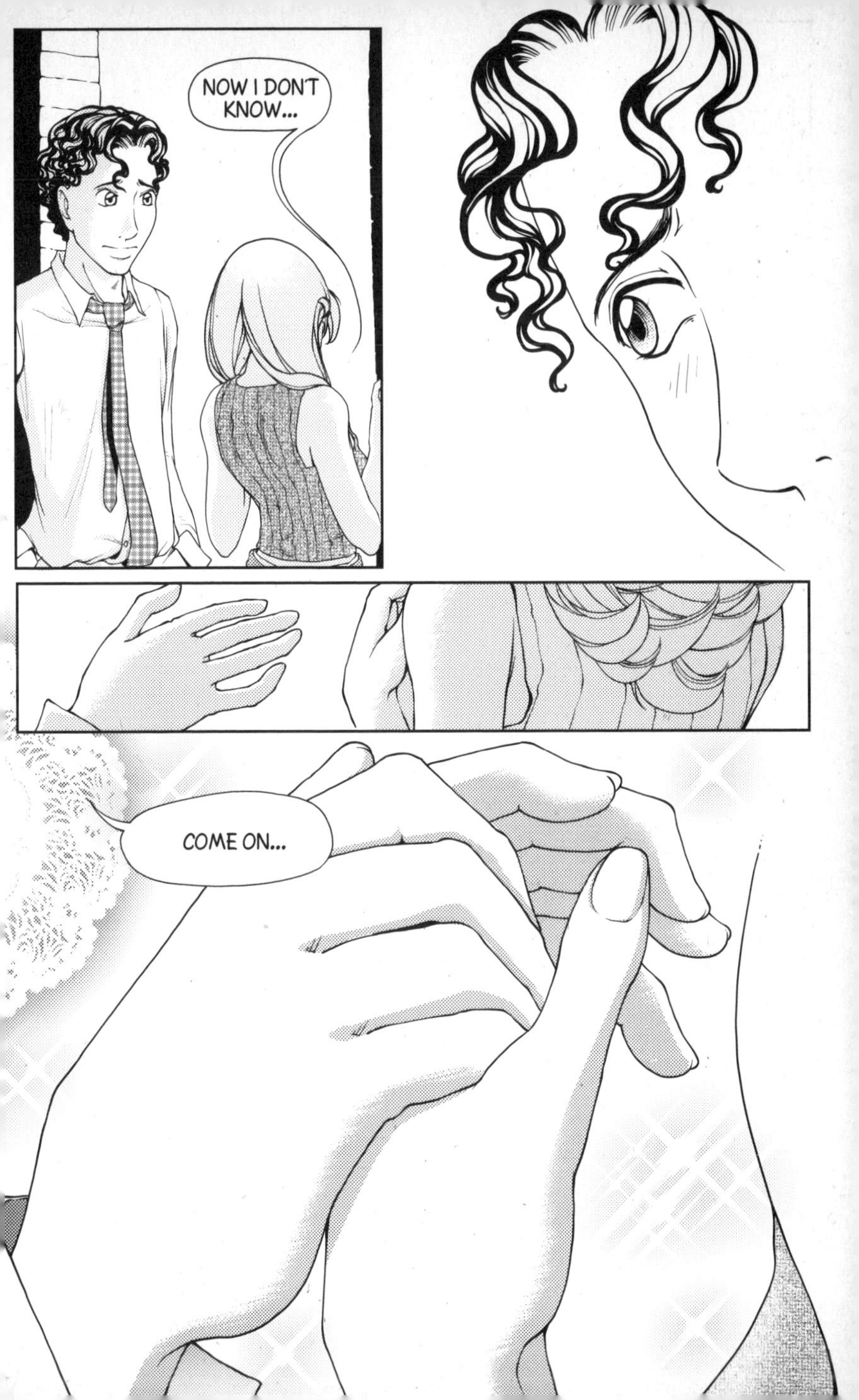
NOW I DON'T KNOW...
COME ON...

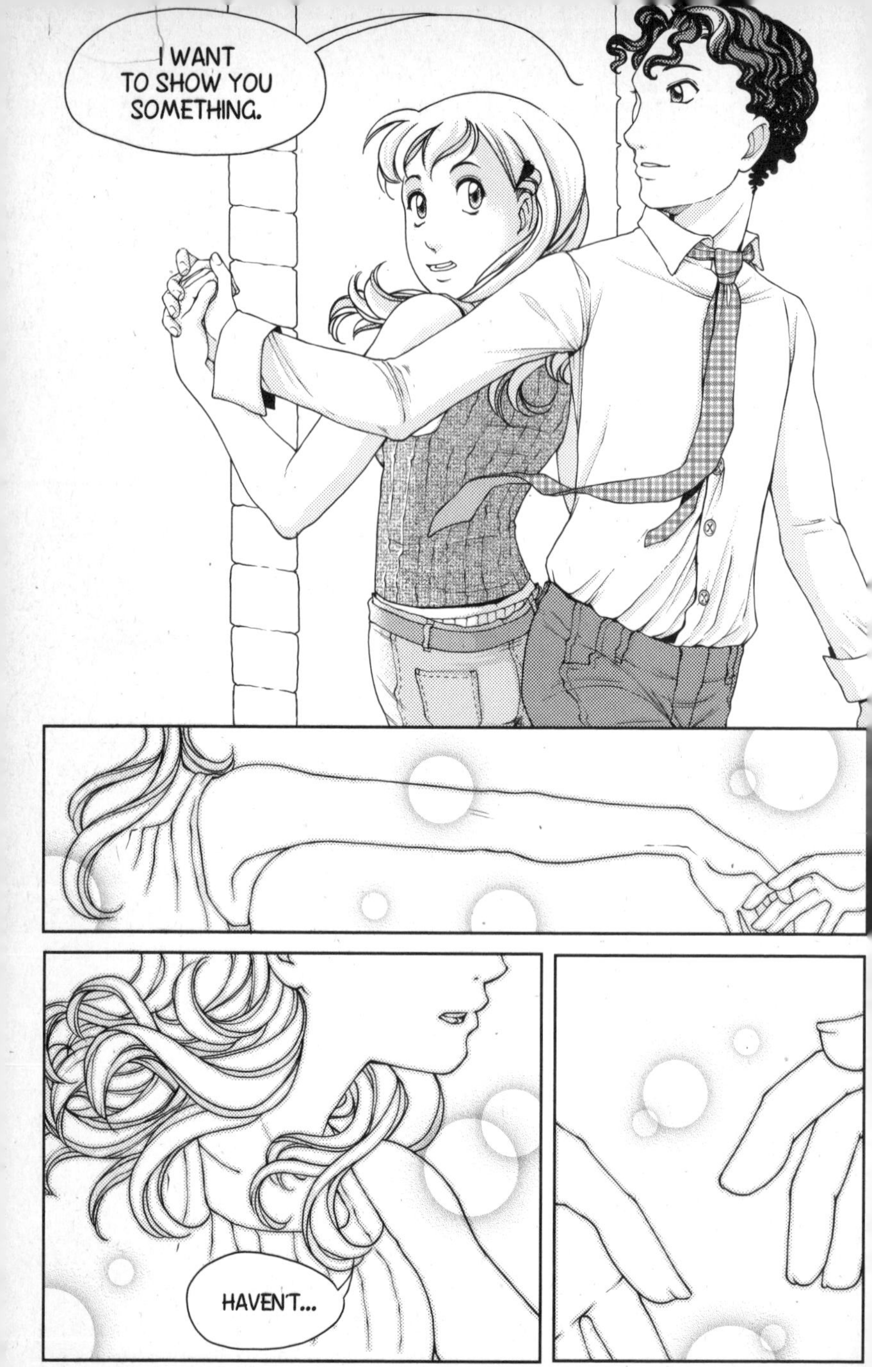
I WANT TO SHOW YOU SOMETHING.
HAVEN'T...

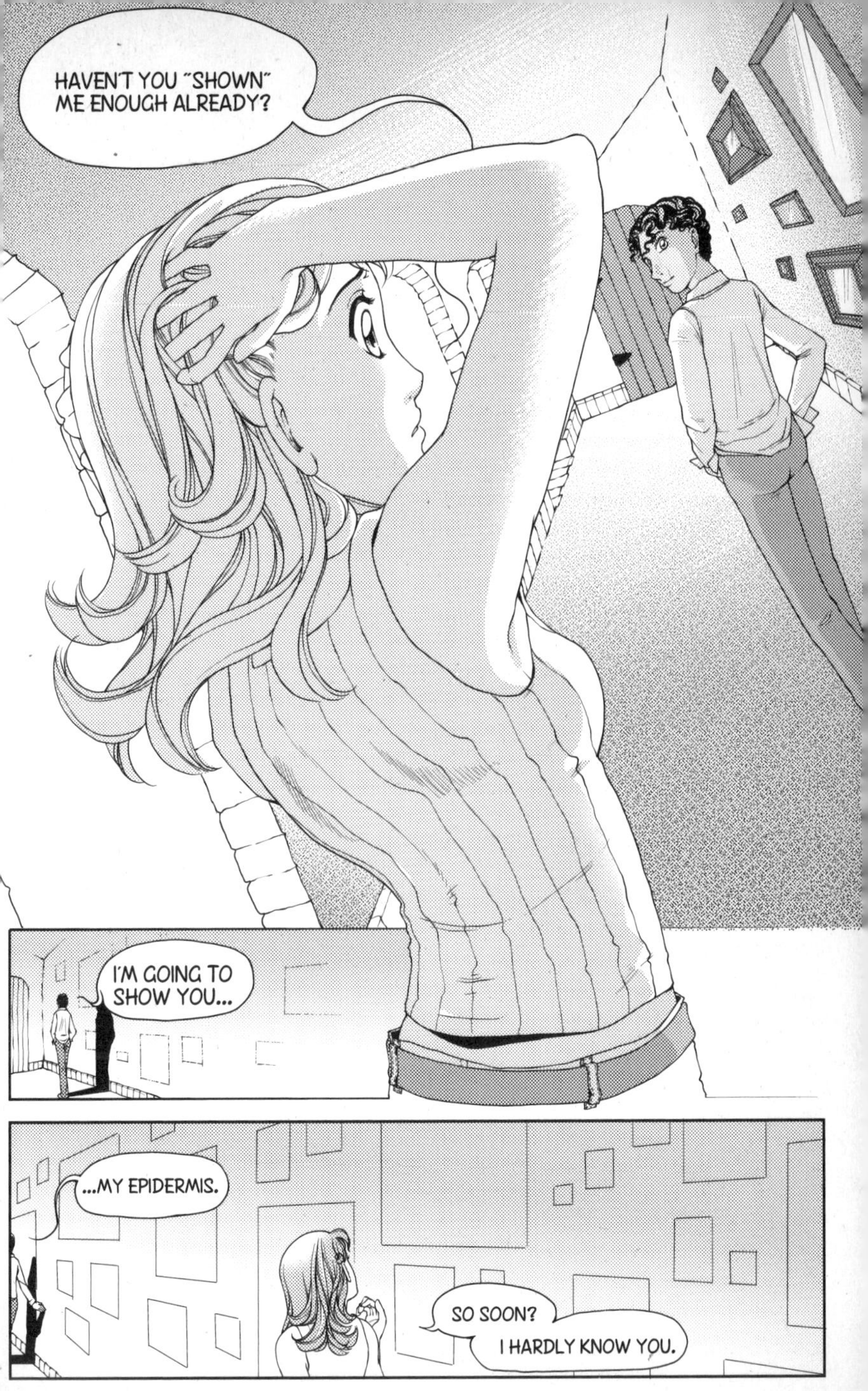
HAVEN'T YOU "SHOWN" ME ENOUGH ALREADY?
I'M GOING TO SHOW YOU...
...MY EPIDERMIS.
SO SOON?
I HARDLY KNOW YOU.

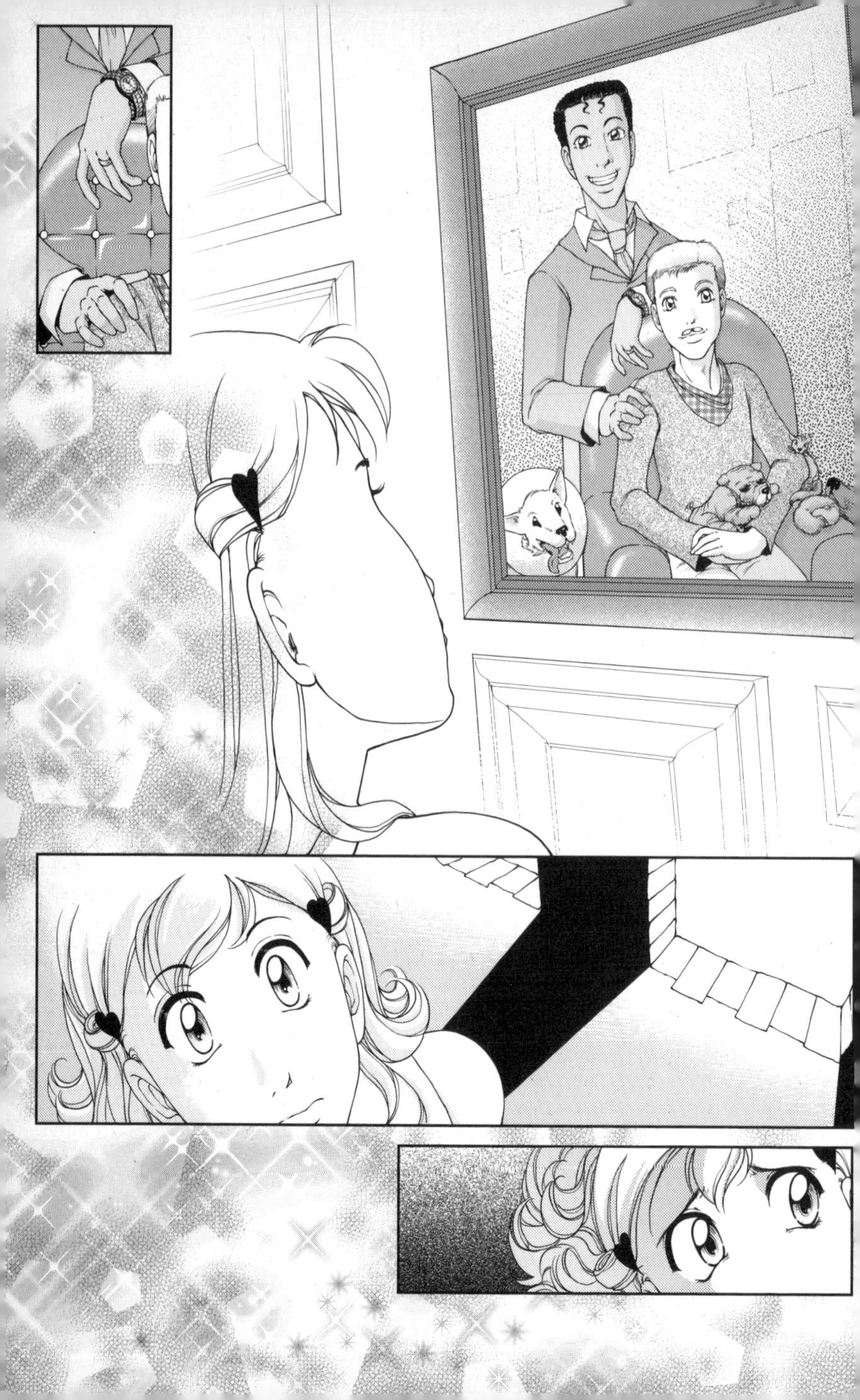

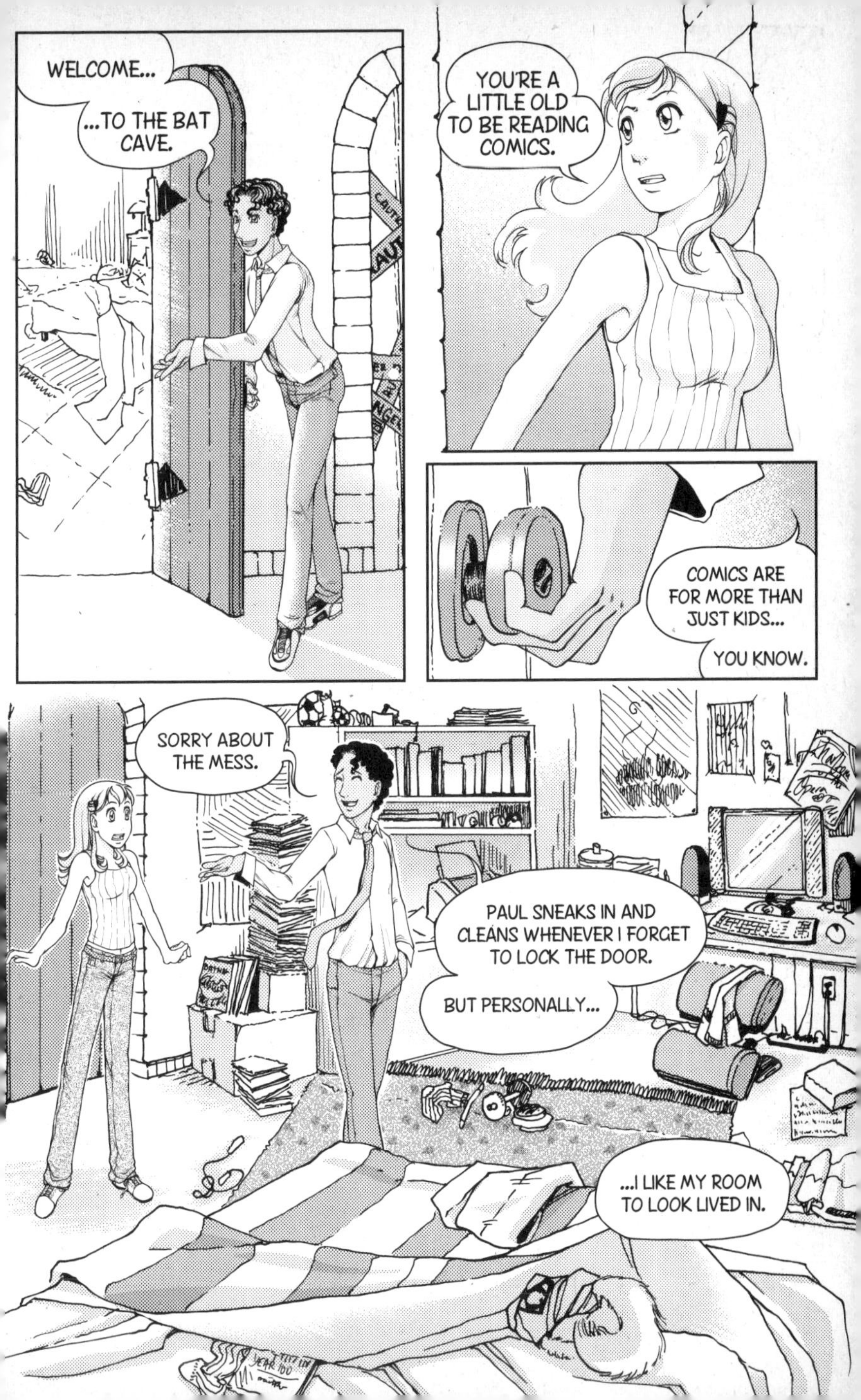
WELCOME...
...TO THE BAT CAVE.
YOU'RE A LITTLE OLD TO BE READING COMICS.
COMICS ARE FOR MORE THAN JUST KIDS...
YOU KNOW.
SORRY ABOUT THE MESS.
PAUL SNEAKS IN AND CLEANS WHENEVER I FORGET TO LOCK THE DOOR.
BUT PERSONALLY...
...I LIKE MY ROOM TO LOOK LIVED IN.

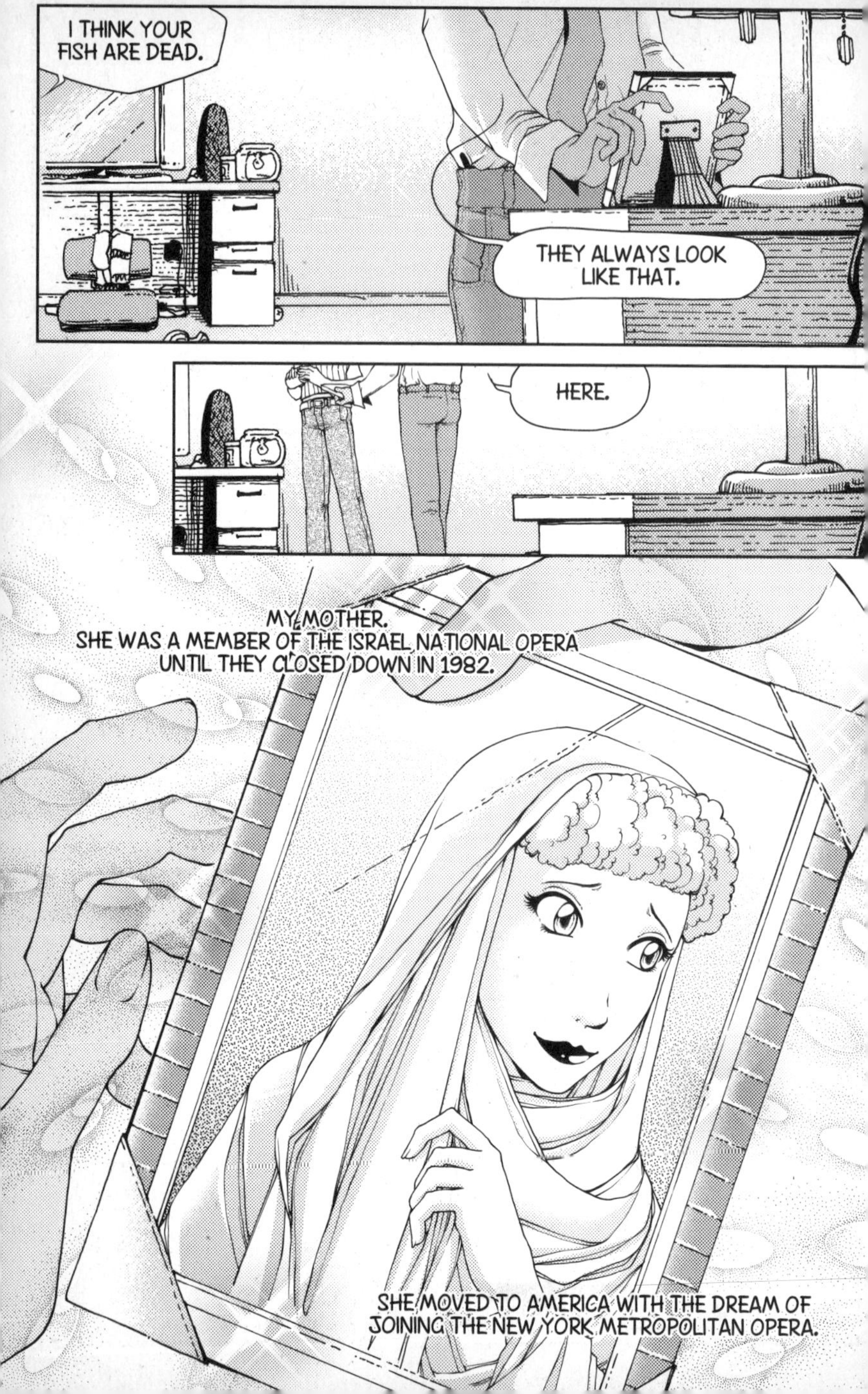

I THINK YOUR FISH ARE DEAD.
THEY ALWAYS LOOK LIKE THAT.
HERE.
MY MOTHER.
SHE WAS A MEMBER OF THE ISRAEL NATIONAL OPERA UNTIL THEY CLOSED DOWN IN 1982.
SHE MOVED TO AMERICA WITH THE DREAM OF JOINING THE NEW YORK METROPOLITAN OPERA.

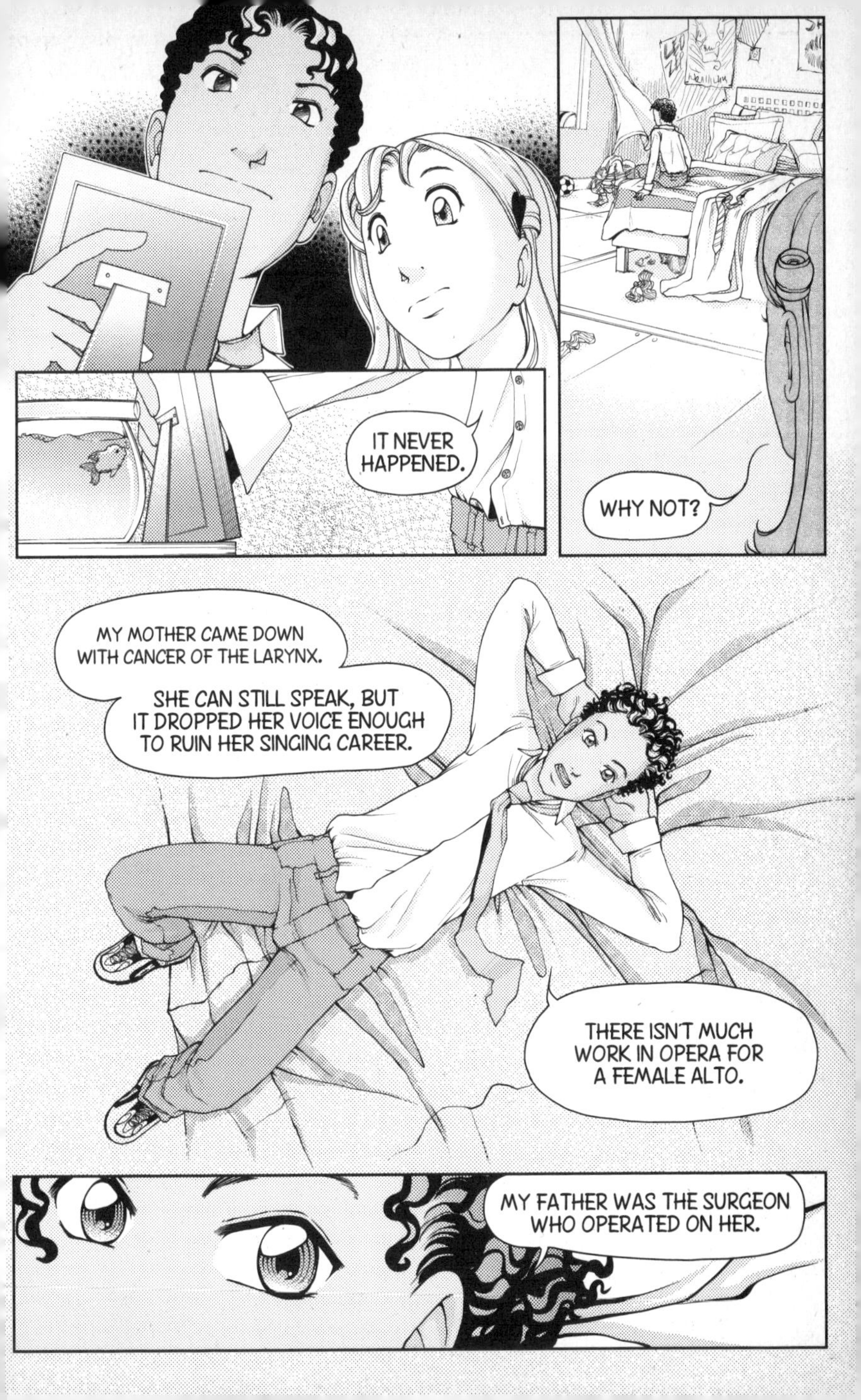
IT NEVER HAPPENED.
WHY NOT?
MY MOTHER CAME DOWN WITH CANCER OF THE LARYNX.
SHE CAN STILL SPEAK, BUT IT DROPPED HER VOICE ENOUGH TO RUIN HER SINGING CAREER.
THERE ISN'T MUCH WORK IN OPERA FOR A FEMALE ALTO.
MY FATHER WAS THE SURGEON WHO OPERATED ON HER.

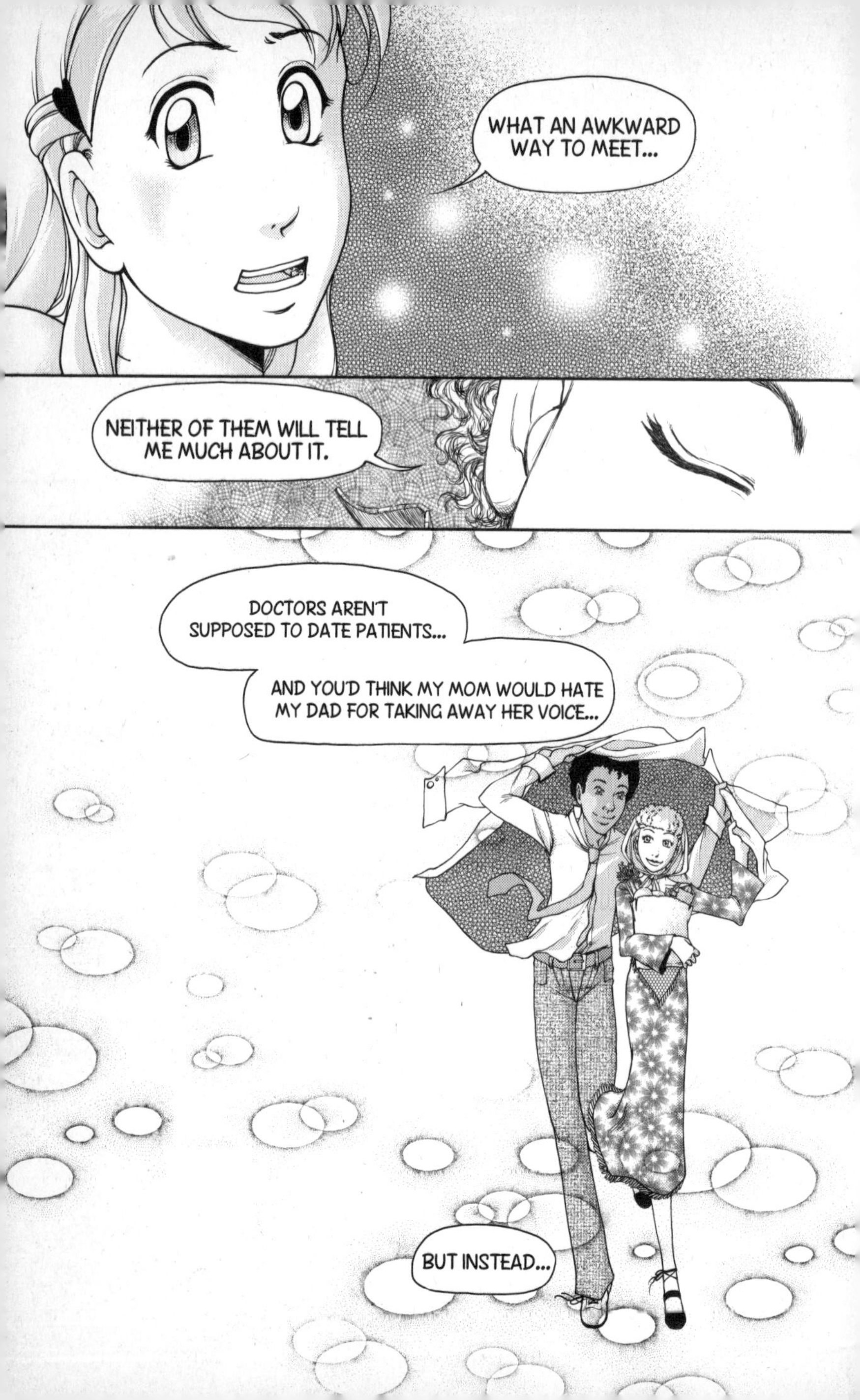
WHAT AN AWKWARD WAY TO MEET...
NEITHER OF THEM WILL TELL ME MUCH ABOUT IT.
DOCTORS AREN'T SUPPOSED TO DATE PATIENTS...
AND YOU'D THINK MY MOM WOULD HATE MY DAD FOR TAKING AWAY HER VOICE...
BUT INSTEAD...

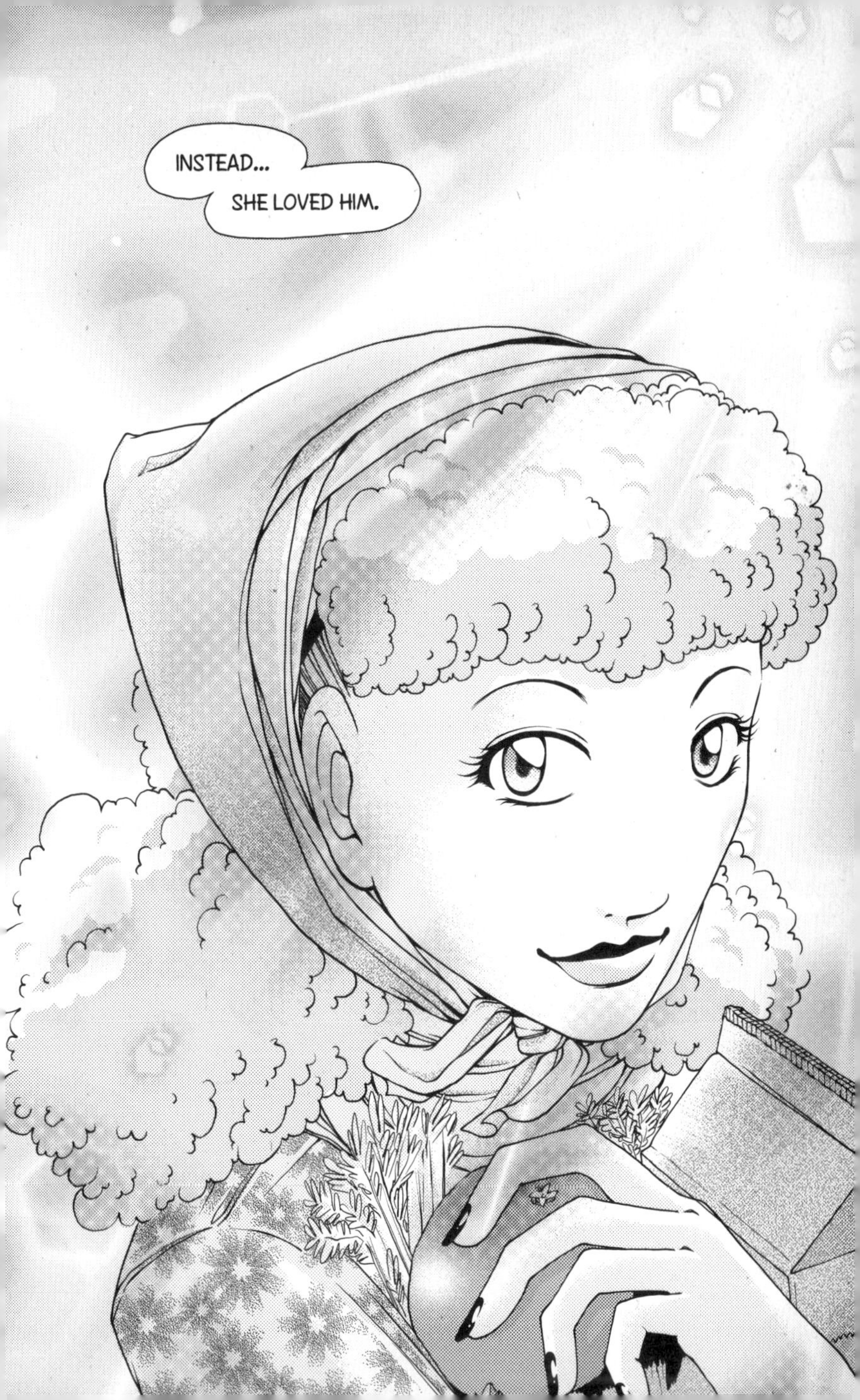
INSTEAD...
SHE LOVED HIM.

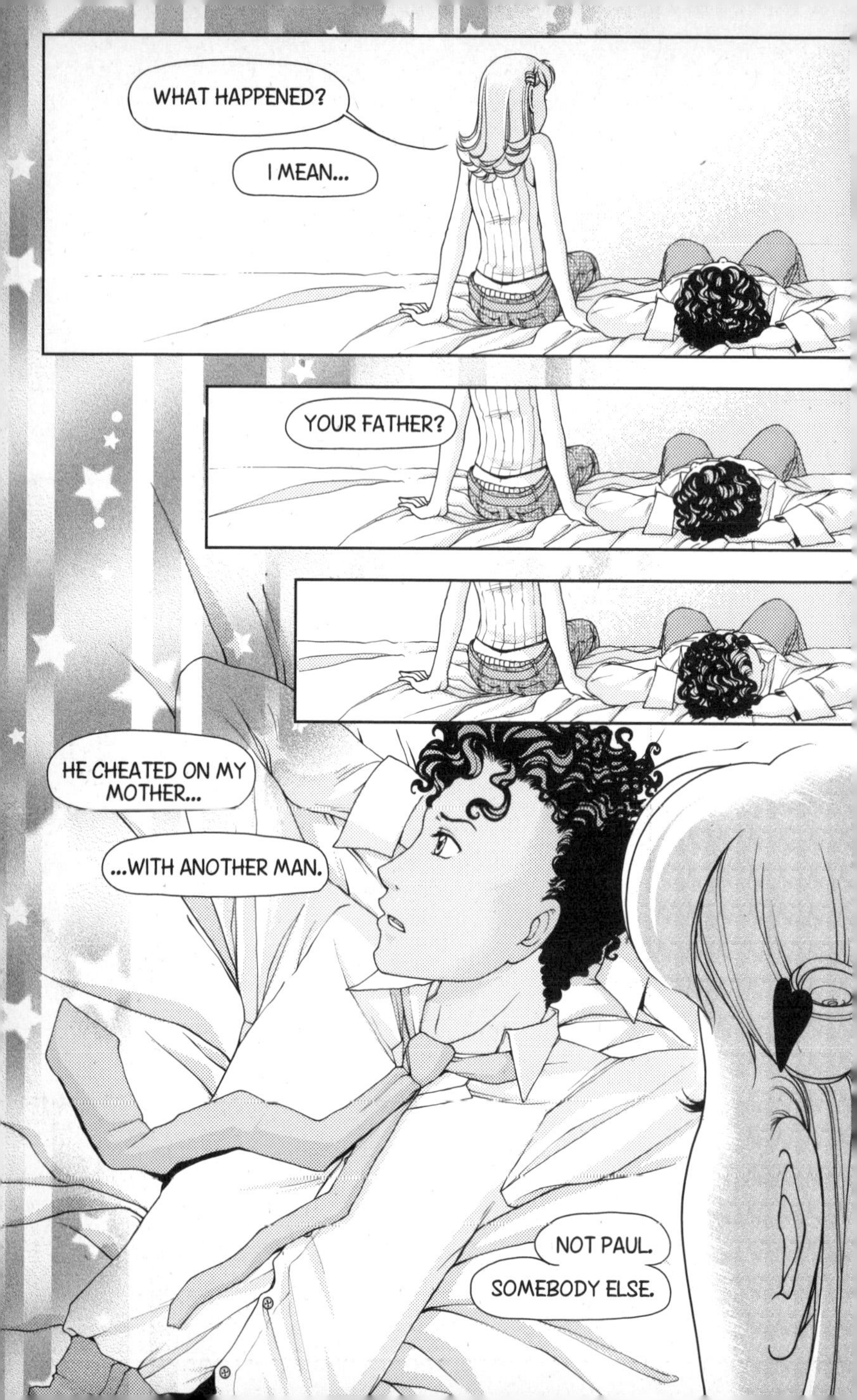
WHAT HAPPENED?
I MEAN...
YOUR FATHER?
HE CHEATED ON MY MOTHER...
...WITH ANOTHER MAN.
NOT PAUL.
SOMEBODY ELSE.

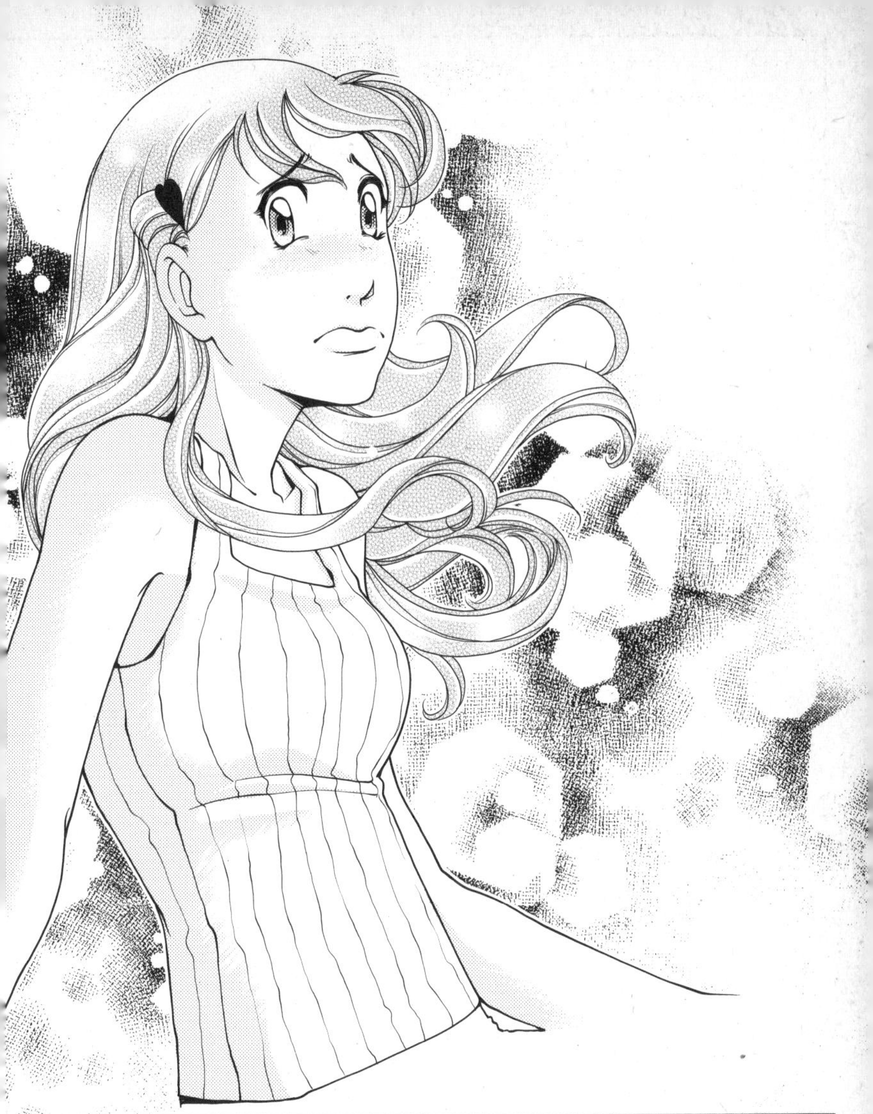
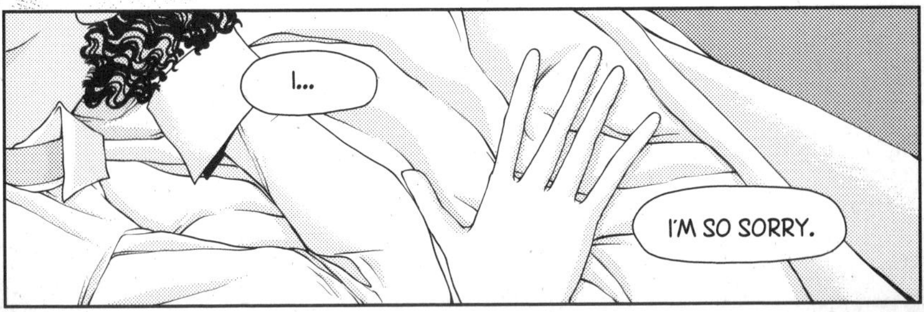
I...
I'M SO SORRY.

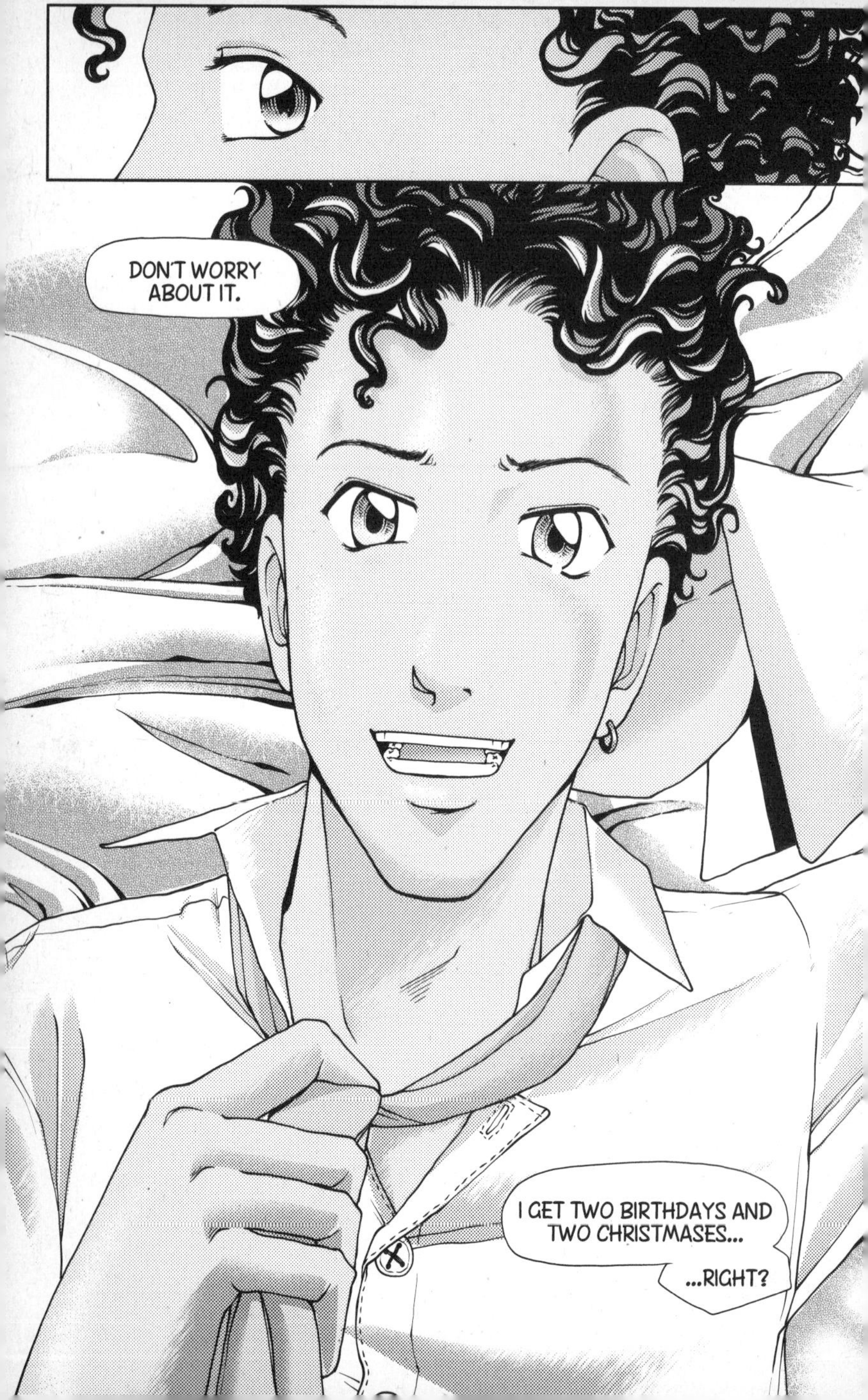
DON'T WORRY ABOUT IT.
I GET TWO BIRTHDAYS AND TWO CHRISTMASES...
...RIGHT?

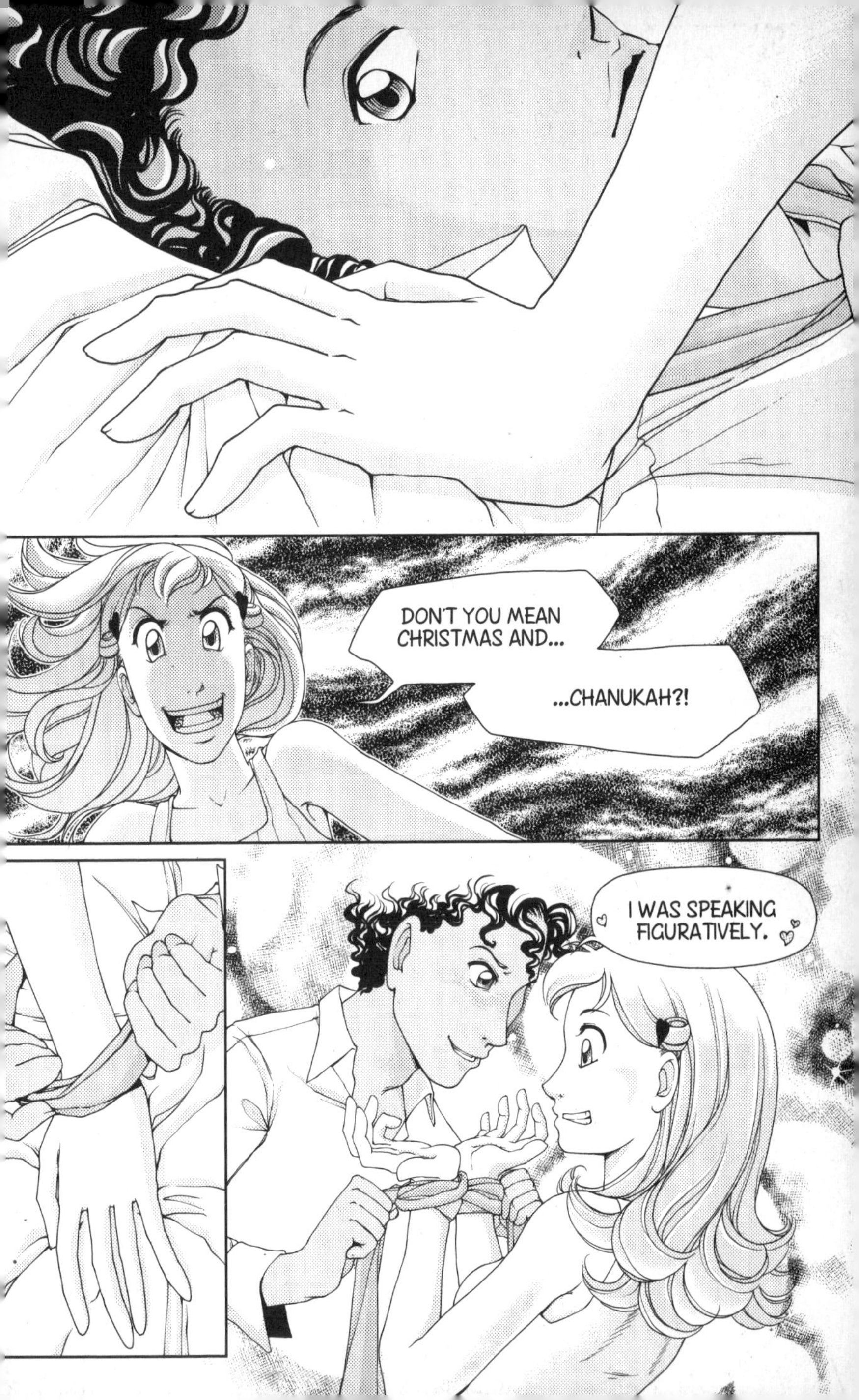
DON'T YOU MEAN CHRISTMAS AND...
...CHANUKAH?!
I WAS SPEAKING FIGURATIVELY.

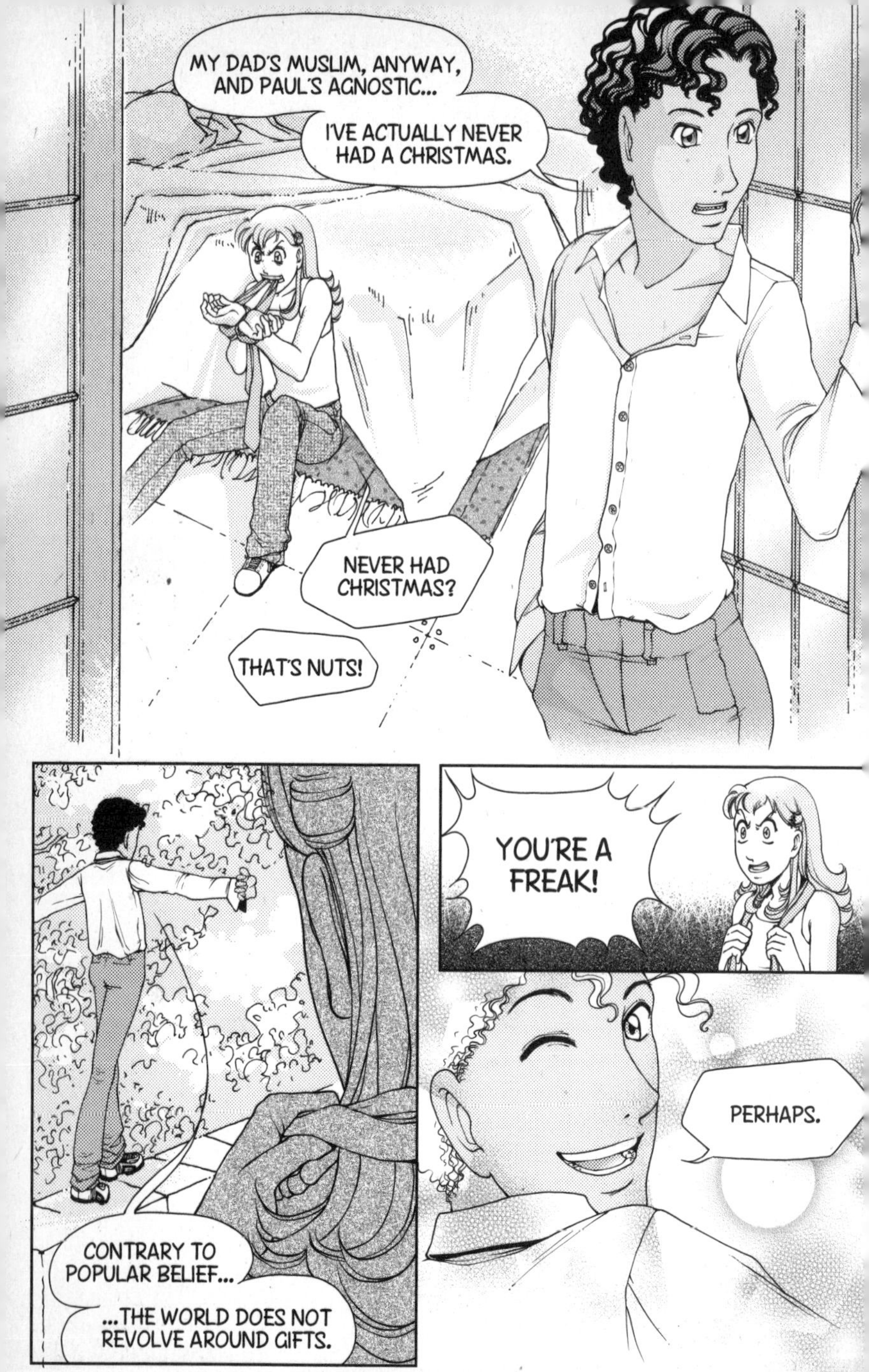
MY DAD'S MUSLIM, ANYWAY, AND PAUL'S AGNOSTIC...
I'VE ACTUALLY NEVER HAD A CHRISTMAS.
NEVER HAD CHRISTMAS?
THAT'S NUTS!
CONTRARY TO POPULAR BELIEF...
...THE WORLD DOES NOT REVOLVE AROUND GIFTS.
YOU'RE A FREAK!
PERHAPS.

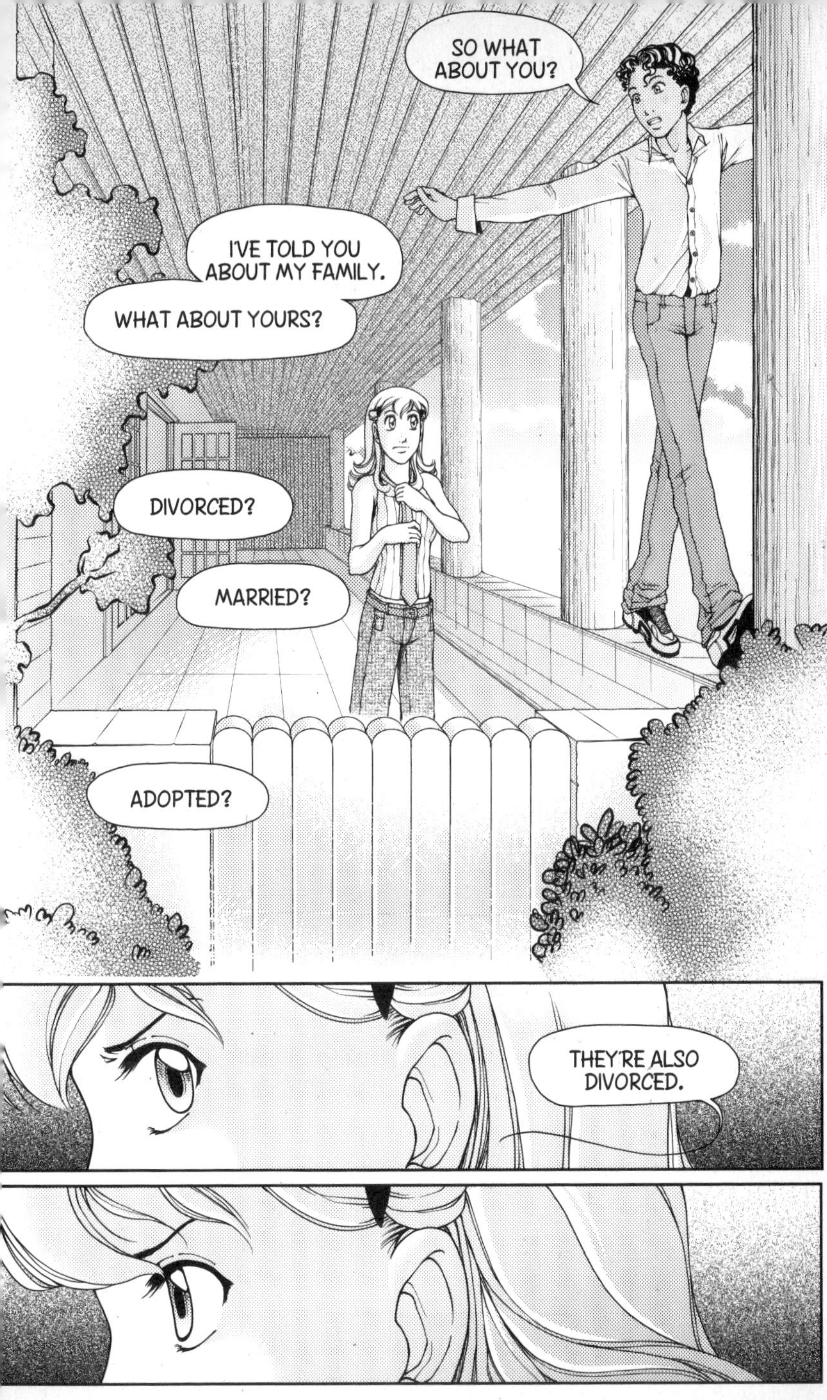
SO WHAT ABOUT YOU?
I'VE TOLD YOU ABOUT MY FAMILY.
WHAT ABOUT YOURS?
DIVORCED?
MARRIED?
ADOPTED?
THEY'RE ALSO DIVORCED.

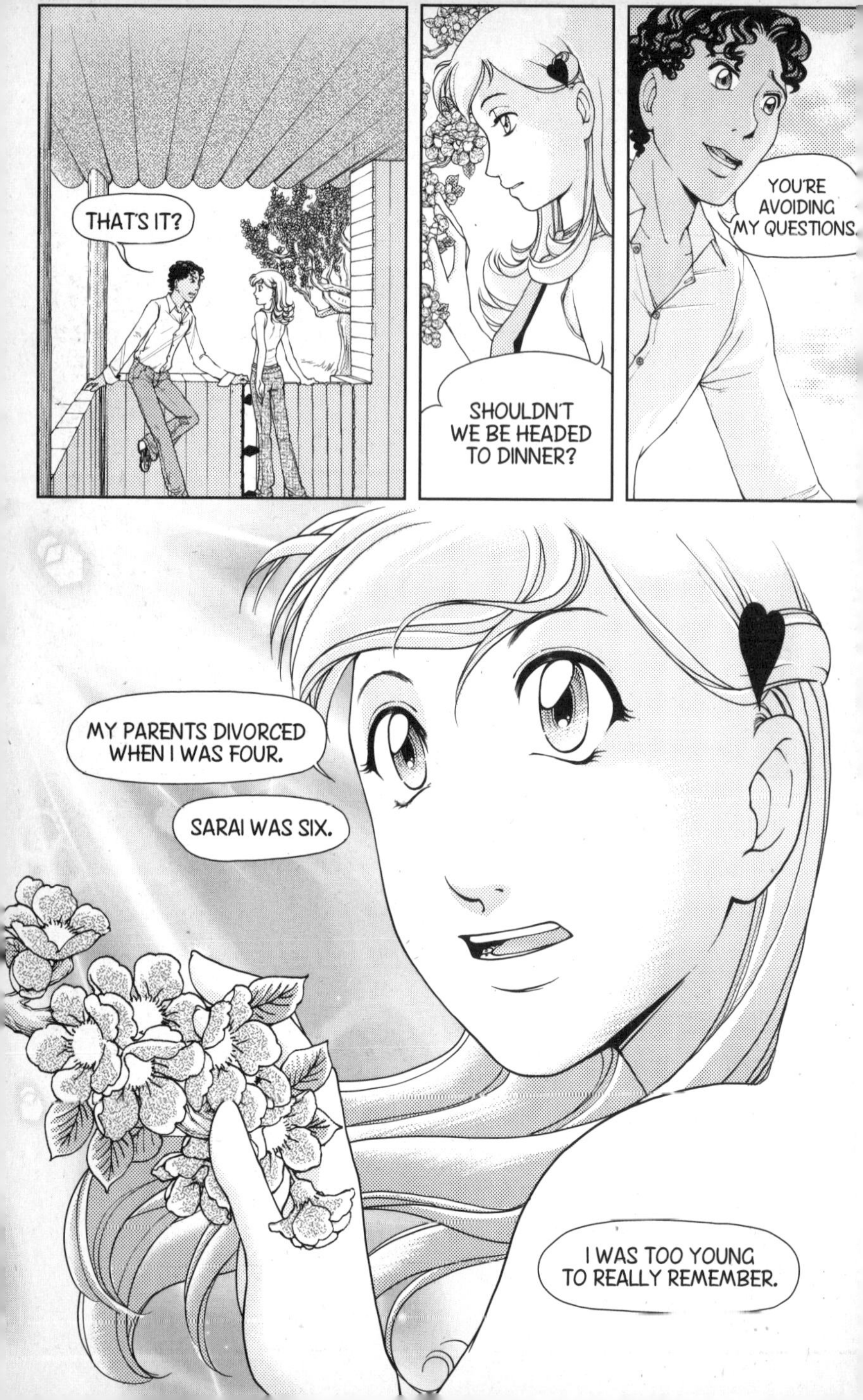
THAT'S IT?
SHOULDN'T WE BE HEADED TO DINNER?
YOU'RE AVOIDING MY QUESTIONS.
MY PARENTS DIVORCED WHEN I WAS FOUR.
SARAI WAS SIX.
I WAS TOO YOUNG TO REALLY REMEMBER.

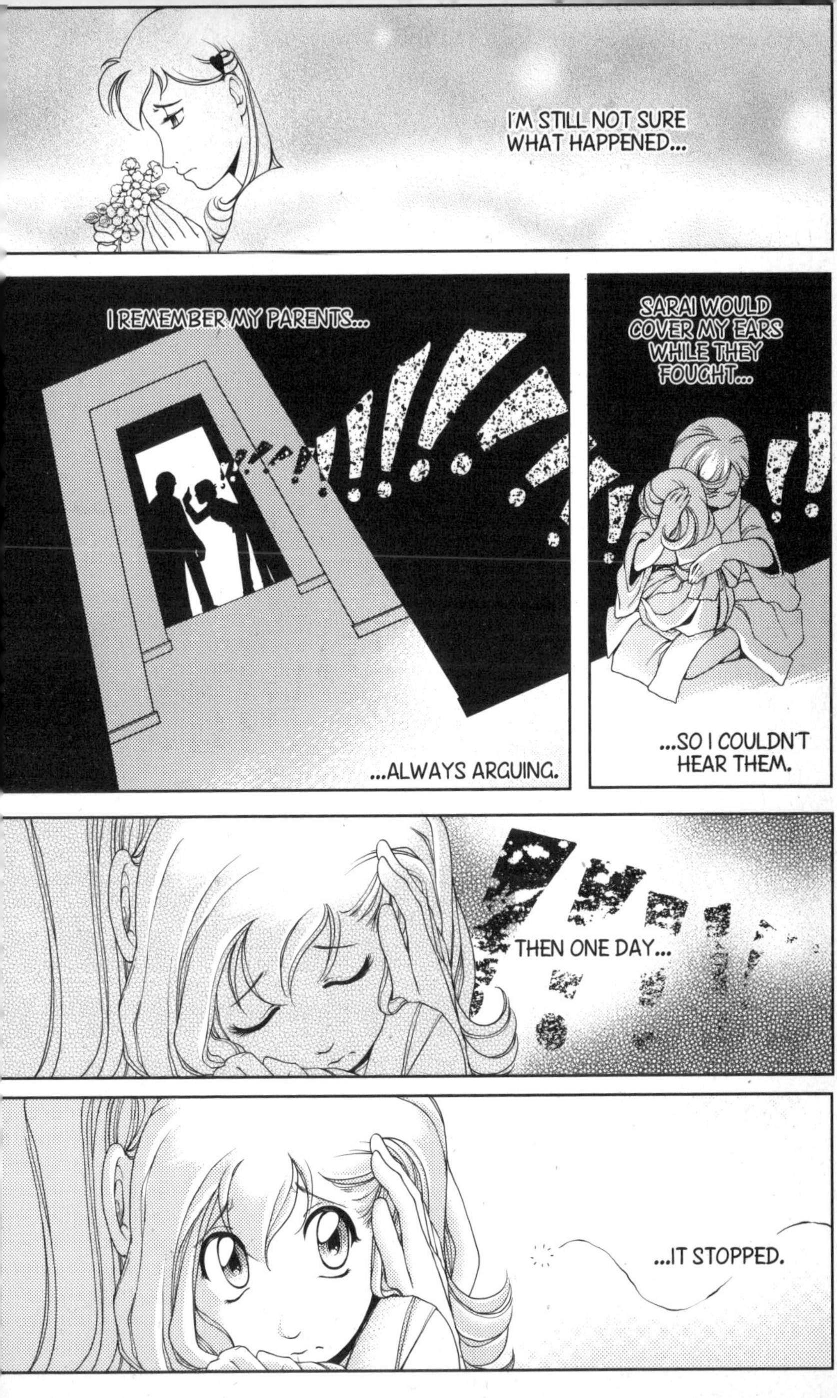
I'M STILL NOT SURE WHAT HAPPENED...
I REMEMBER MY PARENTS...
...ALWAYS ARGUING.
SARAI WOULD COVER MY EARS WHILE THEY FOUGHT...
...SO I COULDN'T HEAR THEM.
THEN ONE DAY...
...IT STOPPED.

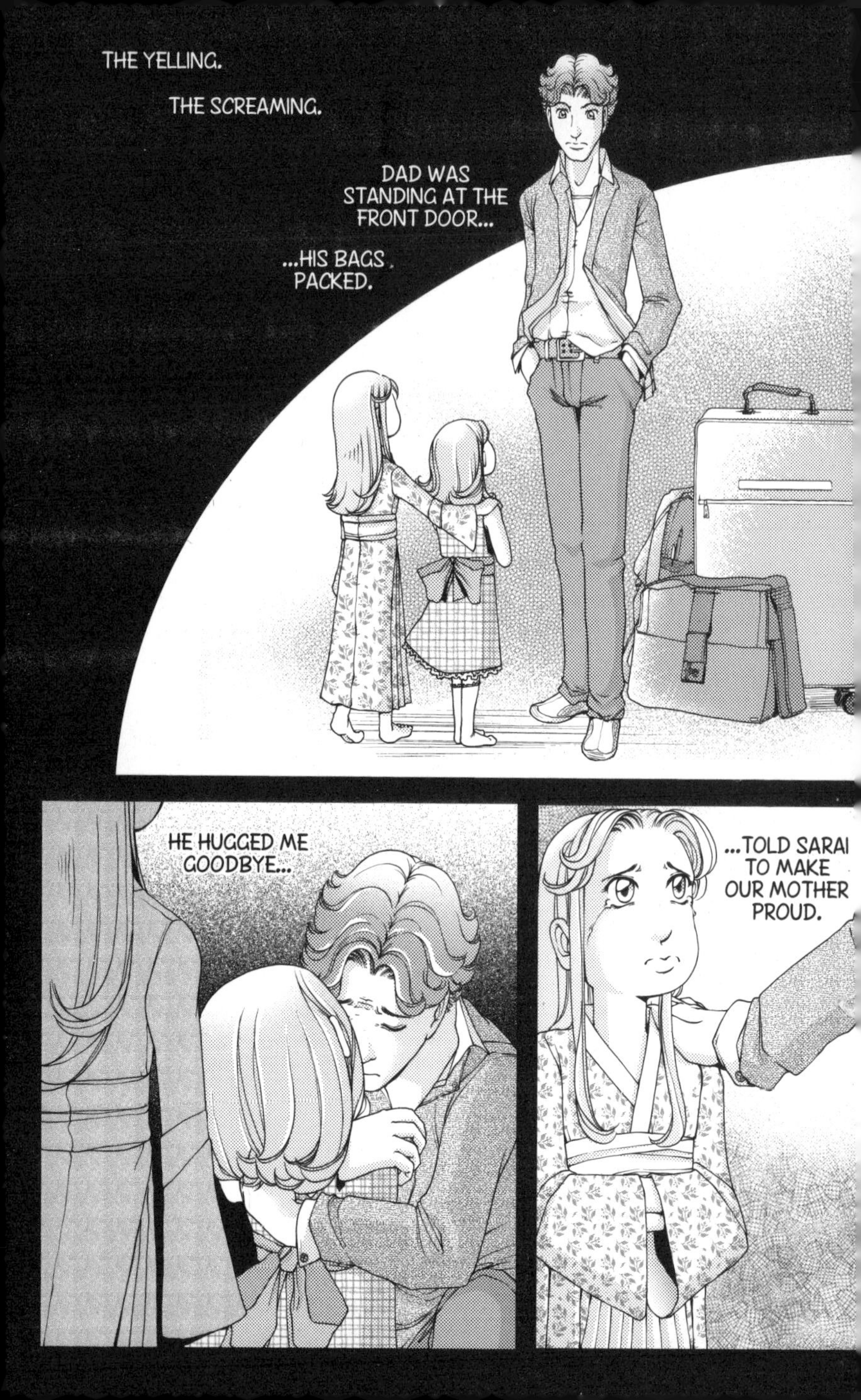
THE YELLING.
THE SCREAMING.
DAD WAS STANDING AT THE FRONT DOOR...
...HIS BAGS PACKED.
HE HUGGED ME GOODBYE...
...TOLD SARAI TO MAKE OUR MOTHER PROUD.

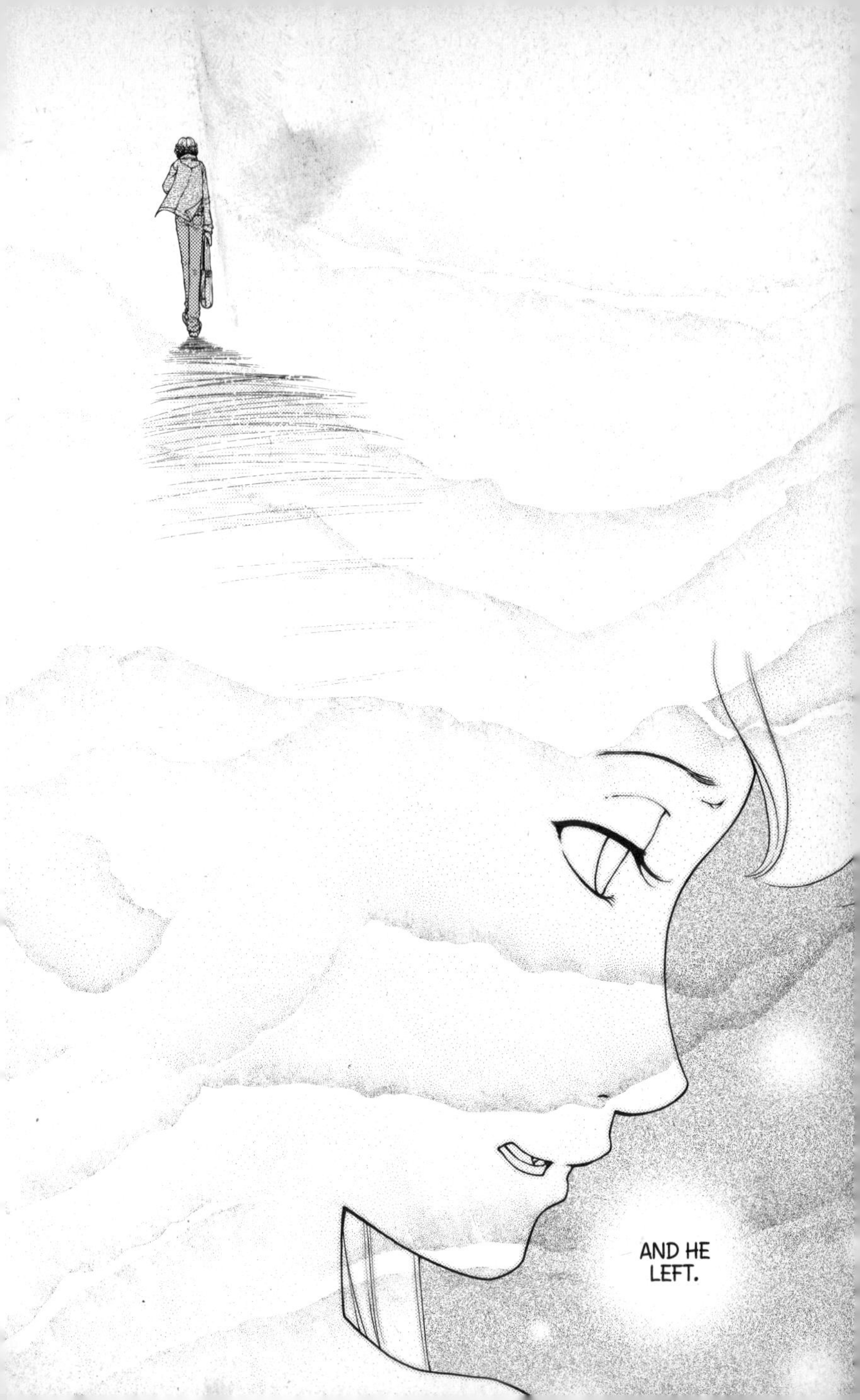
AND HE LEFT.

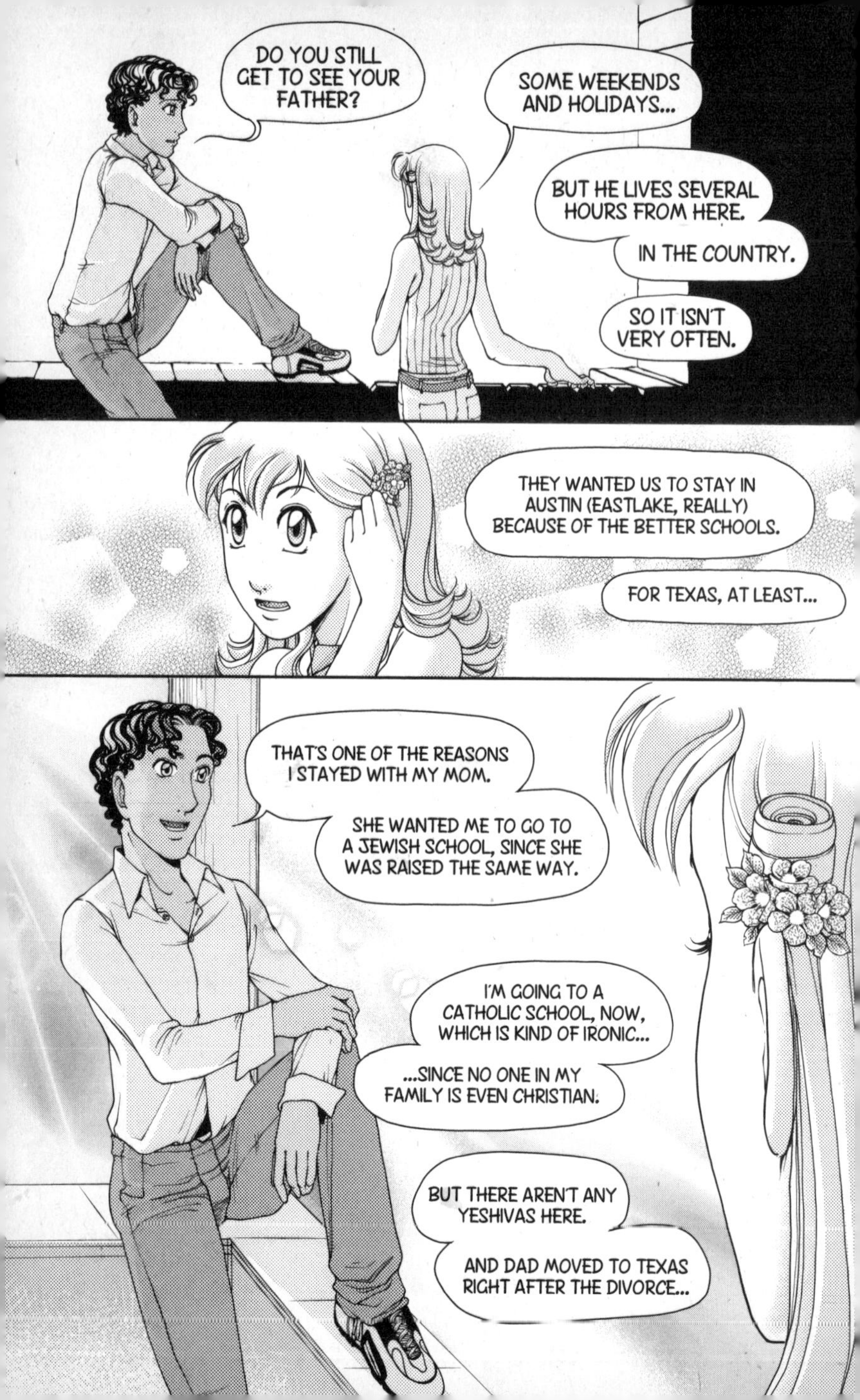
DO YOU STILL GET TO SEE YOUR FATHER?
SOME WEEKENDS AND HOLIDAYS...
BUT HE LIVES SEVERAL HOURS FROM HERE.
IN THE COUNTRY.
SO IT ISN'T VERY OFTEN.
THEY WANTED US TO STAY IN AUSTIN (EASTLAKE, REALLY) BECAUSE OF THE BETTER SCHOOLS.
FOR TEXAS, AT LEAST...
THAT'S ONE OF THE REASONS I STAYED WITH MY MOM.
SHE WANTED ME TO GO TO A JEWISH SCHOOL, SINCE SHE WAS RAISED THE SAME WAY.
I'M GOING TO A CATHOLIC SCHOOL, NOW, WHICH IS KIND OF IRONIC...
...SINCE NO ONE IN MY FAMILY IS EVEN CHRISTIAN.
BUT THERE AREN'T ANY YESHIVAS HERE.
AND DAD MOVED TO TEXAS RIGHT AFTER THE DIVORCE...

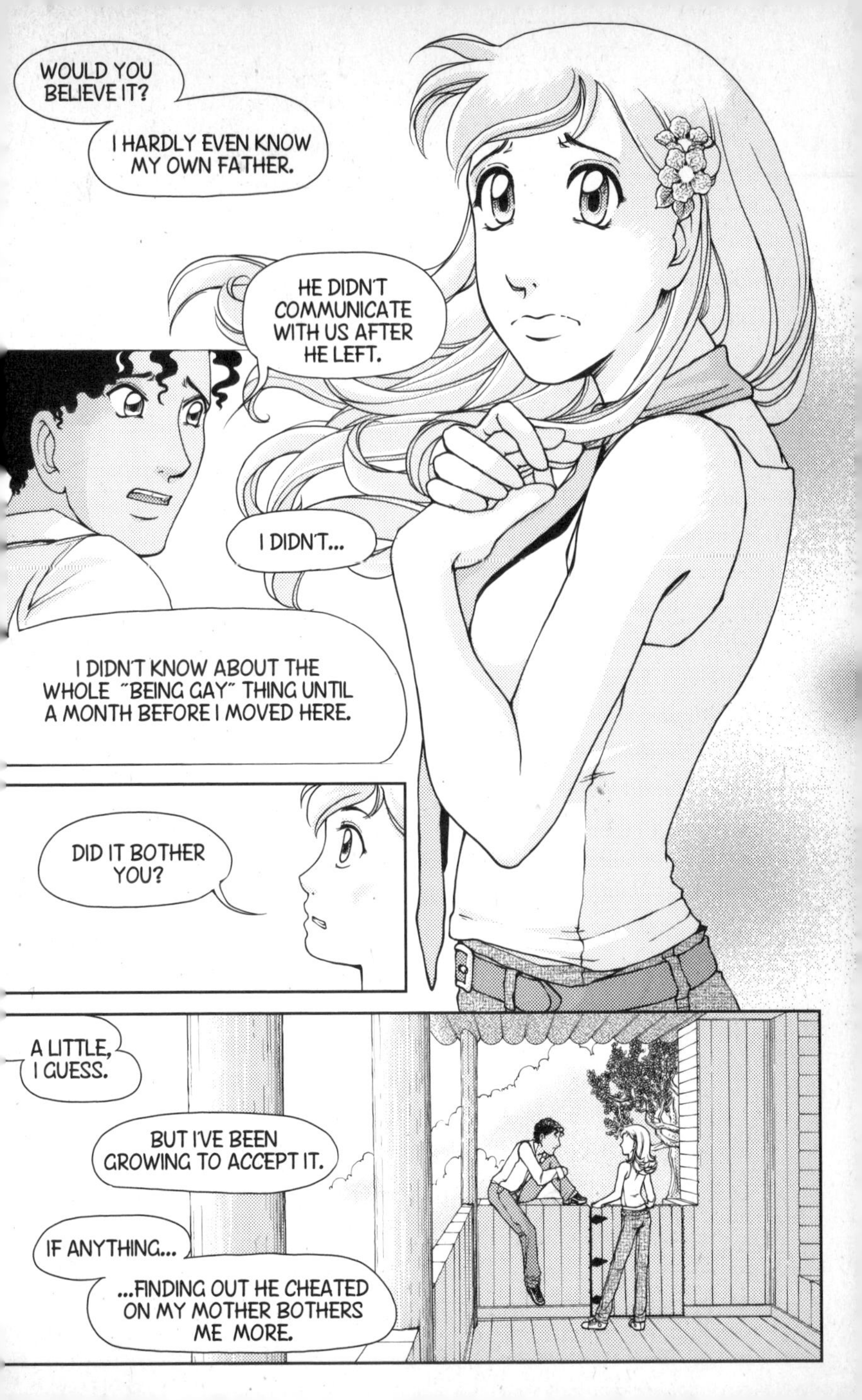
WOULD YOU BELIEVE IT?
I HARDLY EVEN KNOW MY OWN FATHER.
HE DIDN'T COMMUNICATE WITH US AFTER HE LEFT.
I DIDN'T...
I DIDN'T KNOW ABOUT THE WHOLE "BEING GAY" THING UNTIL A MONTH BEFORE I MOVED HERE.
DID IT BOTHER YOU?
A LITTLE, I GUESS.
BUT I'VE BEEN GROWING TO ACCEPT IT.
IF ANYTHING...
...FINDING OUT HE CHEATED ON MY MOTHER BOTHERS ME MORE.

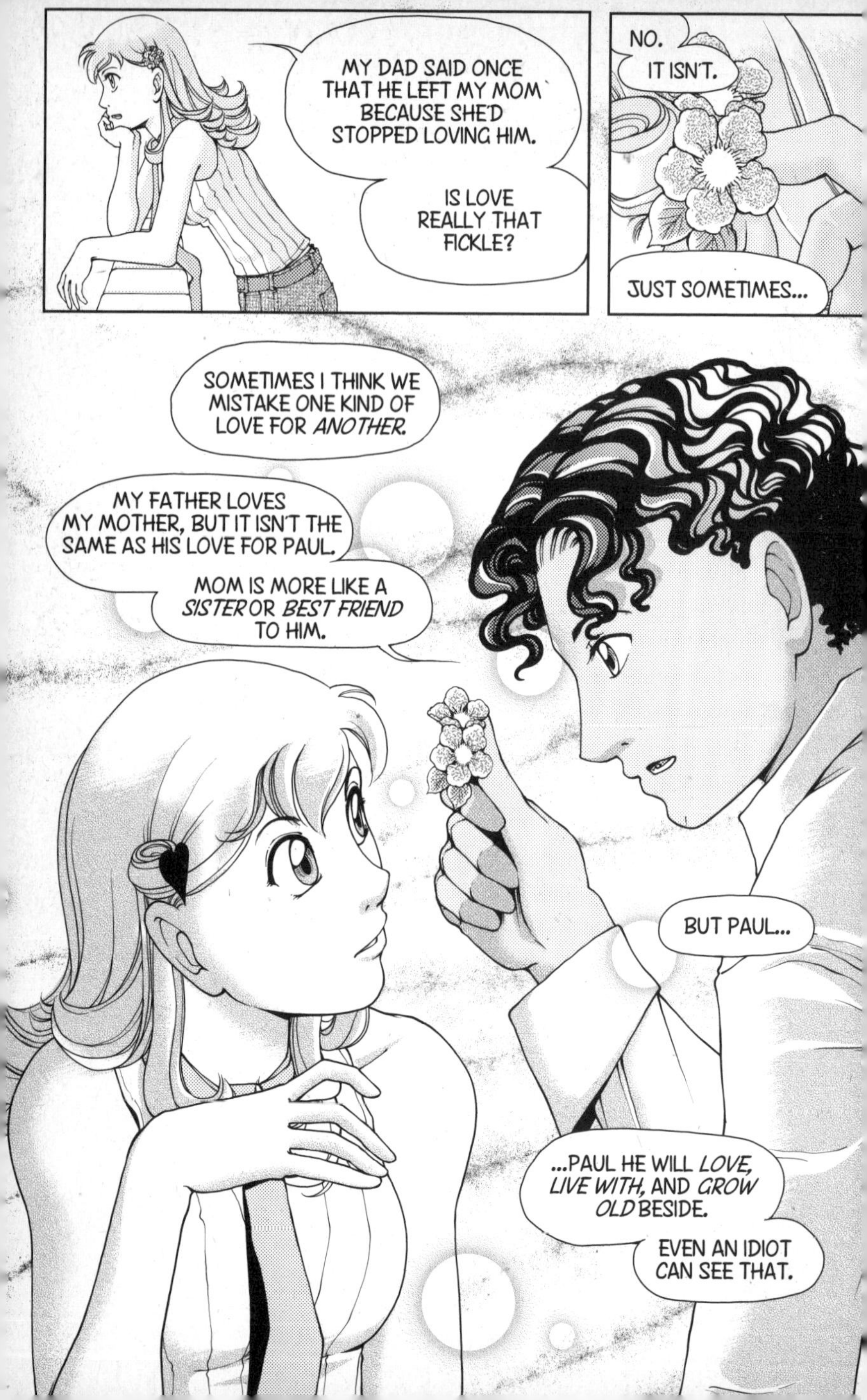
MY DAD SAID ONCE THAT HE LEFT MY MOM BECAUSE SHE'D STOPPED LOVING HIM.
IS LOVE REALLY THAT FICKLE?
NO.
IT ISN'T.
JUST SOMETIMES...
SOMETIMES I THINK WE MISTAKE ONE KIND OF LOVE FOR *ANOTHER.*
MY FATHER LOVES MY MOTHER, BUT IT ISN'T THE SAME AS HIS LOVE FOR PAUL.
MOM IS MORE LIKE A *SISTER* OR *BEST FRIEND* TO HIM.
BUT PAUL...
...PAUL HE WILL *LOVE, LIVE WITH,* AND *GROW OLD* BESIDE.
EVEN AN IDIOT CAN SEE THAT.

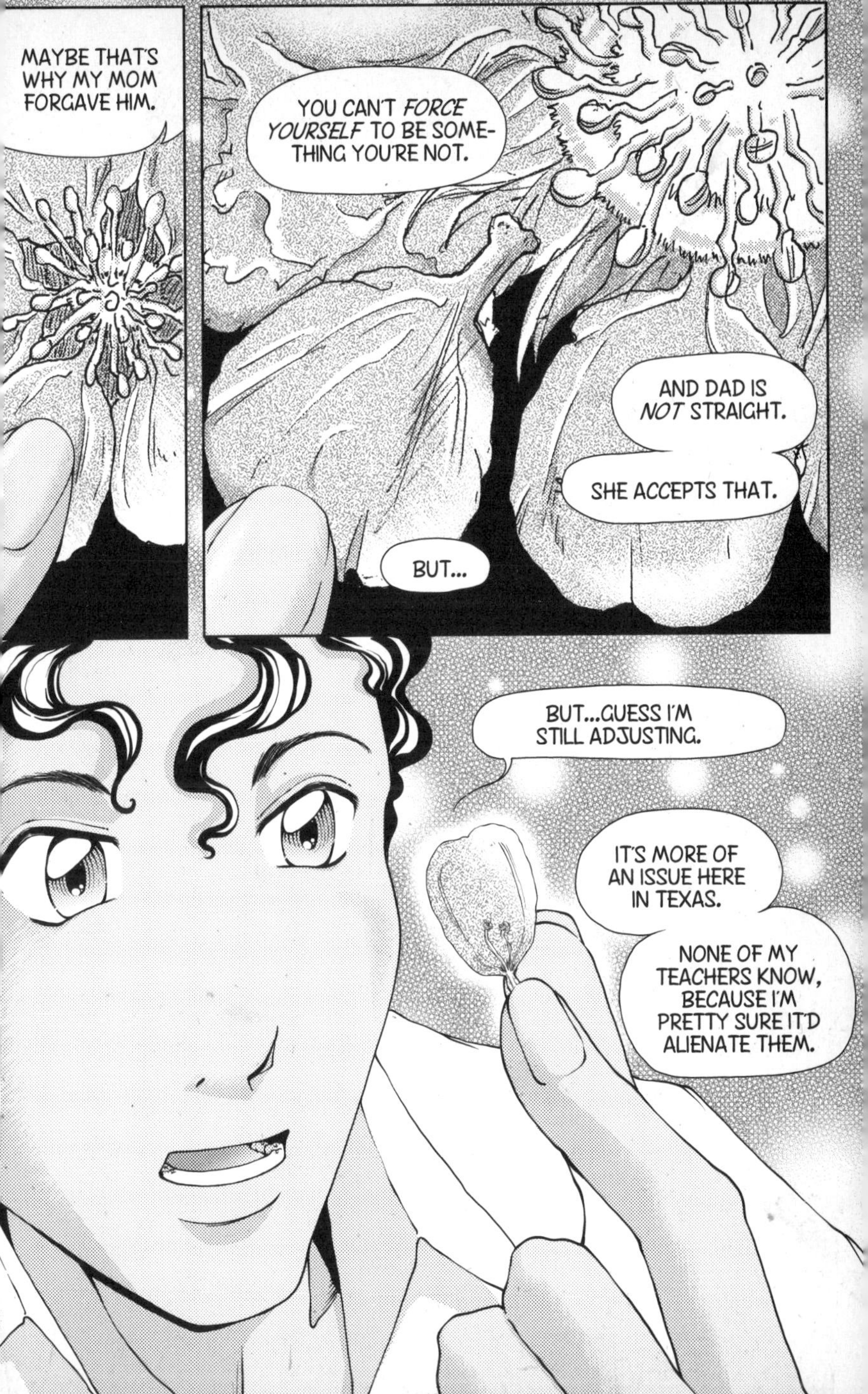
MAYBE THAT'S WHY MY MOM FORGAVE HIM.
YOU CAN'T *FORCE YOURSELF* TO BE SOME-THING YOU'RE NOT.
AND DAD IS *NOT* STRAIGHT.
SHE ACCEPTS THAT.
BUT...
BUT...GUESS I'M STILL ADJUSTING.
IT'S MORE OF AN ISSUE HERE IN TEXAS.
NONE OF MY TEACHERS KNOW, BECAUSE I'M PRETTY SURE IT'D ALIENATE THEM.

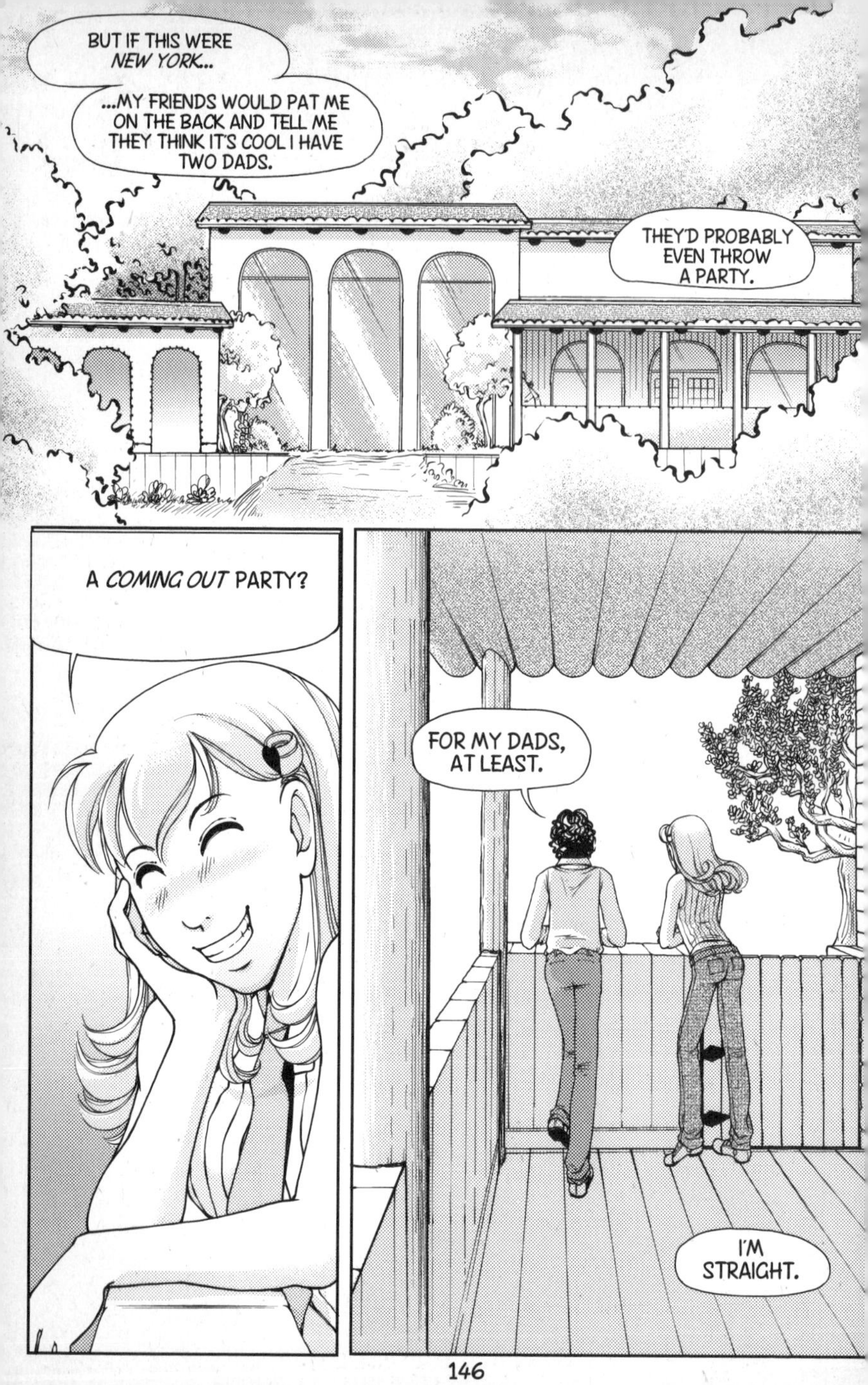
BUT IF THIS WERE *NEW YORK*...
...MY FRIENDS WOULD PAT ME ON THE BACK AND TELL ME THEY THINK IT'S *COOL* I HAVE TWO DADS.
THEY'D PROBABLY EVEN THROW A PARTY.
A *COMING OUT* PARTY?
FOR MY DADS, AT LEAST.
I'M STRAIGHT.

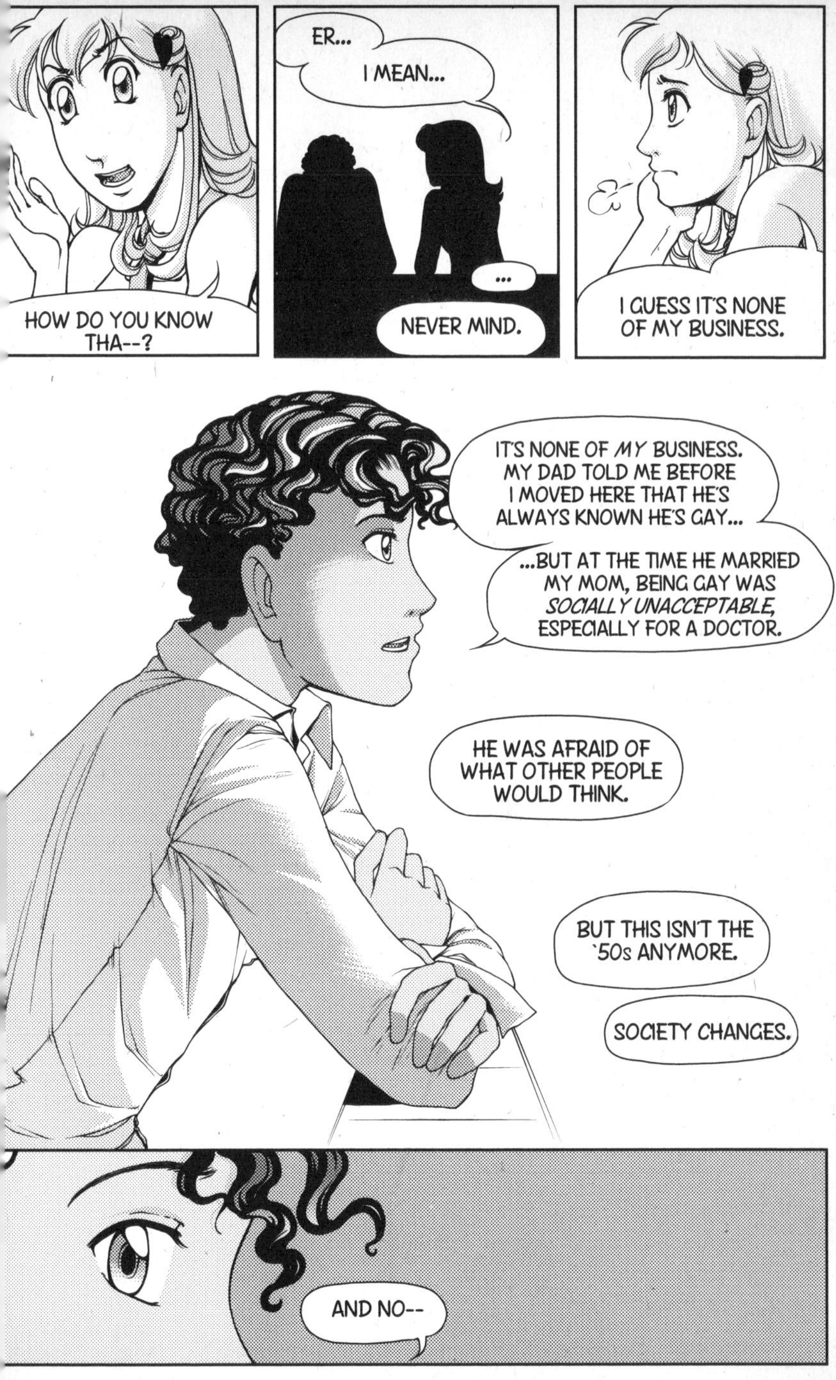
HOW DO YOU KNOW THA--?
ER...
I MEAN...
...
NEVER MIND.
I GUESS IT'S NONE OF MY BUSINESS.
IT'S NONE OF *MY* BUSINESS. MY DAD TOLD ME BEFORE I MOVED HERE THAT HE'S ALWAYS KNOWN HE'S GAY...
...BUT AT THE TIME HE MARRIED MY MOM, BEING GAY WAS *SOCIALLY UNACCEPTABLE*, ESPECIALLY FOR A DOCTOR.
HE WAS AFRAID OF WHAT OTHER PEOPLE WOULD THINK.
BUT THIS ISN'T THE `50s ANYMORE.
SOCIETY CHANGES.
AND NO--

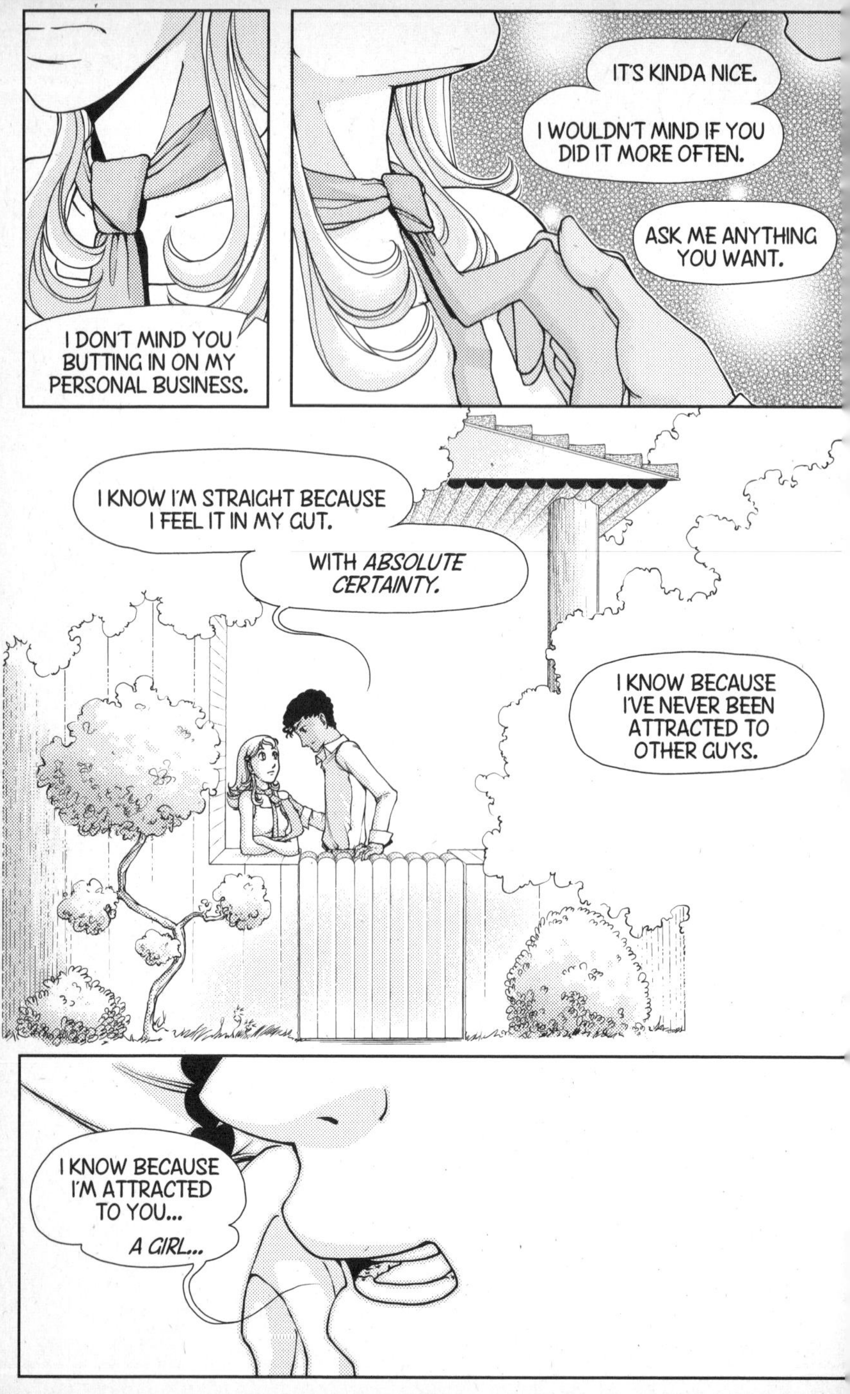
I DON'T MIND YOU BUTTING IN ON MY PERSONAL BUSINESS.
IT'S KINDA NICE.
I WOULDN'T MIND IF YOU DID IT MORE OFTEN.
ASK ME ANYTHING YOU WANT.
I KNOW I'M STRAIGHT BECAUSE I FEEL IT IN MY GUT.
WITH *ABSOLUTE CERTAINTY.*
I KNOW BECAUSE I'VE NEVER BEEN ATTRACTED TO OTHER GUYS.
I KNOW BECAUSE I'M ATTRACTED TO YOU...
*A GIRL...*

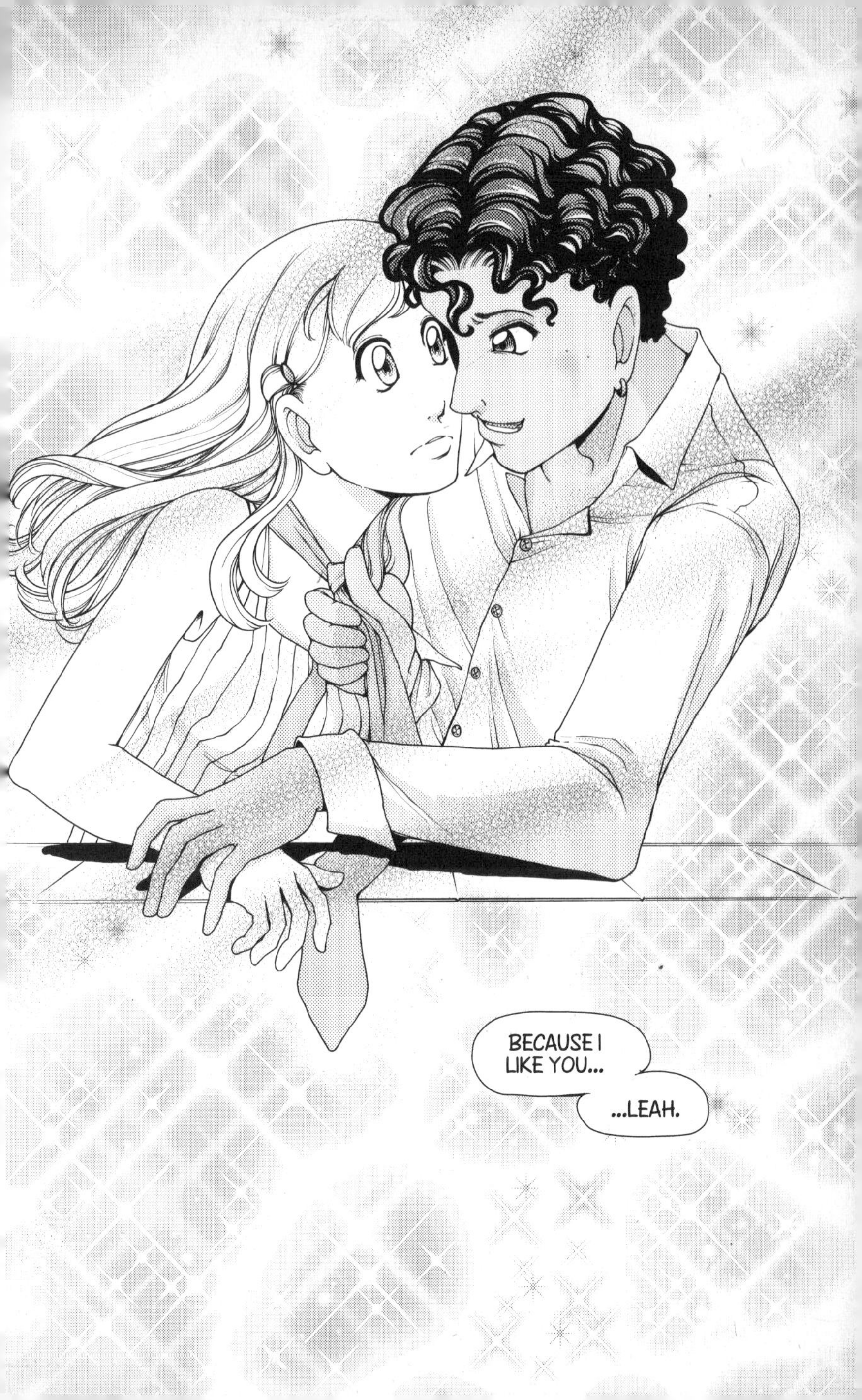
BECAUSE I LIKE YOU...
...LEAH.

Dear God,                                    September 5th
                                                (night)

    Are you there? I'm so confused. This
whole thing with Sarai... I don't
know what to do. I'm so, so, so confused
!!

    I want to do something. I just
don't know what. I don't have anybody else to talk to about it. June's
maybe my best friend, but I actually feel really weird/strange
talking to her about it. And I
can't very well talk to mom or Sarai
about it. Then there's this Elijah
guy... ... ... and I don't know.
    I sorta trust him. I kinda don't.
It's all confuzzled, and I don't know
how to explain it...

    So God, now there's you. I don't
want to believe that you'd think
love could be wrong I mean,
maybe I've never been in love, but
why does everybody think a certain
kind of love is bad ??? At church,
the youth pastor says all gays are
sinners and going to hell... that
it's a choice... but... I love
my sister, and I know she's
a good person. Is she just

September 5th

confused? Can she help it?

I *want* to ask her, but I'm so scared... I don't... I don't want to make her feel bad. Sarai's always been religious, so why would she choose to do something she's always been taught is wrong?

But is it really???

Oh God...!! I'm so, so, so confused! *Why* in the world would you hate people for loving, and if you don't, why does everybody *say* you do?

God is good. God is love.

So how can love be bad?

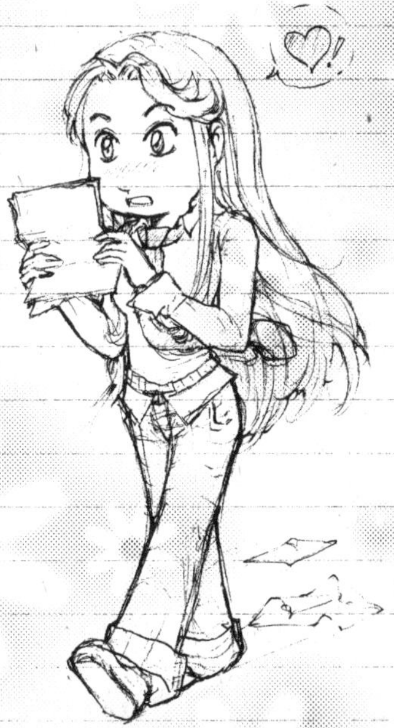

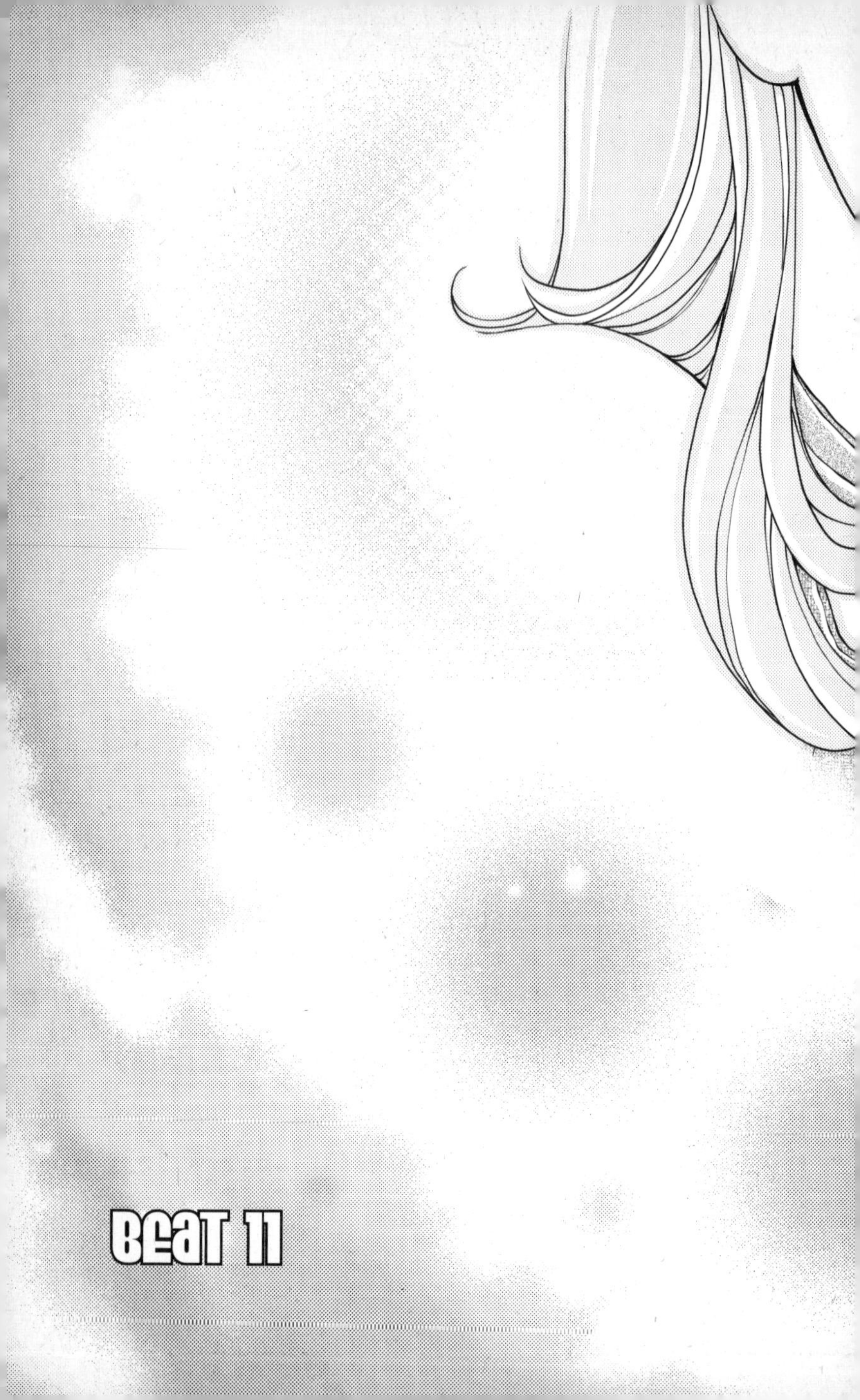
BEAT 11

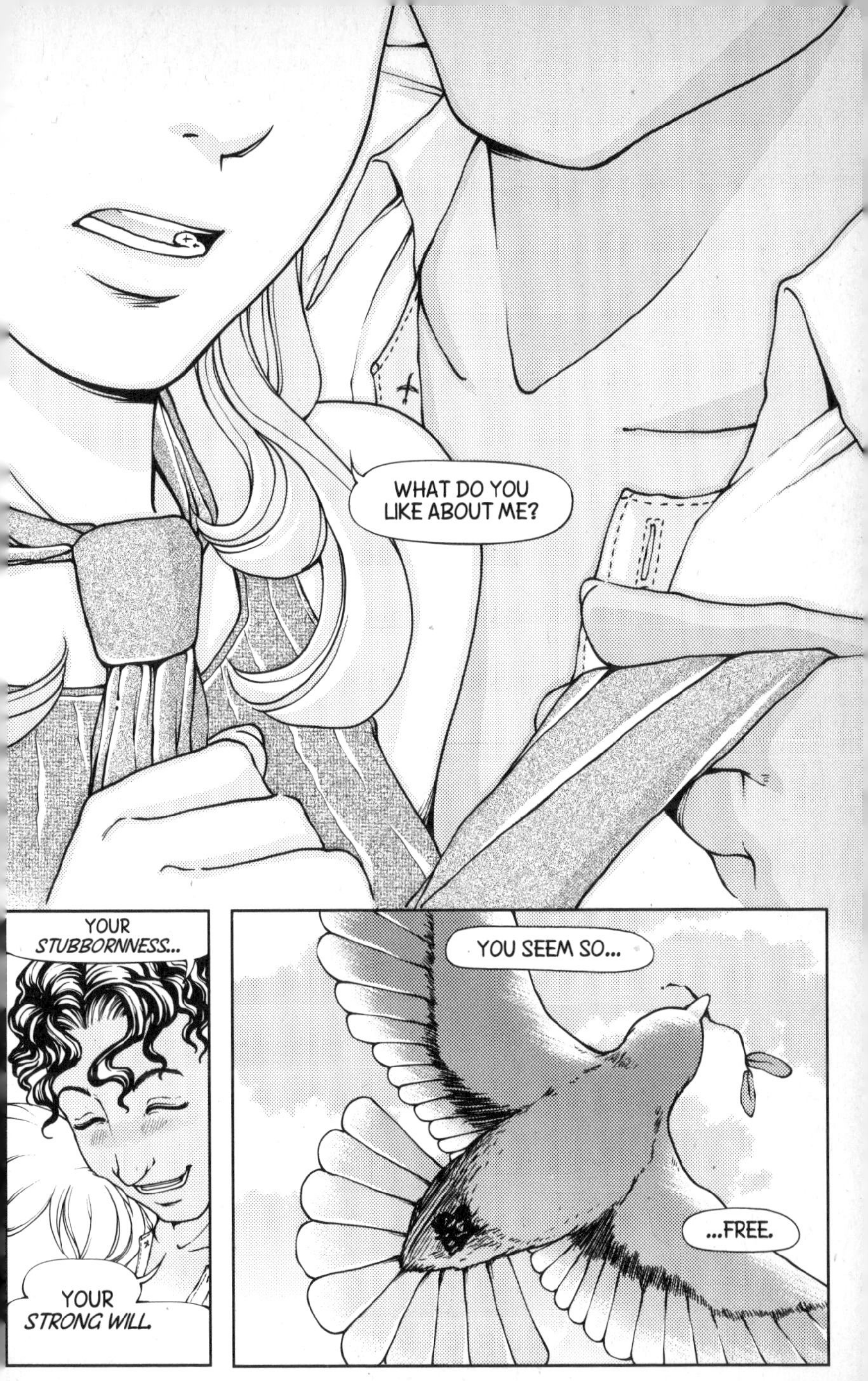
WHAT DO YOU LIKE ABOUT ME?
YOUR *STUBBORNNESS...*
YOUR *STRONG WILL.*
YOU SEEM SO...
...FREE.

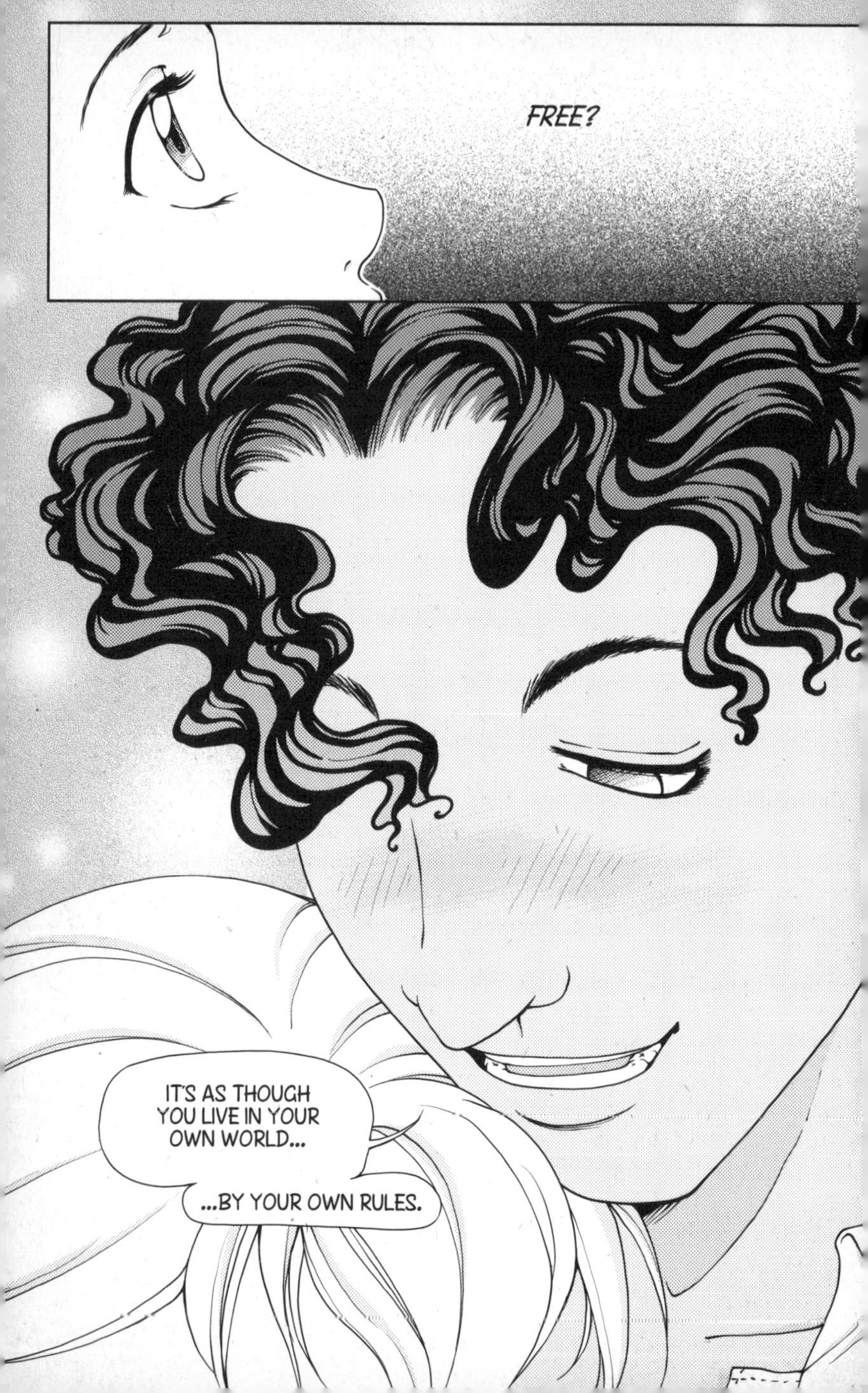
FREE?
IT'S AS THOUGH YOU LIVE IN YOUR OWN WORLD...
...BY YOUR OWN RULES.

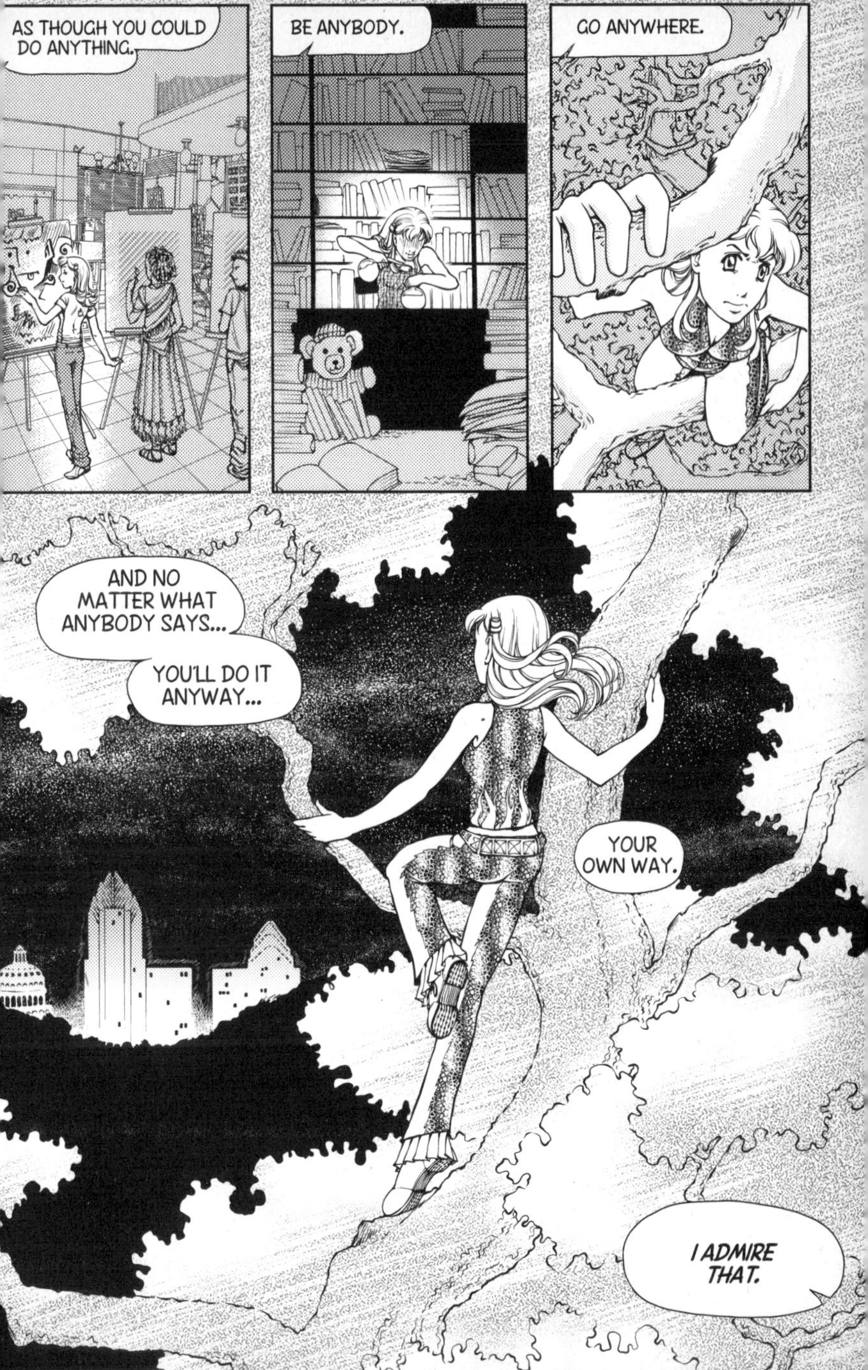
AS THOUGH YOU COULD DO ANYTHING.
BE ANYBODY.
GO ANYWHERE.
AND NO MATTER WHAT ANYBODY SAYS...
YOU'LL DO IT ANYWAY...
YOUR OWN WAY.
I ADMIRE THAT.

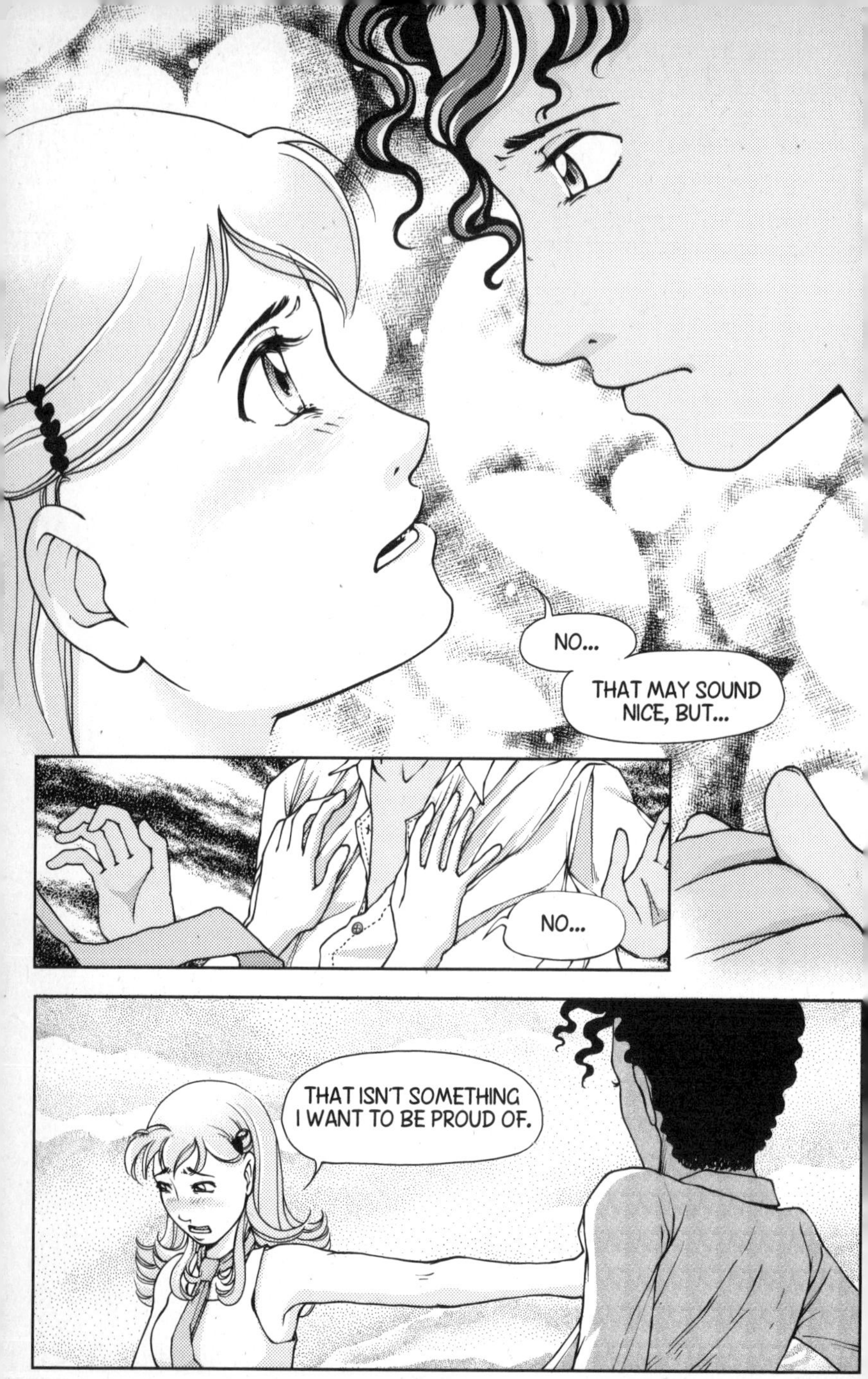
NO...
THAT MAY SOUND NICE, BUT...
NO...
THAT ISN'T SOMETHING I WANT TO BE PROUD OF.

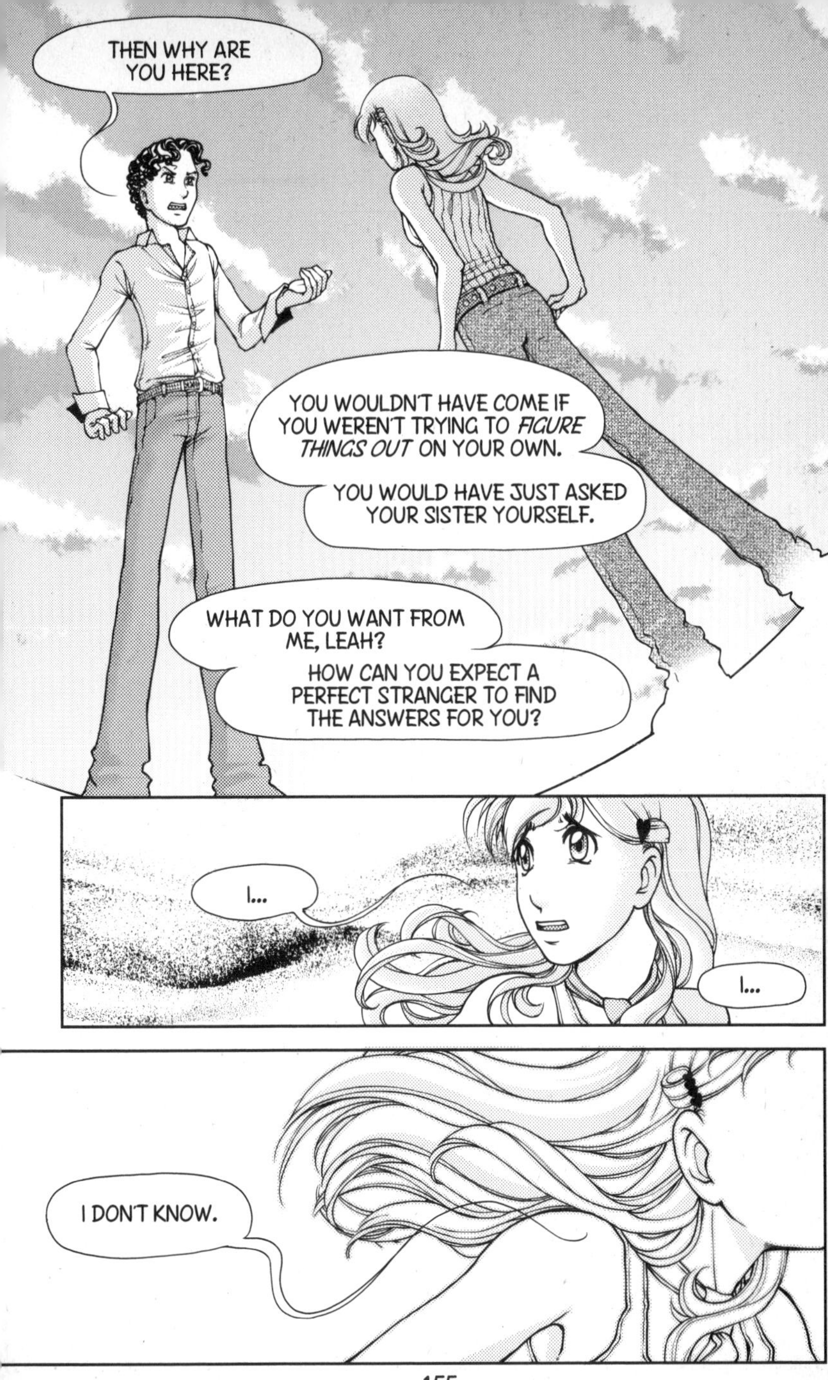
THEN WHY ARE YOU HERE?
YOU WOULDN'T HAVE COME IF YOU WEREN'T TRYING TO *FIGURE THINGS OUT* ON YOUR OWN.
YOU WOULD HAVE JUST ASKED YOUR SISTER YOURSELF.
WHAT DO YOU WANT FROM ME, LEAH?
HOW CAN YOU EXPECT A PERFECT STRANGER TO FIND THE ANSWERS FOR YOU?
I...
I...
I DON'T KNOW.

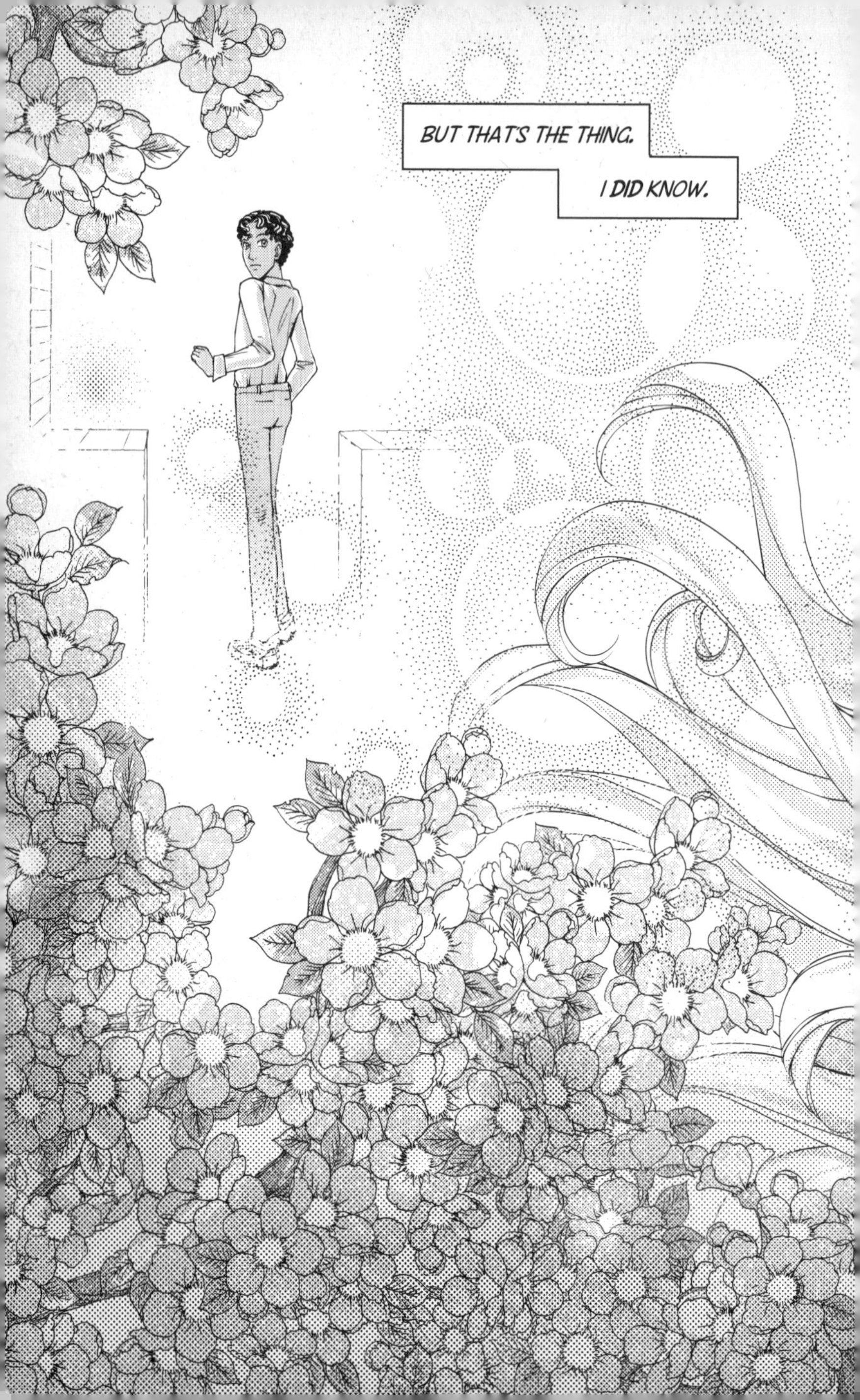
BUT THAT'S THE THING.
I DID KNOW.

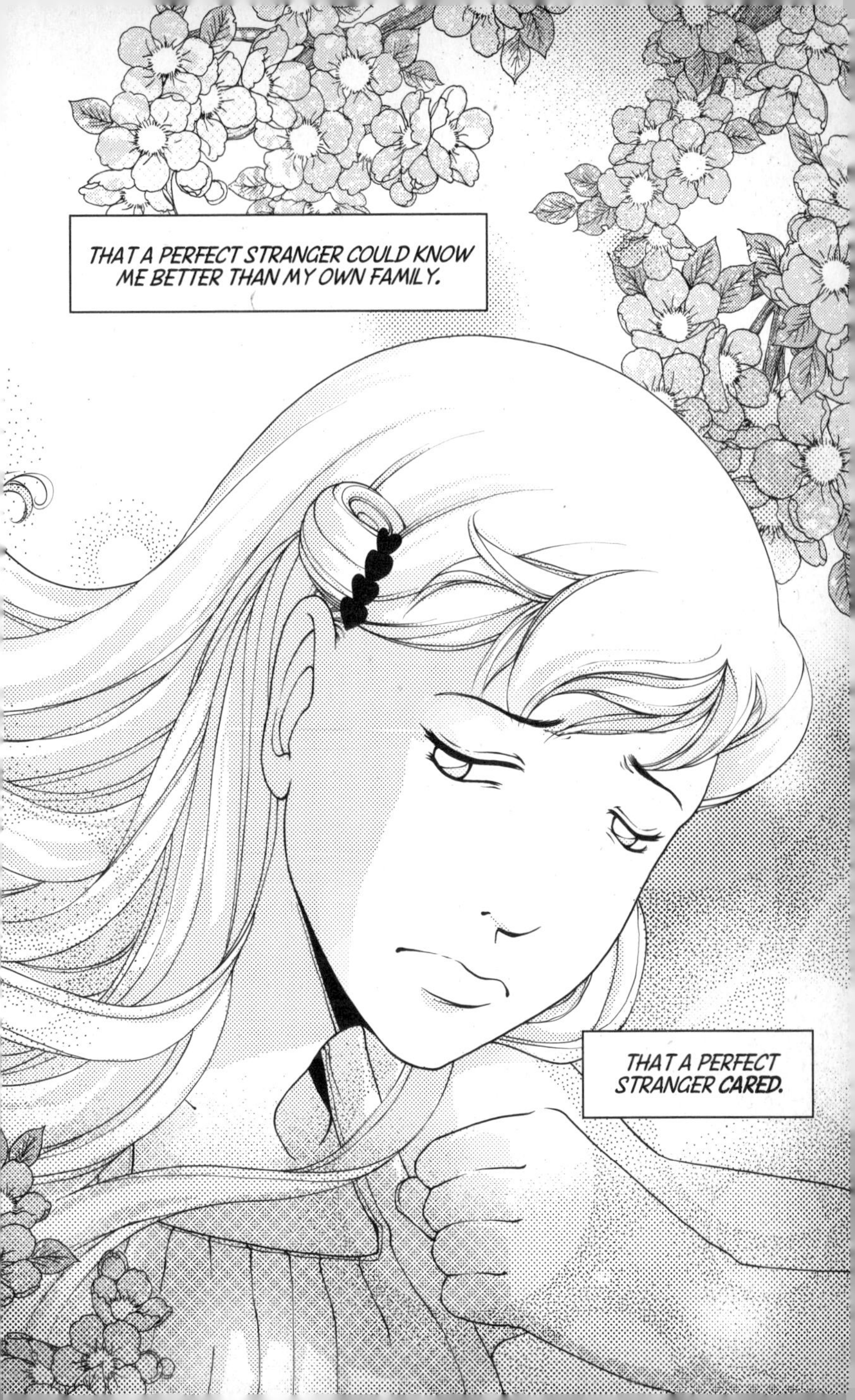
THAT A PERFECT STRANGER COULD KNOW ME BETTER THAN MY OWN FAMILY.
THAT A PERFECT STRANGER CARED.

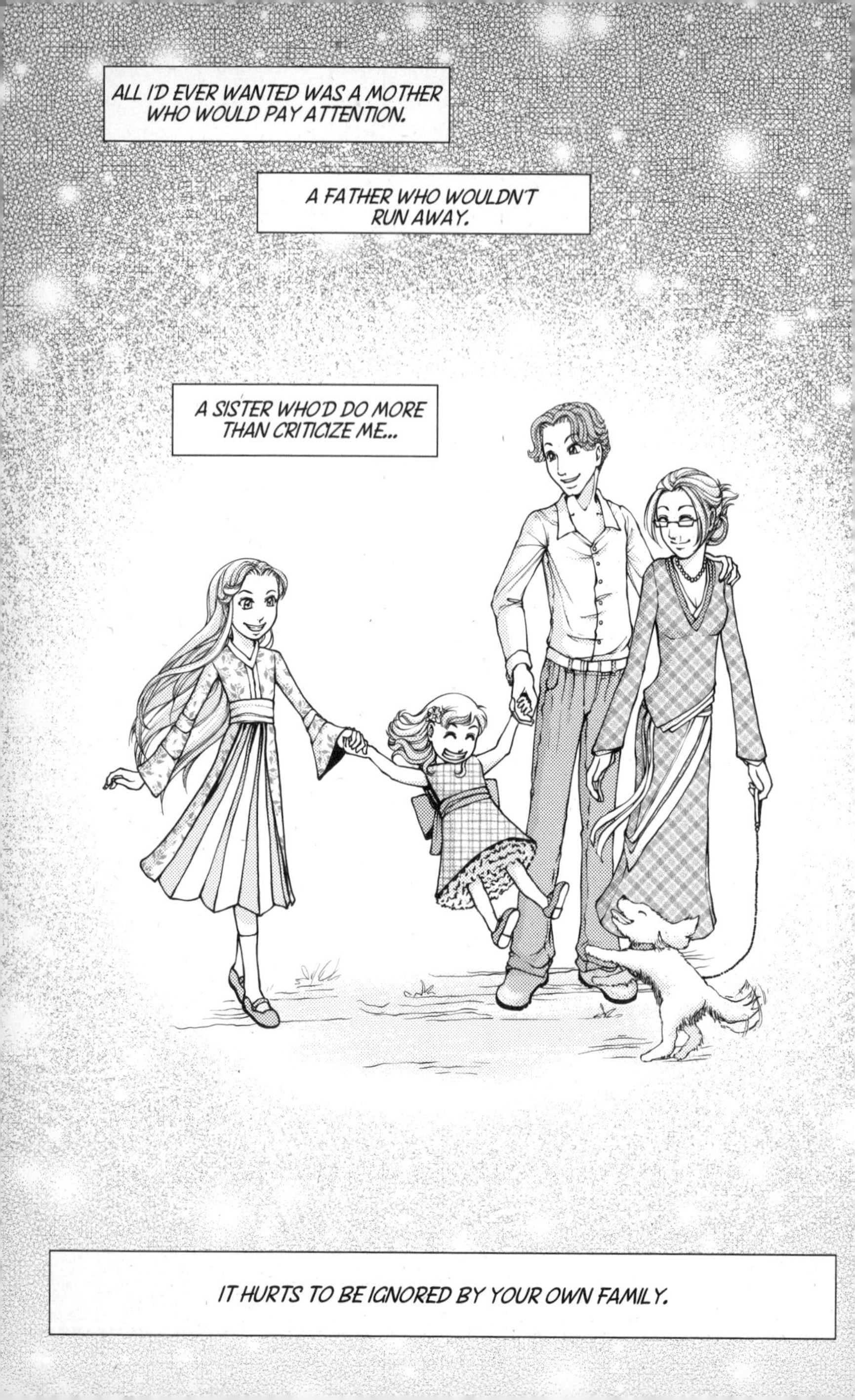
ALL I'D EVER WANTED WAS A MOTHER WHO WOULD PAY ATTENTION.
A FATHER WHO WOULDN'T RUN AWAY.
A SISTER WHO'D DO MORE THAN CRITICIZE ME...
IT HURTS TO BE IGNORED BY YOUR OWN FAMILY.

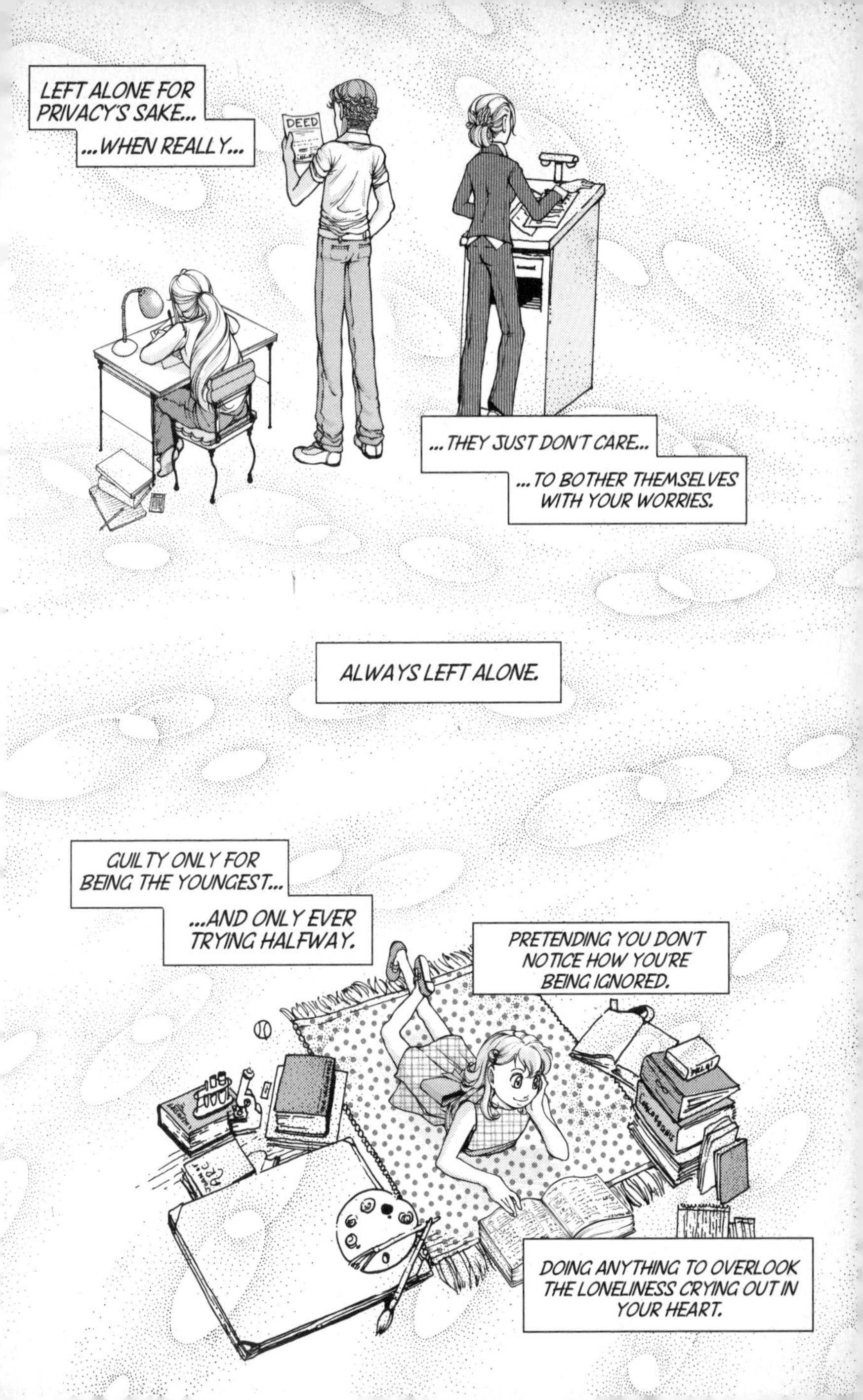
LEFT ALONE FOR PRIVACY'S SAKE...
...WHEN REALLY...
DEED
...THEY JUST DON'T CARE...
...TO BOTHER THEMSELVES WITH YOUR WORRIES.
ALWAYS LEFT ALONE.
GUILTY ONLY FOR BEING THE YOUNGEST...
...AND ONLY EVER TRYING HALFWAY.
PRETENDING YOU DON'T NOTICE HOW YOU'RE BEING IGNORED.
DOING ANYTHING TO OVERLOOK THE LONELINESS CRYING OUT IN YOUR HEART.

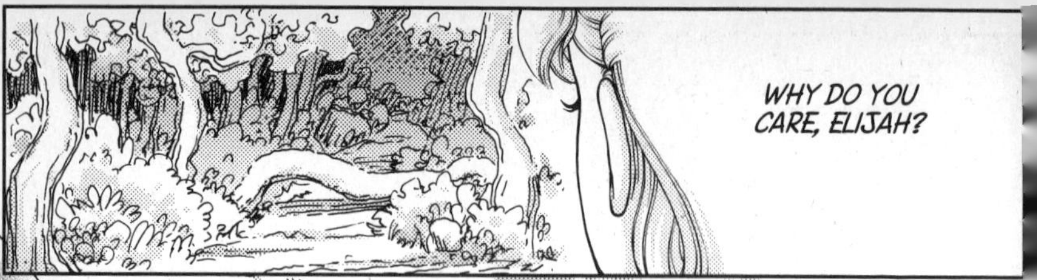
WHY DO YOU CARE, ELIJAH?
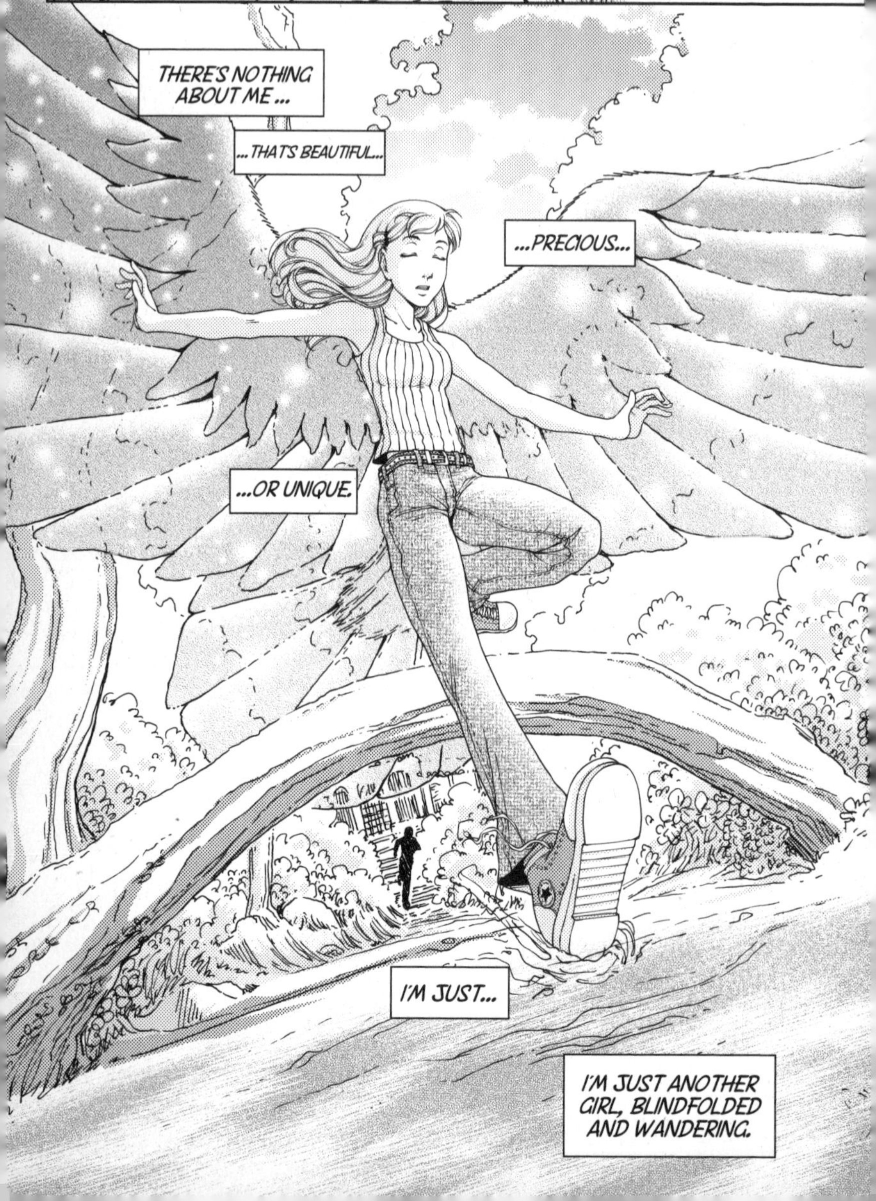
THERE'S NOTHING ABOUT ME...
...THAT'S BEAUTIFUL...
...PRECIOUS...
...OR UNIQUE.
I'M JUST...
I'M JUST ANOTHER GIRL, BLINDFOLDED AND WANDERING.

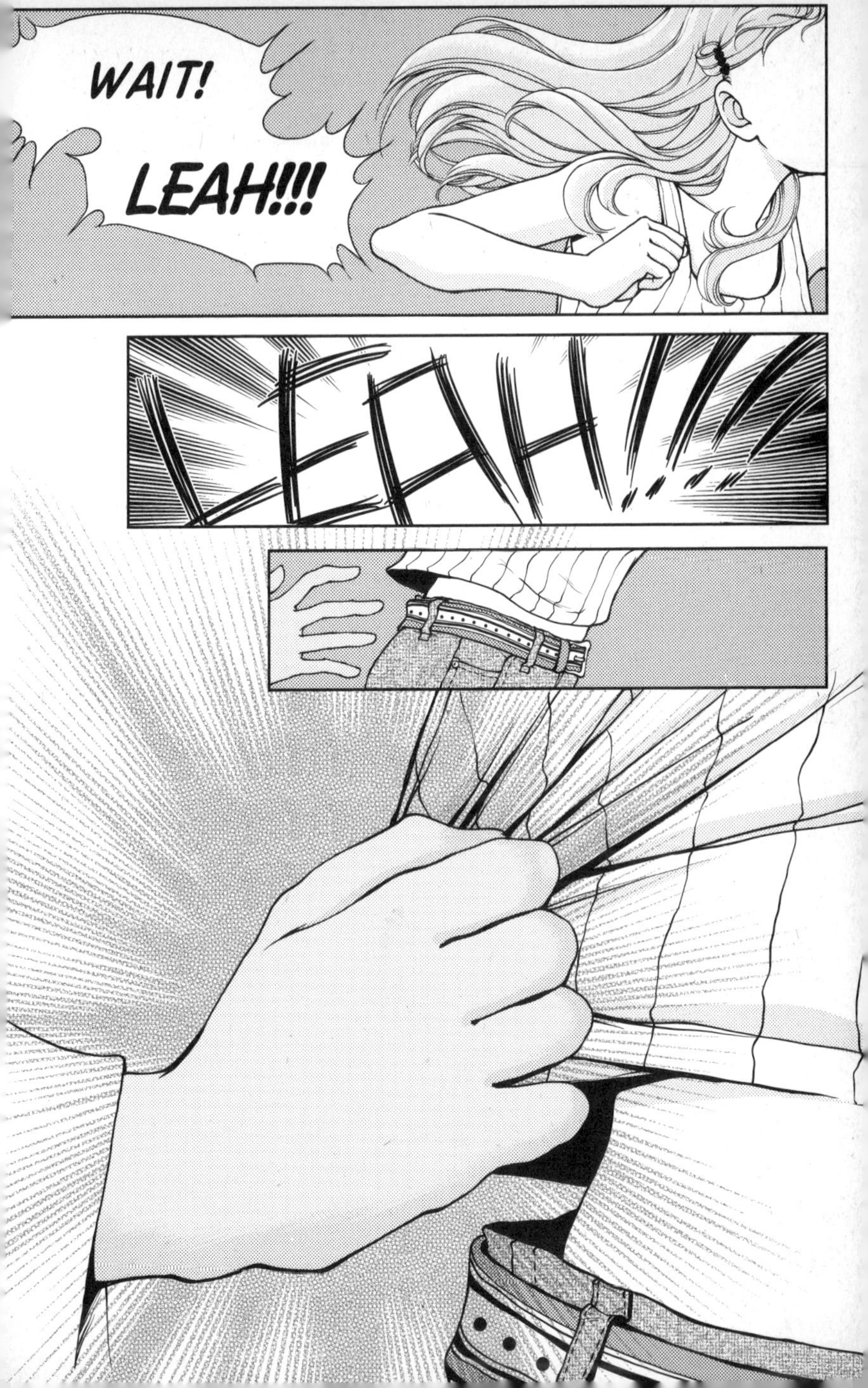
WAIT!
LEAH!!!
LEEAH!!!...

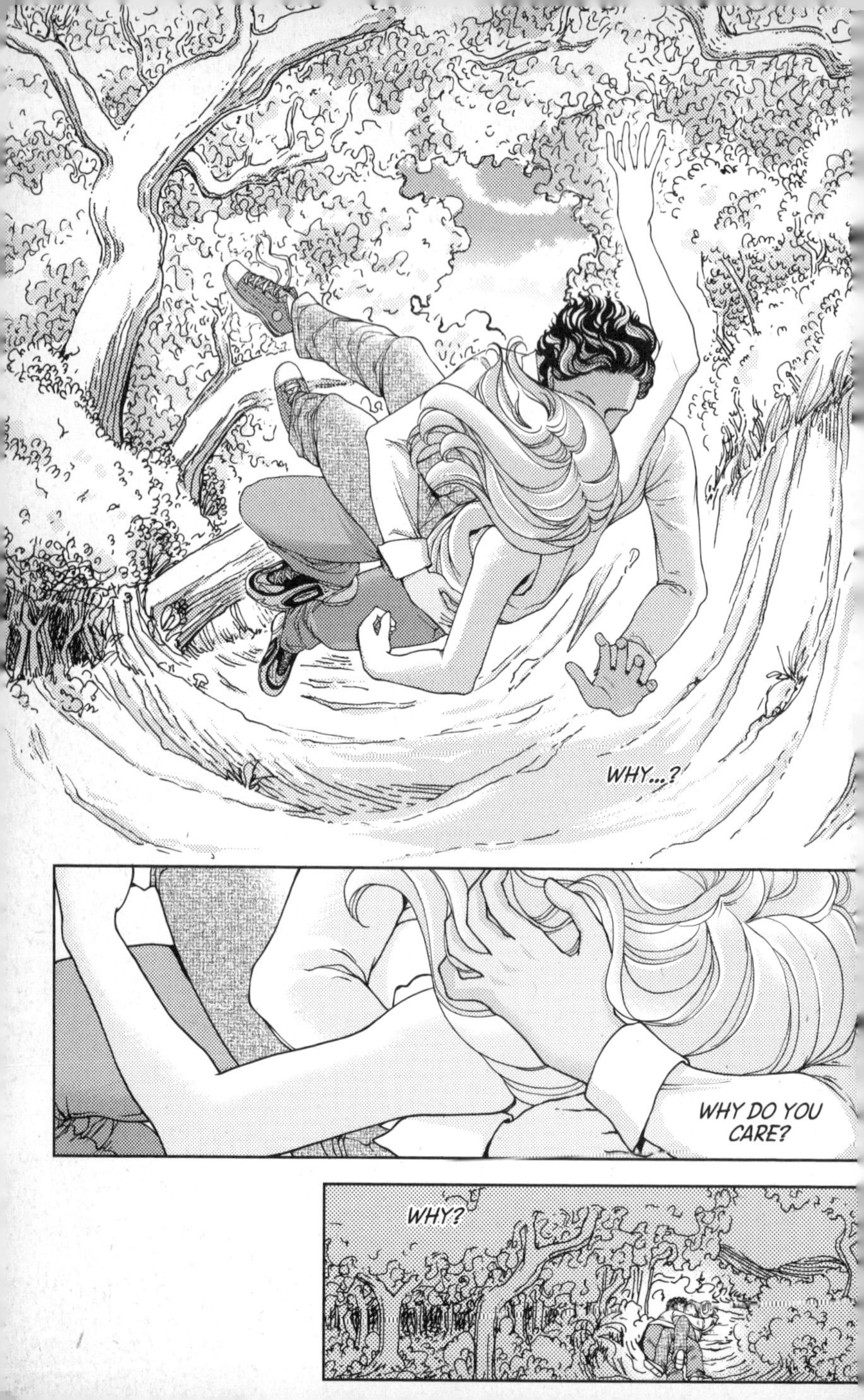
WHY...?
WHY DO YOU CARE?
WHY?

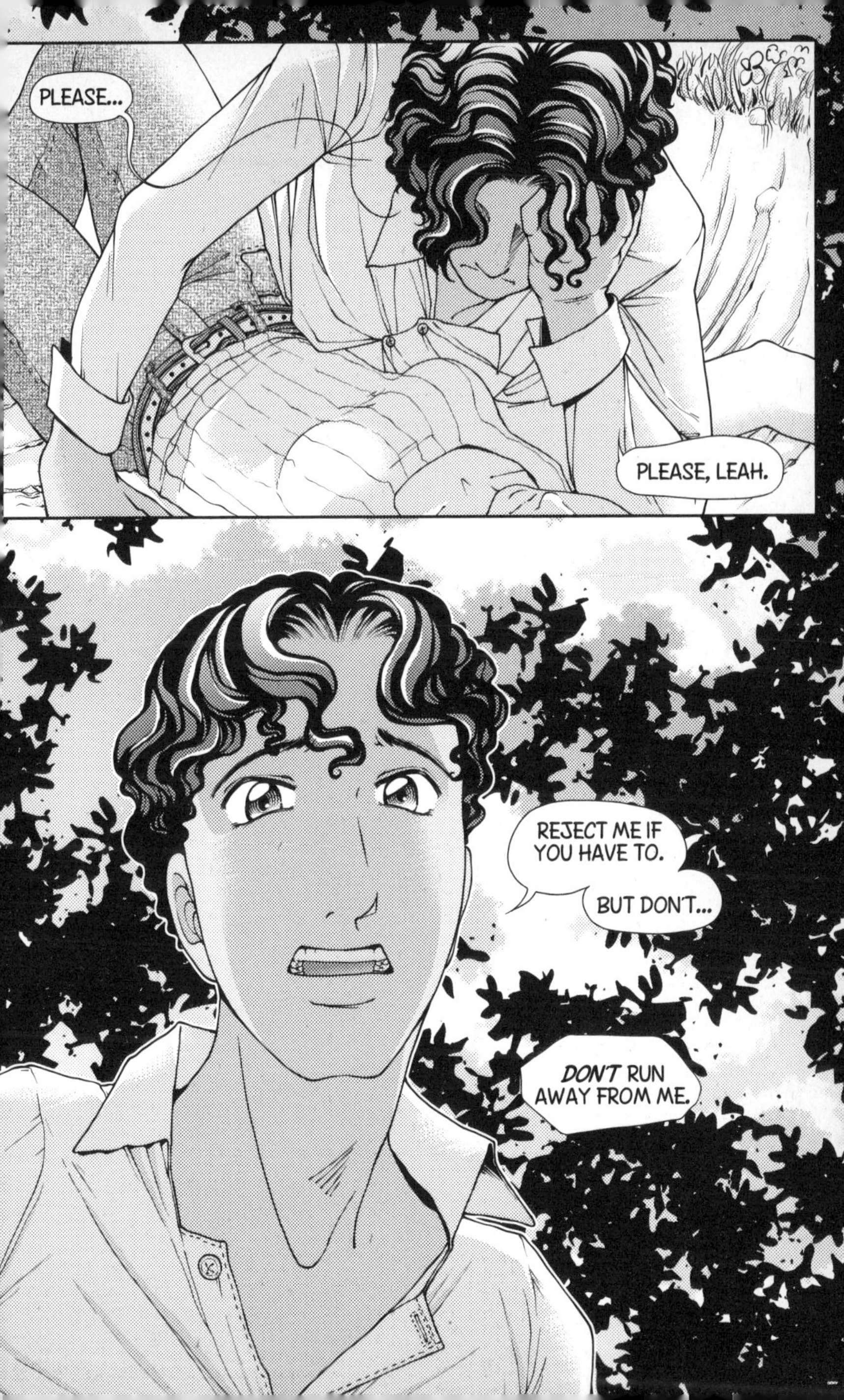
PLEASE...
PLEASE, LEAH.
REJECT ME IF YOU HAVE TO.
BUT DON'T...
*DON'T* RUN AWAY FROM ME.

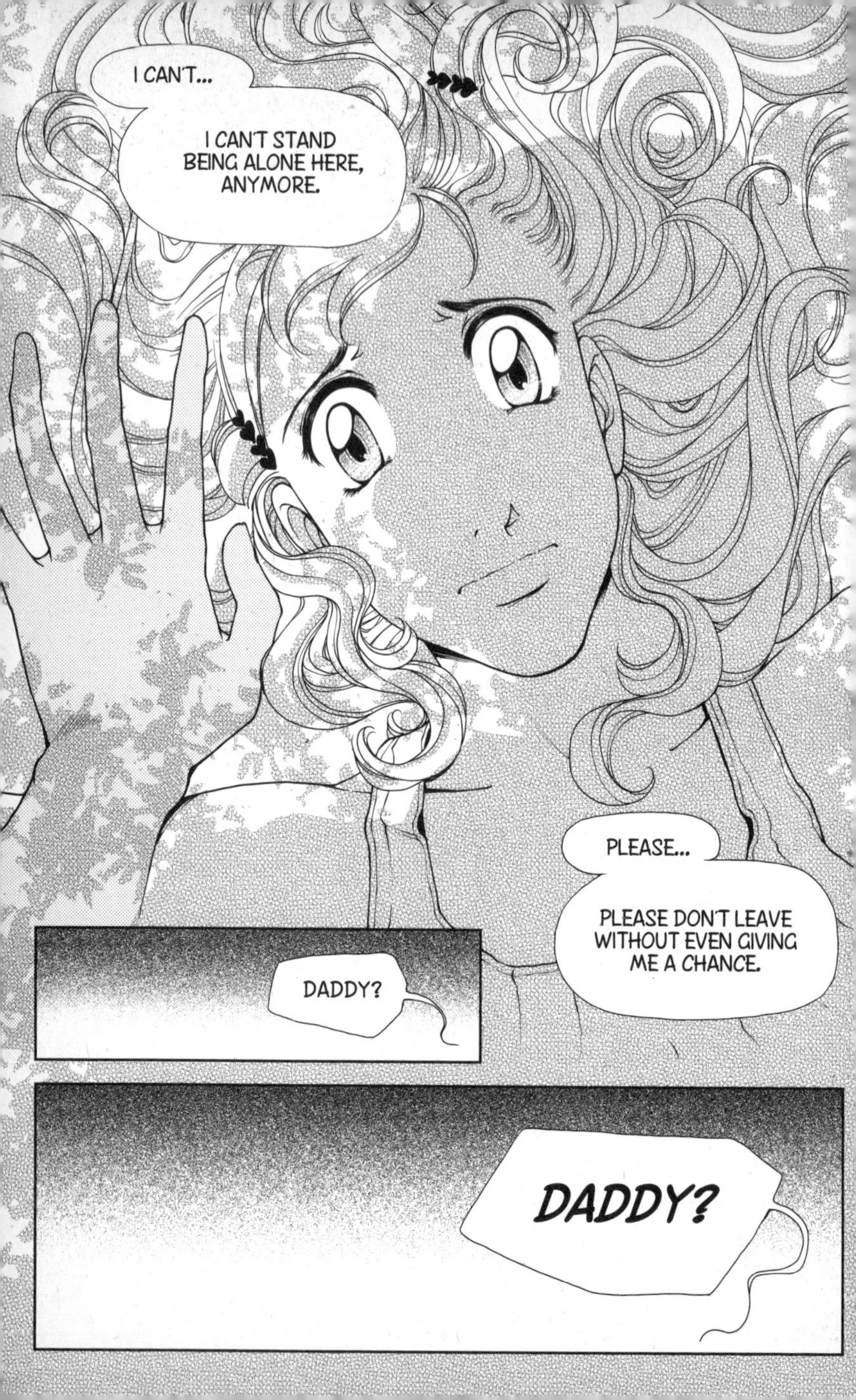
I CAN'T...
I CAN'T STAND BEING ALONE HERE, ANYMORE.
PLEASE...
PLEASE DON'T LEAVE WITHOUT EVEN GIVING ME A CHANCE.
DADDY?
DADDY?

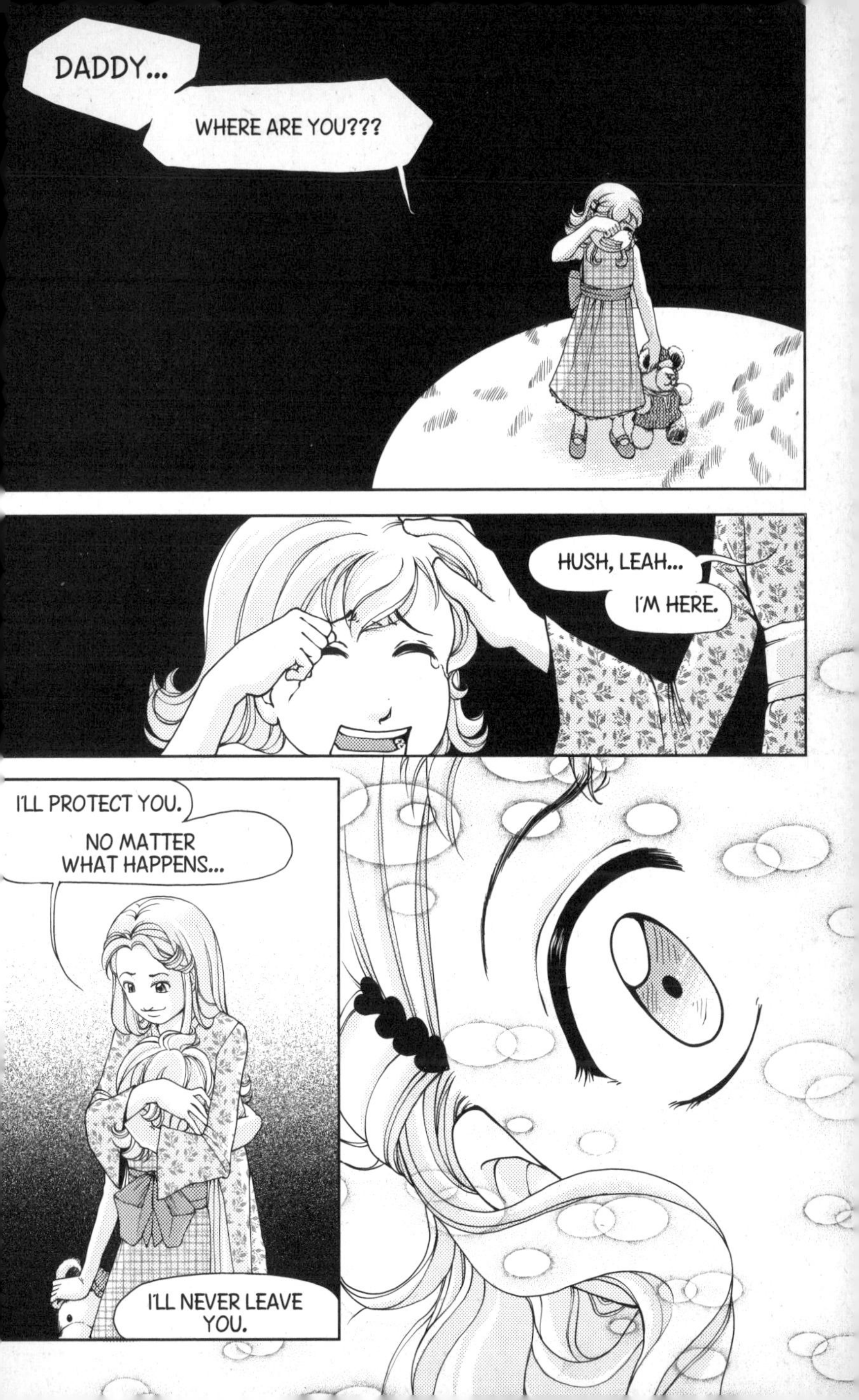
DADDY...
WHERE ARE YOU???
HUSH, LEAH...
I'M HERE.
I'LL PROTECT YOU.
NO MATTER WHAT HAPPENS...
I'LL NEVER LEAVE YOU.

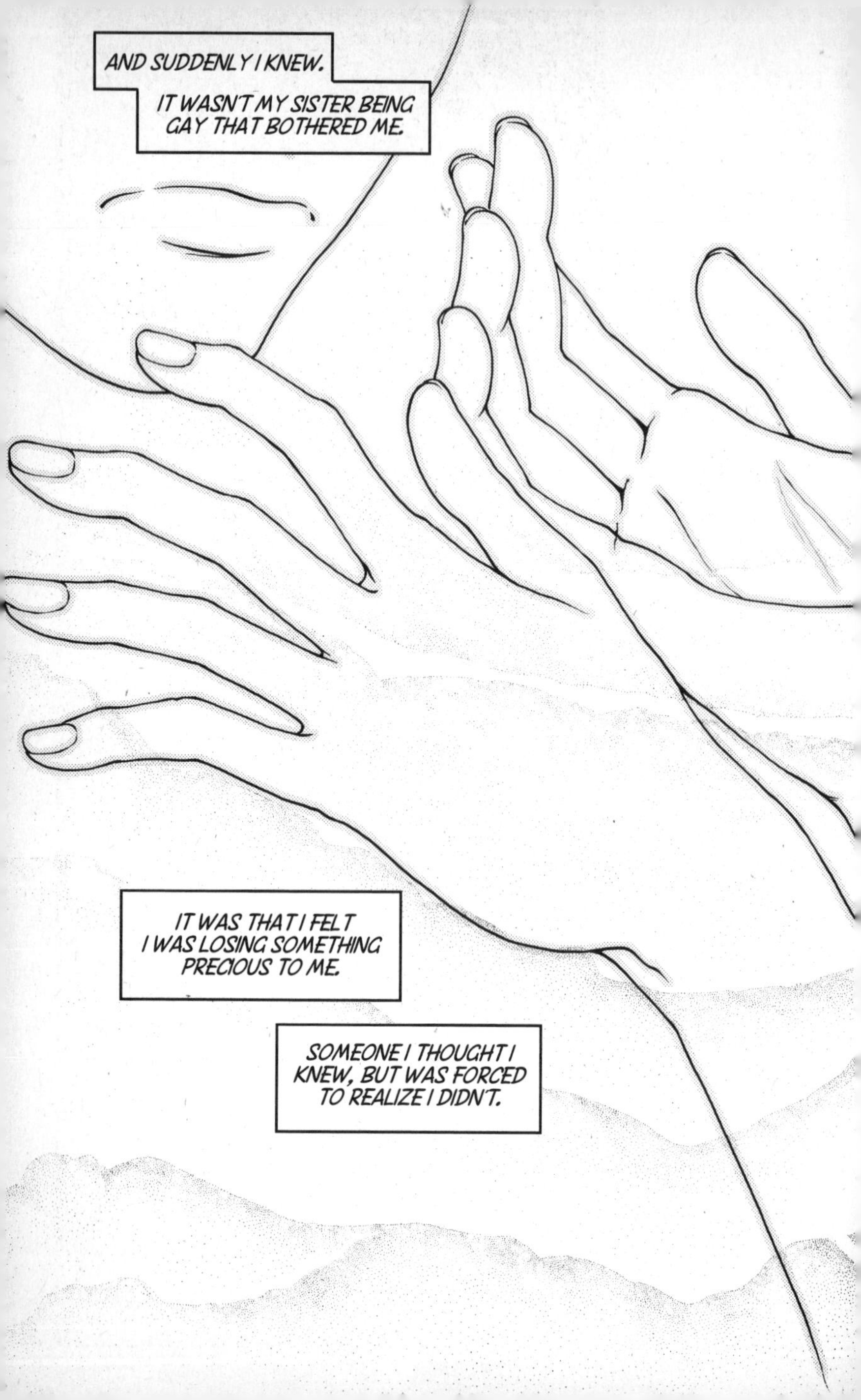
AND SUDDENLY I KNEW.
IT WASN'T MY SISTER BEING GAY THAT BOTHERED ME.
IT WAS THAT I FELT I WAS LOSING SOMETHING PRECIOUS TO ME.
SOMEONE I THOUGHT I KNEW, BUT WAS FORCED TO REALIZE I DIDN'T.

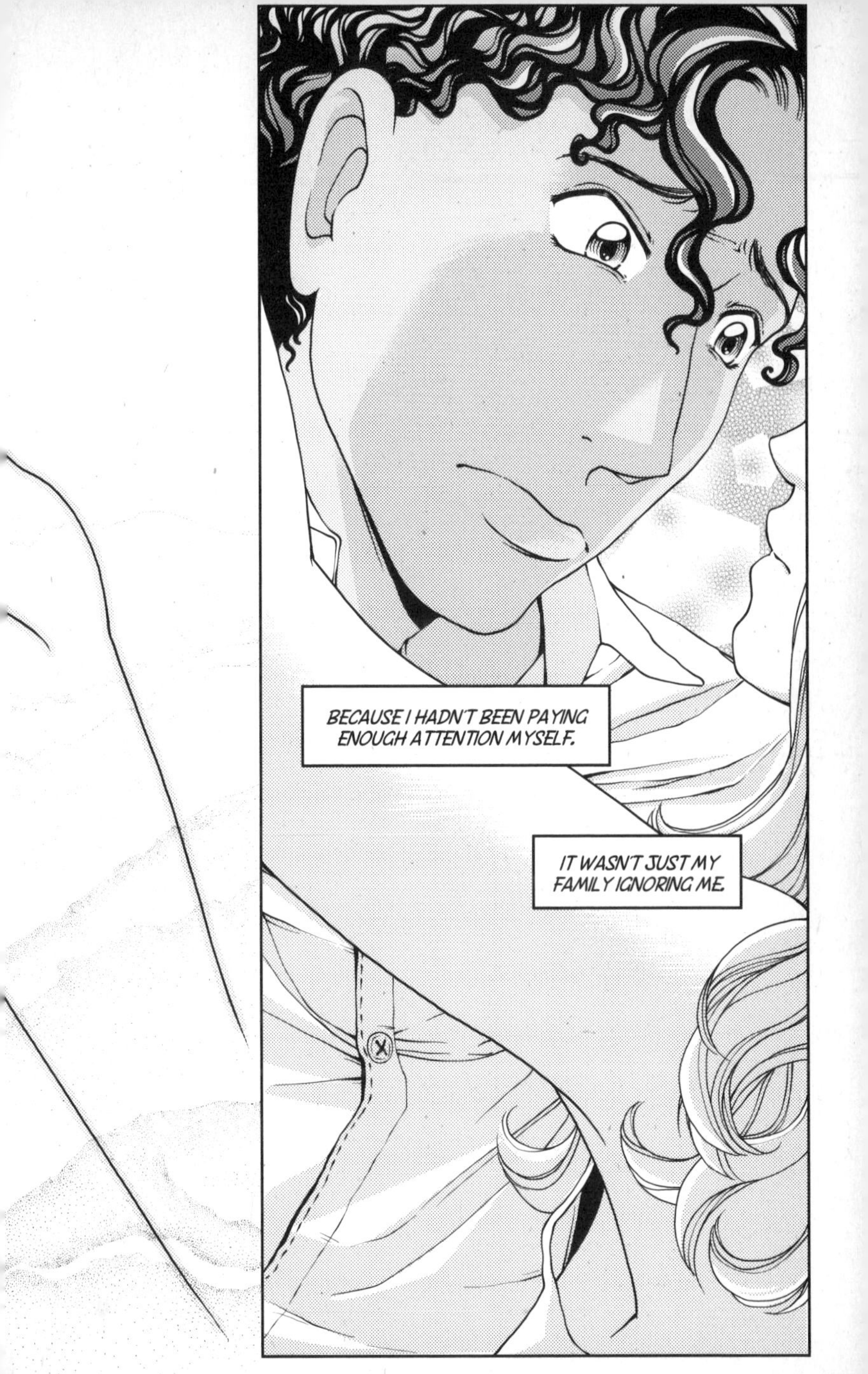
BECAUSE I HADN'T BEEN PAYING ENOUGH ATTENTION MYSELF.
IT WASN'T JUST MY FAMILY IGNORING ME.

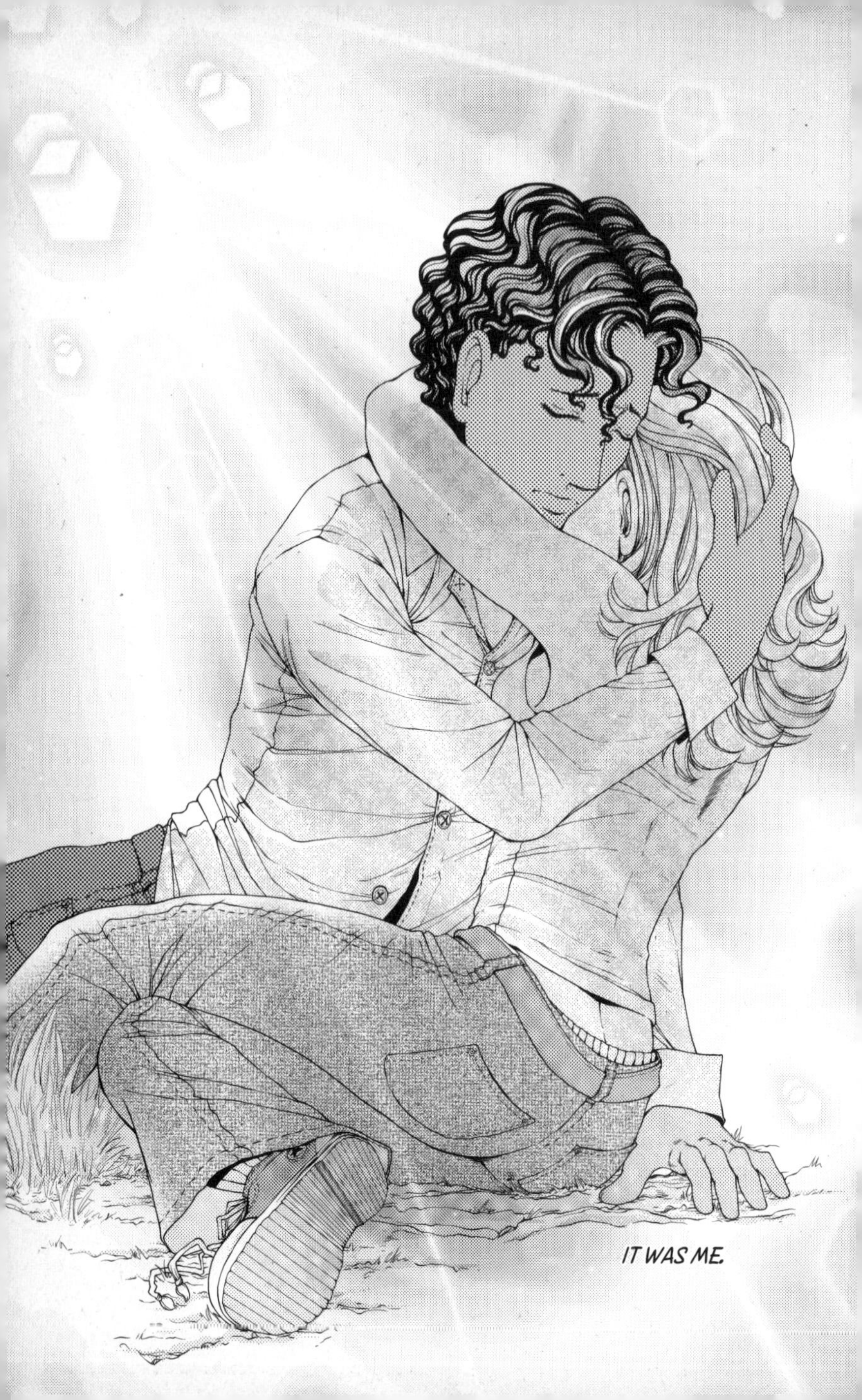
IT WAS ME.

END VOLUME 2

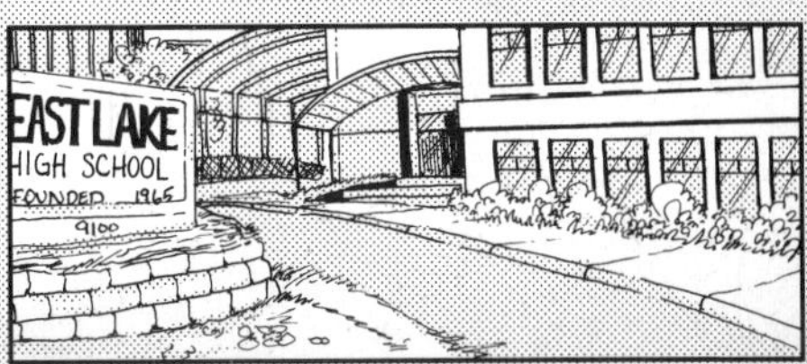
EAST LAKE
HIGH SCHOOL
FOUNDED 1965
9100

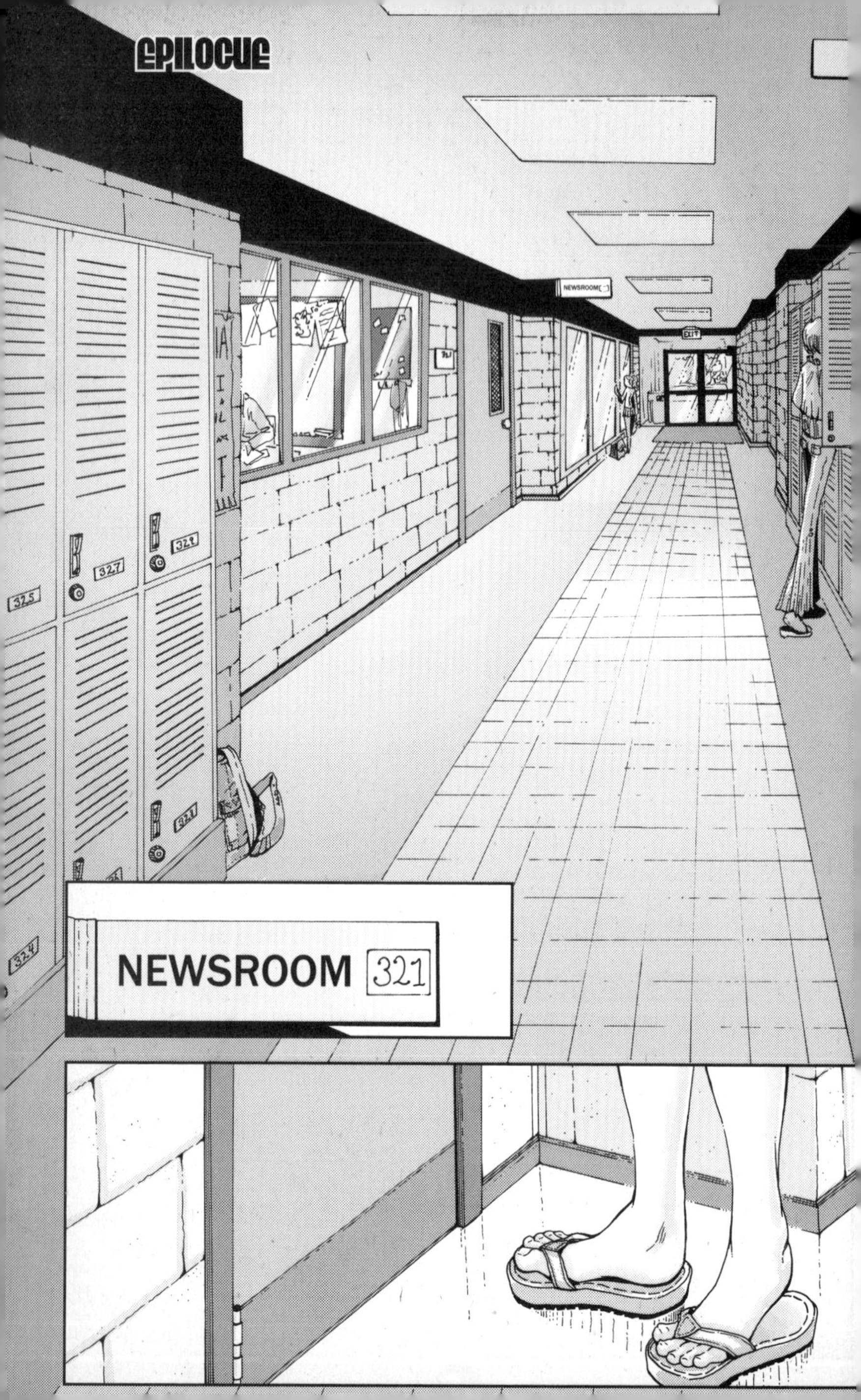
EPILOGUE
NEWSROOM 321
EXIT
NEWSROOM 321

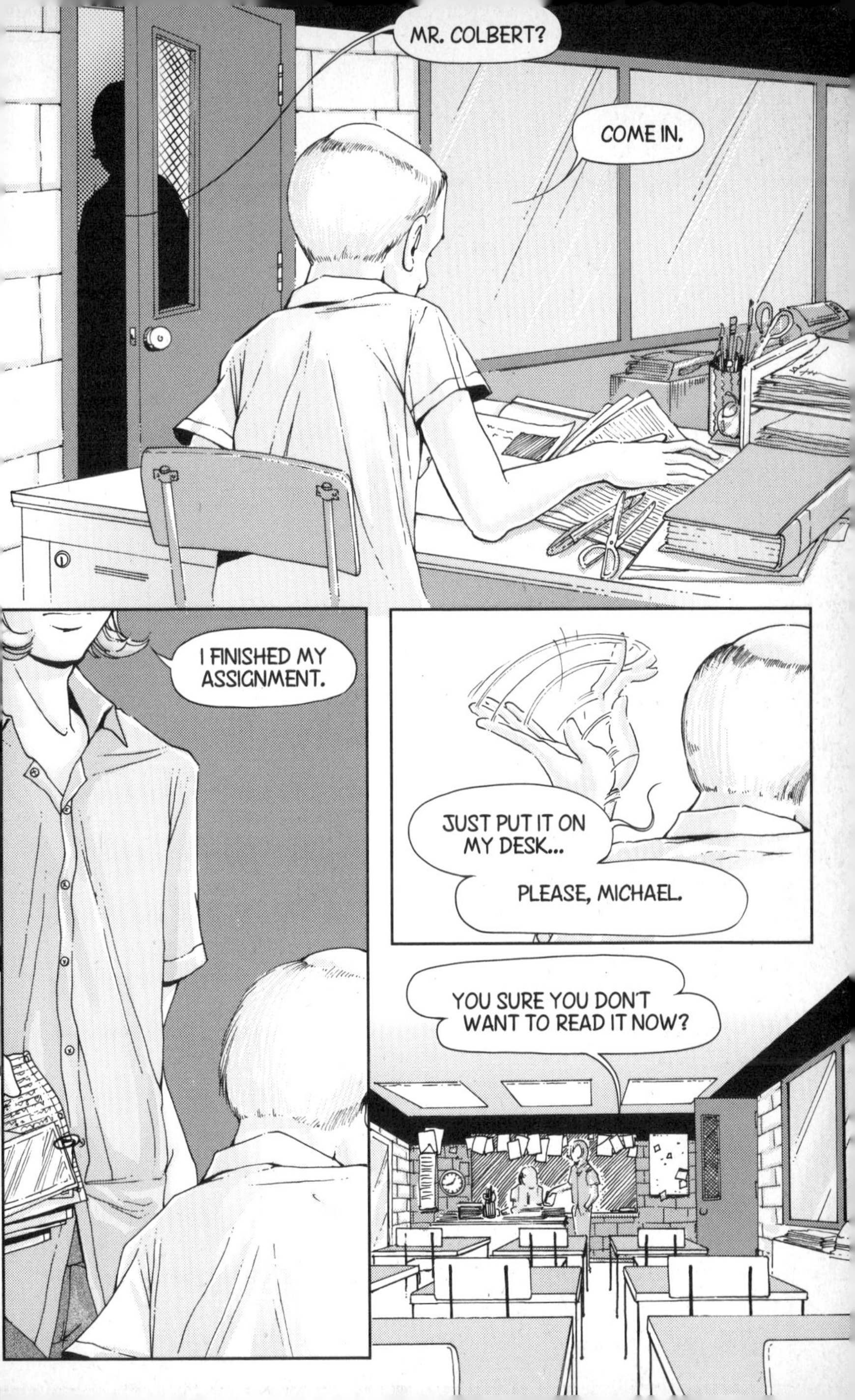
MR. COLBERT?
COME IN.
I FINISHED MY ASSIGNMENT.
JUST PUT IT ON MY DESK...
PLEASE, MICHAEL.
YOU SURE YOU DON'T WANT TO READ IT NOW?

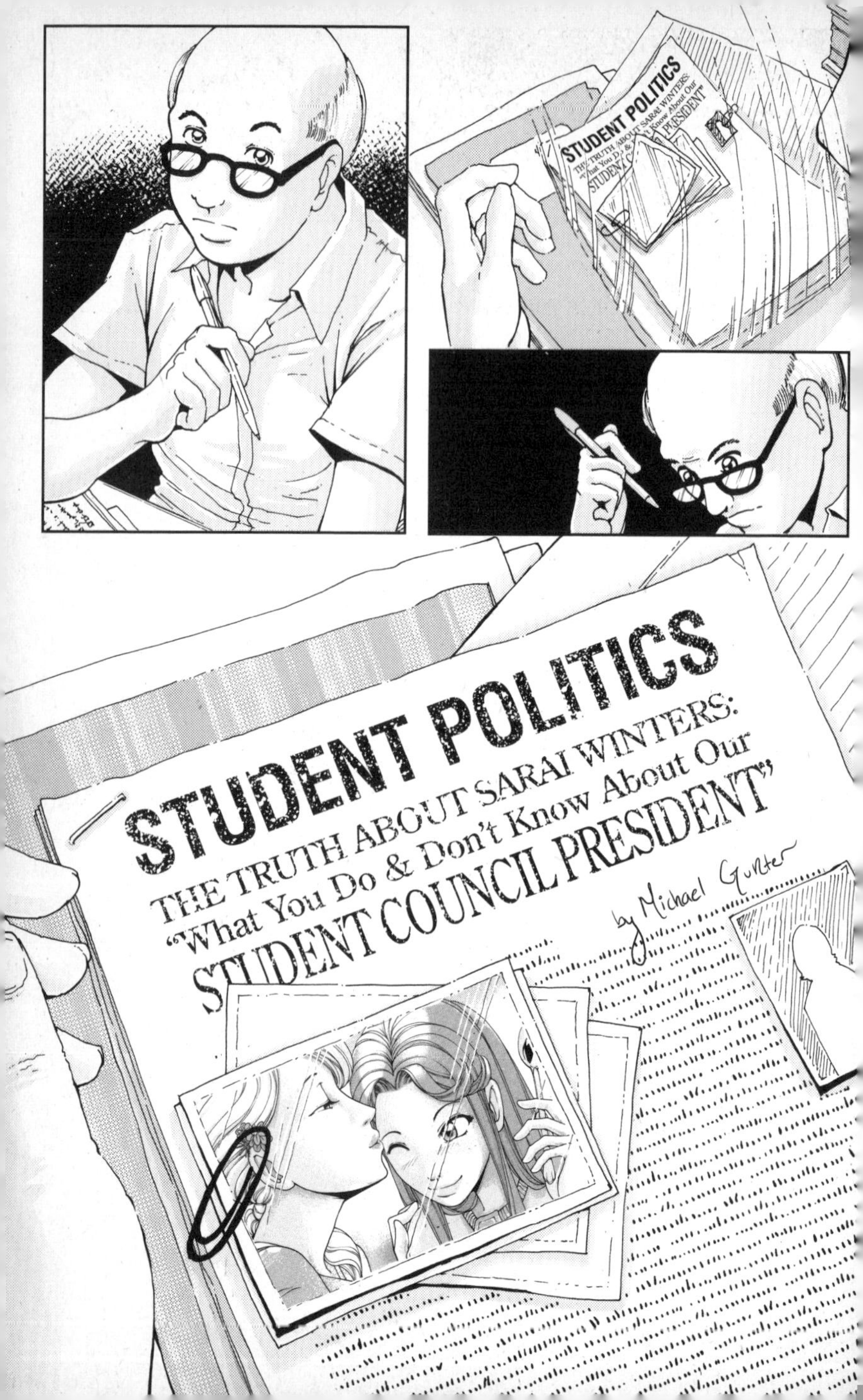
STUDENT POLITICS
THE TRUTH ABOUT SARAI WINTERS:
"What You Do & Don't Know About Our
STUDENT COUNCIL PRESIDENT"
by Michael Gunter

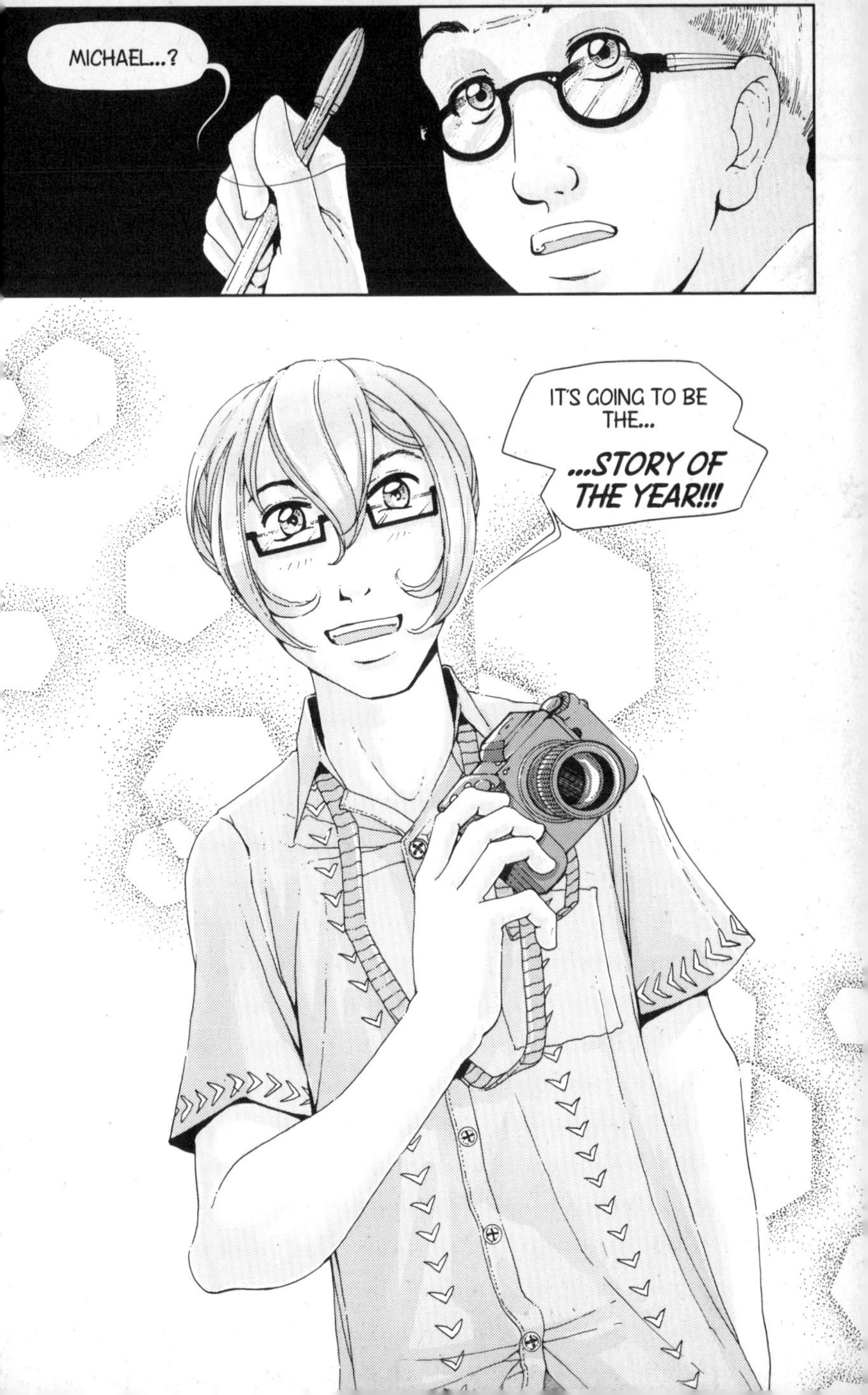
MICHAEL...?
IT'S GOING TO BE THE...
...STORY OF THE YEAR!!!

Dear Me,                              September 6th

What is love? I mean... why do people fall in love? Sometimes it seems like it just messes up people's lives. I think it's stupid, all the girls I see who obsess over their boyfriends and then fall apart when they break up. It all seems so pointless.

I've decided I'm not going to even date until college. All the boys at school are pretty much idiots, and I don't get going out with someone just because they're cute. There's so many better things to do, and it seems like when two people fall in love, they completely forget about those things. Then again maybe that's because it's infatuation and not love? Dad says you know it's the right kind of love when you feel like the one you're with makes you a better person (and vice versa).

I wonder if I'll know it when I see it or if I'll be just as stupid about it as all the other girls in the world?

# IN THE NEXT VOLUME OF

# STEADY BEAT™

SARAI ALWAYS LIVED UP TO OTHERS' EXPECTATIONS--YET SHE'S OVERLOOKED THE SINGLE MOST IMPORTANT THING OF ALL...HERSELF. WHAT DO YOU DO WHEN BEING YOUR-SELF MEANS DISAPPOINTING YOUR COMMUNITY, YOUR CHURCH AND EVEN YOUR FAMILY? YET SARAI MAY HAVE THAT ANSWERED FOR HER. WHEN A SCHOOL NEWSPAPER ARTICLE UNEXPECTEDLY FORCES HER OUT OF THE CLOSET, SHE'S FACED WITH THE DECISION TO EITHER ACCEPT WHO SHE IS OR DENY EVERYTHING TO THE PEOPLE SHE CHER-ISHES MOST.

VOLUME THREE OF *STEADY BEAT* CONTINUES THE STORY OF TWO SISTERS AND THEIR SEARCH FOR TOLERANCE, AC-CEPTANCE AND LOVE IN THE MIDST OF THE SOUTHERN MINDSET.

IT'S A TALE OF SELF-DISCOVERY AND OF THE REALIZATION THAT THE REACTIONS OF OTHERS AREN'T ALWAYS WHAT WE QUITE EXPECT.

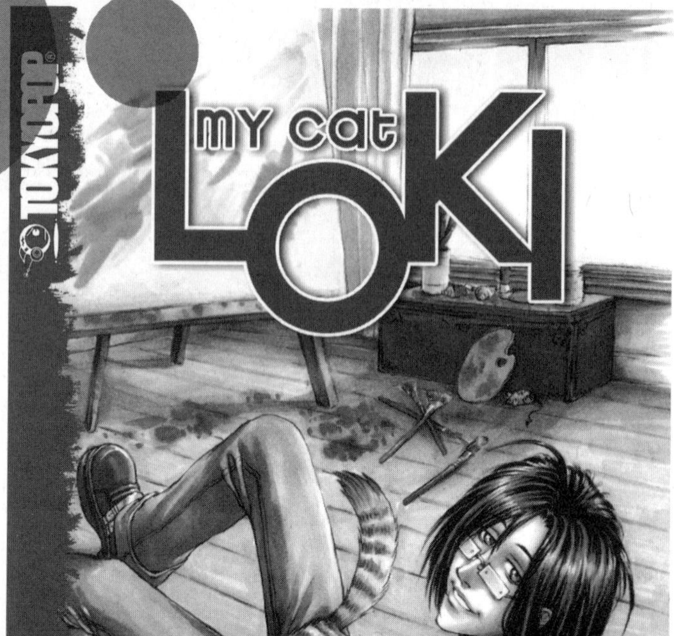
TOKYOPOP
MY CAT LOKI
BETTINA KURKOSKI
1

# And now, an exciting first look at a new manga from TOKYOPOP...

As a child, Ameya had always considered his cat more a sibling than a pet. As the years went by, their bond grew ever tighter. But the day his feline "brother" died was the day Ameya withdrew from the world.

Several years later, Ameya encounters a drenched stray cat in the park. Little does he know what fate has in store for him...

Beautifully rendered and hauntingly crafted, Bettina Kurkoski's heartwarming story will touch everyone who's grown up with a furry friend.

## Available Now!

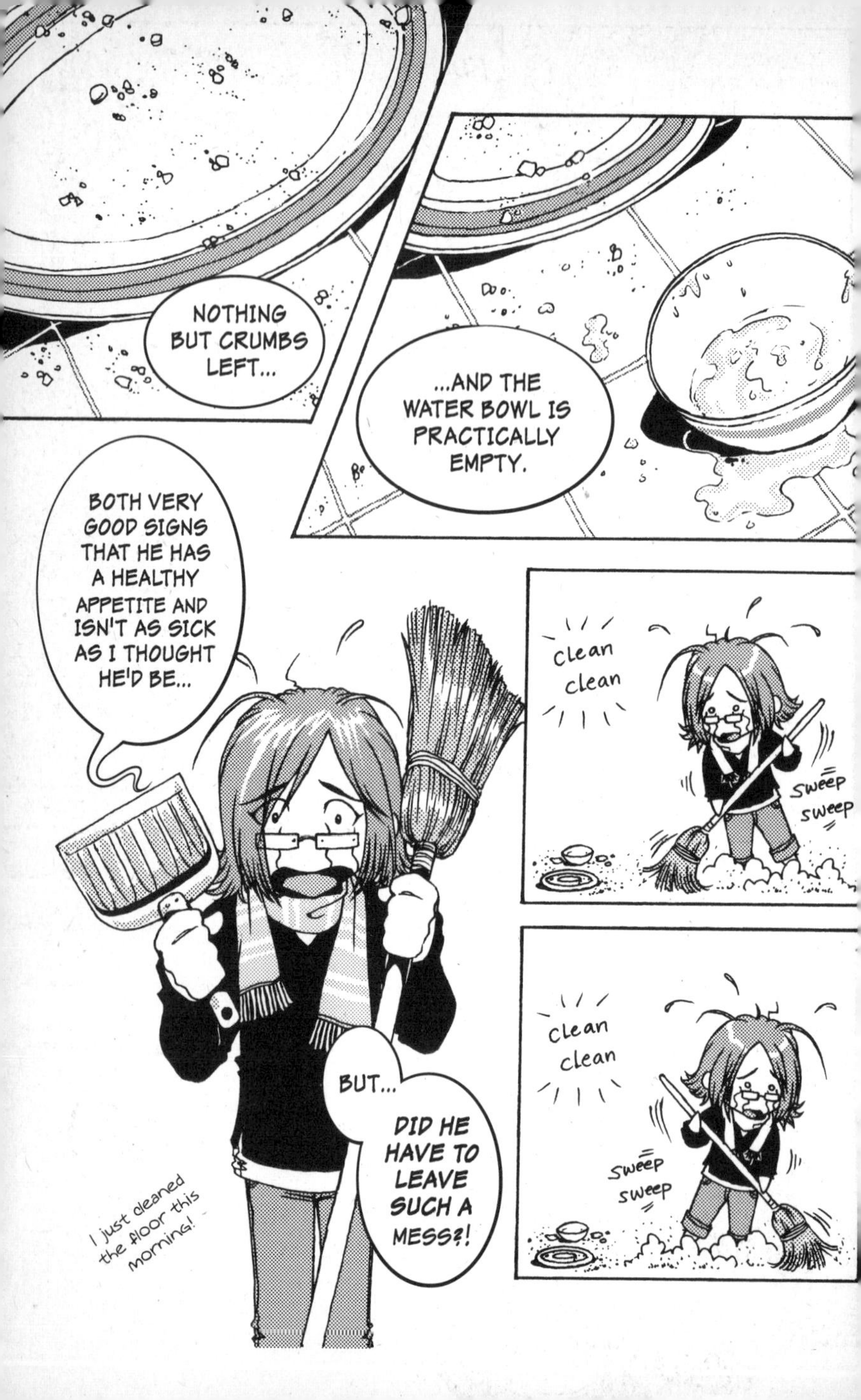
NOTHING BUT CRUMBS LEFT...
...AND THE WATER BOWL IS PRACTICALLY EMPTY.
BOTH VERY GOOD SIGNS THAT HE HAS A HEALTHY APPETITE AND ISN'T AS SICK AS I THOUGHT HE'D BE...
BUT...
DID HE HAVE TO LEAVE SUCH A MESS?!
I just cleaned the floor this morning!
clean clean
sweep sweep
clean clean
sweep sweep

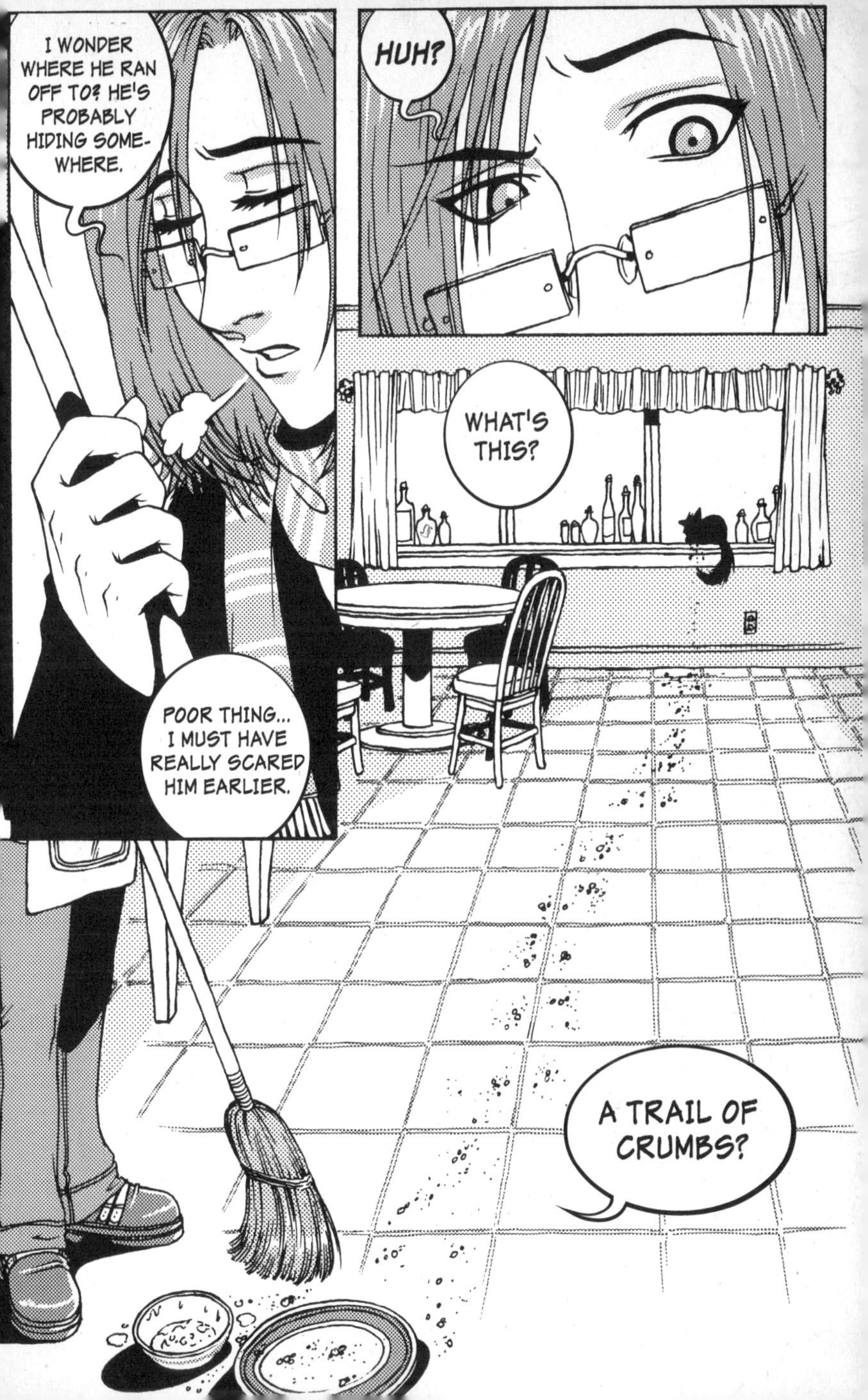
I WONDER WHERE HE RAN OFF TO? HE'S PROBABLY HIDING SOME-WHERE.
POOR THING... I MUST HAVE REALLY SCARED HIM EARLIER.
HUH?
WHAT'S THIS?
A TRAIL OF CRUMBS?

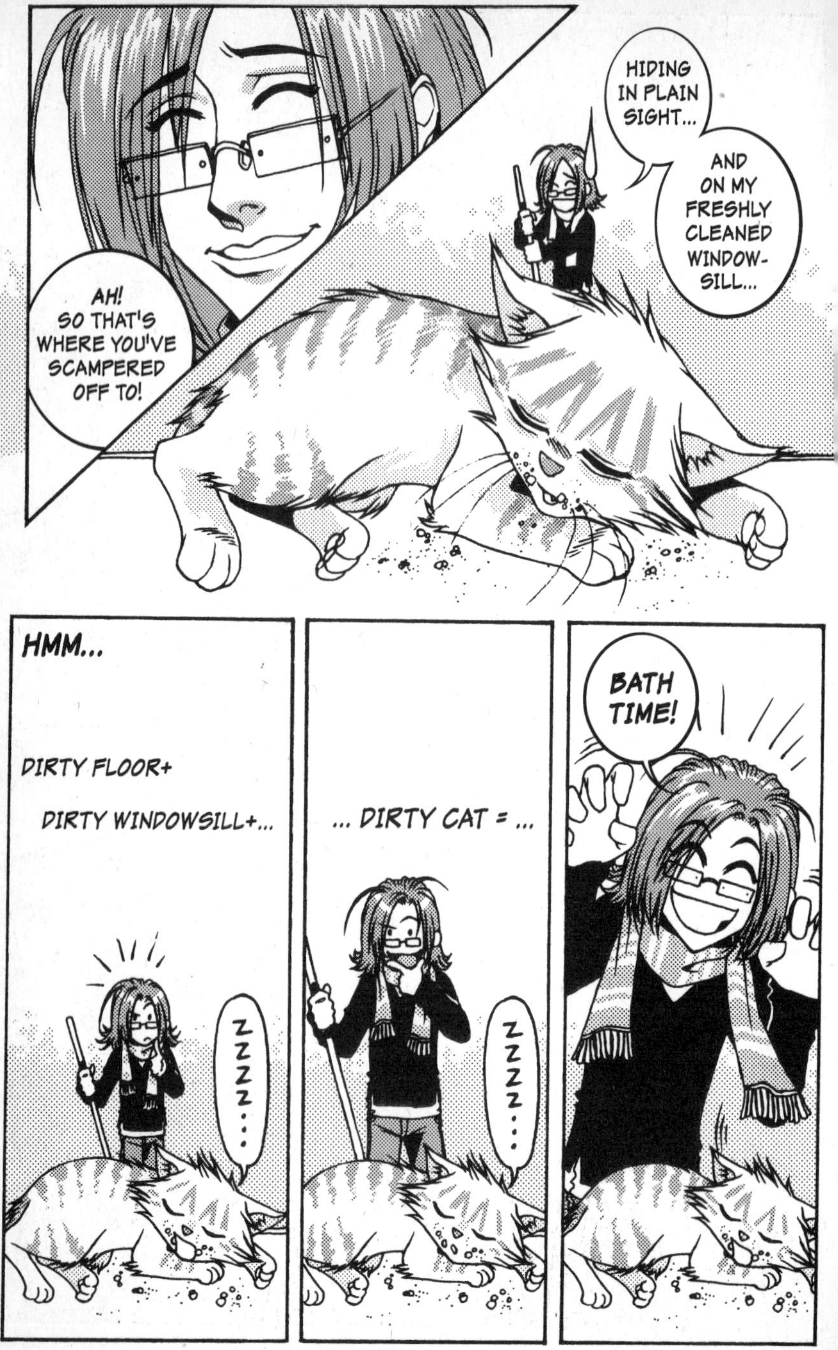
AH! SO THAT'S WHERE YOU'VE SCAMPERED OFF TO!
HIDING IN PLAIN SIGHT...
AND ON MY FRESHLY CLEANED WINDOW-SILL...
HMM...
DIRTY FLOOR+
DIRTY WINDOWSILL+...
ZZZZ...
... DIRTY CAT = ...
ZZZZ...
BATH TIME!

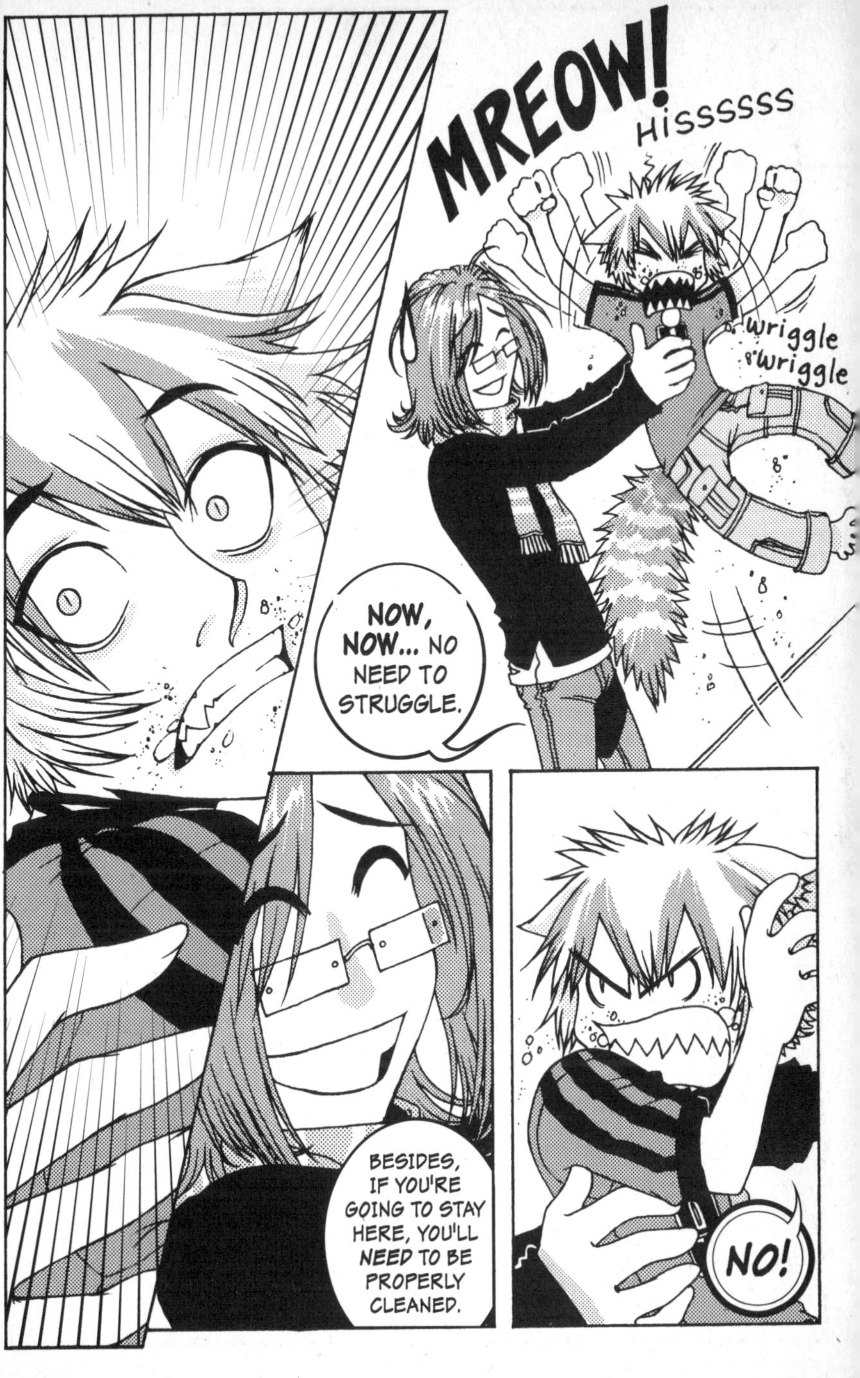
MREOW!
HISSSSSS
wriggle
wriggle
NOW, NOW... NO NEED TO STRUGGLE.
BESIDES, IF YOU'RE GOING TO STAY HERE, YOU'LL NEED TO BE PROPERLY CLEANED.
NO!

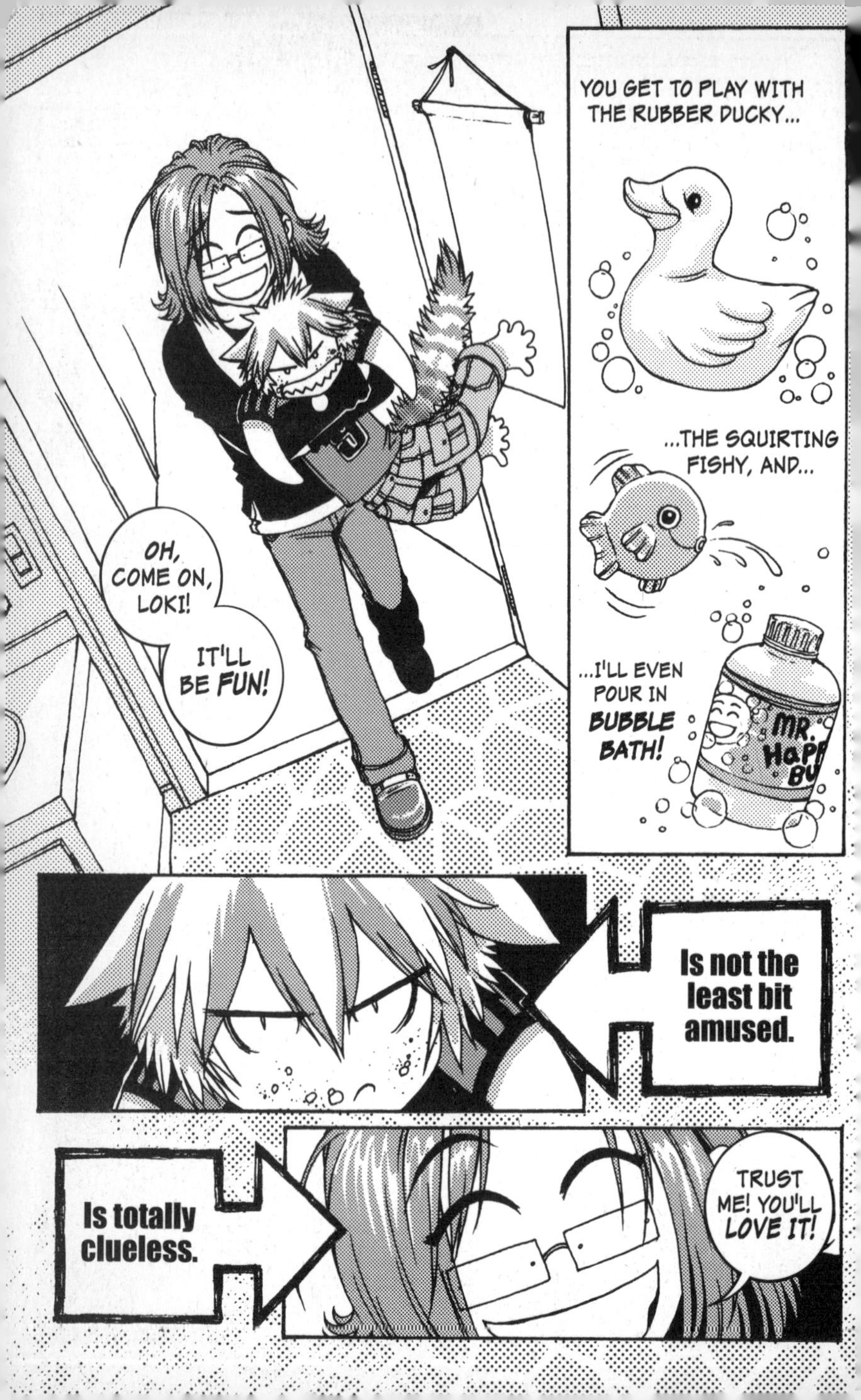

OH, COME ON, LOKI!
IT'LL BE FUN!
YOU GET TO PLAY WITH THE RUBBER DUCKY...
...THE SQUIRTING FISHY, AND...
...I'LL EVEN POUR IN BUBBLE BATH!
Is not the least bit amused.
Is totally clueless.
TRUST ME! YOU'LL LOVE IT!

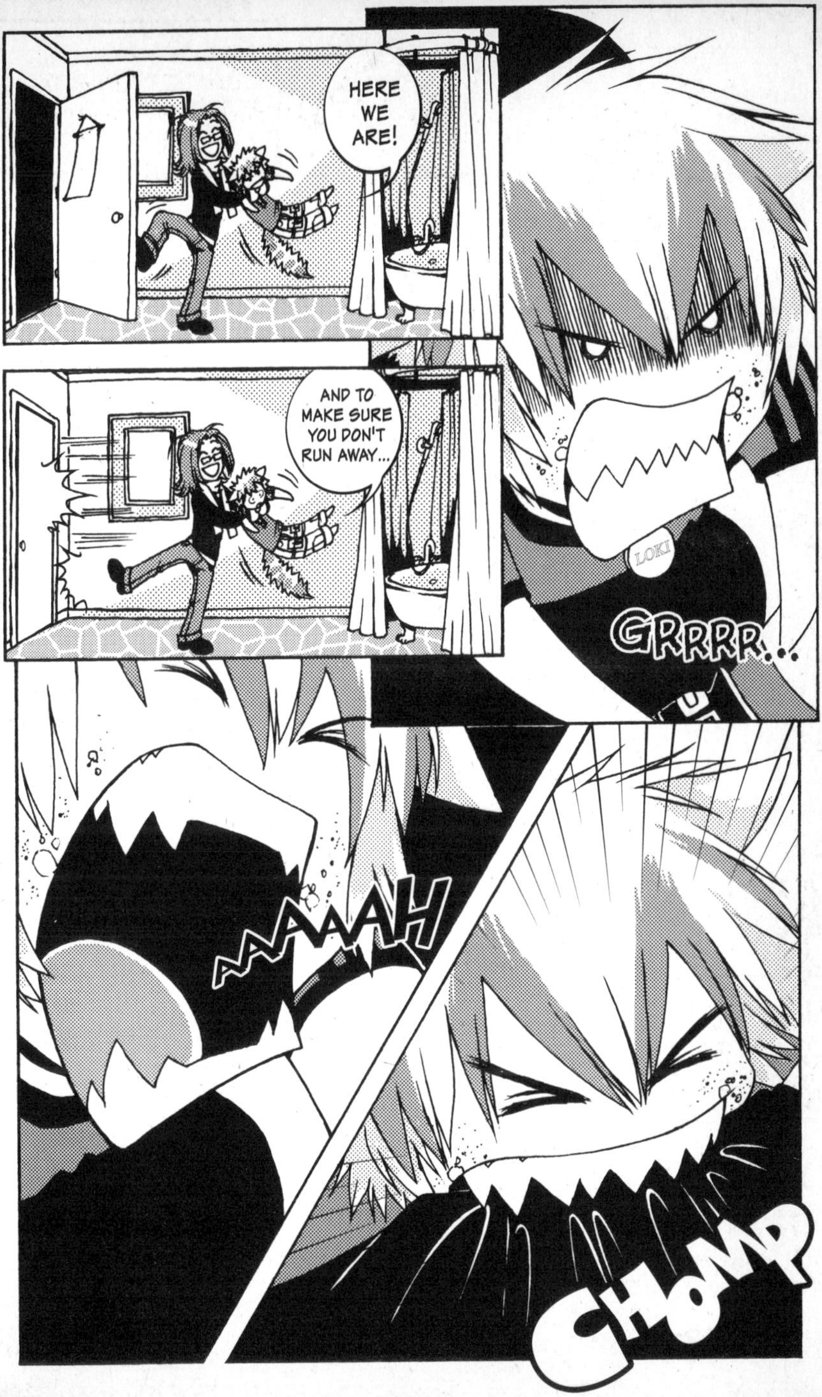
HERE WE ARE!
AND TO MAKE SURE YOU DON'T RUN AWAY...
LOKI
GRRRR...
AAAAAH
CHOMP

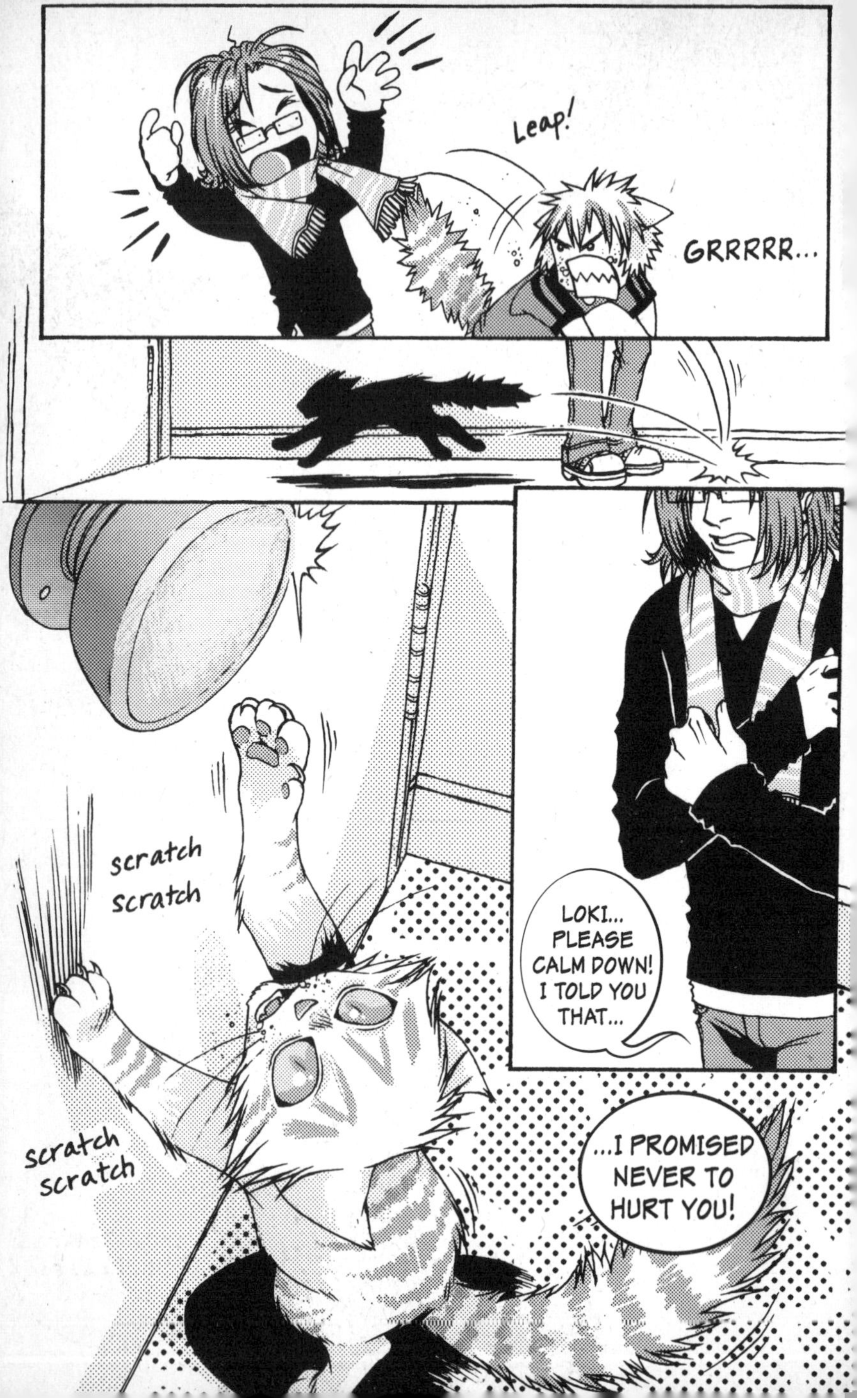
Leap!
GRRRRR...
scratch
scratch
scratch
scratch
LOKI... PLEASE CALM DOWN! I TOLD YOU THAT...
...I PROMISED NEVER TO HURT YOU!

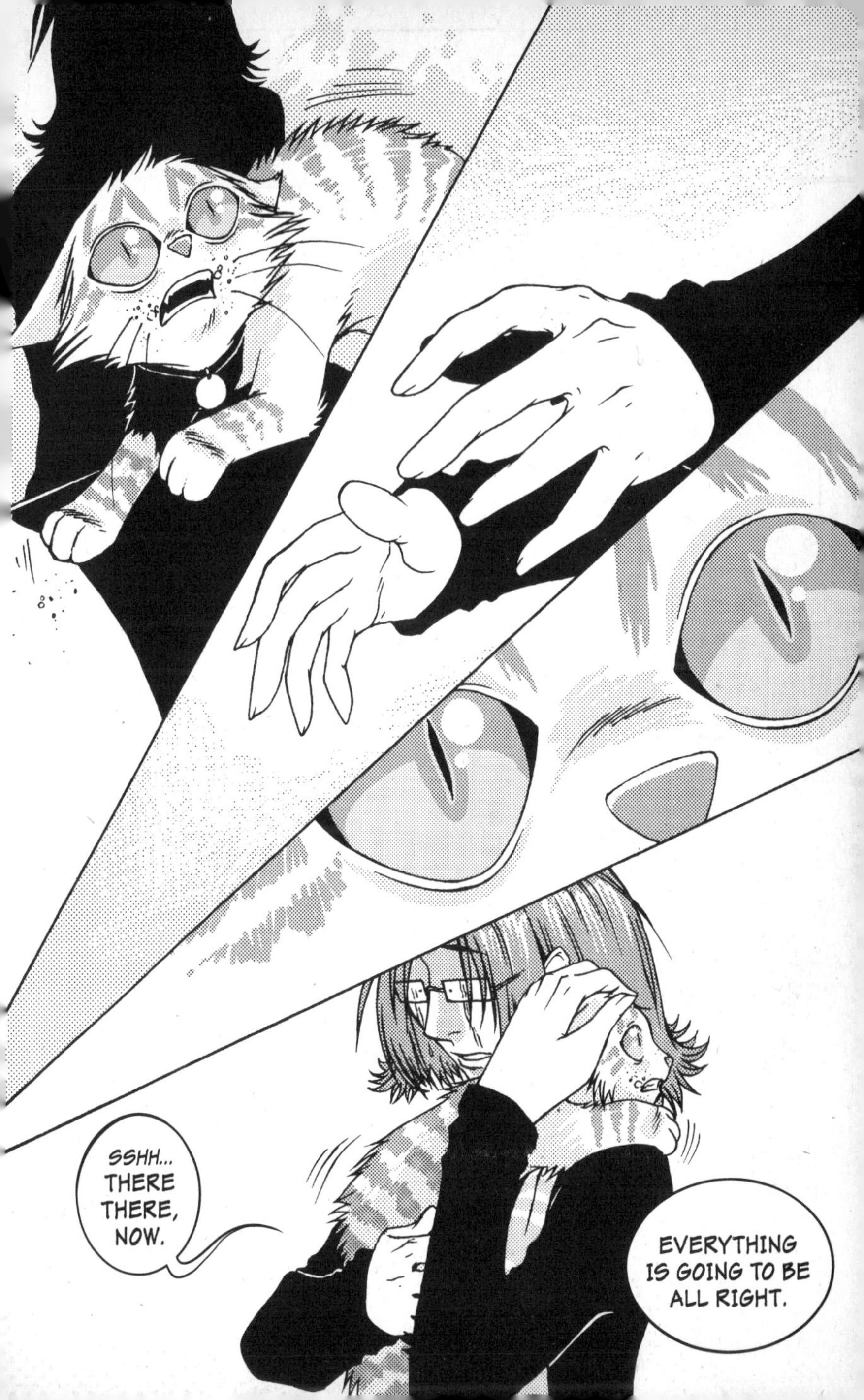
SSHH... THERE THERE, NOW.
EVERYTHING IS GOING TO BE ALL RIGHT.

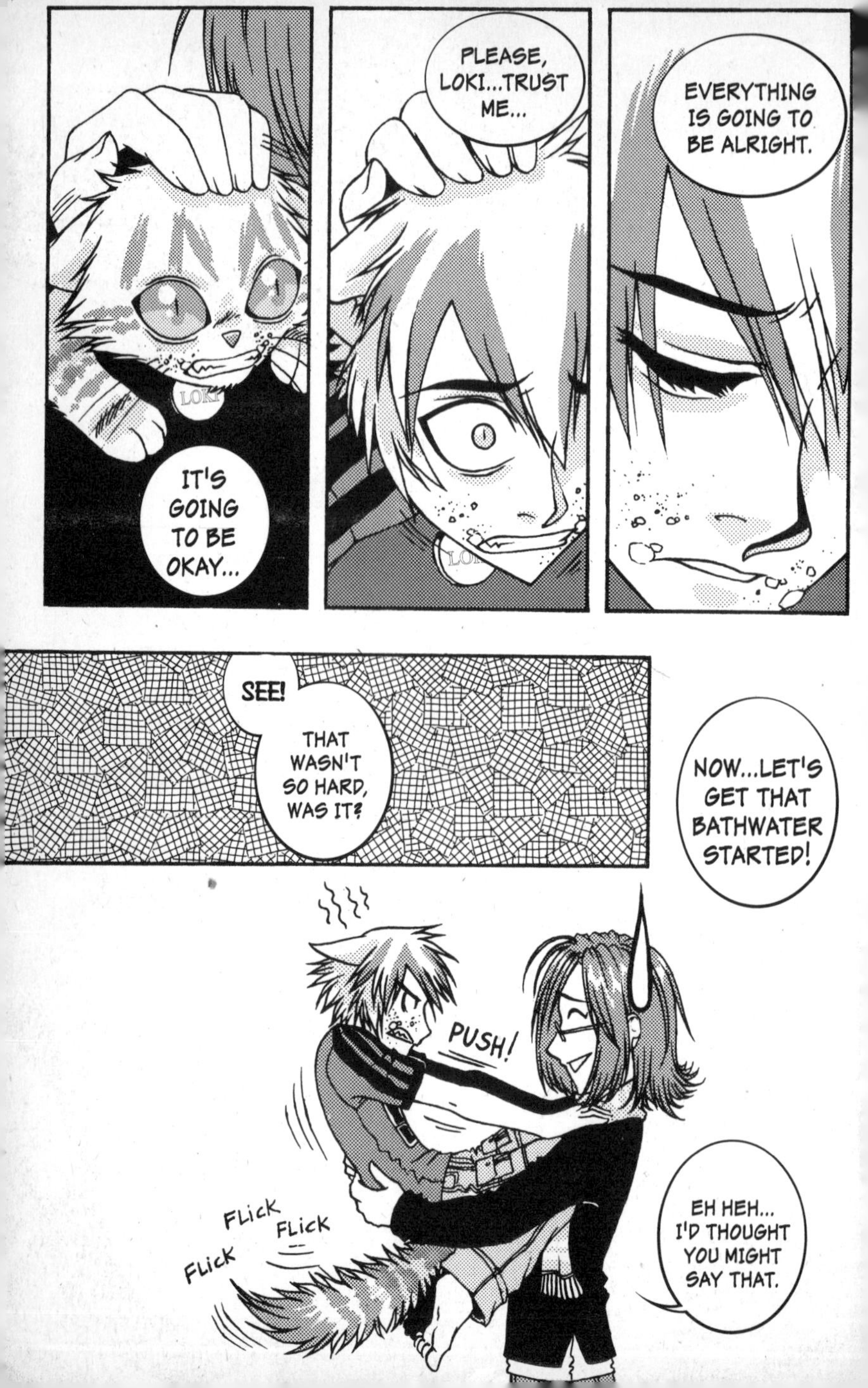
LOKI
IT'S GOING TO BE OKAY...
PLEASE, LOKI...TRUST ME...
EVERYTHING IS GOING TO BE ALRIGHT.
SEE!
THAT WASN'T SO HARD, WAS IT?
NOW...LET'S GET THAT BATHWATER STARTED!
PUSH!
FLICK
FLICK
FLICK
EH HEH... I'D THOUGHT YOU MIGHT SAY THAT.

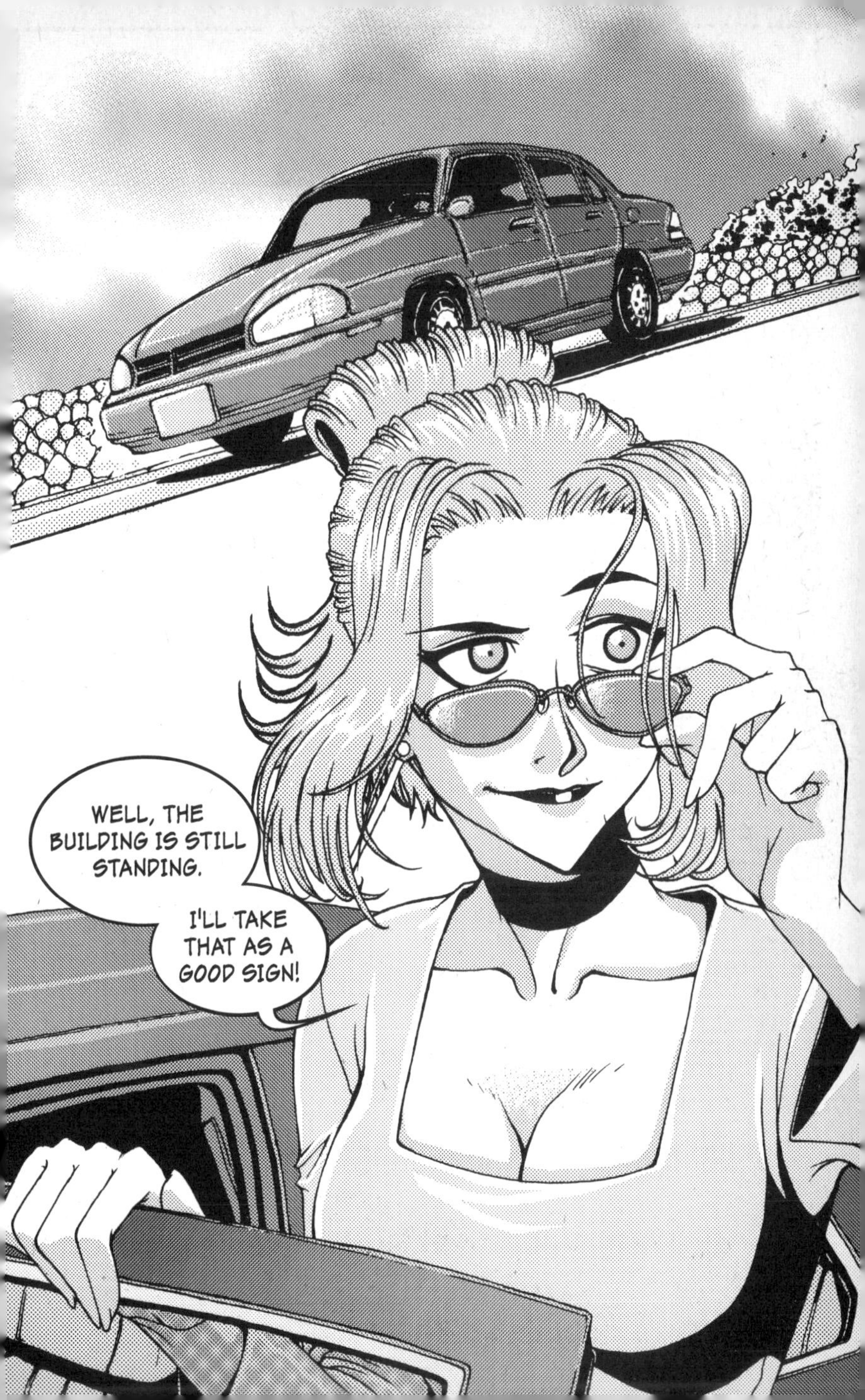
WELL, THE BUILDING IS STILL STANDING.
I'LL TAKE THAT AS A GOOD SIGN!

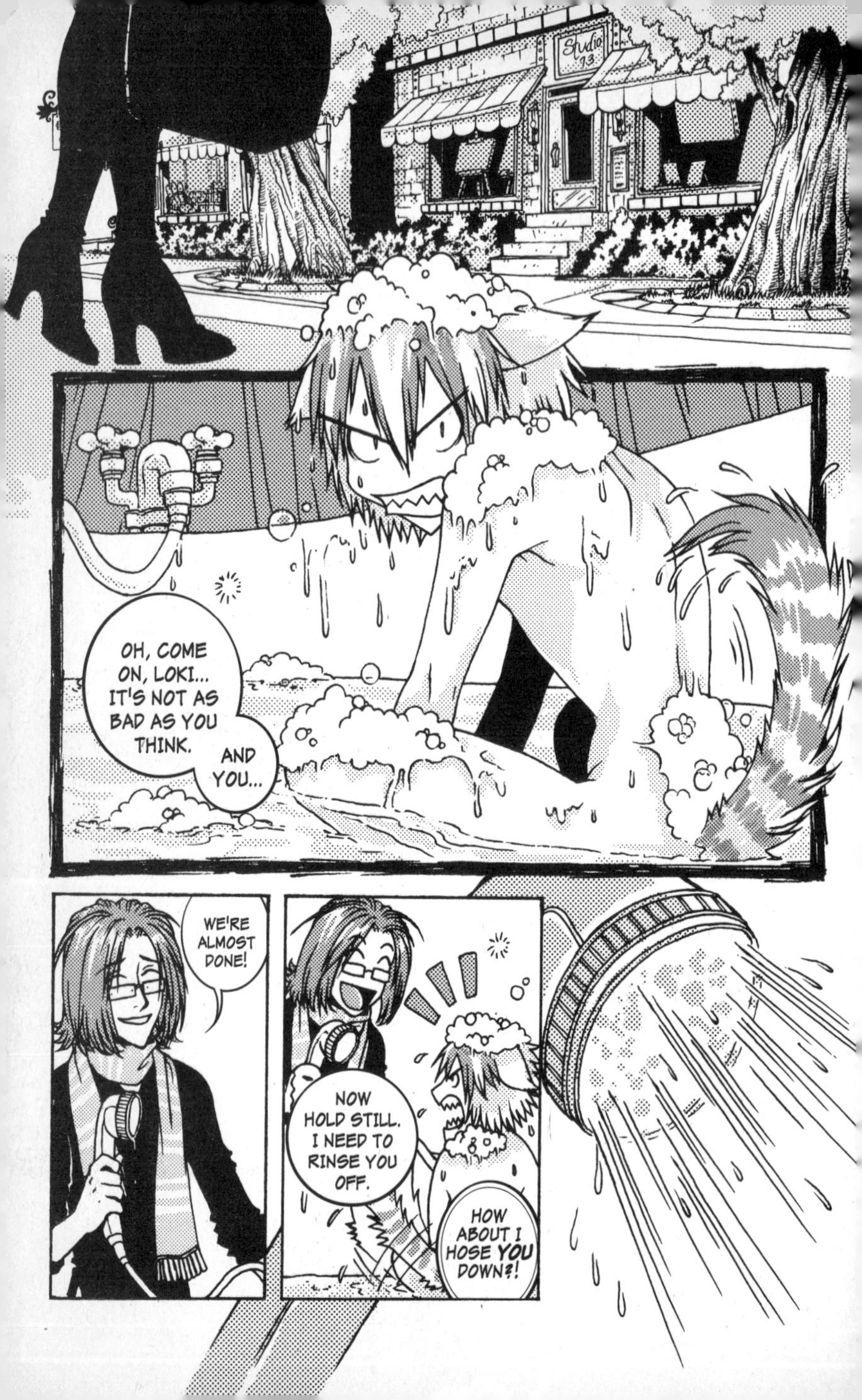
Studio 13
OH, COME ON, LOKI... IT'S NOT AS BAD AS YOU THINK.
AND YOU...
WE'RE ALMOST DONE!
NOW HOLD STILL. I NEED TO RINSE YOU OFF.
HOW ABOUT I HOSE **YOU** DOWN?!

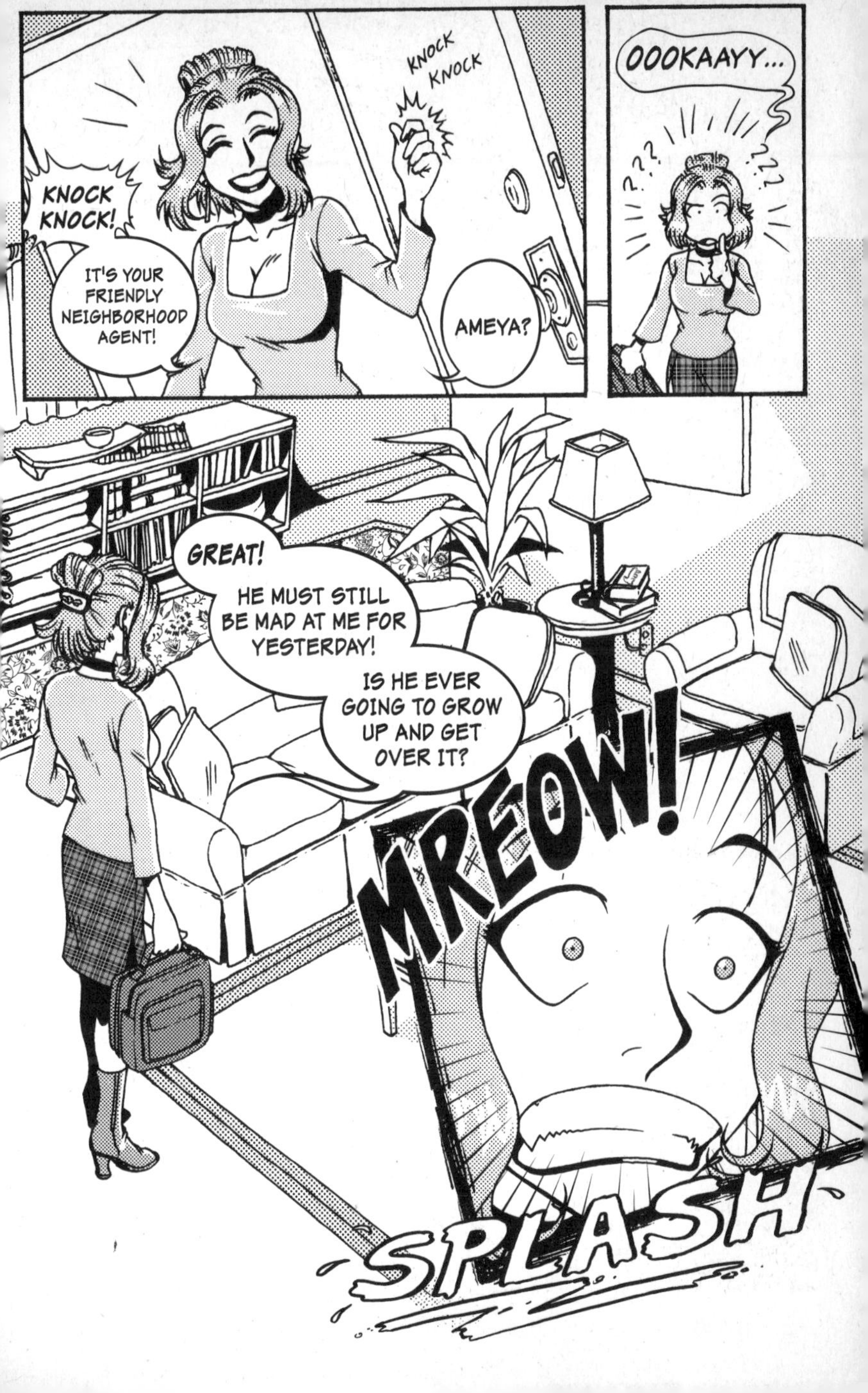
KNOCK KNOCK
KNOCK KNOCK!
IT'S YOUR FRIENDLY NEIGHBORHOOD AGENT!
AMEYA?
OOOKAAYY...
???
???
GREAT!
HE MUST STILL BE MAD AT ME FOR YESTERDAY!
IS HE EVER GOING TO GROW UP AND GET OVER IT?
MREOW!
SPLASH

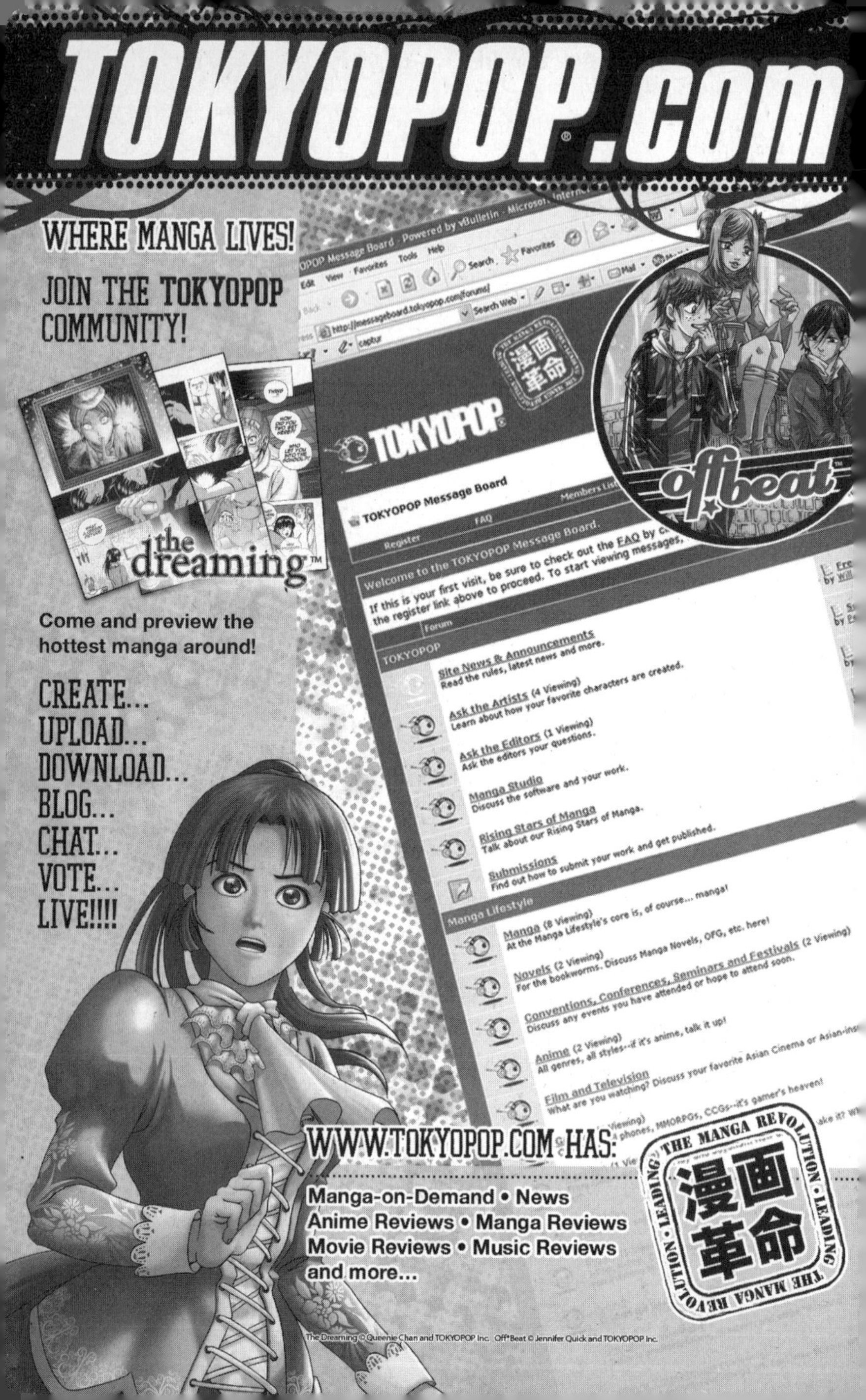
TOKYOPOP®.com
WHERE MANGA LIVES!
JOIN THE TOKYOPOP COMMUNITY!
the dreaming™
Come and preview the hottest manga around!
CREATE...
UPLOAD...
DOWNLOAD...
BLOG...
CHAT...
VOTE...
LIVE!!!!
offbeat™
TOKYOPOP
TOKYOPOP Message Board
Site News & Announcements
Read the rules, latest news and more.
Ask the Artists (4 Viewing)
Learn about how your favorite characters are created.
Ask the Editors (1 Viewing)
Ask the editors your questions.
Manga Studio
Discuss the software and your work.
Rising Stars of Manga
Talk about our Rising Stars of Manga.
Submissions
Find out how to submit your work and get published.
Manga Lifestyle
Manga (8 Viewing)
At the Manga Lifestyle's core is, of course... manga!
Novels (2 Viewing)
Conventions, Conferences, Seminars and Festivals (2 Viewing)
Discuss any events you have attended or hope to attend soon.
Anime (2 Viewing)
Film and Television
What are you watching? Discuss your favorite Asian Cinema or Asian-ins
WWW.TOKYOPOP.COM HAS:
Manga-on-Demand • News
Anime Reviews • Manga Reviews
Movie Reviews • Music Reviews
and more...
THE MANGA REVOLUTION • LEADING
漫画革命
The Dreaming © Queenie Chan and TOKYOPOP Inc. Off*Beat © Jennifer Quick and TOKYOPOP Inc.

© MAYUMI AZUMA

## A SKY PIRATE MANGA BOUND TO HOOK YOU!

Rookie sky pirate Coud Van Giruet discovers a most unusual bounty: a young girl named Ren who is an "Edel Raid"—a living weapon that lends extraordinary powers to humans. But just as he realizes Ren is a very valuable treasure, she is captured! Can Coud and Arc Aile join forces and rescue her without killing themselves…or each other?

## THE MANGA THAT SPARKED THE HIT ANIME!!

ACTION

T TEEN AGE 13+